THE
LAST FULL
MEASURE

The Life and Death
of the First
Minnesota Volunteers

RICHARD MOE

HENRY HOLT AND COMPANY · NEW YORK

To my Mother and Father
And to the memory of Isaac Lyman Taylor,
Patrick Henry Taylor, and the men
of the First Minnesota Volunteer Regiment

Henry Holt and Company, Inc.
Publishers since 1866
115 West 18th Street
New York, New York 10011

Henry Holt® is a registered
trademark of Henry Holt and Company, Inc.

Library of Congress Cataloging-in-Publication Data
Moe, Richard.
The last full measure : the life and death of the First
Minnesota Volunteers / Richard Moe. — 1st ed.
    p.   cm.
Includes bibliographical references.
1. United States. Army. Minnesota Infantry Regiment, 1st
(1861–1864)—History.   2. United States—History—Civil War,
1861–1865—Regimental histories.   3. Minnesota—History—
Civil War, 1861–1865—Regimental histories.   I. Title.
E515.5 1st.M64   1993
973.7'476—dc20   92-32687
                                                       CIP

ISBN   0-8050-2309-7

First Edition—1993

Designed by Victoria Hartman
Maps by Jeffrey L. Ward

Printed in the United States of America
All first editions are printed on acid-free paper.∞

10   9   8   7   6   5   4   3   2   1

CONTENTS

FOREWORD

M ilitary historians are fond of the hoary old adage that, on the
day of battle, naked truths are there for the seeing; very soon
they put on their uniforms. Those of us who served as combat historians in the Pacific were well aware of this warning; hence we
interviewed and observed soldiers before, during, and right after the
fighting. This made for much more authentic history. Even so, something was lacking. The fighting men had their brief moments of glory
and misery, of victory and death, and then passed from the scene.
There was little recording of them as *persons*—as human beings with
individual and regional backgrounds, earlier civilian and military successes and failures—or of what happened to them after their brief
combat appearances on the stage of history.

It is this personal background of human beings in war that Richard
Moe presents so feelingly in his treatment of the First Minnesota
Volunteers. With his own deep roots in Minnesota, the author takes us
back to a fort named for its designer, Col. Josiah Snelling, and located
on a fine military site originally scouted out by an expedition sent by
President Jefferson. We read about the migration into Minnesota
of families from the East and from Europe and about the hardening of
the men—farmers, trappers, loggers, and the like—who would supply
some of the toughest troops for the coming ordeals of the Civil War.

We follow these troops out of their homes and villages, into the hul-
labaloo and optimism of the mustering-in process, the choosing of most
small-unit officers through political means—from Washington patron-

age to election by the troops—as well as through merit, and the soldiers' introduction to the most ancient military experiences—poor food, inadequate equipment, "hurry up and wait." And we follow them further as they journey down the Mississippi, take trains—the first experience for many—to Chicago, and move through cheering villages and then a hostile Baltimore to Washington. They arrive in ample time to experience the devastating defeat and retreat of Bull Run.

The truths in this narrative do not take on uniforms, as Richard Moe pictures the long three-year involvement of the Minnesotans in the bloodiest battles of the Civil War. They do not, because he uses remarkably revealing and moving letters and diaries written by soldiers before, during, and after combat, as well as newspaper dispatches from the front. The letters have a freshness and an immediacy that make us feel close to the human beings who are trying to come to grips with the strangeness and horror of war. But we see more than war through their eyes—we see them looking scornfully at the different agricultural world of Virginia, with soil far inferior to the deep sod of their home state. We view their first encounters with blacks, who were hardly known back home—initially seeing them as wretches far worse off than any people they had known, then finding the humanity and the hope in the black men and women they talked with.

Some chronicles of men at war take on a repetitious quality, especially chronicles of twentieth-century wars, as day after day and month after month, soldiers grind out small infantry, tank, and artillery attacks along the endless front. Not so this story of the First Minnesota Volunteers. Each battle unfolds as a mighty, new drama, with different constellations of forces, context, terrain, leadership, strategy. If at times the reader feels as perplexed as the soldiers did during the roar and chaos of battle, that was the way it was. Like Tolstoy's *War and Peace*, this work sticks close to the men in battle, and hence, like Tolstoy, the author keeps close to the human side of war. Richard Moe captures also the spirit of another classic, Stephen Crane's *The Red Badge of Courage,* in chronicling how men lived as well as how they fought and died—playing games, telling stories, chewing tobacco, foraging for food, feeling homesick, experiencing dread, coming under fire, watching comrades die.

While *The Last Full Measure* keeps the reader oriented to the changing overall military and political context during the Civil War, it does not purport to be a history of that war. Certain broad themes or questions, however, do emerge from the work. One is the nature of leadership in war. Many of these pages reveal how crucial such leadership was, but not merely leadership at the top. Time and again the "common" soldier displayed uncommon leadership as well as valor.

What interests the author above all, I believe, is the most mysterious of all the mysteries of war—why men (and today women) fight. In the case of the Minnesota volunteers it could not have been a fervent belief in abolition—that whole struggle, while important, must have seemed remote to farmers and tradespeople who had rarely even seen a black American. Nor was it a deep hatred of the Southern "secessionists" or "rebs," even though that feeling of course intensified during the long course of the war. Nor was it, certainly, for the soldier's pay, which was paltry, whether disbursed by the federal government or by the state of Minnesota (which had a total annual budget of $100,000 at the time).

What appeared to motivate these men was something so old-fashioned and hallowed as to seem platitudinous—a sense of duty. But the immediate question is what kind of duty, or duty to whom? These men had duties to the families they were helping support, to wives and parents and siblings they loved, to farms they had cleared and had to maintain, to their churches and schools and communities. How could a duty that transcended all that lead men to go to war, never to return to those duties at home? Perhaps it was the example of Abe Lincoln, who reviewed the volunteers in Washington and who might have struck the Minnesotans then and during the war as a man of absolutely steadfast goals and principles, a man whose vision would be given its best expression at Gettysburg and whose own sense of duty undergirded his leadership throughout the war. Lincoln symbolized the nation to which these men also felt a sense of duty. But even more, that soldier's sense of duty was strengthened by the examples of officers who led the charges, of noncoms who took over when officers fell, of comrades who griped and swore but came through when courage and sacrifice were called for.

So through Richard Moe's gifted pen, through his extensive research and historical imagination, we follow these soldiers as they pursue their duty. At the end he brings us home with these men—with the small number that survived—as they retrace their steps from Washington to Minnesota. In one of his most evocative portraits, he describes the hardened veterans, in the final leg of their journey, wrapped in buffalo robes as they ride in horse-drawn sleighs up the Mississippi over three-foot-thick ice. Because they had fulfilled their supreme duty, as they defined it, now they could return to the duties of citizens.

James MacGregor Burns
Williamstown, Massachusetts
1992

PREFACE

L ike most boys growing up in Minnesota at midcentury, I saw the Civil War as ancient and largely irrelevant history. It was simply too remote in time, place, and effect to have much meaning for a youngster preoccupied with the here and now. That began to change one day, however, when, for reasons long forgotten, I was selected to be one of several Boy Scouts to attend church with Albert Woolson, then one of the few living survivors of the Civil War. Woolson was the most honored man in Duluth—within a few years he would be the *only* living veteran of the Union army—and it was impressed on me that it was a very big thing to attend church with him.

Woolson had said that in 1864, at age seventeen, he enlisted in the First Minnesota Heavy Artillery in order to get his "share of the glory." But serving as a drummer boy and bugler doing garrison duty in Tennessee, he didn't find it. ("We were fighting our brothers," he would say toward the end of his life. "In that there was no glory.") As the years passed, he found something else. Until he died at age 109 in 1956, he was a living link to the most important national event since America's founding, and for that he was venerated.

I didn't quite understand it in these terms at the time that I met him, but I did understand from all the attention that was paid him that Woolson was a great man who had participated in a great event. It began to occur to me that the Civil War couldn't be "ancient" history if I had met someone who had served in it. The older I got, in fact, the more "recent" the war seemed, and that progression is still under way.

It also occurred to me that, nearly a century later, people took the Civil War very, very seriously. World War II had ended just a few years earlier, and I understood why people took that war seriously. I had lived through it, albeit as a child, and it had dominated our lives for nearly five years. But the *Civil* War?

The impression that people took the Civil War seriously was strongly reinforced years later, when, as a young man, I worked in the Minnesota state capitol in St. Paul. Like most state capitols, it was—and still is—filled with reminders of the conflict. Paintings, statuary, battle flags, uniforms, and other memorabilia were everywhere. The conclusion was inescapable that the Civil War had to be something very important to warrant all this attention—*still*.

Today, more than a century and a quarter after it ended, the Civil War continues to have a phenomenal hold on Americans. Fought over the profoundly fundamental issues of union and slavery, the conflict severed the country as nothing else before or since. It cost nearly as many American lives as have all other wars combined. The enmities it fostered have taken generations to dissipate, and some of them still linger. But despite all the trauma and pain—in fact, largely because of it—the experience and its result determined the kind of nation that we were to become. More than anything since the Founding Fathers put pen to paper in Philadelphia, the war defined the America that Lincoln and the North sought—one nation, indivisible, with liberty and justice for all.

This part of the Civil War story is well known. It has become deeply embedded not only in our history but in the way we still choose to see ourselves. The part that is less well known concerns the men who actually fought the war. What were they like? Why did they enlist? What were they fighting for? What did they think of their leadership, both civilian and military, and why did they put up with such incompetence? How did they live their lives day by day, and how did they endure as much hardship and defeat as they did? What kept them going year after frustrating year? In short, who were these men?

Fortunately, the answers to these questions are revealed in the literature they left behind. The men who fought the Civil War bequeathed future generations of Americans many legacies, among them a literature in the form of letters, diaries, and reminiscences.

During the war itself, most of the men wrote letters whenever they could for the same reasons that soldiers have always written letters: to assure family and friends that they were well and to assure that they would receive letters in return. The smaller number who kept diaries did so for a different reason: most of them knew that they were engaged in the greatest adventure of their lives, and they wanted to keep a record of it. The reminiscences, of course, came later, after the war was over—sometimes long after it was over—and the motivations here were more complex. Some merely wanted to complete the record of their experiences, but many also wanted posterity to see them in the most favorable light possible. A number of veterans wrote hoping to be published—not all were successful, but many of their writings nonetheless survive—and various degrees of revisionism crept into some of the later accounts. This fact and the fading of memories decades after the event make the reminiscences less reliable than the contemporaneously written letters and diaries.

The letters and diaries by themselves make the Civil War the most literate war in American history. Never before had so many American soldiers been able to write, and never since have they been able to write so freely. In subsequent wars letters home were heavily censored and the keeping of diaries was strongly discouraged. But the security concerns that led to these later measures were minimal in the Civil War; the only real inhibitions the men felt in conveying their thoughts and experiences were self-imposed.

When the Civil War soldier wrote home, Bruce Catton says, he "talked about his officers and about his food, about the irritating absurdities of army life and its deadly monotony, and about the evils of making forced marches across country. . . . He was usually a bit reserved when it came to describing the reality of combat. He was willing enough to tell where his regiment went and what it did, but when it came to saying what fighting was really like, he generally picked his words carefully, apparently on the theory that the man who had been there did not need to be told about it, while the man who had not been there would not understand it anyway."

This book attempts to tell, through their own writings, the story of the men of one remarkable Union regiment, the First Minnesota

Volunteers. The premise of the work is that nothing can convey the experiences, thoughts, and emotions of these soldiers more effectively than their own words. Thus, to the maximum extent possible, the story is told by them, with a narrative added only to provide glue, context, and occasional explanation.

As in most regiments, the officers tended to be better educated and therefore to be better writers than most of the enlisted men. But many of the men—including Isaac and Henry Taylor, the principal story-tellers, both of whom were college graduates—were good writers as well. Isaac Taylor, in particular, enjoyed language and tried hard to make it work for him. Most of the other enlisted men were less accomplished with the written word. Edward Bassett, Mathew Marvin, and Charley Goddard, among others, made numerous errors of spelling, grammar, punctuation, and syntax, although fewer and fewer as they gained experience. But however technically flawed, their writings almost always conveyed clearly the thoughts or experiences their writers intended to convey, and no attempt has been made here to modify the original language unless doing so was necessary for understanding its meaning. As for the less reliable postwar reminiscences, I have used them only when I was reasonably certain that the writer—including the seemingly ubiquitous William Lochren—personally witnessed the events he describes.

Much of the Civil War art and memorabilia I encountered in the state capitol in St. Paul thirty years ago concerned the First Minnesota. I was vaguely aware then that the regiment had had a distinguished record and that it somehow played an important role in the battle of Gettysburg, but my interests at that time were elsewhere and I made no effort to learn more. It was not until many years later that, no longer living in Minnesota, I rediscovered the First. This time I pursued the facts behind the legend and discovered a marvelously human and poignant story of men at war. I also discovered a story of uncommon bravery and heroism, especially at Gettysburg, where, as Catton writes, "The whole war had suddenly come to focus in this smoky hollow with a few score Westerners trading their lives for the time the army needed. . . ." I realized that the story had been largely lost over time, even to most Minnesotans, and that it had never received the attention elsewhere that it deserved.

During the years following the Civil War the veterans of the First were among the most honored men in Minnesota. Their feats were legendary, indeed reached near-mythic proportions in some accounts. But the passage of time took its toll on the legend, and as the veterans disappeared, so did the public recognition for what they had done. Also, unlike the citizens of virtually every other state then in existence, most Minnesotans didn't necessarily experience the Civil War as the most significant event in the years it took place. It was fought largely in the East and the South, and it never touched Minnesota's soil. What did touch Minnesota's soil was the Sioux uprising of 1862, which resulted in the massacre of hundreds of white settlers throughout the southern and western parts of the state. The experience traumatized Minnesotans for years to come, and it is understandable that they would accord less lasting recognition to Civil War veterans than they would have otherwise.

But the story of the First is much more than a Minnesota story; from the beginning I have viewed it rather as the story of the Army of the Potomac during the first three years of the war as seen by the men of one regiment, which happened to come from Minnesota. It is the story of the rush to enlist after Fort Sumter; the early heady enthusiasm dashed by sudden defeat at Bull Run; the pride at being shaped into an army by George McClellan; the frustration at his—and his successors'—inability to defeat Robert E. Lee; finally, the costly victory at Gettysburg, the decisive battle of the war. It is the story, as they told it, of ordinary young men who did extraordinary things.

Richard Moe
Chevy Chase, Maryland
October 1992

ACKNOWLEDGMENTS

O ne of the joys of writing about American history is the opportunity to meet and work with people who love history, whether
they are professional historians, archivists, librarians, collec-
tors, or simply individuals who are drawn to the past. The people whom
I encountered in the course of this project could not have been more
encouraging and more helpful, and I am much in their debt. I wish particularly to thank Ruth E. Bauer and her staff in the Division of Library
and Archives at the Minnesota Historical Society in St. Paul. From the
beginning she was an enthusiastic supporter of the project. She steered
me to the letters and diaries she knew would be of greatest interest and
tolerated with grace and aplomb my unending pleas to her to copy
them and send them east. I also appreciate the assistance of Bonnie
Wilson and Tracey Baker of the Photo Division of the Minnesota
Historical Society.

Minnesota is fortunate in the quality of its county historical societies as
well, and I wish in particular to thank the following for their invaluable
help: Anita Buck of the Washington County Historical Society, Kim
Czech of the Morrison County Historical Society, Marie Dorsch and
Linda Rosenthal Dean of the Winona County Historical Society, Arnold
Madow of the Rice County Historical Society, Patricia Maus of the St.
Louis County Historical Society, Orville Olson of the Goodhue County
Historical Society, and Gary Phelps of the Dakota County Historical
Society. I also received valuable assistance from the archivists of the
Wisconsin Historical Society and the New Hampshire Historical Society.

The Library of Congress is a little-known institution to most Americans, but to researchers it is an indispensable national treasure. I am especially indebted to the professionals in the Archives Division and the Prints and Photographs Division, both of which are superbly organized and staffed by people who are eager to help at every turn. The professionals in the National Park Service—especially those at Manassas, Antietam, Harpers Ferry, Fredericksburg, and Gettysburg—were extremely competent and also eager to help. The men and women of the National Park Service, who serve as stewards of some of our most famous battlefields, represent public service at its best.

Not surprisingly, there are a number of Minnesotans who have made the First Minnesota their avocation. I am especially indebted to Wayne D. Jorgenson of Minneapolis, who furnished me with copies of previously unpublished letters and diaries from his private collection. They added greatly to the breadth of literature I had available for this work. Charles Barden of Prior Lake also made a unique contribution by sharing with me biographical and military information he has collected on the individual members of the regiment. Discovering the existence of his data base was a researcher's dream come true; having access to it was of inestimable help. I greatly admire his work and deeply appreciate his generosity. Finally, Stephen Osman, a historian at Fort Snelling, was kind enough to read the manuscript and offer helpful suggestions.

Three members of the Taylor family provided enormous assistance by sharing with me previously unknown writings of Isaac and Henry Taylor. I made the most valuable discovery of my research when Jeanne Barr of Columbia, Missouri, Henry Taylor's granddaughter, told me that Henry as well as Isaac had kept a diary throughout the war. My joy knew no bounds when she sent me excerpts that had been reprinted in the Cass County (Missouri) *Democrat* in 1934, together with a number of letters the brothers had written during the war. She was wonderfully supportive of the project throughout, and I will never forget her many kindnesses. Two other members of the Taylor family, Frank E. Dubach of Colorado Springs and Edgar Cadwallader of Rockville, Maryland, were also very helpful.

William A. Frassanito, the distinguished photographic historian of the Civil War, was kind enough to share with me a print of the photograph of Isaac and Henry Taylor that appears on the jacket and in the photo insert. Thanks to his decision to make a negative from the original tintype, which has since disappeared from the files of the National Park Service at Gettysburg, a "likeness" of the brothers survives.

I am blessed with a number of literate and knowledgeable friends, and several of them volunteered to read the manuscript at various stages. All who did so—Charles W. Bailey, Alan McConagha, Harry McPherson, Eric Moe, Julian Scheer, Sue Scheer, Guy Struve, Robert Torricelli—offered extremely helpful suggestions, and for those, as well as for their support, I am much in their debt. All remaining short-comings are strictly my own.

I owe deep thanks too to Ken Burns and David McCullough, who, in their superb television series *The Civil War*, reminded me—and millions of others—of the lasting magnificence of the war's literature. The words of the men who fought the war and the battlefields on which they fought it are the two tangible legacies of the conflict that must be preserved if the experience is to have meaning for future generations of Americans.

My thanks also to my agent, Gerry McCauley, and to my editor at Holt, Bill Strachan. Both served me and the work superbly, as did Roslyn Schloss, a gifted copyeditor. Margaret Conley, who used her many talents to help the project along in countless ways, was wonder-ful. And I am especially pleased that Elizabeth Andes, my sister, and Dick Stipe, her partner at North Market Street Graphics in Lancaster, Pennsylvania, were able to do the production. As always, they did a beautiful job.

I must acknowledge as well my debt to three men who wrote earlier histories of the First Minnesota—William Lochren, Return I. Hol-combe, and John Quinn Imholte. Unlike theirs, this book attempts to tell the story primarily through the words of the men themselves, but it was nonetheless aided significantly by the work they did.

Writing this book necesarily took me away from my family for too many evenings and weekends, and I could not have done the work without the support that Julia, Eric, Andrew, and Alex gave me throughout. In their own ways they are all attracted to and skilled in the use of the written word, and they understood that this project was important to me. Their understanding and encouragement constituted a gift for which I am deeply grateful.

R. M.

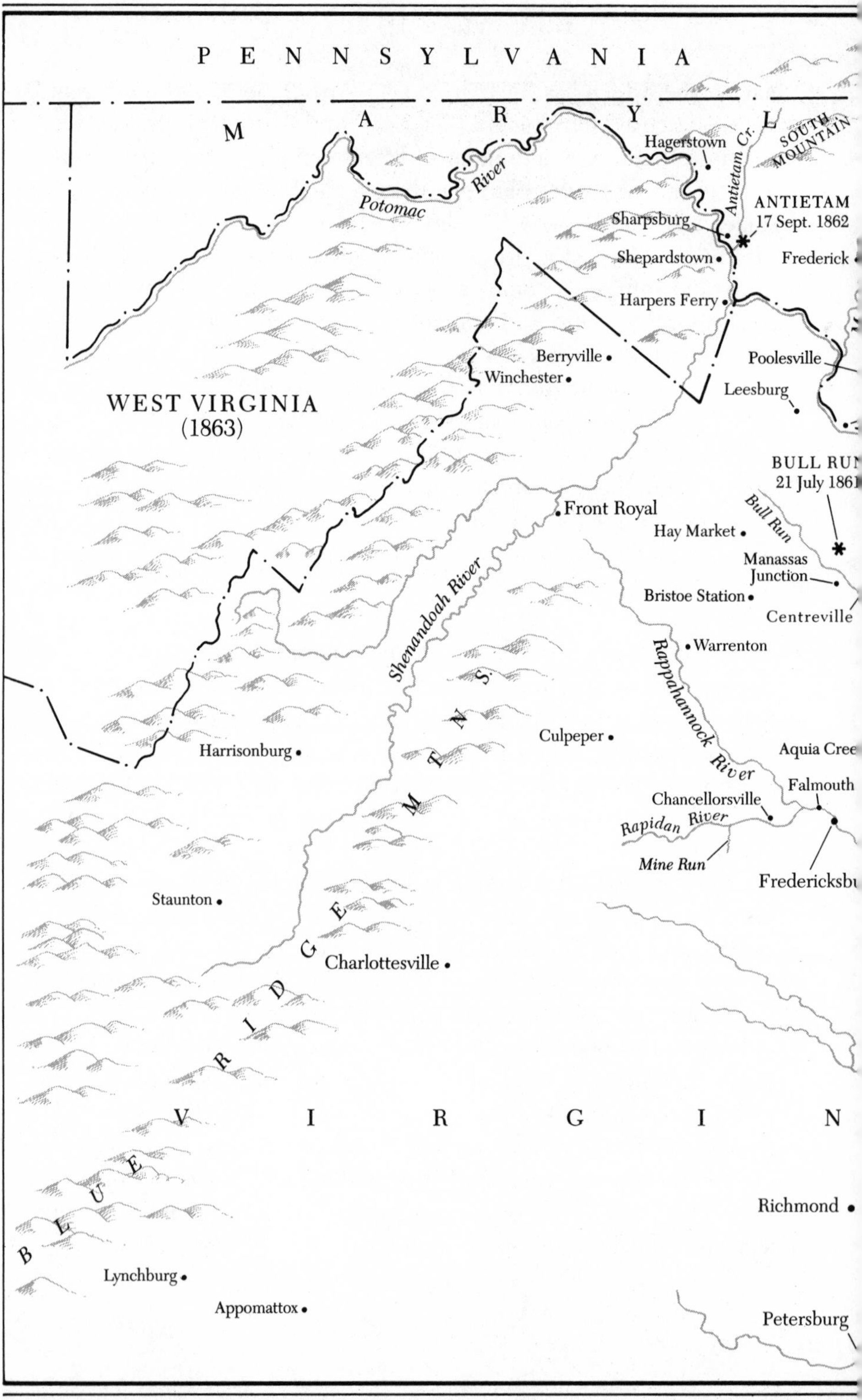

P E N N S Y L V A N I A
M A R Y L
SOUTH MOUNTAIN
Hagerstown
Antietam Cr.
Potomac River
ANTIETAM
17 Sept. 1862
Sharpsburg
Shepardstown
Frederick
Harpers Ferry
Berryville
Poolesville
Winchester
Leesburg
WEST VIRGINIA
(1863)
BULL RU
21 July 186
Bull Run
Front Royal
Hay Market
Manassas Junction
Bristoe Station
Centreville
Shenandoah River
Warrenton
Rappahannock River
Culpeper
Harrisonburg
Aquia Cree
Falmouth
Chancellorsville
Rapidan River
Mine Run
Fredericksbu
Staunton
Charlottesville
BLUE RIDGE MTNS.
V I R G I N
Richmond
Lynchburg
Appomattox
Petersburg

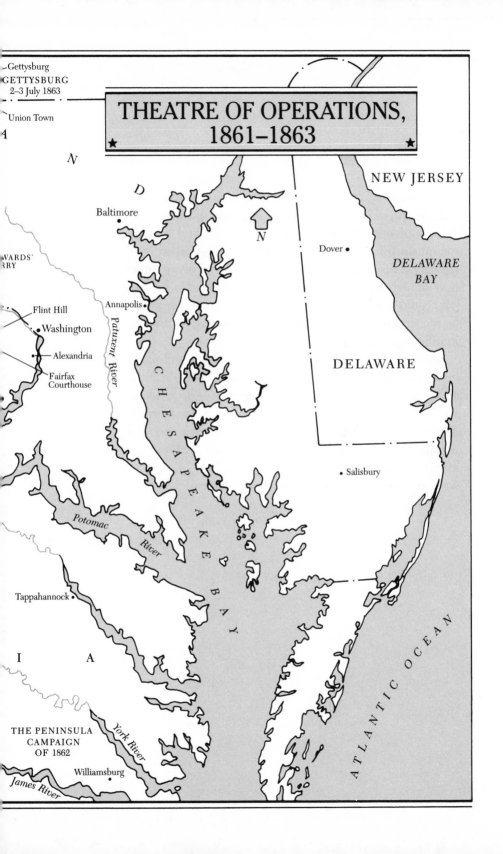

Gettysburg
GETTYSBURG
2–3 July 1863

Union Town

4

N

THEATRE OF OPERATIONS, 1861–1863

NEW JERSEY

D

Baltimore

N

Dover

DELAWARE
BAY

WARDS'
RRY

Flint Hill

Washington

Alexandria

Fairfax
Courthouse

Annapolis

Patuxent River

C H E S A P E A K E

DELAWARE

Salisbury

Potomac

River

B A Y

Tappahannock

I

A

ATLANTIC OCEAN

THE PENINSULA
CAMPAIGN
OF 1862

York River

Williamsburg

James River

Future years will never know the seething hell and the black infernal background of countless minor scenes and interiors, (not the few great battles) of the Secession War; and it is best they should not. In the mushy influences of current times the fervid atmosphere and typical events of those years are in danger of being totally forgotten. I have at night watch'd by the side of a sick man in the hospital, one who could not live many hours. I have seen his eyes flash and burn as he recurr'd to the cruelties on his surrender'd brother, and mutilations of the corpse afterward.

Such was the war. It was not a quadrille in a ball-room. Its interior history will not only never be written, its practicality, minutia of deeds and passions, will never be even suggested. The actual soldier of 1862–65, North and South, with all his ways, his incredible dauntlessness, habits, practices, tastes, language, his appetite, rankness, his superb strength and animality, lawless gait, and a hundred unnamed lights and shades of camp—I say, will never be written—perhaps must not and should not be.

Walt Whitman
"Memoranda during the War"

THE
LAST FULL
MEASURE

1

FORT SNELLING

"I can fight. I know I can."

G en. George Gordon Meade, the commander of the Army of the Potomac, was emboldened by his recent successes against the Confederate army. Not only had he defeated Robert E. Lee several months earlier at Gettysburg, the single most important battle of the war, but just weeks earlier he had prevented Lee from turning his flank as the two armies raced toward Washington from their positions below the Rappahannock. Meade's Union forces had mauled the Southerners first at Bristoe Station and then at Rappahannock Bridge and Kelly's Ford, and Lee had been forced to return to the safety of his camp south of the Rapidan River. Now, on the eve of Thanksgiving Day 1863, Meade decided to seize the initiative from Lee and pursue him across the Rapidan. Believing that he had about a two-to-one advantage in men, he proposed to cross the river on fords far beyond the Confederate right and then swing swiftly to the west and hit Lee's unsuspecting flank. With the Confederates stretched out along a thirty-mile line on the south bank of the Rapidan, Meade intended to bring his full force to bear on only a part of Lee's. The plan was premised on stealth and speed, qualities not always associated with the Army of the Potomac, but Meade was determined to deal Lee the decisive blow he had failed to deliver at Gettysburg and since.

On 24 November 1863, every man in the First Minnesota Volunteer Regiment was issued five days' rations and forty rounds of ammunition before the army marched off toward the Rapidan. But it was a false start, and the men soon returned to their camp. Two days later the operation resumed in the midst of a heavy fog. "At 10:30 a.m. we filed off from the road within a mile of the Rapidan River and are ordered to keep quiet and build no fires," Sgt. Henry Taylor, a 25-year-old former schoolteacher, wrote in his diary. "Crossed the river on a pontoon bridge of eight boats at Germania at 2 p.m. We bivouac some three miles south of the river after dark. This is Thanksgiving Day but I fail to see the roast turkey—pork and hardtack is the soldier's lot."[1]

A series of Union delays caused the crossing to go neither smoothly nor quickly. A scouting report enabled Lee to discover it sooner than Meade had wished, but the Confederate commander was uncertain whether the Union aim was to engage his army or to head east for Richmond. Reminding himself that he had humiliated this same army only six months earlier, at nearby Chancellorsville, he ordered the left wing of his army brought up to join the main force. He soon learned that the Federals were moving westward, and before long, forward units from the two armies became engaged. There would be none of the element of surprise that Meade had hoped for.

"The skirmishers are already engaged and in a short time the tumult swells to a battle," Sergeant Taylor wrote the next day. "I distinctly hear the shouts of the combatants. Late in the afternoon our regiment . . . was ordered to take position on the right, which we did, passing over the 15th Mass. Vol, which was then banging away at the enemy in the pine thicket. Halting our regiment at the edge of the woods, it was deployed and we advanced a quarter of a mile, driving the skirmishers of the enemy before us. The skirmishers of the 1st division fired into our skirmish line about 8 p.m., by error, as they were trying to 'join our right.' "[2] The experience of fighting an enemy at close hand for two and a half years had not eliminated casualties from friendly fire.

Lee ordered a heavily fortified defense line prepared west of Mine Run, a creek flowing north into the Rapidan. The next day he permitted his forward units to be pushed back to the line while the rest of his army was coming up to it. The result was a seven-mile line of earthworks behind an unobstructed slope that provided a clear field of fire down on anyone approaching it. Precisely as Lee had in mind, it offered an opportunity for a massacre like the one that had devastated the Army of the Potomac at Fredericksburg. Meade was nonetheless determined to go forward, and he ordered that an artillery barrage on the morning of 30 November was to be followed by infantry assaults against both ends of Lee's line. The First Minnesota and the rest of the Second Corps, under the command of Gen. Gouverneur K. Warren, would anchor the Union left and would lead the charge.

"Up at 2 a.m. and march without cooking coffee," Taylor wrote on the morning of 30 November, "passing along the plank road towards Orange C[ourt] H[ouse] about two miles and form in battle line—two lines of battle and a line of skirmishers."[3] Edward Bassett, a twenty-one-year-old farmer from Rice County in southern Minnesota, wrote that the plan called for the Minnesotans "to drive in their pickets, go as far as we could and wait for the line of battle to come up. Then we would join them and charge the works. It was cold and frosty and we had to wait about two hours for light. We could see their camp fires, and hear them talking. At dawn it created quite a stir among the Rebs when they saw us. We counted twelve cannon on their works."[4]

William Lochren, a lawyer from St. Anthony, recalled later that once in position the Minnesotans

> could plainly see the line of earthworks on the crest of the gentle slope rising before us. Our position required us to do picket duty during the night, and we could hear the incessant sound of entrenching tools in the enemy's works. We knew that it was expected that we should charge those works, and earnestly wished that the order would come to do so in the darkness, before they were made stronger and reinforced. Near morning the order came that the charge would be made at eight o'clock precisely, on the firing of signal guns from the different corps, and that, in the advance, the First Minnesota should march on the enemy's works, keeping its distance as skirmishers in front of the first line until it should draw the enemy's full fire, upon which the lines behind were to move at double-quick, and the survivors of our regiment were to fall into the first line as it reached them, and participate in the assault. The earthworks in our front seemed very strong, and well covered with artillery, which would sweep every inch of the perfectly open, gentle slope over which we must advance. It was plain that reinforcements were pouring in. . . . The prospect was far from assuring, and, with our orders here, we felt that . . . there would not be enough left of the regiment for a formal muster-out after this charge should be made.[5]

Although the Minnesotans had been at Fredericksburg, they had been spared the slaughter, and they knew how lucky they were. But they had been in the Army of the Potomac since its very beginning, since the first battle of Bull Run, and they had little doubt what was going to happen to them at 8 o'clock the next morning. They believed their chances of being spared again were so remote as to be nonexistent. They had been at Antietam, Gettysburg, and more than a dozen other bloody battles, and the growing ferocity of the war convinced them of that. But instead of the few fleeting seconds they had had in earlier engagements to grasp the danger they faced, now they had all night on the forward line to think about it. They knew that their chances of surviving an assault across a clearing against entrenched artillery and musketry was next to impossible. They knew that if they were wounded even slightly, enemy fire would almost certainly prevent stretcher bearers from reaching them. They knew that if they lay disabled for long in the wintry cold, they could easily freeze to death.

They had time to reflect as well on the strong likelihood that this engagement, no matter how it turned out, would be their last. Almost certainly both armies would go into winter quarters in December, and by spring the Minnesotans' three-year enlistments would be up. But there was no way, virtually all of them concluded that night, that they would live to see themselves mustered out.

The frigid temperatures made the waiting even worse. Water in the men's canteens turned to ice, and the soldiers on both sides had to move constantly to keep from being frostbitten. "The severe cold drove [the Confederates] out of their pits for exercise," Lochren remembered, "and as we did not fire on them, they also abstained from firing, and soon they and we were running and jumping about, within pistol range, to keep from chilling."[6]

The assistant adjutant general of the Second Corps, concealing his rank under an overcoat, ventured out to the skirmish line to hear what the men were thinking: "I asked an old veteran of the noble First Minnesota, on picket, what he thought of the prospect. Not recognizing me as an officer, he expressed himself very freely, declaring it 'a damned sight worse than Fredericksburg,' and adding, 'I am going as far as I can travel, but we can't get more than two-thirds of the way up that hill.' "[7]

Shortly after 6:00 a.m. Gen. Alexander Webb, the division commander, began making the rounds of each of his regiments. According to
Henry Taylor, he

> caution[ed] them to reserve their fire until they are fairly upon
> them—says the enemy has 63,000 men and we have 80,000, and
> that the first grand assault is to be made by the left wing of our
> army, consisting of 28,000 men, and that a division of A.P. Hill's
> Corps—15,000 men—is all that is in front of us. The morning is
> cold and very chilly and we are anxious to have the dreadful hour of
> "8 o'clock" come when we are to charge.
>
> At 7:30 a.m., the two lines of battle and the line of skirmishers are
> seen picking up their knapsacks, preparatory to the charge. Every
> man seems determined to "wade in." Officers pass along the line
> and speak of the "big thing, if we are successful," and caution us to
> fall in with the first line so as to have the 1st Minnesota among the
> first to enter the works. This deep silence of 28,000 men, waiting for
> the order to storm the Rebel works, is one of the most sublime
> scenes I have witnessed. How anxiously do the men, every few min-
> utes, ask "What time is it?" Eight o'clock and all quiet—perhaps my
> watch is fast—8:10 and cannonading commences far away to our
> right, perhaps three miles off, and gradually works toward us. I hear
> the remark, "Boys, she will soon reach us"—but in the course of 15
> minutes, all is yet quiet. Since daylight, the enemy has been bring-
> ing in troops and strengthening their works in front of us.

It was the waiting that was the worst, at least for Lochren: "We were
nerved up for the rush and the sacrifice, and the suspense was almost
painful."[8]

General Warren saw the same reenforcements that Sergeant Taylor
had seen. Assessing the situation anew, he concluded that an assault
would not only fail but be suicidal. He sent for Meade to come and
make his own assessment. At the last moment Meade agreed. He called
off the attack on both ends of the line. The lesson of Fredericksburg had
been learned after all: it was sheer folly to send men up an open slope
against artillery and entrenched infantry. The tenet was obvious, but it
had almost been lost. Because it wasn't, the Minnesotans were spared.

"Curiosity was aroused as to the cause of the delay," Lochren wrote
later, "and after a half hour of intense expectation of instant signal to

move, came the rumor, soon confirmed, that Warren had decided that the assault could not succeed, and that he would not order the slaughter. This was relief indeed, and every man commended the decision." Bassett agreed: "Thus we got out of another bad spot. I believe that if we had charged, as first ordered, not ten men of our Regt. would have come out alive. It was one of the worst places that I have seen. We were lucky. I shall never forget Nov. 30th 1863."[9]

Charley Goddard had managed to enlist in the regiment when he was only fifteen years old. Now, at seventeen, a battle-hardened veteran who had just returned to the regiment after being severely wounded at Gettysburg, he wrote his mother that he had seen "some fighting, been in some hot places, but never in my life did I think I was gone up the 'spout' until the order came to charge those works and I was as shure as I set here writing to you that if I went up in that charge Chas. E. Goddard would be no more . . . Such awful suspence I never experienced before in my life. I thought it was the longest day of my life."[10]

When Charley Goddard, Henry Taylor, Edward Bassett, and their comrades had responded to President Lincoln's call for volunteers some thirty months earlier, Minnesota was still America's northwestern frontier. A decade of extraordinary growth during the 1850s, however, was beginning to change it in profound ways. Land cessions conferred by the Sioux and Chippewa in a series of treaties opened millions of acres to farming, timber harvesting, and land speculation, a combination that drew thousands of ambitious men from the East and abroad. In 1856 alone, at prices as low as $1.25 an acre for surveyed land, public sales totaled more than two million acres. But many of the newcomers didn't bother to wait for the surveyors; they simply took possession and started cutting trees, plowing fields, and building homes.

The territorial government sought to attract new settlers by every means possible. Advertisements were placed in European newspapers, a special exhibit was sponsored at the New York World's Fair, and a "commissioner of immigration" was dispatched to New York to persuade newly arrived immigrants to settle in Minnesota. These efforts were wildly successful. The population soared twentyfold in just over a decade, from fewer than 10,000 in 1850 to over 200,000 in 1861. More than two-thirds of the new Minnesotians, as they were then called, were native-born Americans, drawn primarily from New England, New York State and the Midwest, but a large number were foreign-born. Of these, Germans represented the largest number, with the Irish, Norwegians, British, and Swedes following behind.

By the end of the 1850s more than four hundred cities, towns, and villages had been established, and eleven of them had populations over a thousand. An entrepreneurial spirit thrived in the new communities, with new shops and businesses springing up everywhere. By the time statehood was granted in 1858 there were more than thirty banks and nearly ninety newspapers. The telegraph had arrived and, with it, an important link to the outside world. The railroad, however, had yet to make its appearance. Until it did, the principal means of transportation was by water. In 1855, St. Paul saw a hundred steamboats come up the Mississippi; three years later, there were more than a thousand.

Most of the newcomers shunned the cities and towns and headed instead for the rich virgin farmland in the southern part of the territory. Despite innumerable obstacles there were some 18,000 farms by 1859, and more farmers were coming all the time. Most of them settled in family units, but some came together to organize farming colonies or, occasionally, towns. They cleared the land, built sod or log houses, and planted crops. They survived long, cold winters, scorching summers, constant isolation, and the fear of Indians. For their efforts, most of them barely eked out a living.

Although they didn't know it, a number of these new Minnesotans were in the process of developing precisely those qualities they would soon need to fight a war. They endured great hardship, but they persisted with resourcefulness, hard work, and a conviction that they would ultimately prevail. They demonstrated a degree of toughness and self-reliance that would help see them through ordeals they could not yet imagine.

On 13 April 1861, Alexander Ramsey, the second elected governor of Minnesota, happened to be in Washington to discuss patronage with the new Lincoln administration—like many governors of his time and since, he was preoccupied with the subject—when the electrifying news reached the capital that Fort Sumter had been fired on by South Carolina militia and had surrendered. The next morning Ramsey, a popular Republican whose strong ambition was well served by a keen political instinct and an eye for opportunity, rushed to the War Department to see the secretary, Simon Cameron, an old acquaintance from Pennsylvania. As Ramsey later told the story, he "found the Secretary with his hat on and papers in his hand, about to leave his office. I said, 'My business is simply as Governor of Minnesota to tender a thousand men to defend the government.' 'Sit down immediately,' he replied, 'and write the tender you have made, as I am now on my way to the President's mansion.' "[11] Ramsey wrote out the offer as requested, thus earning for Minnesota the distinction of being the first state to tender volunteer troops to preserve the Union.

The news from South Carolina was not unexpected. The previous December, following Lincoln's election, seven Southern states declared they were seceding from the federal union. In January South Carolina militiamen fired on a U.S. ship sent to resupply the isolated garrison at Fort Sumter, and the next month the Confederate States of America was officially pronounced. Lincoln warned in his inaugural address during the first week of March "that no state, upon its own motion, can lawfully get out of the Union," and he vowed that federal laws would be "faithfully executed in all the states."[12] Lincoln pleaded for reconciliation, but armed conflict seemed inevitable.

The standing peacetime army numbered approximately sixteen thousand troops in 1861, and obviously many more men than that would be needed to put down the insurrection. It was then the practice to raise and train volunteer regiments through the states at times of national need. Once the War Department determined its requirements and apportioned them among the states, the governors would issue a call for volunteers to form the regiments requested.

President Lincoln had not yet called on the states to provide volunteers when Ramsey offered his thousand men. The governor apparently thought Lincoln had, however, and he further believed that Minnesota was not among the states asked to comply. Ramsey may have thought he could have the distinction of being the first governor to tender troops without actually having to provide them, at least not right away. In any event he did not allow his patriotic ardor to interfere with his responsibility for the state's limited finances, for he placed certain conditions on the tender. Since the legislature would not convene until the following year, he wrote Cameron, "May I ask whether you would feel justified in saying that the reasonable expenses that may be involved will be furnished by the general government?" He took the liberty of answering his own question when he wired his adjutant general back in Minnesota later that day that "the expense of uniforming and of transportation will be borne by the government here."[13]

The next day Lincoln called for 75,000 three-month volunteers to suppress the insurrection "and to cause the laws to be duly executed."[14] Cameron notified Ramsey that Minnesota would be expected to provide one infantry regiment of 780 officers and men. Ramsey instructed his adjutant general to issue a proclamation "in my name, calling for volunteers under a requisition of the President of the United States for one regiment of infantry, composed of 10 companies, each of 64 privates, 1 captain, 1 lieutenant, 4 sergeants, 1 ensign, 4 corporals, 1 fifer or bugler, to report at St. Paul forthwith." Ramsey's prickly lieutenant governor, Ignatius Donnelly, sensing a plot to slight him, insisted on issuing the proclamation himself. He did so as governor ad interim, indicating that preference would be given to the "volunteer companies already organized" and that enlistments would be for three months "unless sooner discharged."[15]

Minnesota already had eight volunteer militia companies scattered throughout the southern half of the state. In theory the militia included 26,000 men between the ages of eighteen and forty-five, but in fact there were only 147 officers and about 200 privates. Their ostensible purpose was to support regular army units garrisoned in frontier forts to protect against Indian attacks, but in practice their function was at least as much social and fraternal as it was military. Most of the militiamen, it soon became evident, had a decidedly dim view of being activated into federal service. Being a part-time soldier at home was one thing, but actually going off to war was quite another. A majority of militiamen in virtually every company rejected the idea of activating their units in response to Donnelly's proclamation; usually they argued that if both the regular army and the militia went off to put down the rebellion, whole areas would be left unprotected from Indian raids. Whatever their real reasons for rejecting federal service, the fear of Indian raids was justified, as the tragic events of the Sioux uprising the next year would confirm.

Three militia companies—the Minnesota Pioneer Guard from St. Paul, the St. Anthony Zouaves, and the Stillwater Guard—were permitted to offer their unit names and as many of their members as wanted to volunteer because, unlike the other companies, they had not formally rejected the proposal to join the regiment. Each of these units was filled out to the required number of men with new volunteers. At public meetings around the state, would-be officers formed seven additional companies, including another from St. Paul and the Lincoln Guard from Minneapolis, a small but promising community of 2,500 across the Mississippi from the capital. The balance came from the river towns of southern Minnesota—Red Wing, Faribault, Hastings, Wabasha, and Winona.

Despite the reluctance of most militiamen to join up, other Minnesotans responded with such swiftness and enthusiasm that the ten companies were accepted by the state adjutant general on 27 April, only eleven days after Donnelly's proclamation. In Winona, for example, so many of the town's citizens attended the public meeting that the hall couldn't accommodate them all. At the urging of Henry C. Lester, a leading citizen, the group adopted and signed an enlistment agreement: "We, the undersigned, mutually agree to unite ourselves together as the Winona Volunteer Company and tender our services to the state adjutant-general for the purpose of sustaining the government of the United States in pursuance of the call of the government; the details of subsequent action to be arranged upon receipt of proper instructions from the adjutant-general's office at St. Paul."[16]

But they didn't bother to wait for "proper instructions" from St. Paul. The next morning they started signing up volunteers and made provision for those families that would require financial assistance while a husband or son was gone. Within a week the company had seventy-six enlistments. They included Mathew Marvin, a twenty-two-year-old native New Yorker who had come to Winona two years before to work as a clerk in a leather shop; Sam Stebbins, thirty-one, who wrote for the Winona *Republican;* and Charley Goddard, the lanky and mischievous youth of fifteen who followed the company to Fort Snelling, told everyone he was eighteen, and got away with it. Lester was elected captain, and on 28 April the eager volunteers boarded the steamer *Golden Era* for the trip up the Mississippi to Fort Snelling, where the companies were assembling.

Goodhue County organized its company in much the same way. The first "war meeting" was held on 25 April in the courthouse at Red Wing, where the crowd was sustained by rousing patriotic speeches well into the night while a committee of five drafted resolutions to express the sentiment of the community. Attending the meeting were a number of professors and students from Hamline University, one of the few institutions of higher learning west of the Mississippi. When the speeches were finished and the resolutions adopted, the presiding officer issued a call for volunteers. At least two men in the audience, Edward Welch and William Colvill, believed that great honor would attach to the first man to sign up, and they both sprang from their seats and leapt over chairs in a race to the front of the room. Welch appeared to be the winner until he fell bounding over the last chair, making a valiant effort to reach for the pen on his way to the floor. Colvill got to it first, however, calmly telling Welch, "You are next, Ed." More than fifty men followed them to the front of the hall, according to one account, "pledging their lives, their fortunes and their sacred honor in upholding the stars and stripes against the rebellious assaults now made upon them."[17]

Within five days the company's ranks were oversubscribed, and some had to be turned away. A number of the Hamline students and their professors signed up, together with farmers, tradesmen, and clerks. Local enthusiasm for the cause ran so strong that a large number of citizens signed a petition to the county commissioners urging that $500 be appropriated to support the families of the volunteers while they were gone. The commissioners, wishing to be both responsive and frugal, voted the sum of $300 and appointed a committee of three to direct its use as needed.

William Colvill III was elected captain of the Goodhue County Volunteers, as they preferred to call themselves in these early days—soon they would be known simply as Company F. Edward Welch was elected first lieutenant, or second in command. More than mere honor was at stake, apparently, in the race to be the first to enlist. Although only thirty-one and a Red Wing resident for barely seven years, Colvill was already a leading citizen in the community as an attorney and newspaper publisher. His father had arrived in America in 1820, the product of the best education Scotland had to offer—among other things, he had studied with Thomas Carlyle at the University of Edinburgh—and he was determined that his son should have the same. The family settled in Forestville, New York, where young William attended the Fredonia Academy before moving to Buffalo, where he read law in the office of

Millard Fillmore. Admitted to the bar at twenty-one, he practiced in Forestville for three years before restlessness and the lure of the West drew him to Red Wing. By the time war broke out, he had established a successful law practice and served briefly as editor of the Red Wing *Daily Republican* before founding his own newspaper, the *Sentinel.* But for all his education and achievement, Colvill was without the things he now needed most—military training and experience. More than a hundred lives would soon depend on his leadership, and yet at this point he had no better idea of what war was about than his men did. They would learn together, and in the end Colvill's performance would vindicate their decision to choose him as their leader.

On 27 April, the fresh Goodhue County recruits, most of them of Scandinavian descent, were seen off by a large, enthusiastic crowd. A brass band made the trip with them, and when they reached the capital, according to the St. Paul *Press,* "an immense crowd of citizens were at the levee to welcome their arrival, and as the companies filed through the streets to their quarters, the sidewalks were lined with ladies and gentlemen, who kept up a continuous cheer as the brave volunteers passed along. The ranks returned the salutations with hearty goodwill. The Red Wing brass band . . . added materially to the enthusiasm of the occasion. The company is more than full, and composed of the very bone and sinew of the stalwart farmers of Goodhue county."[18]

The same sequence of events—enthusiastic rallies, patriotic resolutions, the rush to volunteer, emotional partings—was repeated in Faribault, Hastings, and Wabasha. The pattern varied some in St. Paul, where patriotism overcame past political divisions. Approximately half of those signing up had been members of the Republican Campaign Uniformed Club, known locally as the St. Paul Wide Awakes, and had campaigned the year before on behalf of Lincoln. A smaller number had been members of the opposition Democratic Club, known as the Little Giants after the candidate they had supported against Lincoln in 1860, Stephen A. Douglas. The election decided and a national crisis now bringing them together, they asked William H. Acker, the state adjutant general, to resign his post to become the company's captain. Although only twenty-six, Billy Acker was "possessed of a brilliant intellect, had an admirable military carriage and was so affable in his nature as to captivate all with whom he came in contact," according to Thomas

Pressnell, an eighteen-year-old who had been one of the first to join the new company. "[I]t required but little persuasion on the part of the old 'Wide Awake' and 'Little Giant' elements in our new company C to induce him to become our Captain and he was unanimously elected to that position."[19]

The pattern varied again at Stillwater, where the existing militia formed the core of the new company. The unit had a heavy concentration of woodsmen from Maine and Switzerland and, consequently, fewer farmers and Scandinavians than those from the other river towns. Edward A. Stevens undertook his own census of the company and reported that thirty-nine of its members had been born abroad and forty-seven in the United States. The fact that not a single member had been born in Minnesota underscored the newness of the state. He also reported that the average age, probably higher than that of most of the other companies, was "26 years and 8 months. The average age of foreigners is 28 years, and that of natives a fraction over 25 years. Twenty are over 18 and under 22, 29 are over 22 and under 26, 16 are over 26 and under 30, 22 are over 30 and under 35, 8 are over 35 and under 40, 5 are over 40 and under 46."[20]

The men who formed these new companies had responded enthusiastically to President Lincoln's call for volunteers to suppress the rebellion. The rallying cry in western states such as Minnesota was not slavery but secession, and in this respect the westerners reflected the views of the president, who, coming from Illinois, was one of them. Preoccupied with the harsh demands of life on the frontier, most Minnesotans did not get caught up in the abolitionist cause that had gained such a firm foothold in the cities of New England. They tended to oppose extending slavery into new territories, but they were not inclined to interfere with it where it already existed. Lincoln had carried Minnesota overwhelmingly in 1860, but he had done so largely on the issue of federal land policy, for most citizens a much more immediate and compelling issue than slavery.

In calling for volunteers Lincoln had appealed "to all loyal citizens to favor, facilitate and aid this effort to maintain the honor, the integrity, and the existence of our National Union, and the perpetuity of popular government; and to redress wrongs already long enough endured."[21] The great and urgent need, in short, was to preserve the Union; all else was secondary. Fort Sumter had been fired on and federal property had been seized by the insurrectionists. There was no alternative but to deal with the rebels swiftly and, if need be, harshly.

A great patriotic fervor swept through the North, and the residents of Minnesota, just three years a state, were determined to prove themselves as full participants in the nation's struggle. "We have reason to thank God that Minnesota is represented in this Grand Army," Pvt. Jasper Searles wrote; "that she has this opportunity of defending (as it has become necessary) that Constitution under which she was born and under whose benign influence she has become what she now is—a prosperous, flourishing state."[22]

They enlisted for a variety of reasons. For some, it was purely a matter of patriotism and hatred for the secessionist "traitors." For most, however, the motives were more complex. The prospect of excitement, adventure, travel to new places, and even financial improvement usually came together with patriotism to impel young men to sign up. In the end, as Shelby Foote has said of new recruits both North and South, it was the thing to do.

For whatever reason they enlisted, ten companies were subscribed and accepted so rapidly that there was no room to accommodate seven others, some of them not yet fully formed but all eager to be part of the new regiment. Eventually more than twenty-two thousand Minnesotans would wear federal blue uniforms, forming a total of eleven infantry regiments and assorted other units.

At that point on the upper great plains where the Minnesota River flows into the Mississippi, the bluffs overlooking the two rivers— formed over the centuries by their confluence—reach more than one hundred feet above the water. Offering control of the waterways as well as a sweeping view of the surrounding prairie, the site was an obvious one for a frontier fortification early in the eighteenth century. On an expedition for President Thomas Jefferson's administration following its purchase of the Louisiana Territory, Lt. Zebulon Pike decided that the United States should build an outpost there to establish its authority and protect the growing fur trade in this untamed part of the Northwest. Designed by Col. Josiah Snelling in the shape of a diamond anchored by three defensive towers, the fort was built of limestone blocks that gave it an imposing and impregnable look.

When Gen. Winfield Scott visited in 1824, he was so impressed that he later persuaded the War Department to name it after Snelling.

For the next thirty years the fort not only fulfilled its military purpose but also became the hub of economic and social activity in the vast northwestern territory. It served as a trading center for the entire region, and it housed the first school, the first library, and the first hospital in what was to become Minnesota. With the emergence of St. Paul as a major city just six miles away, however, Fort Snelling gradually diminished in importance, and ultimately it was sold to a private developer. When war broke out in 1861, Ramsey commandeered it back into military service as a training facility for Minnesota's volunteer troops.

By 29 April the ten companies had all reported to the fort, which, they quickly discovered, had seriously deteriorated from years of disuse. Nor was its size adequate: the Stillwater Guard found itself assigned to a large barn outside the fort. Every man was given a heavy blanket, a flannel shirt (usually red), a pair of woolen socks, and the promise of a regular uniform within a fortnight. Because supply logistics could not keep pace with events, it would be several months before the promise was fulfilled. A local physician made a pretense of giving each volunteer an examination, which was primarily intended—though it was not very successful—to weed out those not yet eighteen years old. Few were eliminated for any reason, but one who was rejected for defective eyesight was a young man from St. Paul named James J. Hill, who would become one of the railroading giants of the Northwest. Despite his rejection, Hill developed close relationships to the men of the regiment that he maintained for the rest of his life.

During the next two days the volunteers were mustered into the United States Army by a regular officer, who read aloud the articles of war—which spelled out severe punishments for specific transgressions—before administering the oath of allegiance.

The volunteers came from every part of the state and virtually every walk of life. Josias R. King of St. Paul, twenty-nine, had rushed to the meeting of the Pioneer Guard, immediately enlisted, and thereafter claimed to be the Union's first volunteer. Peter Hall, a Swedish-born lumberman working at Taylor's Falls, built a raft to carry him and three others down the St. Croix River to Stillwater to sign up. Newton Brown, a young farm boy from Waterville, walked barefoot the sixty-five miles to St. Paul to do the same. Emmet Jefferson, who had just built one of the first houses in a new settlement at the head of Lake Superior known as Duluth, packed up his wife and baby daughter and headed for Fort Snelling, 150 miles to the south. Traveling by stagecoach and canoe through dangerous Indian territory, he arrived at the fort only to be rejected for reasons that do not survive.

William Lochren, twenty-nine, would become the regiment's official historian. Born in County Tyrone, Ireland, he came to America with his widowed mother and lived in New England and Canada before arriving in Minnesota in 1857. He had studied law along the way and went into partnership with two others in St. Anthony. When war broke out he enlisted in Company E and was immediately promoted to sergeant.

Even Chief Pug-o-na-ke-shick of Minnesota's Chippewa Nation wanted to help. He wrote Secretary Cameron that he was "deeply impressed with the sentiments of patriotism" and that, "grateful for the aid and protection extended to him and his people," he wished to offer "the services of himself and 100 [or more] . . . of his headmen and braves to aid in defending the Government and its institutions against the enemies of the country."[23] There is no record of the secretary's response.

And there were the Taylor brothers: Isaac, who was sometimes known as Ike, and Patrick Henry, whom his family called either Henry or P. H. Isaac was born in 1837 and Henry a year later in Franklin County, Massachusetts, the fourth and fifth of Jonathan and Alvira Taylor's thirteen children. In 1855 the family moved to Fulton County, Illinois, where it established a household and took up farming. By all accounts it was a prosperous and happy family, actively involved in its church and community. Henry lost the use of one eye as a child when a flying woodchip from his father's chopping block struck him, but the handicap never inhibited his activity. Nearer to each other in age than they were to any of their other siblings, Isaac and Henry became especially close.

The Taylors believed strongly in education and saw to it that their children were afforded opportunities not readily available to their Illinois neighbors. The two boys graduated from an academy at Prairie City before going on to Burlington University, a Baptist school in Iowa. Isaac, one of the first to attend the new university, concentrated on the study of science in the "gentleman's department." Deciding on a teaching career, he returned to Fulton County to pursue it. Henry also was determined to teach, but he set off for Minnesota, and his decision would ultimately lead both of them to the First Minnesota Volunteers.

A decade earlier Jonathan Taylor's sister and her husband, both mission teachers, had founded a school for Chippewa Indians at Belle Prairie, some fifty miles north of Fort Snelling on the Mississippi River. Various branches of the family had helped support the school for years, and a number of Taylors, including Isaac and Henry's older brother Jonathan, had settled nearby. Henry arrived in Belle Prairie in 1859— a year after Minnesota was admitted to the Union as a state—after he and Jonathan undertook a five-hundred-mile journey by birchbark canoe down the Red River and the headwaters of the Mississippi. He taught both whites and Indians in the public school, keeping in constant contact with Isaac by letter.

When war broke out two years later they both got caught up in the patriotic fervor and, like most young men at the time, agonized as to what to do. But by the time Henry had decided to enlist he was told the First Minnesota was already fully subscribed. "We are not sufficient in no.s here to form a military co.," he wrote Isaac, "or I, too, should enlist to try what I could do for the 'Stars & Stripes' of which I hope to be ever proud. If you can do anything—go ahead. . . . Some from here have gone 20 miles to enlist & then could not from the fact that Min. has more ready now than have been called for. If I am wanted by & bye I shall go, I think, if my eye don't prevent."[24]

By a stroke of luck Henry got his opportunity. On a trip to St. Cloud, he chanced on a traveling recruiter for the First Regiment and eagerly signed up. The next day he wrote his parents in Illinois: "The spirit of patriotism prompted me to volunteer to go and fight for my beloved country. I gave in my name last eve. I'll start next Monday for St. Cloud to drill and shall be gone a week and then return and continue teaching until the Co. is accepted. I go for the flag of 39 stars."[25]

There was to be only a slight change of plans, as he indicated when he wrote his parents again five days later:

> I have heard that it is doubtful about the St. Cloud company being accepted for some time at least, and as more men are wanted to fill up the First Regiment which has already been accepted for three months, but now wanted for three years or during the war, I have given my name to go in that Reg. I am to start for Fort Snelling (near St. Paul) in the course of three hours. It is now 7 o'clock A.M.

I am the only one who goes from Belle Prairie. I have taught
two weeks on my term at Little Falls, but you know schools come
after Law and Government. I shall probably take the oath day after
tomorrow. The "Star Spangled Banner, o long may it wave." I
should be pleased to see you all before I go, but I cannot. The same
God who has thus protected me will not withhold his guardian care
in future. I go feeling that I am right and in a good cause, and if that
be the case, I will not fear. Tell all my brothers and sisters to stand
firm by the Union and by the glorious liberties which, under God,
we enjoy.[26]

Henry resigned his teaching post and traveled south to Fort Snelling
to join the regiment. He was the first of the Taylors to enlist, but five of
his brothers would follow. More restless than ever, Isaac went north to
Minnesota to assume Henry's teaching duties; he tried to concentrate,
but his thoughts kept coming back to his brother's great adventure as
Henry wrote of his training and his new comrades. It would be only a
few months before Isaac joined him.

Henry decided to keep a diary beginning on the day he left for
Fort Snelling. His first few days' entries reveal both his excitement
and his uncertainty: "May 22, 1861—Left Belle Prairie, Minn. at
11 a.m. by stage, arriving at Sauk Rapids at 7 p.m., the boys drilling
in the opening. May 23—St. Anthony, 7 p.m. Put up at 'St. Charles.'
May 24—Took buss for Fort Snelling via Minnehaha Falls. Was sworn
into the U.S. Army at 2 p.m. to serve three years or during the war.
Ho, Ho, for the wars! May 25—On guard, but I don't know 'beans'
about a sentinel's duty. May 26—Rains. No religious service. Most of
the boys pay very little respect for the Sabbath. I am reminded of the
kindly restraining influence of women. Assigned to Company E under
Capt. G.N. Morgan, First Minnesota Volunteers."[27]

Tradition and state law permitted the governor to appoint the colonel
commanding the regiment as well as the other field officers. Captains
and lieutenants were elected by the men of each company, and in
Minnesota, as elsewhere, the person who took the initiative and
demonstrated leadership in organizing the unit was frequently elected
captain. Military experience was not considered a prerequisite for company command, but it helped. Billy Acker's service as state adjutant
general, for example, was an obvious credential. But there were few

others with similar qualifications, and if there was no one with prior military experience, it was simply assumed that a captain or lieutenant would learn his job along with everyone else.

Governor Ramsey apparently felt some pressure to appoint a military man as the regiment's colonel although he was not required to do so. He entertained the idea of appointing at least two others—even Lieutenant Governor Donnelly had some interest in the job—before he finally settled on Willis Arnold Gorman of St. Paul. Having represented Indiana in Congress for two terms and having served as the second territorial governor of Minnesota—he had been appointed by President Franklin Pierce to replace Ramsey in 1853—he was a familiar and respected figure in the state. More to the point, he had led two Indiana regiments with distinction during the Mexican War. Among other things, he looked the part, having by most accounts an impressive bearing and a commanding presence. Lochren said he "acquired a reputation for sterling, unbending integrity, and of being one of the most effective orators in the country. His voice was a marvel of flexibility and power." Although an unabashed admirer of Gorman and at times even his apologist, Lochren conceded that he could be "rough in manner and eloquent in vituperation."[28] He also had a proclivity for generating controversy, as he would soon reveal.

His major drawback, as far as Ramsey was concerned, was the fact that he was a Democrat, and an active one at that. The public support for Gorman and his obvious qualifications made him impossible to ignore, however, and Ramsey hid whatever reservations he had and made the appointment. Having conceded the top position to a Democrat, Ramsey was determined to name Republican loyalists to the remaining regimental posts. Patronage was something he took seriously, and these appointments were unmistakably a matter of patronage. He selected Stephen Miller of St. Cloud, a close political ally, as lieutenant colonel, the number two position in the regiment. Miller had edited a Whig newspaper in Harrisburg, Pennsylvania, until 1858, when he moved to Minnesota for health reasons. He became deeply involved in the politics of the new state, and during the 1860 campaign, as a Republican elector, he and his Democratic counterpart debated the merits of Lincoln and Douglas in more than fifty joint appearances throughout Minnesota. His efforts strengthened his ties to Ramsey and won him a coveted appointment in the U.S. Land Office.

The governor named William H. Dike of Faribault a major. Dike had been elected captain of the Faribault company after serving as its chief organizer, but neither he nor Miller had any previous military training or experience. There is no evidence that Gorman was consulted on these or other regimental appointments, but he was permitted to select his own staff, which soon included two of his sons. Political and blood ties counted when it came to making officers. It was to be that kind of army, at least in the beginning.

On 30 April, exactly two weeks after the state's call for volunteers, Gorman informed Ramsey that "the First Regiment of Minnesota Volunteers has been duly mustered into the service of the United States, and are now ready for duty, and await the orders of the Secretary of War." The governor wrote Secretary Cameron the same day that "one regiment of nine hundred men has been detached from the militia of Minnesota, and is now . . . ready for active service."[29]

The First Minnesota, as it would be known, may have been deemed "ready for active service" but it was a regiment in name only. The men began their training immediately, performing squad, company, and regimental drills daily. Joseph Spencer, the orderly sergeant of Company G, summarized his daily routine: "My duties . . . are such that I have no time to spare. I have to get the boys all up every morning to call the roll at 6 am, have to make my report at the Colonel's office at 7 am. Drill from 9 to 12 and from 2 to 5. The balance of my time is occupied in keeping the boys strait and asking ten thousand questions that I don't know any more about than they do themselves."[30]

Since only a few officers had had any prior experience, they learned the basics of drilling along with the enlisted men and with the help of Hardee's *Tactics* and other manuals. Those who had served in the old militia units helped teach the manual of arms to the newcomers. "The whole business was extremely tiresome," Thomas Pressnell said, "and, in fact exasperatingly so at times."[31] But despite their lack of training, equipment, and uniforms, the men "presented a very creditable appearance," according to Edward Stevens, reporting for the Stillwater *Messenger* under the byline "Raisins." "One thing is certain, it would be difficult to find a hardier, better natured, or a *better looking* set of men, anywhere except in the great northwest."[32]

Although ammunition was scarce, the men learned to fire their muskets and rifles at targets up to nine hundred yards away. Fortunately, there was an ample supply of weapons from the militia arsenals. The best shoulder arm then available was the .58 caliber Springfield rifle, which fired "minié" bullets. There were enough of these to arm three companies, while the others had to settle for .69 caliber rifled muskets. Both were muzzle-loading weapons.

Morale was high among the men at Fort Snelling. They cleaned out the musty barracks and brought in straw bedding, which made sleeping two to a bunk more comfortable. "We are all well Generally and enjoying ourselves first rate," Pvt. Edward L. Davis wrote in early May. "We have had a good time ever since we left home."[33]

The men quickly became the focus of admiring public attention, and life at Fort Snelling took on something approaching a holiday atmosphere. Visitors swarmed into the fort nearly every day, among them "the soldiers' relatives, friends and neighbors, who were often charged with distributing articles of comfort and convenience prepared by the ladies of different localities throughout the state," according to Lochren.[34] In the evenings there were often dress parades, which invariably drew appreciative civilian audiences. One day the women of Minneapolis and St. Anthony treated the regiment to a banquet on Nicollet Island, after which, according to Pressnell, Gorman put the regiment through maneuvers "principally for the purpose of 'showing us off' to the ladies."[35] A week later the men assembled in front of the capitol to hear flowery speeches and receive the regimental flag from the governor's wife. After the ceremony the regiment moved on to yet another banquet before enjoying a leisurely steamboat ride back to Fort Snelling. A few days later a half dozen coaches carrying young women from St. Anthony visited the fort. "The life of the First at Snelling," Private Searles would remember, "was all the people could make it in point of comfort and encouragement."[36]

The business of preparing for war under these circumstances was not altogether unpleasant, but neither was it trouble-free. The first food provided by local contractors was so bad that it provoked what came to be known as the "bad beef riots." After the men took out their ire on the cooks by pillorying them with plates and the malodorous meat,

Colonel Gorman threatened drastic measures. "The rations furnished the men were of the poorest quality," "Raisins" wrote,

> consisting of beans, dry bread, bull-beef, chicory coffee, turnips and salt. The beans are the most valuable and nutricious article of diet to be found, being boiled for dinner on one day, and on the next such as are not used are made into soup—17½ beans to a pint—should any soup be left it is strained, the beans picked out, dried, roasted, ground and made into Java coffee for supper. Much complaint was made to the Colonel concerning the rations, and on Wednesday he gave Messrs. Eustis & Lamb, the "grub" contractors, notice that unless an immediate improvement was made in the quality thereof, the contract would be revoked or a Court of Inquiry ordered. The result of this prompt action on the part of our energetic Colonel is, that yesterday and to-day our rations will compare favorably with those of the State Prison convicts . . . or any other body of hard working men.[37]

The problem of inadequate clothing and equipment was not as easily remedied. In addition to the blanket, shirt, and pair of socks each man was given on arrival at Fort Snelling, he later received a pair of black pants and a slouch felt hat. Only the men from Company K had anything resembling a uniform; they wore the light gray suits made by the patriotic women of Winona. "They do not look very well," "Raisins" observed, "being almost white."[38] Proper uniforms were ordered for the regiment, but their arrival was delayed by endless bickering between Governor Ramsey and the quartermaster general in Washington over who was to pay and, if it was to be the state, how soon reimbursement could be expected. In Ramsey's defense, the state government had almost no resources—the entire budget for 1861 was slightly more than $100,000 and the state had just $675 in its treasury at the beginning of that year. But Ramsey had signed a joint resolution of the legislature in January, when Fort Sumter was being threatened, promising men and money from the state to support the authority of the national government. What's more, the governors of states just as financially strapped were finding ways to clothe and equip their regiments properly. Ramsey was harshly criticized for not doing more. The need was so great that John B. Sanborn, the state's new adjutant general, whose annual salary was $100, spent more than $2,000 of his own money to purchase equipment. Other private gifts were gratefully received. The problem would not be resolved until the regiment had been through its first major battle.

Not all the men took to army life, and some of them felt themselves less than fully bound by the terms of their enlistments. "Four good-for-nothing rascals concluded camp life was rather a hard kind of living, and deserted on Monday evening," "Raisins" reported to his readers. "Col. Gorman sent a squad of men after them with orders to take them dead or alive. They were found in St. Paul, and after some little resistance concluded to come back peaceably. They were alive in every sense of the word, so much so that they appeared to be moving, when perfectly still. What was done with the culprits I have not learned, but rumor has it that they were kicked out of camp, minus the buttons on their coats. 'A good riddance of bad rubbish.' "[39]

Some of the independent frontiersmen, moreover, had a difficult time adjusting to authority. The men of Company C briefly considered resisting the arrest of a few of their number who had been charged with being "drunk and disorderly" and "speaking in a disrespectful manner to and of their superior officers." The men thought better of it, however, and, according to "Raisins," "graciously allowed them to be taken 'prisoners of war,' " but not before the sergeant of the guard received a bayonet wound from one of the prisoners. "Those arrested—a half dozen—were put in the guard house and there remain."[40]

In early May the regiment received two disturbing pieces of news. On the fourth, it was ordered to send detachments to the frontier posts—Fort Ripley, Fort Ridgley, and Fort Abercrombie—to replace regular army troops, which were needed back east. The despondency at Fort Snelling was universal; these men had enlisted not to sit out the war in remote outposts but rather to put down the rebellion. The news threw "a decidedly wet blanket over our patriotism," Thomas Pressnell recalled.[41] Gorman responded that he would comply with the order as soon as practicable, but he also convened a meeting of his commissioned officers. They promptly agreed to send a resolution to Ramsey, who was about to leave again for Washington, urging that the order be reversed.

Three days later Lieutenant Governor Donnelly received a communication from Secretary of War Cameron indicating that all regiments mustered into federal service but still remaining in their home state should be mustered in again, this time for three years. Any three-month volunteers refusing to reenlist would be replaced by new three-year recruits. The administration had concluded that the war might not be over quickly after all. Donnelly notified Ramsey, by then in Washington, and Ramsey replied by stating that no other regiment had been honored by a request to serve for three years—which was untrue. He asked Donnelly and Gorman whether the regiment would comply. Before he got the answer he told Cameron the regiment would be available for a three-year term. He was eager, it seems, to offer up the men for a period twelve times longer than the one they had agreed to.

The men themselves, when the time came for each to decide, had mixed views on the matter. According to "Raisins," it had become the "all-absorbing topic" among the men:

> The most prevalent opinion . . . is that it would have been better to have served out the three months enlistment, and then if thought advisable again enlist. Certain it is that the First Minnesota would not desert "our dearly beloved Uncle" in the hour of need. The probability of being sent to the various forts in this State throws a damper on the project, so far as a large number is concerned, who would readily enlist could they be sure of a glimpse at the elephant. As it is one-half, perhaps two-thirds will "go it blind." The Regimental staff and most of the commissioned officers are keen to go. With the privates it is not so unanimous—the feeling being to wait and see whether orders for re-enlistment arrive (when they arrive they wish to know it), and then each man act for himself.[42]

Harboring grave doubts about the duration, if not the severity, of the conflict to come, more than 350 of the men opted out. Of the 600 or so who chose to stay, many were no doubt motivated by the same patriotic reasons that prompted them to enlist in the first place. Others were already caught up in the adventure of the enterprise and were not yet prepared to return to the predictable routine of a farm, shop, or classroom. Still others were reportedly susceptible to the officers' threats or enticements, the latter usually in the form of drink. "Suffice it to say that [some] felt that they had been tricked into re-enlisting for three years," Pressnell recalled years later.[43]

The Stillwater Company, "Raisins" recounted, was "drawn up in line, and all who were ready and willing to enlist for three years or during the war, were directed to step forward three paces. Out of about 80 present 62 stepped forward, and it is expected that when the absentees return, enough will volunteer to form a new company out of the old ranks. The beer had long since disappeared, no signs of it were visible, and all enlisted in their sober senses without undue excitement. The charge of 'cowardice' has been retracted, and is heard no more. So far, we have the largest list in the garrison, and we mean to keep it so."[44] The regiment undertook a new recruiting drive, primarily in the communities that had produced the original companies, to replace those who had concluded three months was long enough to serve. By early June the unit was back up to full strength.

"It is at last decided that some of the companies are going to the frontier forts to fight mosquitoes and 'injuns,'" "Raisins" wrote at the end of May.[45] On the twenty-eighth, Company B (the Stillwater Guard) and Company G (the Faribault Guard) left Fort Snelling and headed up the Minnesota River to Fort Ridgley. The next day Company A (the Pioneer Guard of St. Paul) began the march up the east bank of the Mississippi to Fort Ripley, to be followed a week later by Henry Taylor and the rest of Company E (the St. Anthony Zouaves). Companies C (the St. Paul Volunteers) and D (the Lincoln Guard of Minneapolis) started up the opposite bank several days later, toward the more distant Fort Abercrombie.

The two-day trip up the Minnesota River aboard the *Frank Steel* to Fort Ridgley was slow and pleasant. The men were met by a company of regular army soldiers eager to be relieved and facilities much to their liking: "We found the quarters here much better than in Fort Snelling in every respect," "Raisins" reported. "Our beds last night consisted of a pine floor and blanket with a pillow of soft maple for each man. Today, however, we will have our bed-ticks filled with hay and then we can sleep easier."[46]

The men didn't really believe they would stay at the forts for "three years or during," as they referred to their terms of enlistment, and they immediately began to speculate about how soon they would leave. "How long we will remain in the wilderness we know not," "Raisins" wrote. "We hope only until Fall at latest, but are sorely afraid we will not leave here until the war is over, but if otherwise 'it is a consummation devoutedly to be wished for,' and we will soon be very glad of a chance to do our share towards showing the traitors of the South that the nerve and steele of 'mud-sils' form a slightly disagreeable mass to swallow. Minnesota, in such a case will look with pride upon her regiment, for 'retreat' is not down in our vocabulary."[47]

The food as well as the accommodations may have been more appealing, but the Stillwater correspondent wrote that the routine of army life in an isolated wilderness fort quickly led to boredom: "Now that all hope of going South, at least for some time to come, is given up, many of the boys almost hope that the Indians will get just a little troublesome in order that we may have a brush and get our hands in; but nothing of the kind is anticipated." To pass the time, he reported, "the boys amuse themselves between drill hours in stowing away rations, buying eggs, chewing tobacco, foot racing, jumping, boxing, playing ball, fishing, swimming, killing snakes, cleaning guns, singing, telling yarns, and waiting for the mail. A debating society is about being formed, and a Thespian Association is talked of."[48]

Garrison duty gave some of the men time to reflect anew on why they chose to be in uniform. "Our country is imperiled by civil war," Sergeant Spencer wrote his sister in Vermont. "Everything which the Christian and patriot holds dear is in jeopardy, our country's flag is dishonored. Our Government is defied. Our laws are broken. Bitterest hatred is kindled between sections of a common country. Brother is arrayed against brother. Everything seems to foreshadow the most awful strife. . . . Our only hope in this day of peril is to stand firm as loyal and lawabiding citizens. Every tie of party, friendship and kindred, sinks into insignificance before the impending danger." Spencer knew that he would be tested in battle, and he did his best to convince his sister, and probably himself as well, that he would meet the test: "When I enlisted my weight was 172, now it is only 138 which is rather light for me, but I can fight. I know I can."[49]

No one in Minnesota was pleased by the prospect of its first regiment spending the war in these outposts, and pressure built on Ramsey and the state's two U.S. senators, Henry M. Rice and Morton S. Wilkinson, to get the decision reversed. While in Washington, Ramsey had lobbied his friend Cameron hard but without success. Rice, a Democrat, thought he would try a new tack. He proposed that Cameron accept a second Minnesota regiment, this one led by Daniel B. Robertson, also a Democrat. Clearly more interested in getting troops to Washington than in Minnesota political maneuvering, Cameron told Ramsey he would accept a second regiment if it was prepared to leave Minnesota within ten days. But Ramsey would have none of it. His wire of 12 June to Cameron was blunt: "Do you want Minnesota regiment? If so, Colonel Gorman's is well drilled and armed and can be in Washington in ten days. A full regiment could not be got up in ten days, but I can have the forts relieved in less time. Answer."[50]

He got his answer two days later, and it was the one he wanted. A wire from Cameron ordered the First Minnesota to report to Harrisburg, and another wire the same day instructed the unit to travel directly to Washington. When word reached Fort Snelling at ten o'clock that night, nearly everyone was asleep. Colonel Gorman "fairly howled with joy" when he tore open the official envelope and read the order. "The news soon spread to the quarters of the company officers and then to the men," reported the St. Paul *Pioneer and Democrat* a few days later, "and such rejoicing took place as had never before occurred since the regiment was mustered in. The men did not stop to put on their clothing, but rushed around hurrahing and hugging one another as wild as a crowd of school boys at the announcement of a vacation."[51]

Couriers were immediately sent to retrieve the companies at the forts. The detachments intended for Ridgley and Ripley had already reached their destinations, but the one headed for Abercrombie was overtaken near St. Cloud, less than halfway there. The men of these companies were as delighted by the news as their comrades at Fort Snelling had been, indeed more so since it spared them a tour of duty in the wilderness. Henry Taylor was out on a pass when he received the word: "I hasten back as I learn our regiment is ordered to Washington, D.C. All hands busy packing up our 'duds.' "[52]

When the "unexpected but wished for announcement" reached Fort Ridgley, according to "Raisins," it set off a boisterous celebration. "The noise made by us can be in some measure imagined," he wrote, "when I state that about three hours after we had got through, wagon-loads of citizens arrived from the country around—chiefly from New Ulm, a town fifteen miles from here—to ascertain what the firing was occasioned by, and where the engagement had taken place. . . . Some few cases of sickness were on the Doctor's list, and it is astonishing what a marvelous effect the news had on the poor sinners—not one but is able to 'take up his bed and walk.' . . . The order just suits all concerned. Everybody is in the best of spirits."[53]

Apparently the order didn't "just suit" quite everyone, however. At least two members of the regiment decided that fighting in the East was not for them. "Our readers will notice the advertisement of Col. Gorman, for the arrest and return to Fort Ridgley, for punishment, the two cowardly deserters who escaped from Fort Snelling immediately after the regiment received order to proceed to Harrisburgh," ran an article in the Faribault *Central Republican* in late June. "Men who will desert under such circumstances, after having taken the oath to serve their country, are fit food for powder, and should be sent back, if caught, to meet their fate. Boyd is said to reside some three or four miles from here, North of the Cannon River. Hetherington is a resident of Cannon City. We have never thought that Boyd had honesty, decency, and manhood enough about him to make a soldier. Hetherington we don't know and don't wish to. We understand there are patriots on the look-out for them, and if they return here they may look out for justice."[54]

Within a week the First was back at Fort Snelling except for Company A, which remained at Fort Ripley, and twenty-five men from Company G, who stayed at Fort Ridgley until they could be relieved. The members of Company E marched all night on their trek back from Fort Ripley to be certain the regiment didn't leave without them. "Fort Snelling, arriving 7 a.m.," Henry Taylor recorded in his diary.[55] With little sleep but more than enough enthusiasm, he and his comrades got there just in time.

The more than nine hundred men who fell into ranks on the parade ground of Fort Snelling on the morning of 22 June 1861 were beginning to look like soldiers despite their red flannel shirts, black pants, and black felt hats. They were young, mostly in their late teens and early and mid-twenties, and their appearance suggested that a good number of them made their living with their hands. Just a few months before most of them had been farmers, but there were also trappers, lumbermen, schoolteachers, and clerks in the ranks. The day before many of them had said their final farewells to weeping mothers and sweethearts. Now, less than two months after enlisting, they were off to war.

The men were addressed by their chaplain, the Reverend Edward Neill. He urged them to see their mission in a determined but charitable light. "Your errand is not to overturn, but to uphold the most tolerant and forbearing government on earth," he said. "You go to war with misguided brethren, not with wrathful, but with mourning hearts. . . . To fight for a great principle is a noble work. We are all erring and fallible men; but the civilized world feel that you are engaged in a just cause, which God will defend."[56]

When the brief departure ceremony concluded, the men marched down the bluffs to the wharf, where two flat-bottomed steamers, the *Northern Belle* and the *War Eagle,* were waiting to take them to St. Paul, the state capital as well as its largest city. On reaching the upper levee they disembarked and proceeded to march through the main street. Although it was only seven o'clock in the morning, most of the town's ten thousand citizens had turned out to see the regiment off. There were more emotional farewells, and the women of St. Paul gave each man a havelock, a cloth covering designed to keep the neck from getting sunburned.

The young Thomas Pressnell, who had taken ill and who was confined by his doctor to a room in St. Paul two blocks from the parade route, managed to slip away to see his comrades depart: "When Co. C came along the boys recognized and accosted me with friendly greetings. I halloed back that I was a little under the weather just then, but that I would be with them later. . . . [W]hat a sight it was to see the boys, arrayed in their black felt hats, black pantaloons and bright red shirts—with their guns, carried at a right shoulder shift, glistening in the sun-light as they were marching toward the front, and to duty. I never have seen, never expect to, and, in fact, never want to see a more glamorous one."[57]

Within a half hour the men were back on the boats and steaming south. "The separation of soldiers and friends was a thrilling and affecting scene," the Stillwater *Messenger* wrote, "but just such as has been witnessed all over the country. That all of them will return to home and kindred, is not within the range of probability; that most of them will, is the sincerest prayer of thousands of sympathizing hearts. The bearing of officers and men on departing was just what might be expected. They bore up manfully, and as the boats cut loose from their moorings, the air was made to vibrate with the shouts of the exulting soldiers. Determination, courage, patriotism, were visible in every eye and in every movement. May God in his mercy deal gently with our glorious First."[58]

As the boats moved slowly down the Mississippi they made brief stops at Hastings, Red Wing, Lake City, and Wabasha, where the companies organized in those places were permitted still more good-byes. When the *Northern Belle* reached Winona, the southernmost Minnesota town on the river, it was greeted by several thousand cheering citizens. "There were occasional instances of unrestrained emotion" when the men disembarked for their final farewells, according to the local newspaper. As the soldiers filed back up the gangplank to depart, they were followed by shouts from their friends: "Don't let them shoot you in the back!" "Give the traitors hell!" "Go in to win, boys!" "God bless you boys!" "Be sure to thresh the rebels!" "The Union and victory!"[59]

The regiment left Minnesota behind as the two steamers steered toward the Wisconsin bank of the river. At LaCrosse and Prairie du Chien the men boarded railway cars for the trip to Chicago. Riding "the cars" was a new and exciting experience for many of them, and the "sumptuous" meals provided by the railroad company contributed to a holiday atmosphere. As Mathew Marvin wrote a short time later, people turned out virtually everywhere to show their support: "At each station we wer met by crowds of citizens who cheered us enthusiastically."[60] It was to be an especially festive trip for Lt. William B. Leach, twenty-seven, a successful lawyer from Hastings whom Gorman had named the regimental adjutant, and his new bride. They had been married just before leaving Fort Snelling, and they were now spending their honeymoon traveling east with nearly a thousand volunteer soldiers.

The regiment was reunited at Janesville and then continued to Chicago, where a huge crowd greeted it the evening of 23 June. Mayor "Long John" Wentworth gave a warm welcoming speech before he joined in leading the regiment on its march across town to another railroad station. Since it was Sunday, there was no cheering, but one Minnesotan noted that "plenty of 'kids' applauded in the most approved style, while compliments not a few, were passing round us on all sides."[61] By all accounts Chicago was impressed. The *Tribune* reported the next morning that "there are few regiments we have ever seen that can compare in brawn and muscle with the Minnesotians, used to the axe, plow, rifle, oar and setting pole. They are unquestionably the finest body of troops that has yet appeared on our streets."[62]

Then it was back on the cars and on to the East—more crowds, more cheering, more first-class meals. Pvt. Jasper Searles described the atmosphere of celebration: "All along the road through Wis., Ill., Ind., Ohio, Penn., Md, we were cheered from almost every home. The boys tired themselves more yelling than from anything they had to perform. . . . At every station we found old men and women ready to greet us . . . and in one instance an old lady, grey headed and trembling sat in her door as we passed and blessed us in words & actions so fervently that she resembled a spiritual medium passing through her gyrations."[63]

Newspapers in several of the towns in which the companies had been organized had signed up special correspondents among the enlisted men to send back news of the regiment. Sam Stebbins, who in civilian life had written for the Winona *Republican,* continued to report as a member of the Winona Volunteers; Edward Stevens wrote for the Stillwater *Messenger* as "Raisins"; and a correspondent known to his readers only as "D" sent dispatches back to the Faribault *Central Republican.* The trip east was their first opportunity to write of the world beyond Minnesota, and they made the most of it.

On the twenty-fifth, the men pulled into Harrisburg to camp overnight. The crowds, the cheers, and the comforts were behind them now. At three o'clock in the morning they were rousted out and loaded onto filthy cattle cars for the ride to Baltimore. Sgt. William Lochren saw the transition from comfortable coaches to cattle cars for what it was: "We found we were approaching a region where soldiering was less of a holiday matter than it had been with us."[64]

Baltimore was home to a strong secessionist element, and the Minnesotans witnessed the first signs of hostility as they approached the city. A "comely maiden," apparently a domestic servant, stopped sweeping to wave her handkerchief at the troops as their train passed a large house. "A lady, apparently her mistress, stepped quickly from the door, took the broom from the girl, and shook the handle menacingly at us," Lochren recalled. "The act was so sudden, unexpected and unlike any manifestation of feeling we had met with, that its impotent spitefulness was answered with cheers and shouts of laughter."[65]

Other regiments had come under armed attack when passing through Baltimore, and the First Minnesota was taking no chances. The men marched from one train station to another with weapons loaded and bayonets fixed. The crowds lining the streets were surly but restrained, and the regiment reached its destination unmolested. "Suffice it we met nothing worse than cross looks," Marvin reported. According to Pvt. Edward Bassett, the only excitement occurred when one of the Stillwater men "collared a man who was cheering for Jeff D[avis], and ordered him to cheer for the Union or he would knock his damned head off. He complied with the order."[66]

While waiting for the train to get under way, Edward Stevens displayed the callous curiosity of many of his comrades, who had seldom if ever seen blacks. Reporting as "Raisins" he wrote:

> I put my head out of the window, and seeing an old negro wench whom I had just heard addressed as "Dinah," and wishing to hear her talk, I said "Good bye, Dinah, take care of yourself till I come back." Her answer rather surprised me, and looked as tho' the negro race have an idea that this war is to inure to their benefit. She opened her mouth to its fullest extent, and approaching the car window, spoke in a low voice as follows, in short, distinct jerks: "Good bye, massa—God bless yer honey—Take keer o' yerself—I knows what yer arter—kill 'em all—When yer come back bring a purty little yaller gal wid yer—De Lor's a watchin' ye—Look to him in de hour of trouble and keep yer eyes skinned." With this benediction, she left and I saw her no more.[67]

As the Minnesotans rode the cars on the final leg of their trip to Washington, they were already thinking of home. Bassett, who had never been far from his family farm, showed the first unmistakable signs of homesickness when he wrote in his diary that he had "not seen any country to compare with Minnesota for soil, except Wisconsin, since I left. The red sand hills of Maryland, the clay bluffs of Ohio nor the clay stone points of Penn. Not even the noted prairies of Illinois or the old farms of Indiana, I think can compare with Minnesota. There will be a large immigration to Minnesota when the war is over."[68]

It had been a long and arduous trip but as the men neared the capital they were still in a state of excitement. "Taking it all together we got along very well considering the distance and time—over 2,000 miles in five days, a thing unparalleled in the whole history of war," Jasper Searles wrote. "Sunday the boys were entirely without food excepting a slice of raw salt pork, . . . but through all that the boys kept up their spirits well."[69]

What awaited these barely trained volunteers in Washington and beyond they could only imagine. To a man they felt proud to be in the service of their country and excited by the prospect of danger; they almost certainly felt protected by the invincibility of youth. Many had never been more than a few miles from home, and this already was proving to be a great adventure. What's more, like many Northerners they believed that the South was seriously outmatched by the resources of the North as well as by what they saw as the rightness of its cause. They were confident that the rebellion could be suppressed within a matter of months. Others knew better and said so, but many refused to listen or to believe.

The men of the First Minnesota were no different from the men of other Northern regiments in their expectation of what the future would bring, but they would experience the brutal and unforgiving nature of civil war in ways that none of them could have foreseen. Few of them suspected that they were destined to do extraordinary things. They were ordinary men for that time and place, susceptible to human weaknesses as well as possessed of great strengths. Both qualities would be evident in their early experiences, but as time went on the strengths prevailed. The fact that they did would change them, and it would change their country, forever.

2

BULL RUN

"Stonewall Had His Trap Set."

The train carrying the First Minnesota pulled into Washington near midnight on 26 June. There to greet it was Col. Cyrus Aldrich, one of Minnesota's two congressmen, "followed by a large squad of colored servants, bearing pails of hot coffee, baskets of sandwiches, and other refreshments."[1] It appears that the "other refreshments" included brandy, which later caused some to denounce Aldrich as a "demoralizer" and an "encourager of intemperance." There is no indication, however, that his generosity did anything but improve his standing with most of the men, one of whom said, "It seemed to be a repetition of the biblical incident of the loaves and fishes. The more we eat, the more there was to eat."[2]

"Raisins" reported that the First Minnesota was "cordially received, and when it became known that we were from 'away out in the wilderness,' enthusiasm ran high. It being late and we all being more or less fatigued, we did not pitch our tents that night, but were provided with quarters by the authorities,—companies B, C, D, and E in the Washington Assembly Rooms on Pennsylvania Avenue, and companies F, G, H, I and K in the old Plymouth Church near by. They proved to be first rate quarters, although not erected specially for that purpose."[3]

The next morning the men set up camp a half mile east of the Capitol and resumed the routine of daily drilling. "We are now drilling exclusively in light infantry tactics, according to Hardee, in which we are making considerable progress," "Raisins" wrote a few days after they arrived. "We have also commenced learning the bayonet exercise.

34

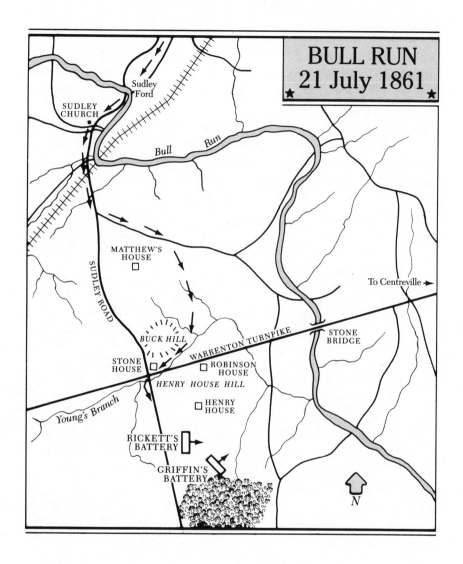

BULL RUN
21 July 1861

Sudley
Ford

SUDLEY
CHURCH

Bull Run

MATTHEW'S
HOUSE

SUDLEY ROAD

BUCK HILL

To Centreville →

WARRENTON TURNPIKE

STONE
BRIDGE

STONE
HOUSE

ROBINSON
HOUSE

HENRY HOUSE HILL

HENRY
HOUSE

Young's Branch

RICKETT'S
BATTERY

GRIFFIN'S
BATTERY

N

We are evidently intended as skirmishers." President Lincoln reviewed the Minnesotans, and for Jasper Searles, at least, the event achieved its purpose. "The 1st Min. produced a very favorable impression with the Pres. and all," he wrote. "The Col. tells us that 'Old Abe' has confidence in us, and *we shall not betray it.*"[4]

From the moment the regiment arrived there were tension and anticipation. There was also a plentiful supply of rumors, most of them wrong. "A battle is liable to take place at any hour, in which 300,000 men may be engaged," "D" wrote his readers on his second day in Washington.

> But be not surprised if we return home without having cut our way to glory, for such a thing is probable. Jeff. Davis has not only deluded his followers, but he has deluded himself. But does he not begin to realize his situation? He is being daily drawn into Gen. Scott's meshes. Is he waiting in conscious superiority, or with a hope of compromise? It is rumored that he expects by the intrigues so frequently used heretofore, in carrying corrupt measures through Congress, to effect a compromise; but he has broken the golden egg of opportunity—deluded soul! Any member of Congress who will favor any measure short of a complete and unconditional surrender to Federal authority, and the death of two hundred traitors, will consign their names to eternal infamy.[5]

On 28 June the detachment from Fort Ripley—Company A— rejoined the regiment. Speculation abounded as to the unit's next move. "Their is some hoopes of our being the presidents body guard as Col. Gorman is a favorite of theirs," Mathew Marvin incorrectly speculated.[6] One day, according to Edward Bassett, a number of Southern sympathizers "were bold enough to come spying around the camp" of a nearby Vermont regiment and managed to disarm one of the guards. After he got his weapon back "one of the Rebs was shot thru the head and killed."[7]

"We are fast getting to be adept in camp life," "Raisins" reported. "Two years and ten months more experience at 'laying around loose' and we will be prepared to 'live and let live' in any and all manner of ways. During the few days we have been here we have had a first rate time getting rested. Col. Gorman is enforcing strict discipline, and all who wish matters to go on in a proper shape are rejoiced thereat."[8]

The men were allowed out of camp only a few hours each day, and most of them used the time to explore and sightsee, especially in the Capitol itself, where the dome and the Senate wing were still under construction. To keep them out of trouble an improvised form of frontier justice was propounded. "To prevent such of the boys as may be disposed to follow the poor example set by the more reckless members of other regiments," "Raisins" continued, "our order has been given which amounts to this: If any member of the regiment behaves in an improper manner in the city, or gets drunk, or attempts any mean tricks toward other members, the orderly and well-disposed members are authorized to arrest the offender and deal with them when, where and how they please. In addition to such punishment as he may receive by this order he is to be detailed for double guard duty."[9]

In the summer of 1861 Washington was not the impressive city it would become. "I was greatly disappointed in the looks of the city of Washington," Jasper Searles noted. "With the exception of the Public Buildings it is a second or third class city." Pigs and other animals ran loose in the unpaved streets. Loaded wagons became mired in the ever-present mud. William Lochren complained of the shabbiness of the place and especially of the "old, dilapidated and neglected" shanties and of the "malarious and foul smells" emanating from the canal. It was nonetheless a "right smart little town" to Private Bassett, the farm boy from near Morristown, who had never been east. Edward Davis found the capital "a very pleasant city altho it did not half realize my expectations."[10]

"Raisins" told of an incident illustrating "how little is known in this section regarding Minnesota. . . . One of our boys was asked by an Irishman hereabouts, as we are by all, 'Where is your regiment from?' 'Minnesota,' was the reply. 'Yes, I know the name, but where are you from?' The same reply was given with just a little show of a smile on the part of the Minnesotian. A little perplexed that he could not make the soldier understand him, as he thought, he made plain his question in the words: 'Yes, I know it's Minnesota, but *what State?*' He was informed, and departed in peace, just in time to save hearing an awful explosion."[11]

"Washington is full of soldiers and while we stopped there were coming in at the rate of 10,000 per day," Joseph Spencer wrote his sister.[12]

At last the capital seemed secure. Only a few months before, immediately after the fall of Fort Sumter, near panic gripped the city when reports arrived that fifteen thousand Confederate troops were near Alexandria and another eight thousand at Harpers Ferry. Government workers and many others fled. Even President Lincoln feared that the city, protected by a meager handful of regular troops and only a few militia units, would soon fall into rebel hands. But the regiments Lincoln had called for finally began to arrive in late April, and by the end of May the point of greatest danger had passed. Lincoln felt sufficiently confident to send his forces across the Potomac to clear rebel troops from Alexandria and Arlington Heights and create a buffer zone between the rebels and Washington. Army engineers began building a thirty-seven-mile ring of earthworks and forts around the city, and soon everyone breathed easier.

But a secure Washington was not enough. The dynamic of the conflict dictated that the North take the offensive. Having seceded from the Union, the South maintained that it only wanted to be "left alone." That was an unacceptable result for the North, and Lincoln had no choice but to invade the South if he was to reassert federal authority. The Northern press and public were demanding a quick end to the war, and the rallying cry became "Onward to Richmond." Nearly everyone assumed that if the new Confederate capital one hundred miles south of Washington could be taken, the war would soon be over. But as Lincoln was beginning to suspect and as the country would soon learn, destroying armies would count for a good deal more than capturing capital cities in this war.

While Lincoln needed little encouragement to take the offensive that summer, his generals needed a good deal. Gen. in Chief Winfield Scott, the hero of the Mexican War but now seventy-five years old and infirm, advocated what came to be known as the Anaconda Plan, designed to gradually isolate and strangle the South by driving down the Mississippi and then pulling the coil tighter. But it was too timid a plan for Lincoln (although he would eventually adopt key elements of it) and for most everyone else in the government. Gen. Irvin McDowell, who had been appointed to command the thirty thousand troops assembling in Washington, was no more eager than Scott to fight an early battle. His troops were inexperienced, a third of the Union officer corps had gone south, and he didn't even have an adequate map of Virginia. But Lincoln was determined to go on the offensive, and he ordered McDowell to draw up a plan to attack Gen. Pierre G. T. Beauregard's force of twenty thousand, gathered at Manassas Junction, some thirty miles southwest of Washington. His intention was to destroy the Confederate forces at this important rail and communications link between Richmond and the Shenandoah Valley and then to launch a swift and decisive drive on the Confederate capital.

Although his heart wasn't in it, McDowell proposed a flanking movement to force the Confederates out of their defensive positions. McDowell was an experienced and intelligent officer and his plan was sound, but it had one large caveat. Its success depended heavily, if not entirely, on keeping Gen. Joseph E. Johnston's eleven thousand Confederates pinned near Harpers Ferry to prevent their reinforcing Beauregard at Manassas. When he presented his plan to the cabinet on 29 June, McDowell pleaded for more time to implement it. Lincoln countered that the Confederates were just as unprepared as McDowell's forces: "You are green, it is true; but they are green also; you are all green alike."[13] The president ordered the general to go forward.

Some fifty infantry regiments, including the First Minnesota, were directed to assemble in northeastern Virginia in preparation for an assault on Beauregard's army. "We are now ready packed to march—we know not where—under sealed orders, with forty rounds of ammunition in our cartridge-boxes and one day's rations, in our knap-sacks," "D" wrote his editor.

> The Col. came around to each company telling them that ours was considered the best volunteer regiment in the United States! that we must take care of our legs, or they might carry us off when we received the first fire, that we were not surgeons, and therefore must leave any one who falls by our side alone, and much other advice for our benefit. We were going to march he said, but it was not our business where; it was our duty to follow our officers. He said he would not rush us into unnecessary danger, but we would be liable to a fight at any time. We are ready to strike our tents at the toot of the bugle. . . . A few of the boys are unwell, but none will be left behind. We were all furnished with a new military, cloth cap this morning, and we are soldiers, playing a part in one of the greatest Revolutions America has ever seen. We will do our duty, if I do not mistake the spirit and pluck of the boys.[14]

On the morning of 3 July the regiment broke camp on Capitol Hill and proceeded to the Navy Yard, where it boarded two steamers for the short trip down the Potomac to Alexandria. Celebrating the fact that they were on Confederate soil for the first time, the men cheered as they marched through the nearly empty streets of the historic town. Henry Taylor, for one, was not impressed: "Marched through that old secession hole. . . . Poor, stony, deserted town."[15] A few blacks who ventured out to witness the strange sight of yelling Union soldiers appeared astonished by what they saw.

After General McDowell inspected the Minnesotans they marched one mile west and set up camp on the Alexandria–Fairfax Court House Road. Once again they settled into the routine of daily drilling, but now it was broken up by the new routine of picket duty, in this instance to guard the railway and telegraph lines. In enemy territory, the Minnesotans were understandably nervous but sometimes also trigger-happy. One day a man from Company H shot at and killed a man who he thought was an enemy soldier but who Bassett said turned out to be a "seccesh civilian preacher."[16]

The men knew the Confederates were nearby, and some wrote home to say that they were eager for action and confident of the outcome. In doing so they were also ratcheting up their confidence. Cpl. Sam Stebbins passed on news of Company K to the Winona *Republican* and explained what guard duty was like. He concluded, "Before long we expect to move forward to attack the rebels, and if they don't run we shall have some fun. We are anxious for a chance to meet the scamps on an open field."[17] Distant artillery fire brought the regiment out one morning at three o'clock, but it was a false alarm. Stebbins would have to wait for his "fun."

"D" too wrote to his readers that the regiment was ready:

> We know not the day nor the hour we may have orders to march. An advance movement of course is contemplated from this side of the Potomac, to which troops are crossing from Washington in great numbers. Probably the grand march, cleaning out Fairfax and Manassas Gap on the passage—the troops presenting a wide front, to be concentrated around Richmond, where the rebels will make their grand fight, if any—will commence as soon as the army is supplied with army wagons, which are under contract now. . . . We who have volunteered do not fight under discouraging circumstances.

What if we do live rough, eat hard bread, and pork, and drink water and muddy coffee! What if we are aroused from our troubled slumbers by midnight alarms, march with heavy packs strapped to our shoulders, in a Southern climate! What if we leave our friends with the certainty that many of us will never return to our adopted country? . . . Conscious that we have been foremost in the ranks of nations, are we not proud that her name will be more illustrious in the future, while internal peace and universal good-will will unite a prosperous and happy people? We perform no reluctant task.[18]

There were false alarms almost every night, as the jittery and untested commanders were taking no chances. Any sign of enemy activity was sufficient reason to call out the entire unit. The regiment's camp, according to "D," was "surrounded by spies and scouts. They have been distinctly heard by the guards, signalling in the grain fields and bushes, and two were seen and fired at night before last. Last night they were heard, but the night being very dark, could not be seen. One guard was fired into by two men with pistols. . . . Our regiment took two men in custody as spies, who however upon investigation were liberated.—Several suspicious characters are around in the day time. Some of them will be taken care of some of these days, if they don't keep quiet."[19]

Spencer wrote that "there is a skirmish about every night" and that they were looking for an attack momentarily. "Each man has 40 rounds of cartridges in his cartridge Box," he added, "and does not pretend to take his pants off at night. We don't calculate to be taken by surprise." He assured his sister that "a soldiers life agrees with me. I never felt better in my life. I am just spoiling for a fight."[20]

The regiment celebrated the Fourth of July, according to "Raisins," "in a far different manner than by others. We had a grand burlesque Indian War Dance, executed in a style which would do justice to any set of savages wherever congregated." Some of the men chose to celebrate the occasion by having a local delicacy—crabs—for dinner. But Searles, who said they "look like fury," noted a slight problem: "None of us know how to cook them—awful fix." At night, "D" wrote, "the sky in the direction of Washington, was lit up with the fireworks displayed on that occasion. We hope before another anniversary of our independence rolls around, to be at home enjoying the blessings of peace and the prosperity which will follow."[21]

The Minnesotans were curious about this new country, especially about blacks. One day a group went to a nearby poorhouse, where Bassett saw "the most miserable looking creatures that I have ever seen. The blacks and whites mingle together without distinction." On another day a former slave claiming to be 110 years old walked the half mile from the poorhouse to visit with the men. "He says he is the first man that beat the drum for Gen. Washington," Bassett recorded. "Says that Washington brought him up, and his mother before him. T[h]e General treated him well, sent him to school, and treated him like his own child. He was owned by 13 different men since the death of Washington, and has been abused. He is very patriotic. When we left, he took off his hat, made a polite bow and said, 'Success to you, God Bless You.' . . . Very interesting to visit with."[22]

"D," in Virginia only a few days, tried to articulate what he saw in a larger context:

> A mighty change has been wrought in the spirit of the people we have all so highly respected. The rule of slavery has done its work. The people have become demoralized and infatuated. The ch[i]valry of Alexandria have left their homes, by thousands, in the care of their wives and domestics, and attached themselves to the rebel army. The property they have left behind is nearly worthless. The people are beginning to reap the just reward of disloyalty and rebellion.— It is to be desired, but not hoped, for it cannot be expected, that private property will not suffer for it is impossible for armed hosts to be encamped in a country like this, surrounded by persons from whom the North have received insult and injury, unparallelled in civilized nations, without committing some depradations, and the loyal are as likely to suffer as the rebel.— A house was burned a few rods off the other day. It was unoccupied, but of some value.[23]

Only the quality of the food dampened the men's spirits—the Winona company protested by conducting a mock funeral to bury its breakfast—but the arrival of a regimental sutler helped. Oscar King and his wagon went everywhere that the regiment did, offering cakes, pies, and other "delicacies" for a price, usually a handsome price. Knowing that the men could spend their money nowhere else, he was usually willing to extend credit until payday.

King also provided liquor for the officers, a service that understandably rankled many of the enlisted men. One night several of them decided to liberate a keg of whiskey from King's tent. Without detection they carried it to a nearby field, where it was tapped, half emptied into the men's canteens—it is not recorded how much disappeared on its way from the keg to the canteen—and then buried for future retrieval. The theft was soon discovered, and the lieutenant of the guard was dispatched to apprehend the guilty parties. Alarmed, the perpetrators sought the help of their sergeant, who had not been part of the plot. He reproved them for the act, but he was not about to let them down. He observed that the lieutenant was making his way down the row of tents, determining the number of occupants in each, and then calling for that number of canteens.

Returning to his own tent, the sergeant discovered that only two canteens besides his own were empty, so he had to think fast. According to Lochren, the lieutenant "soon approached and called for him. 'Sergeant, how many men have you?' 'Fourteen.' 'Pass out their canteens.' With a peremptory order from the sergeant to the men to pass up their canteens rapidly, an empty canteen was passed to the officer, smelled of, and dropped at his feet as a second one was handed him, while a man, lying down where he could reach safely in the darkness, passed the dropped canteen back to the sergeant, to be presented to the officer again, and thus the three canteens were each examined five times and nothing found." The culprits were never discovered, although the experience "frightened the boys, and made them careful in the use of the liquor."[24]

On 13 July the detachment from Fort Ridgley arrived, and once again the regiment was up to full strength at slightly more than one thousand men. Two days earlier Gorman had reported to Governor Ramsey that the Minnesotans were ready for the fight they knew was coming, and he took the opportunity to boast that his troops were better trained than others nearby: "I say to you, sincerely, we are the best drilled, best disciplined regiment in the service, and such is the judgment of the regular officers who have seen us."[25]

McDowell was scheduled to begin moving his forces toward Manassas on 8 July. He put off his departure date, however, until he could be assured of adequate supplies and until he could organize the independent regiments into a workable command structure. For the first time the Minnesotans were fit into a larger unit and thus into the Army of Northeastern Virginia. With two other infantry regiments and an artillery battery, they became part of Col. W. B. Franklin's First Brigade of Col. Samuel P. Heintzelman's Third Division. Setting up command and control structures on the very eve of battle meant that unit commanders would have virtually no experience dealing with one another, a fact that would prove costly to the Union effort.

The Minnesotans were ordered to pack their knapsacks for storage in Alexandria and then to be ready to march. "We take our coats, one pair of socks and roll in our blankets, in a long roll and tie the ends together," Bassett explained to his family. "We throw this over our shoulder and carry it very nicely. This with three days cooked rations, and forty rounds of ammunition is called light marching order."[26] Leaving behind fifteen-year-old Charley Goddard and almost one hundred other comrades laid low by dysentery, diarrhea, and assorted other illnesses, the regiment broke camp on 16 July, joined up with the other units, and headed for Manassas.

Because most of the regiments were new to their brigades and divisions, there was a good deal of sorting out to do as the unruly and strange-looking procession assembled. Adding to the confusion was the fact that there was no common uniform but, rather, various colored shirts, with the Minnesotans still standing out in red. Once the units got under way the line of march behaved much like an accordion, crowding up in places when there was a halt at the head of the column. As a result, the men, unused to marching in such large numbers, were forced to spend long periods standing on dusty roads under a hot sun waiting for the march to resume. An abundance of ripe blackberries and streams along the route was their chief consolation, and they did not hesitate to break ranks to get their fill of fruit and water. The lack of discipline greatly agitated McDowell, who later complained that the men did pretty much as they pleased. The column made twelve miles the first day and sixteen the next, when they reached Sangster's Station. "As we came into this place," "D" wrote, "we could see the smoke of bridges burned by the retreating army."[27]

The Minnesotans, accustomed to the vigor and productivity of midwestern farmers, were unimpressed by what they saw. "This is a miserable country, thinly settled, the buildings poor and old, without paint, but some are whitewashed," Bassett recorded. "The water is poor, the people poor and ignorant. Not half of them can talk anything but the Virginia dialect." Chaplain Neill reported seeing "here and there a clearing, and with a poor log farmhouse and an apology for a barn in the shape of a few pine logs loosely put together and half decayed. The inmates are what the Virginians call 'poor whites.' The mother stands at the door, a tall, vacant, gaunt, care-worn woman; the children pale and buttonless; the father ill clad and looking as if he were half ashamed to hold up his head in the presence of decent people."[28]

On the second day some of the men, not yet disciplined enough to make their rations last, decided to see what they could find to eat in the countryside, although foraging was strictly forbidden. "A large number of the boys had eaten all of their three days' rations in two days," Sam Stebbins reported,

> and with no prospect of getting any more, they considered it a des-
> perate case, and early in the morning several of them took their
> guns and started to see what they could find, but for some time they
> had no success. At last they found a nice fat heifer, and one of the
> boys looked sharply at her neck just behind the left ear, and ere
> long she made a half right wheel and grounded arms, and we had
> plenty of meat, but no salt. I went to a number of farm houses for
> salt. The people seemed very much frightened, but treated us
> kindly, and would give us anything we asked for. They said they had
> been told we would burn their buildings and destroy their property,
> and probably kill them; they seemed to have a particular dread of
> the Fire Zouaves and when I told them that the celebrated Fire
> Zouaves were camped within two miles of them they shook with
> fear and begged us to stay and protect them, but we assured them
> there was no danger.[29]

As the men advanced toward Manassas Junction it was evident that they were getting close to the enemy. Lieutenant Colonel Miller led Companies A and B on a scouting expedition and reported back that he had seen an enemy battery of five or six guns about three miles away. Rebel pickets who hadn't received the word that their units were pulling out were captured and paraded through the Union camp. The Confederates, alerted by spies in Washington that McDowell was on the march, felled trees and created other obstacles to slow his progress. "Started northwest, cutting our road clear some of the way," Henry Taylor wrote in his diary, "routing the 'Secesh' pickets and came up to the railroad track just in time to see the rear of the rebels as they ran, burning bridges after them."[30]

"We soon came to deserted picket posts," Chaplain Neill remembered, "and in a little while at an abandoned camp ground there was a great dense smoke and we learned that the rebels had left in haste this morning, burning up all the stores they could not carry with them." Finally, on 19 July, the troops marched into Centreville, where McDowell's entire army was gathering. For the next two days, according to "D," "we remained inactive, each half hour enlivened by some new rumor, camp gossip, the capture of some new specimen of the 'sesesh' tribe, whom Madame Rumor had dangling from a distant tree in less than half an hour."[31]

The Union commander had already lost a day marching, and now he lost another resupplying the troops with food and ammunition and personally scouting the terrain and enemy defenses. The delay would cost him dearly. Learning of McDowell's intentions, Beauregard had pleaded for reinforcements from Johnston's forces in the Shenandoah Valley, and his request was granted. Johnston eluded the Union forces shadowing him and boarded railway cars for Manassas Junction. Their arrival in a few days would mean that McDowell had lost his huge numerical advantage; the two armies would be virtually identical in strength.

Bull Run creek stood between McDowell's and Beauregard's armies. Its deep water and steep banks made it impossible for artillery and difficult for infantry to cross except at a few well-known fords. As a result, Beauregard established strong defensive positions along six miles of the south bank with breastworks supported by cannon at each of the crossings. McDowell could either charge these heavily defended fortifications head-on or go around them. He chose to go around them. He would feign an attack down the Warrenton Turnpike across Stone Bridge and send his main force, including Heintzelman's division with the Minnesotans, on a broad circling movement to the north. McDowell intended to catch the rebels unawares and take them from behind. All the plan lacked was experienced commanders and seasoned troops to carry it out.

■ ■ ■

At two o'clock on the morning of 21 July the First Minnesota was up and ready to march, and every man knew that he would see combat. After a delay of several hours—the Union forces were constantly behind schedule at Manassas, a major factor in the events of the day—Heintzelman's and Gen. David Hunter's divisions made their way from Centreville down the Warrenton Turnpike toward Bull Run, six miles away. Well short of Stone Bridge and after crossing Cub Run, they left the road and veered sharply to the north on a wagon trail. "The march was very tiresome," Stebbins wrote, "as it was a warm day and very dusty. I could form no idea of the number of soldiers, as I could not see either end of the line. The road seemed like a living river of soldiers."[32] At eleven o'clock, two hours late but having covered more than ten miles, they forded Bull Run near Sudley Church, far beyond the Confederate left.

During the last several miles they had heard cannon and rifle fire to the south, and they were aware they would soon be in the thick of it. The sounds they heard were from the diversionary effort at Stone Bridge, which was proving wholly unconvincing to the Confederate forces defending the bridge. They saw the feint for what it was, and after sounding the alarm they rushed north to meet the two Union divisions to stall them until reinforcements could be brought up.

McDowell's plan was not working perfectly, but it was working. The Confederates had not expected the flanking movement, and for two hours they were steadily pushed back over the rolling countryside by forces that outnumbered them by better than two to one. McDowell had every reason to believe that the day would be his. True, the assault of the Union forces was not well coordinated, with most units fighting in isolation from the others, but the element of surprise and the numerical advantage augured well for a Union victory.

Colonel Gorman was ordered to lead his Minnesotans, who thus far had been held in reserve, to several different positions on the battlefield, including one "near the front and centre of the enemy's line, in an open field, where we came under the direct fire of the enemy's batteries," according to Gorman's official report.[33] It was already a blistering hot day, and many of the men threw away their blankets and some even their canteens, to lighten their loads. The regiment was soon directed to support Capt. James Ricketts's battery, the artillery unit with which it was brigaded, on the far right of the Union lines. To get there the men had to march double-quick time directly across the front of the rebel lines. Fortunately for the Federals, the enemy's artillery pieces were aimed too high and the shells missed their mark. But nonetheless the march was the Minnesotans' first exposure to hostile fire, and through it they showed the steadiness and resolve that would characterize their behavior later that day.

Their objective was Henry Hill, which commanded the approach of the Union forces down Sudley Road from the north. Followed by the artillerymen with their horses and cannon, the troops swung sharply to the right and crossed Warrenton Turnpike where it intersected with Sudley Road so that they could approach the hill from the west. On the way, the men encountered the first corpses of their brief war experience as they passed several Zouaves who had been killed by shelling just moments before.

"We filed left into the field," recalled Capt. William Colvill, whose Company F was leading the advance, "and then up the hill, coming by company into line, and then forward into line, with intent to form on the brink of the hill, the batteries to pass through the line at the centre, taking position a short distance in front."[34]

Coming over the crest of the hill, with the Blue Ridge Mountains to their backs, the Minnesotans faced a rolling plateau of waist-high grass spotted with thick clumps of scrub pine and oak. Several hundred yards opposite them and bending around to the regiment's extreme right, dense woods concealed the Confederate troops of Gen. Thomas J. Jackson, who was about to make his presence felt. "Stonewall had his trap set," Colvill said later—using the legendary name that Jackson would acquire that day—"and did not choose to disclose it."[35]

Ricketts's battery of six artillery pieces, ten-pound Parrotts, passed through the regiment to take up its position, and in doing so it split the Minnesotans into two separate forces. Company A and Colvill's Company F, together under the command of Lieutenant Colonel Miller, slid off to the far right and effectively lost communication with the rest of the regiment for the entire engagement. Gorman formed a line of battle for the main force extending left from the battery, which was the southern tip of the Union position. There was great confusion everywhere. "One of the cannons stood directly behind me," Stebbins wrote, "and I heard the officer of the gun order his man to shoot us down if we did not get out of the way; and as I saw him about to execute the order I stepped forward out of the ranks and to the right, when the gun went off, and nearly knocked me down."[36]

The batteries and the Minnesotans, it quickly became evident, were far in front of the rest of the Union line and thus in a highly exposed position. Once over the crest of Henry Hill they were easily within sight and range of the rebel batteries, themselves effectively masked by scrub pine just outside the woods opposite the First. Even more threatening was the presence of Confederate infantry deployed behind a ridge, much closer than anyone had initially thought. Gorman reported several days later that his men were "within fifty or sixty feet of the enemy's line of infantry, with whom we could have readily conversed in an ordinary tone of voice."[37]

Dust from the horses, and the similarity of Northern and Southern uniforms, compounded the confusion on both sides. The new Confederate flag, moreover, bore a strong resemblance in color and design to the Stars and Stripes. It was virtually impossible to tell which units belonged to which side.

Colonel Heintzelman, the division commander, appeared on the scene and ordered Miller's separated Minnesotans to "feel in the woods for the enemy." "We responded by volleys, and then by a continued fire," Captain Colvill later recorded. "It would have been more sensible to have pushed a few skirmishers into the wood, who, in two minutes, would have notified us of the near approach of the enemy." Gorman reported that Heintzelman "rode up between our lines and that of the enemy, within pistol shot of each, which circumstance staggered my judgment whether those in front were friends or enemies, it being equally manifest that the enemy were in the same dilemma as to our identity."[38]

So great was the uncertainty that Lieutenant Colonel Boone of the Second Mississippi responded to the fire of Companies A and F by approaching the units and ordering them to stop shooting at their "friends." He had mistaken the red shirts of the Minnesotans for those of the Fourth Alabama. Javan B. Irvine, a civilian from St. Paul who was traveling with Company A—such was discipline at this point in the war—asked Boone if he was a secessionist. The colonel responded that he was a Mississippian, whereupon Irvine brandished his bayonet and took as his prisoner the highest-ranking Confederate officer captured during the battle.

At least one of Jackson's regiments, however, knew who and where the enemy was. The Thirty-third Virginia emerged from the woods on the far right, opposite the Minnesotans, and started toward them. At that moment Confederate artillery fire fell on Ricketts's battery with devastating effect. "They had barely unlimbered, and got in altogether two or three shots," Colvill recalled, "when the concentrated fire of all the enemy's guns had killed all their horses and many of their men, practically disabling . . . the batteries."[39]

The "quiet and deliberate" approach of the Virginians caught the attention of a companion battery, Capt. Charles Griffin's, which was on the right of Ricketts's and therefore well positioned to stop the advance. Inexplicably, however, Griffin ordered his men to hold their fire before they too were disabled. The failure of the battery to fire would have disastrous consequences for the Minnesotans, and they would not soon forget it.

Gorman, too, apparently believed the Virginians to be Union forces, and he refused to allow the Minnesotans to fire, despite the desperate appeals of Edward Davis, his sergeant major. Suddenly the field erupted, as the rebels unleashed their fury on the Minnesotans and the remaining artillerymen at close range. The regiment staggered back, reeling under the powerful and unexpected blow. Capt. Lewis McKune of the Faribault Guards, "his arms raised up encouraging the boys on," took a bullet through the heart and fell dead. Asa Miller, the flag bearer of Company G, "was hit by three balls before he fell and after that he loaded and fired some three or four times" before finally succumbing to his wounds. Henry Taylor wrote that he "was wounded in left hand and wrist by a musket ball and bomb shell." He would recall that "the piece of shell that did the work broke one side of the swivel that held the upper end of the gun strap & left quite a scar on the gun stock."[40] Men everywhere went down. Thirty in the color company alone were killed or wounded and the colors themselves were "riddled with bullets." This was the critical moment for the men of the First Minnesota. If they were to break and run, now would be the time.

They did not break. On the contrary, for the first time they displayed the "coolness" under fire for which the regiment would be praised repeatedly in official reports throughout the war. Their first task was to avoid the rebel fire, and in taking cover they became so crowded together that they found themselves lying on top of each other. "As we had special orders not to fire until ordered," Edward Bassett wrote his parents two days later, "we all dropped down. I did not see the boys drop at first and stood up until they had all laid down and I looked around first on one side, then on the other and could not see the enemy as the bullets were flying about as thick as raindrops. I thought that the safest place for me would be flat on the ground. We laid there about ten minutes when the order was given to retreat firing. By this time the enemy had come up in sight and the boys fired into them and killed them off pretty fast."[41]

According to Sam Stebbins, who a few days earlier had hoped for "some fun" when he met the "scamps," the bullets began to come in his direction

> about as thick as hail, and I could see the rebels' heads sticking up over a bank about ten or fifteen rods in front of us. I took as good aim as I ever did in my life and fired at them. Then I heard the order to all lay down, and tried to do so, but it was impossible, for our line was broken and we stood in a perfect crowd at our end of the regiment. There were so many that had obeyed the order to lay down before I had fired that I could not get down; so I jumped out of the crowd to the rear, and loaded and fired my gun standing up. As I was commencing to load the next time a man that stood behind and a little to my right was shot and fell forward, sticking his bayonet into the instep of my right foot, and throwing me down. I looked at him and saw that he was dying, and tried to push him off, but he died instantly, laying on the breech of his gun and holding it fast. It was one or two minutes I should judge, before I could liberate myself.[42]

As minié balls whistled by, the men quickly took up positions behind the crest of the hill. The task of reloading was time-consuming and awkward, especially for soldiers who were lying on their backs to escape enemy fire. They tore open the cartridges with their teeth, spreading black powder around their mouths, and then forced the charge down the barrel with a ramrod before rising to fire. "They fired, retreated behind bushes and fired, loaded and fired, &c, and undoubtedly did great damage to the enemy," "D" wrote later of the Minnesotans' response. "Our boys . . . loaded and fired with as much coolness as though they were shooting chickens," said Sergeant Spencer.[43]

But reloading from a supine position did not always ensure safety, as Mathew Marvin learned. He wrote his brother that "the nearest I came to being wounded was after loading my gun & turning over on my left side a secesh bullet struck a stick about 3 feet from me & bounded & struck my thigh tearing a hole in my pants without injuring my leg atall. I had quite a number strike close by in the ground & roll under me & stop."[44]

Jackson's artillery maintained a continuous raking fire of grape and canister—the men thought it sounded like heavy thunder when combined with rifle fire—but the Minnesotans rallied and held their positions, even though they were still heavily exposed. The Confederates, by contrast, were able to employ the terrain effectively. "Their ground was carefully selected," "Raisins" wrote after the battle,

> and was composed of valleys and hills, covered with forests and a thick growth of dwarf pine. Their batteries had been planted with great care, under the supervision of able and experienced renegade engineers, in various positions, and so arranged that when one battery was silenced there was another and another in the rear, to open fire on those who captured the foremost ones. They were nearly all masked, and no one could tell their position until they had opened their murderous fire. Our troops were mainly infantry; our batteries, although well managed, were no match for the larger calibre of the enemy's cannon. The rebels had a most decided advantage in position and guns—they knew it, and used them with fearful effect. The bravery of our troops was superhuman, they could not meet the unerring and unceasing fire which came sweeping from almost every tree and bush.[45]

Miller's two separated companies, still off to the far right, escaped the brunt of the shelling, as well as the ground attacks, and hit the advancing force's flank with great effect. Captain Colvill described what was happening in his sector:

> [The Confederates] pushed over the batteries, pretty well jammed up, and finally faced about toward us, and we expected their volley. Instead came a frantic waving of arms and fearful yells, of which we could not distinguish the words because of our fire, which was kept up till the enemy faced to the rear, and after awhile gained distance enough to step out, and then to run, when we broke through the fence to follow along side. We found the woods full of fleeing Alabamians, and we picked up half a dozen too demoralized to

run. . . . We followed the enemy to the thicket, where they disappeared. Our two companies then extended to a skirmish line, penetrating the thicket by cattle paths, and keeping up a lively skirmish fire as any of the enemy were seen dodging about. Then came the real rebel yell, as from their cover, down through the fields outside the woods, charged Beauregard's whole command . . . to the guns. Now came the struggle . . . for their possession.[46]

The guns of Ricketts's battery had become the focal point of both armies, with first one side taking them and then the other. Back and forth it went through the afternoon over ground littered with dead and dying men and horses. The fire was so concentrated on the Minnesotans that when someone counted the holes in the regimental flag after the battle, he found that it had been shot through by "one cannon ball, two grape shots and sixteen bullets, and one in the staff."[47] Lt. Nathan Messick of Company G decided to save his flag by ripping it from the staff and wrapping it around his body, thereby inviting enemy fire. Miraculously, he was not hit.

The wounded Stebbins, who had thought momentarily that Ricketts's guns might offer "a little protection," quickly changed his mind. "At this time the artillerymen had left the cannon and every horse was dead, and the Minnesota regiment had moved to the right and left me," he said.

> I loaded and fired several times while standing there.—There were several of the Minnesota Regiment lying dead in front of me, but they all lay on their faces, so I could not tell who they were, and the fire was too hot for me to stop and examine them. At last an officer of the Zouaves ordered us to retreat and take to the woods, but as I ran down the hill I saw the blood running out of my shoe. I sat down to examine my foot, and when I got my shoe on again I saw our boys coming back, and the rebels had possession of the cannon that had been left by our artillery, and were turning them against us.—As I was lame, I thought it best for me to take care of myself, and accordingly started with a man that had a shot through his arm for the hospital, but he could travel faster than I, and left me as I was passing off from the field.[48]

Eventually the greater Union numbers pushed the rebels back all across the front, and it appeared that victory was imminent. "Three times in succession," McDowell reported, "was [the enemy] repulsed and driven back, the third time it was supposed by us all that the repulse was final, for he was driven entirely from the hill and so far beyond it, as not to be in sight, and we were certain the day was ours, they were evidently disheartened and broken."[49] Great importance was attached to capturing the enemy's colors, and during one of the "repulses" to which McDowell referred Sgt. John G. Merritt of Company K took brief possession of a rebel flag. He would be awarded the Medal of Honor for his action.

First Sgt. Josias R. King of Company A, who claimed to be the Union's first enlistee, recalled the scene when the firing had stopped and the Confederates had cleared from the field: "There was a general rejoicing and exultation prevailing, and we all had concluded the battle was over and the victory ours, officers and men cheering and huzzaing, every one was feeling elated over our success; I saw brigade and field officers shaking hands, congratulating each other; the heat and fatigues of the day were for the time being forgotten." A rumor swept through the ranks that McDowell had sent for the wagon train at Centreville, the obvious implication being that he intended to go into camp right there. Some men wandered off to the creeks to refill their canteens while others went sightseeing, according to King, "looking at dead Confederates, picking up pieces of exploded shell, or anything they could find, as souvenirs. . . . It was but a very few minutes before all regimental organization was entirely gone."[50] John McEwen of Company A was among those looking for souvenirs, especially for Confederate revolvers, which were highly prized among the men. He actually found several "but threw them away thinking that I might find a better one," he wrote a cousin who was eager to have one.[51]

During this interlude Captain Colvill experienced a moment that would stay with him: "Long after . . . all sounds of battle, had ceased, being restive and anxious for news, I left my command and came back to the guns, which stood, powder-stained and grim, in the midst of slain men and horses. They looked forsaken; not a living creature was in sight in any direction."[52]

The rejoicing that King witnessed was premature; the Southerners were far from defeated. They were demoralized, to be sure, but the arrival of Johnston's reinforcements from the Shenandoah rallied them. Johnston himself led an attack on the left flank of the Union forces, at the other end of the battlefield from the Minnesotans, and it took the

Northerners completely by surprise. The charge was accompanied by the rebel yell, a high-pitched, piercing screech that sent fear through those who heard it. The Federals were first stunned by the Confederate charge, then confused, and finally afraid for their lives.

"An attempt had been made to rally the men," King remembered, "and form line regardless of regiments, but every one was giving orders, and pandemonium reigned supreme. The enemy had now approached within a hundred yards and poured a volley into this howling mob; it was then 'Skiddoo,' every man for himself and the devil take the hindmost. There was nothing else to do but to get up and git out of the way; we could do nothing; it was an utter impossibility to restore order."[53]

Although the Minnesotans did not receive the brunt of this attack, Gorman saw that the Union forces around him were retreating. If he held his position the entire regiment could be jeopardized. Jackson's artillery and the Virginians' assault had already taken a heavy toll on his men. He ordered his companies to retire, and they did so in orderly fashion to the foot of Henry Hill. On their way off the field, Gorman reported, "the enemy attempted to make a charge with a body of perhaps five hundred cavalry, who were met . . . and repulsed with considerable loss to the enemy, but without any to us."[69] Private Bassett of Company G also remembered the clash with the horsemen: "In the retreat, we rallied severel times, and charged to hold the Rebs back. Their Black Horse Troop of cavelry, the flower of their army, charged us several times, but were beaten back and badly cut up."[54] The regiment regrouped and headed back north along the same path it had come that morning.

Sam Stebbins, meanwhile, found himself part of a growing tide of wounded making for the rear, but he too encountered the same rebel cavalry:

> I saw a great many wounded men who asked for water, of which I had a canteen full, which I gave them. When I arrived at the hospital I sat down in front a while as the doctors had plenty of worse cases than mine to attend to. I had been here but a few minutes when I saw a regiment of infantry on a hill about half way from the hospital to the enemie's batteries, and a large body of the rebel Black Horse cavalry charged on them and scattered them in every direction; but the cavalry didn't stop there, but dashed up on the hill to the hospital, where there were several hundred, perhaps a

thousand of our men who had brought in wounded men, and some who were slightly wounded, and we all sprang to the rail fence that partly shielded us from their fire, and when they were within a short distance one of the Zouaves that was wounded gave the word and we opened a fire that mowed them like grass, and there were but very few of them left to retreat, but what few there were, fled with the greatest possible speed. I thought it was not best for me to stay there any longer as the shell and shot began to come a little too thick, and for the first time in the whole day I began to think we were going to be whipped. I started for Centerville."[55]

After several skirmishes with the Confederates, Lieutenant Colonel Miller discovered that his two companies, still separated from Gorman, were virtually alone on the battlefield and would have to make their own way back. "Soon a lonesome feeling came over us—no other men in sight, and most of us suffering greatly from thirst," Colvill recalled. "The men began to fall off, and Miller, with a reluctant glance toward the guns, gave the order to retire." But not everyone was eager to leave. "Even then some lingered for a parting shot," Colvill said. "The last, perched on a fence, and there himself a good mark, stayed till I insisted on his leaving. This poor fellow, Fred Miller [no relation to Stephen] of my company, had advanced furthest to the front of any man that day, and was at one time cut off from us by the enemy. On leaving the field he came across three of his comrades carrying a fourth to hospital, and helping, was captured before the hospital was reached."

Colvill himself had a harrowing experience withdrawing from the field:

As I was about to start from the scene of the last action, near the guns, I heard a man crying, and saw . . . a soldier sitting on the ground, and went to him. He had dragged himself from the wood and was crying at seeing us leave, thinking himself abandoned. His leg was broken, the bone protruding. I quieted him, and, seeing a troop of our cavalry, hurried back. . . . Just then one of the cavalry exclaimed, "The devils are coming," and every horse whisked about, and the cavalry was off like a streak. I turned to see what was the matter, as a platoon of the enemy was making a wheel out of the woods to the right into the road. Their sweep would have taken me in. Instinctively, I broke for the ravine. . . . As I reached it I heard the chuck of the muskets, as they fell forward into the left hands, and dropped on my back on the slope, as the bullets buzzed like a nest of hornets past my head. I sprang up and, glancing back, saw a row of blank faces, astonished at seeing me break down the ravine, soon out of their fire. When I reached the brook three or four of our men were drinking. A Wisconsin man dropped dead in the brook as we started. A Fire Zouave jumped the brook at my side, and ran up the hill. He also dropped, but with my help reached the top and the shelter of a tree.[56]

The soldier crying for help was presumably taken prisoner.

Colvill eventually made his way to the head of the retiring Union column near the Warrenton Turnpike, where he saw General McDowell, "his face turning alternately red and white with every pulsation." This was not to be McDowell's day after all. From his vantage point Colvill could still see the battered guns of Ricketts's battery on the hill above him and two brigades of enemy troops advancing "in fine order" toward them. After the column had withdrawn toward the Sudley ford, at McDowell's order, Colvill took a final look back: "As I passed along a fence a glance showed the enemy making a final charge on, and leaping with huzzas upon, our abandoned guns, from which they had been thrice driven, twice by our regiment alone."[57]

The Union retreat to the Sudley ford was carried out in growing confusion as regiments became entangled with one another. Colvill's company arrived at the ford to meet up at last with Gorman, and the regiment was made whole again. A field hospital had been set up at Sudley Church, where the two surgeons of the First, J. H. Stewart and C. W. LeBoutiller, were treating the regiment's wounded. The most seriously wounded would have to be left behind, and the surgeons elected to stay with them, knowing their decision would mean certain capture and months, if not years, in a Confederate prison.

Governor William Sprague of Rhode Island, in temporary command of one of his state's regiments, "rode up with information," according to Sergeant Lochren, "confirming our fears, that the general result of the battle was disaster." Deciding to head back to Centreville, Gorman offered the Minnesotans as the rear guard, but Sprague refused him the honor, claiming it for himself. The regiment marched "in perfect order, in column by platoons," until a Union cavalry unit smashed through their ranks "and our men had to break to the right and left to let them pass, and did not afterward try to keep in regular order," Lochren wrote.[58]

Private Searles remembered the retreat as "headed by many civilians, mostly politicians, who had come out from Washington to see their demand of 'on to Richmond' obeyed by the military forces. The haste with which they changed that cry to 'on to Washington,' and the sweat and alacrity that characterized their execution of the movement, afforded the soldiers about the only consolation to be derived from the movement on Manassas."[59]

Some of the men became separated from the regiment and proceeded back toward Centreville alone or in small groups. First Sergeant King and five other men from Company A were among the latter. When they reached Bull Run they found a young lieutenant and a corporal "in a quandry" about how to get a wounded officer across. "I saw his dilemma; giving my musket to one of my men, I jumped into the creek, took the wounded officer on my back, and carried him across, the Lieutenant and Corporal crossing on the log and took their wounded comrade from me." King learned a few days later from his parents in Washington that the young lieutenant, who had paid a call on them and relayed the story of the rescue, was his second cousin. It was a small war.

After crossing Bull Run, King came to Cub Run, where he found a Union ambulance mired and abandoned in the mud. "Fortunately for us," he wrote, "we struck the ambulance before the Johnnies; suspecting that there might be some contraband goods in the ambulance, I got inside, regardless of the shelling that was going on, and it did not take me long to dig out a box of good old hospital whiskey, nor did it take me long to get the top of that box off. I handed out a quart bottle to each of my comrades and, knocking off the neck of another bottle with my bayonet, we each took a long steady drink. Talk about an 'Oasis in the desert,' this whiskey at this particular time knocked 'em all silly!"[60]

Also separated from the main force, according to a dispatch filed a few days later by "Raisins," was H. A. C. Hines of St. Paul:

> He was considering which way to turn, when a trooper came along and stopped near him, saying, "Well, we are giving 'em fits at last— see them run." Hines was unarmed, but quickly demanded, "who are you?" "Virginia Cavalry," was the reply. A pause ensued, during

which Hines felt a little nervous—he wanted to run too. Cavalry man bethought himself perhaps his neighbor was a Unionist, and propounded the same question, "who are you?" Hines answered "I'm all right," and went toward the horseman to shake hands. On nearing, however, instead of shaking hands he snatched the rebel's sword from its sheath, and demanded his revolver, after which he made him dismount. He was surrendered to a captain in one of our regiments near by.[61]

Sam Stebbins called the retreat "the worst of the battle." Limping along on his wounded foot, he said, he "went very easily for a mile or two and stopped at a church which was used as a hospital. I remained there but a few minutes, for the word came that the rebel cavalry were coming, and all who had any arms would be killed if taken. I was advised to throw mine away, but I thought better, re-loaded and started on. I saw a number of our boys, but they could travel faster than I could, and as they could not help me, which they volunteered to do, I advised them to go on, as I might be the cause of them all being taken prisoners."[62]

Retreating with the main force, Private Searles witnessed "a confused mass of empty wagons, ambulances loaded with wounded, wagon and artillery horses carrying two and sometimes three men, fatigued soldiers, without weapons, equipments, or knapsacks, with torn clothes and bleeding wounds—a hurrying stream of unarticulated humanity, no man knowing his neighbor."[63] As they approached Centreville, Confederate artillery fired on the column, reminding the men, if they needed reminding, that they were engaged in a humiliating retreat.

It was evening now, and the Minnesotans were tired and demoralized. A mood of deep depression pervaded the ranks. They had been marching and fighting since two o'clock that morning, and on reaching their bivouac of the previous night they were "so much fatigued that most of the men dropped to the ground, and were asleep at once, expecting a renewal of the battle the next day." After only a half hour of rest, however, the men were wakened by the cooks, given fresh coffee, and told they had been ordered to set off immediately for Alexandria. "This was the hardest of all," Lochren recalled. "We knew we had met with a repulse, but had not realized that it was to be accepted as a defeat, and the prospect of a march of twenty-five miles, after such a day of phenomenal heat, long marches and hard fighting, seemed an impossible undertaking. How it was accomplished cannot be told. The writer, carrying knapsack, haversack, musket, and complete soldier's outfit, was, on this march, several times awakened from deep sleep by stumbling against some obstruction."[64]

They reached Alexandria shortly before noon the next day and collapsed in their tents for several hours of sleep. In the afternoon they were awakened again and ordered to march the six remaining miles to Washington through a driving rain. "It was the hardest days work I ever expect to do," Edward Davis wrote a few days later. "We marched 12 miles from Centreville to the Battle ground, fought over 2 hours hard fighting & then retreated to Alexandria 42 miles doing all inside 31 hours and only 2 hours sleep during the time & going without food for 24 hours having thrown off our rations before going onto the field of action."[65]

Finally arriving in the capital, Lochren said, "we were compelled to stand on the street more than an hour, in torrents of rain, when churches and halls were assigned for temporary shelter." At Lochren's shelter "our constant friend, [Congressman] Aldrich, appeared promptly with a troop of colored servants, bearing pails of hot coffee, baskets of eatables, and other comforts, most acceptable in our drenched and exhausted condition. The regiment never had a warmer or more efficient friend than Col. Aldrich."[66]

As difficult as the retreat had been for Lochren and Davis and the other Minnesotans, it was preferable to the experience of two other members of the regiment still on the battlefield. Twenty-one-year-old John Alderson had been shot through the breast and was unable to move until the following afternoon. Staggering a half mile toward the Union lines, he sighted a group of soldiers and breathed a sigh of relief, believing that the North had carried the day. He asked for directions to the nearest U.S. hospital, only to discover too late that the men were Confederates. He quickly became their prisoner. J. O. Milne, twenty-three, had also been seriously wounded and left for dead when the Union forces withdrew from Henry Hill. He would lie on the field, semiconscious from the loss of blood, for two days before a Confederate burial party discovered him. They put him on a cattle car packed with other prisoners bound for Richmond.

Sam Stebbins, meanwhile, was still trying to make his way back alone. He managed to evade several detachments of Confederate cavalry looking for stragglers, but eventually he could go no farther on his disabled foot and sought refuge in what he called "a respectable-looking house":

> A black girl came to the door. I asked her if the master of the house was in. She said no, and that his name was Brown. I told her my condition—that I was wounded, tired, wet and hungry, and could travel no farther. I was invited to come in and in a short time Mr. Brown came and I told him my circumstances. He smiled and said he was a seccessionist, but as I looked like an honest man, was welcome, and he would do the best he could for me. I told him that I had no money. He said it made no difference, and ordered the black girl to dress my wound, which she did in the best manner. My foot had swollen much and was very painful. Brown was sociable but differed with me in opinions and said if the South could not gain its liberty without him, he was willing to shoulder his musket and fight for them. He said he hoped I never would come back, but I told him my regiment came back and I was able and should be with them. He was a first-rate fellow and treated me well, giving me lodging and breakfast, and urged me to stay longer, but not feeling perfectly safe, I thought it best to try and reach Washington. The people along the road were mostly in favor of the Union, but were surprised to hear of the treatment I had received from Mr. Brown, who they said was a rank seccessionist.

Stebbins soon found a camp of Rhode Islanders and a wagon ride to Washington, where the next day he was reunited with the Minnesotans. At the end of a long dispatch to his newspaper, he concluded simply, "I felt very different in battle than I expected."[67]

Governor Sprague had been right on the mark—the battle was a total disaster for the Union. Despite a sound battle plan and sufficient troops to implement it, the North's cause was decisively undermined by delayed movements and especially by the failure to prevent the arrival of Johnston's reinforcements. Both sides had difficulty coordinating units for maximum effect, but the Confederates managed the task more effectively. They were also able to engage a greater percentage of their troops in actual combat. The battle was an inauspicious beginning for the North, and it would change the way the two armies, and the whole country, thought about the war. To most Americans, North and

South, it was now apparent that the contest would be long and bloody. It would ultimately become total war, a concept never before experienced, and probably never even imagined, by anyone on the American continent.

The Minnesotans performed well under the circumstances. They fought bravely and they did not panic, as many other untested units did. W. B. Franklin, the brigade commander, said in his official report that the regiment "behaved exceedingly well," and Colonel Heintzelman, the division commander, noted that, of the four regiments engaged around Ricketts's battery, only the First Minnesota, among the last to leave the field, retired in good order.[68]

The men themselves agreed that they had fought well. Some were even a little astonished at just how well they had done. "Colvill fought like a tiger & took 7 prisoners," Edward Davis wrote of his company commander. "I was surprised at the bravery & courage the boys all showed and manifested." But many of the men did not believe that they had been adequately led. "An obvious fault . . . consisted in putting the troops into action in small detached bodies," Lochren observed, "without properly ascertaining the position or strength of the opposing force, or even properly regarding what was in plain view. The result was that in almost every attack our force there was too small, and was beaten in detail." Lieutenant Colonel Miller was even more blunt in a private letter to Governor Ramsey, which quickly became public: "So insane an attack by civilized men I never heard of."[69]

The men were also highly critical of those regiments that did not fight well, and especially of those at the foot of Henry Hill, such as the Fourteenth New York, that did not fight at all. "Is it not strange that during all the while that our regiment was hotly engaged but a few rods in front," Colvill asked, "this regiment was held out of fire, to be stampeded (Griffin says), a few minutes later, by a few rebel horsemen?" Sergeant Spencer of Company G expressed to his sister what many of the men believed: "If we had been properly supported we would have gained the victory."[70]

Some inevitably questioned the regiment's deployment: "It is hard to understand why we and the two batteries were put on that plateau at all," Lochren said, "swept as it was by so many Confederate batteries, so near and plainly in sight." Finally, they were bitter that fire was "senselessly" withheld by Griffin's battery as the Thirty-third Virginia approached and that the battery had placed itself in such a vulnerable position. "After Griffin's . . . blunder in going into the concentrated fire of twenty-six guns at close range, and not unseen, and by the side of a wood filled with the enemy," Colvill complained, "their batteries were disabled in a minute. Yet they claim the guns were lost for lack of support. Were they not well supported when such an overwhelming and sudden attack was repulsed effectually by our regiment?"[71]

Summing it all up, "Raisins" quoted a "wag" as saying that "the name 'Bull Run' was a very appropriate one for the scene of the late battle. He says the commanding officer made a 'bull' of the thing in attacking the rebels as he did, and that the 'run' was engaged in with a will by both of the combatting parties. He will do to travel."[72]

Because the Minnesotans had the bad luck to be at the epicenter of the battle, they paid a terrible price. Citing the "gallant conduct of my regiment," Gorman reported he had lost 49 killed, 107 wounded, and 34 missing.[73] Most of the missing were the wounded left behind at Sudley Church. In short, more than twenty percent of the regiment had become casualties, the heaviest loss sustained by any Union regiment at Bull Run.

Whatever else the experience that day did for the Minnesotans, it rid most of them of any lingering romantic notions about the war in which they were engaged without diminishing their ardor. "I know what it is to be on the battle field and have my friends shot down by my side," Joseph Spencer wrote soon after the battle. "I know what it is to stand where musket balls are thick as hail, and to have cannon balls, grape shot and bomb shell falling in every direction. I know what it is to have our lines broken and our men scattered, and to have them rally again around the good old stars and stripes. I know what it is to have our forces defeated, but *thank God* not a *cowardly* or *shameful* defeat."[74]

Sam Stebbins recalled the strange effect the battle had on him:

> When we first began to meet the wounded coming from the outposts of the engagement, it looked hard but they all seemed in good spirits, and it didn't affect me in the least. As we got nearer, there was a man lying beside the road wrapped in his blanket, and I opened the blanket to see if he was dead or alive; he was dead, and looked most frightful. It sent a shudder over me like a shock of electricity; but it was only for a moment, for the next minute we were

where the cannon balls were flying over our heads, and it was all excitement. There was no time after that when I felt any fear. I saw men with their heads shot off, and others who had lost their arms and legs; and looking on the fight, saw them fall in different directions with a supernatural coolness, the like of which I never before experienced. It is impossible for me to describe it so that one who never witness a similar scene could understand it aright. Several times I thought I should be wounded or instantly killed, but I felt *no* fear such as I have felt at other times in my life when I thought there was danger. There was no time during the battle that I would not laugh at anything comical, and when the man stuck his bayonet in my foot I put my hand against his head and pushed with all my might; and although I knew he was dying, yet I did it with as much indifference as if he were a horse."[75]

3

EDWARDS' FERRY

"Them Dam Blue Bellies."

On 23 July the regiment returned to its campsite on Capitol Hill, where the Minnesotans used the humiliation at Bull Run to give voice to all their frustrations. "Here . . . for the only time in the service of the regiment, was manifested some slight feeling of discontent and lack of *morale*," Lochren recalled years later with characteristic understatement. High among the complaints was "salt beef that defied mastication, and ancient hard tack, on which the brand 'B.C.' was claimed by the boys to mark the date of baking." Moreover, the long-promised new uniforms had still not arrived, leaving the men in "rags and tatters, reminding one of the uniform of Falstaff's vagabonds."[1] By no means least, the men had yet to be paid.

Dr. Daniel Hand joined the First on 27 July as the new assistant surgeon and found the men "badly demoralized. . . . They were tired, disheartened, and homesick, and my first experience at sick-call was in listening to the sorrowful tales of those who wanted to go home. They found many reasons why they were not fit for soldiers,—weak back, lame knees, sore feet, palpitation of heart, rupture, night-blindness, etc. It took most of my time to convince them they were not total wrecks."[2]

"D" wrote openly of the men's disgruntlement to his readers in Faribault, and he made no effort to conceal the identity of the man whom he believed to be its cause: "A change has come over the spirit of our Regiment, as deplorable as it is evident. Col. Gorman is very unpopular. For weeks ill feeling against him has been increasing, and rapidly since the memorable 21st. The boys complain that he takes no interest in the affairs of his men, any further than it serves his own interest. They complain also that our rations are not what our venerable Uncle Sam furnishes his agents for us; that clothes we should have had, have not been furnished, and that our payment has been delayed solely because of the dereliction of duty, on the part of some one. I am sorry all of these complaints are not groundless."[3]

The matter of new uniforms became a symbol of the men's discontent. It had consumed the attention of state, regimental, and U.S. Army officials for months, but its resolution always seemed to fall victim to bureaucratic bungling. Governor Ramsey had ordered uniforms from New York, but they failed to pass inspection. Another shipment missed the regiment at Harrisburg, and when it was sent on to Washington it was "appropriated by other regiments," according to Gorman. The men decided to get results on their own. "Yesterday a committee of gentlemen of Minneapolis called upon me and represented that ten letters from privates in the First Regiment of Minnesota Volunteers, now in Virginia, had been received at that place, complaining of the insufficient clothing of the men of the regiment," Ramsey wrote his state adjutant general, John B. Sanborn, in late July. At the same time newspaper stories on the matter began to appear "reflecting quite severely upon the officers of the gallant First, the state and the general government," according to regimental quartermaster George H. Woods. Ramsey dispatched Sanborn to Washington to "remedy all reasonable complaints and deficiencies."[4]

The long-awaited uniforms finally came, perhaps not so coincidentally, two days before Sanborn reached Washington. When Sanborn arrived everyone in authority denied responsibility. "To find fault at such a time is to bay at the moon, without remedy, and without fault of anyone," Gorman wrote Ramsey. "A few men wore out their pants and tore them, so as to render them unfit for duty. Several of the men were excused from duty owing to their want of clothing. This has occurred in all regiments and in all armies, and perhaps a thousand times." Chaplain Neill pleaded ignorance. "I have no idea that there has been any suffering among the regiment for the lack of proper clothing," he told Sanborn.[5]

Indeed, underlying most of the discontent in the regiment was a lingering depression stemming from the defeat at Bull Run. The men would come out of it eventually, but not before they took out their frustrations on Colonel Gorman and on the enlistment process, which some felt had been used to mislead them.

In rationalizing their defeat, the Minnesotans, like their comrades throughout the Northern army, complained of the rebels' "unfair way of fighting" and accused them of committing atrocities. "It is reported or rumored rather that the enemy burnt the Hospital & killed the wounded in the field," Joseph Spencer wrote a friend a week after the battle. "I believe it. They are a set of barbarians at the Best."[6]

But some also sought a scapegoat, and Gorman quickly became the leading candidate. Critics accused him of cowardice, claiming that he had virtually disappeared from the battlefield after the initial fighting on Henry Hill. William Croffut, a three-month enlistee who was close to the Minnesota congressional delegation (whose members were Republican rivals of Governor Ramsey) wrote the *New York Tribune* that Gorman's performance at Bull Run "is not favorably spoken of by his command, most of them asserting that they *did not see him* after the first charge."[7] The article, no doubt intended to embarrass Ramsey, who had appointed Gorman, became the subject of much controversy throughout the regiment as well as back in Minnesota. The fact that Gorman was not in front of his regiment at Bull Run, where the men could see him, caused many of them to conclude that he was a coward. Experiencing their first combat, they did not understand that his proper place was behind them, where he could direct their movements.

Gorman defended himself against the charges as best he could, suggesting that the men were actually unhappy over the lack of proper food and clothing, but the controversy lingered. More than six weeks after he had been wounded on Henry Hill, Sam Stebbins wrote his hometown newspaper that he doubted there were "ten men in the regiment who have one bit of confidence in Colonel Gorman, as an officer or as a man. I have heard as many as one hundred swear they will never go into another battle under him, they say they will desert first."[8] Charley Goddard went even further in a letter to his mother: "There is men in the Reg that hate him [enough] to shoot him as quick as looked at him   he is an old tyrant . . . if there is any little thing goes rong he will throw down his cap and curse and sware like a trooper & it is a shame the way such an old man should sware so and when our Reg was coming down the river he got as drunk as a fool and hardly could stand up."[9]

The accusations against the beleaguered colonel were largely unfair; there is no credible evidence of cowardice at any time in his military career, including that Sunday at Bull Run. He had the bad luck, however, to be compared with his lieutenant colonel, Stephen Miller, whom the men credited with great bravery in leading Companies A and F after they were separated from the regiment. In most men's assessment of effective military leadership, personal courage outweighed virtually all other qualities combined, and Miller did nothing to dispute the notion when he wrote Ramsey, his patron and political ally, in early August: "I did as I now think, place my life in peculiar and perhaps very indiscreet peril, by rushing before my men; but let me say to you *in the strictest confidence*, that it was a necessity, in order to save the credit and reputation of our State and Regiment. . . . I know that I and many of my men fought well."[10]

Miller also demonstrated that individual initiative, even when undertaken contrary to orders, was a more highly prized quality than modesty. "When ordered by our superiors to retreat we retreated under orders, in different directions," he reported to the governor. "After a few minutes I went back *without orders* retook and reoccupied our original ground and went ten or fifteen paces beyond, and fought the enemy again until all others left the field. In this I probably did wrong, but we were a representative Reg't, and I determined that my State make her mark and have a reputation or lose her Lieut. Col." Miller's fellow field officers in the regiment supported Gorman throughout, but the company officers and enlisted men were nearly unanimous in their criticism.[11]

Similar discontent in the ranks fueled a dispute over the legality of the three-year enlistments. Even before Bull Run some of the men maintained that the three-year enlistments ought not simply replace the three months the men had first sworn to. Once the three-month tour of duty expired at the end of July, they argued, the regiment would have to be mustered in anew for a three-year stint. Obviously this interpretation meant that the men would be free to go home after three months' service, which was precisely what some of them had in mind. According to "D," there were those, privates and captains alike, who would never reenlist under Gorman. "It is not to be supposed, however, but that there are some who enlisted for fun, or without a full consideration of what they were doing, and who would avail themselves of any pretext to quit the service. The battle from which they have just returned, and the hardships of those few days on the soil of Virginia, have convinced them that it is not a very funny affair. But as we get well of our sores, get our money, which they promise soon, get on some new clothes, and are allowed the liberty of looking at a few of the sights of our National Capital, we will all, most probably, feel much better than at present, and again go forth to do our duty without a murmur."[12]

"D's" prediction ultimately proved correct, but it would be some time before conditions permitted the men to "feel much better." When the end of July passed, and with it the three-month deadline, three companies requested their discharges from Gorman. The colonel declined but said he would pass the request on to a higher command. At the same time, nearly half the men in the regiment signed a petition to Secretary of War Cameron asking for an investigation. Unwilling to wait for an answer to these inquiries, the Stillwater company convened a meeting of both officers and enlisted men to debate proposals for taking things into their own hands. A few vocal members wanted to march on Washington—the regiment, having left on 2 August, was by this time forty miles away—to demand their rights, but the majority finally settled on a more measured course. They decided to send a single representative to the capital.

The choice of Edward A. Stevens, the Stillwater *Messenger*'s "Raisins," was a curious one. He had written of the enlistment controversy early in July, and he was thoroughly familiar with the technical legal arguments. Together with his ability to articulate the case, this fact may have accounted for his selection. He was one of the few enlisted men in the entire regiment, however, who still defended Gorman, and that distinction could not have endeared him to many. He also had a tendency to change his views unexpectedly; one day he abruptly dropped his support for the regimental officers and another day he switched his position on the legality of the enlistments.

Stevens visited the state's congressional delegation but received no encouragement for his mission. When a trip to the War Department was also unavailing, he decided to exercise the authority given him by

Company B to retain legal counsel. He engaged one Richard S. Coxe for "a fee in proportion to his services" contingent on success. Coxe had been approached earlier by others regarding the matter and he was both familiar with its elements and persuaded of its merits. On 10 August he filed a petition with Supreme Court Justice James M. Wayne for a writ of habeas corpus demanding that Stevens be released from the army.

Adj. Gen. Lorenzo Thomas was initially inclined to look into the request for discharge and, if he could, to act favorably on it. He immediately had second thoughts, however, and decided that it was better to let the courts decide the issue. On receiving the writ directing him to produce Stevens, Gorman sought direction from Gen. in Chief Winfield Scott, who ordered the colonel to respectfully decline to comply and even drafted a proposed response for Gorman to send the court. Scott soon perceived the full significance of the issue, however; he reversed his order and took the matter to the highest levels of the government. President Lincoln and Secretary of State William H. Seward decided that the government had no choice but to defend vigorously its position and they asked former Attorney General Edwin M. Stanton to argue its case.

Stanton, whom Lincoln would name shortly to replace the hapless Simon Cameron as secretary of war, understood that losing the lawsuit could mean the rapid departure of thousands of volunteer soldiers from the Union army. "We must not have a wrong decision," Seward reportedly told him. "A right one will strengthen the hands of the Government." Stanton responded, "But you can't 'coerce' a Judge of the Supreme Court of the United States to make a right decision; nor even to tell you how he is going to decide." "No," Seward replied, "but we can prevent a wrong decision from being carried into execution. The nation's life is greater than the dignity of the nation's court."[13] The administration had already suspended habeas corpus, and it was prepared to stretch, if not breach, the Constitution in other ways to preserve the Union.

But in this instance that wasn't necessary. Justice Wayne rejected Coxe's argument, which was based on technical irregularities in the mustering process, and sided with Stanton, who maintained that Stevens was estopped from disavowing the legality of his enlistment contract since he had benefited from it. Wayne also ruled that the act of Congress retroactively approving Lincoln's call for three-year volunteers was constitutional and, thus, that enlistment contracts entered into pursuant to the call were valid.

Stevens summarized his view of the case for his readers:

> Mr. Coxe claimed the discharge on the ground that false inducements were held out, and that in no one particular had the Army Regulations been respected. Mr. Stanton for the government, claimed that the Army Regulations did not apply to volunteers, and that while the government threw safeguards around the regular forces, the volunteer must look out for himself. He concluded by an appeal to the patriotism of the Judge, and ended about as follows:—"These Minnesotians, who begged to get into the service, and kept far better men away and are now keeping them away, now ask you to discharge them. The enemy is at the very gates of the capital—if you discharge the petitioner, you must discharge the whole regiment; if you discharge the regiment you must discharge the whole army; and if you do that, what next? This beautiful edifice must fall into the hands of the rebel foe."—Logical, wasn't it? I thought so, especially his trying to keep the "poltroons," as he called them, here, when they are "keeping better men away." Well the judge decided that I was held, and remanded me back to the Marshal to be handed over to the Colonel of the regiment.[14]

It soon developed that Stevens stood to lose a good deal more than his legal case. General Scott ordered him arrested on charges of sedition and encouraging desertion, and he was taken to the Central Guard House in Washington. Stevens later maintained that Gorman refused to seek his release unless he was willing to "correct" statements he had made about the colonel's conduct at Bull Run. "I told him when I found I had done wrong I would correct them," wrote the headstrong "Raisins." "I have not done so as yet. He then commenced a tirade against newspaper correspondents in general and me in particular, and suddenly broke out as follows: 'As sure as there is but one step between me and hell, you incitors of this rebellion shall suffer.'—What did he mean?—he was talking of my correspondence and threatened to punish me and others for rebellion. I leave it for Minnesotians to draw their own inferences."[15]

So it was in an army where virtually every volunteer regiment had enlisted men who doubled as newspaper correspondents and who, writing in that capacity, felt no constraints in criticizing their officers. Stevens was one of a half dozen correspondents with whom Gorman had to contend, and as he learned to his regret, they almost always managed to have the last word. Stevens not only had the last word but also got out of jail without Gorman's help. Ramsey and others interceded for him as enthusiasm for a court martial waned, and after a month the correspondent was allowed to return to the regiment.[16]

Meanwhile, having broken camp on Capitol Hill at the beginning of August, the First began its march up the Potomac River. The prospect of a new destination took the men's minds off some of their complaints, but not all of them. The fact that they hadn't been paid prompted a modest insurrection in the ranks: the men said they wouldn't march until they received what was due them. There followed an extraordinary set of negotiations between Colonel Gorman and his men. "Took up our line of march at 9 oclock A.M.," Mathew Marvin recorded in his diary on the day they left Washington. "The boys are rather reluctant to strike their [tents] because they are not paid & have hard grub. The Col promises to go 4 miles & incamp in a good place & stay until we get our pay & when we get to our journeys end we shall have a whiskey ration if a maj[ority] want it." The paymaster finally arrived the second day out, but he had enough money to pay only half the regiment. "Agreed to march 1½ miles to the woods & their stay until every man get his pay & plenty to eat," Marvin wrote two days later. "Received our pay & wagons came with grub & Blankets. I got $30.36."[17]

The men received eleven dollars in gold and treasury notes for each month's service—as a corporal, Marvin received more—and they were elated. This was more money than some of them had ever seen. "One can hardly imagine how rich a fellow feels when he has two gold eagles in a pocket which has long been innocent of having a cent," "Raisins" wrote. "And that in a camp where one has not had at all times too great a variety to eat, and luxuries 'nary a one.' " "Discontent vanished at once," Lochren remembered.[18]

About the only thing available to spend their money on was food, home cooking at that, and the men wasted little time going after it. "I went up to a farmhouse and tried to buy my dinner," Edward Bassett wrote. "I had $22.89, in the pure quill, right from the mint. There were others before me, so I only got two pieces of bread, some molasses and a bit of ham. The woman had been cooking until she was tired out, and had cooked up everything in the house. Went back to camp, and there were severel wagons there loaded with pies, cakes, etce. I bought some cake and ½ a pie and ate it and began to feel like myself again."[19] The men learned that they could invariably rely on the entrepreneurial skills of sutlers and Maryland farm wives when payday arrived.

The regiment passed through Rockville—"a pleasant village, with a rather disloyal population," according to one Minnesotan—and Seneca Falls, where it spent several pleasant days. The tranquillity of the countryside was already having an effect on the men. Twenty-one-year-old John Thorpe of Company K wrote his father in Rollingstone that he wished he could stay "for two or three weeks, as this is a beautiful country and there is plenty of good spring water, which we prize more than anything else. The health of the camp is a great deal better than it was when we were in Virginia. Some of our men are pretty well used up by exposure and fatigue, but I have stood it first-rate so far, and so have all the Rollingstone boys."[20]

A few days later the Minnesotans reached their destination of Edwards' Ferry, one of the principal crossings on the upper Potomac. The river was about a quarter of a mile wide at that point and shallow enough that boats could be poled across. The Baltimore and Ohio Canal, which ran parallel to it, about a hundred yards inland on the Maryland side, was one of the main avenues of commerce between Washington and the nation's interior; keeping it open was deemed vital to the war effort. Both banks of the river were covered with a heavy growth of trees and brush. Except after torrential rains it flowed peacefully in a bucolic setting, and over the coming months the men would become attached to it.

The regiment's new home became Camp Stone, named for Gen. Charles P. Stone, the commander of the division containing the Minnesotans. It was situated in a wheat field on the gently rolling Maryland countryside two miles north of Edwards' Ferry and an equal distance south of the village of Poolesville. "Our camp is quite pleasantly situated on a slope, which allows the water to run off freely after every shower," "D" wrote several weeks after the regiment arrived. "The streets are ditched on both sides, and are swept every morning, and every offensive thing removed, which gives a tidy appearance to our village. Evergreens have been planted on a few of the streets, green houses built, and high poles at the head of the streets have nailed to them the names of the streets, thus: 'A Street,' 'Pell Place,' and 'Winona Avenue,' meet the eye."[21]

In this pastoral setting of undeniable beauty and serenity, it was sometimes difficult to remember there was a war to fight. The Minnesotans, who were unimpressed by most of what they had seen since leaving home, were much taken with it. One of them wrote his hometown newspaper of "a fine wooded country bordered on both sides with waving fields of corn and rich orchards, while elegant dwellings dot the landscape. In some places, where orchards lined the sides of the narrow road, the branches (drooping under the heavy load of apples and peaches) formed natural arches of foliage and fruit."[22]

The five-month encampment at Edwards' Ferry proved the most peaceful and comfortable of the regiment's three-year experience. It was made all the more so by the friendliness of the locals, who, though mostly sympathetic to the South, usually didn't admit it. "For the past few days I have been around to quite a number of the farm houses, and have made some acquaintances," "D" told his readers shortly after arriving. "There seems quite a sympathy for those on the other side of the Potomac. But few, however, express it by words. They all have 'friends' or 'relatives' on both sides, and wish a compromise could be made—'War is such a cruel thing.' And it is a fact, these farmers near the Potomac are in continual dread."[23]

"The people all claim to be union," Bassett wrote, "as long as the Feds, are here, the Nigs say." Searles recalled that the local population was "chiefly 'secesh,' although so tempered by circumstances and association that the ladies, in many instances, before the winter passed, showed an increasing appreciation of a 'Yankee' in [an officer's] shoulder-straps."[24] For the remainder of their service the men would look back on their time in Maryland with longing.

The mission of Stone's division was to prevent the Confederates from crossing the river and moving northeast to isolate Washington from the rest of the country. The capital was still nervous, and after Bull Run everyone in authority took seriously the threat of an encircling movement by rebel forces. Guarding against such a possibility meant constant picket duty on the Potomac, which is how the Minnesotans spent a good many of their waking hours—"one-third of the time," according to Henry Taylor.[25]

"I like this guard duty first-rate," Sam Stebbins—not yet fully recovered from his wound but well enough to resume normal activity—wrote to the Winona *Daily Republican*.

> There is something exciting about it. It takes three companies for picket guard at a time. The companies whose turn it is to go on duty put their knapsacks in a wagon, take two days rations in their haversacks and march down to the Ferry, which is headquarters for the guards. Then we are distributed to the posts, six or seven in a place except at the Ferry, where besides the guard there are twenty or thirty men left as a reserve. The posts are half a mile apart. In the daytime we can all sleep except one at a time, but at night we all have to keep wide awake, with our eyes and ears wide open. The river here is about 80 rods wide and the enemy has pickets on the other side; but there are trees and brush on the banks of both sides, so we can keep out of sight of one another, save when we go down to the water. We have a little skirmish almost every day, but as yet there have been none of our regiment killed or wounded, although there have been several narrow escapes.
>
> We can see our enemies every day and sometimes we can talk with them. The other day some of our boys were working in the river when two of the rebels came along on the other side and asked them where their guns were. Our boys replied that they had them close by, and inquired what kind of gun the others had. The rebels responded that they had Minie rifles [which had greater range and accuracy than unrifled weapons], and one of our boys told them it was a "d- -d lie." The rebels thought it was an insult, so they instantly fired at our boys, and then ran into the bushes and out of sight. At the Ferry our boys have a swing put up among the trees and I have often seen them sit and swing for a long time right in sight of the enemy. In fact, none of us would take any pains to keep out of sight of them were it not for the strict orders of General Stone. We are told by the men on the other side of the river that they have the same orders over there, so all of our little battles must commence in disobedience to orders.[26]

In a similar report for his Faribault readers, "D" made clear how much the men of Company G enjoyed the new experience. He concluded that they "had a jolly time of it. We feasted on boiled and roasted corn, unsweetned apple sauce, and a small quantity of bread, with such pies as each choose to purchase of the farmers at a 'levy' a piece. We slept under the canopy of heaven, or one of leaves, as we chose, we generally chose the former as being better ventilated! And the soft sand was our bed, unless like Ed Bassett, we constructed a hammock of grape vines, suspended between two trees. The boys were not anxious to leave their duty as picket guards. They had to answer no 5 o'clock roll call, do no police duty or drill."[27]

A month after Stebbins wrote his first account of picket duty he wrote another, this time detailing his personal experiences:

> We are posted about a half mile below the Ferry. The river and canal at this place are about 30 feet apart, and the canal is about 10 feet the highest. There is nothing to mark the spot, except some logs that are piled up for a sort of brestwork. About 8 o'clock I divided the men into three watches, two in a watch—one to keep guard here, and one about twenty rods below; and as I had only five men, I took the third watch at this post myself, and at 9 o'clock I was ready to retire, when I spread my rubber blanket on the smoothest place I could find, and rolled my gun in one side of it. Then placing my knapsack for a pillow, I lay down, but it was some time before I could go to sleep. The insects here are very numerous, and I had not lain but a few minutes when a beetle came walking over my face; and after I had brushed him away, and got nearly to sleep, I felt something scratch my knee. On an examination I found that a large bug had crawled up the leg of my pantaloons. At last I went to sleep, and dreamed of rattling drums and roaring cannon, and a battle, and victory.
>
> These dream-land sensations, however, were soon exchanged for the reality, by my being aroused, at 2 o'clock, to occupy my place on guard. So getting up, I wiped away the dew which had fallen on my cap while I slept, and taking a careful glance at my gun to see that the powder had not also got damp, assumed my post of duty. The night was a bright moonlight one, and as I looked up and down the river, it was undisturbed by a single ripple as far as I could see in either direction. On the opposite side a thick clump of trees and bushes cast a dark shadow on the water, and hid the rebel guards from my sight. Yet I knew that they were there, and it is probable that they watched for me quite as closely as I did for them. The

scene was one well calculated to inspire emotions of a varied nature, and to beget feelings which even the minds of the sternest could not repress, even if they desired to check them.

But a short time elapsed before I heard footsteps behind me and stepping back in the shadow of a bush, I could distinctly recognize the well-known step of Lieut. P. I ordered him to halt, but he, wishing to try the guard, did not stop. With a second command to halt, my gun was brought to a level with his body, and although he could not plainly see me, yet he could *hear* sufficient to make him understand that the guard was equal to his duty, and that for him to advance another step was instant death. Having then commanded: "Who comes there?" I received the reply: "The officer of the guard." The countersign was demanded and given in a whisper. After a few hurried words of conversation, Lieut. P. proceeded to the next post to repeat the experiment with the guard there. And so the night passes.

A few nights ago, while watching on guard, Charles North was approached by an object which, in the darkness of the night, he took to be a man. Having addressed it three times without receiving a reply, and the stranger still drawing near, the guard raised his piece and promptly shot the intruder down. A subsequent examination revealed the fact that the unfortunate intruder was but a rambling cow, whose ignorance of the rules of war led her to an untimely end.[28]

When stray cows weren't available to break up the boredom of picket duty during their first weeks on the Potomac, the Minnesotans, still smarting from the defeat at Bull Run, sought out the real enemy and frequently took potshots at rebel pickets when they appeared. "We send our compliments over to them in the shape of musket balls every time they came in sight on the opposite bank," Joseph Spencer wrote his sister in early September, "but as the river is about 90 rods wide we cannot do much harm." "One half of their bullets dont come across," Mathew Marvin wrote, but with more than a little bravado he added, "But ours make either the bark on the trees or the blood fly. We have got the old harpers ferry rifled musket."[29]

From time to time the two sides engaged in artillery duels. Marvin had little liking for the practice: "The shells get so close that I can all most smell them as they go by. . . . The bloody little things make a noise like a *nite hawk* only a goodeal more so. A person not yoused to this kind of business mite think it was tuff laying down flat on the grass watching for moore than the usual number of pickets be fore we can fire at them. The artillery are having all the fun & we have to lay here out of sight & let them shoot over our heads."[30]

Because neither side could do much harm to the other, an unofficial truce was declared. "Confederate pickets come down to the river and talk to our pickets," Edward Bassett wrote. "They made a bargain, not to shoot, as long as each kept to their respective grounds. We have just as good shooting irons as they have. They call the Minn. boys the 'Blue Bellies' on account of our shotting so savage."[31]

"Raisins" described how pickets on opposite sides of the river typically struck up a conversation:

> [The Confederates] walked out on the sand banks and conversed as friendly as they would have done a year ago.—First passed the usual morning salutations, then a few questions as to the price of whiskey on the Virginia side. Then followed a Union sentiment from both sides—"the Union as it was"—which was expressed in a wish to have a little whiskey. Secesh then asked the day of the week, and one of our boys who happened to know, answered that it was Sunday on this side. After a little more bantering they entered into a general conversation. Both parties were in the Bull Run fight, and the only overcoats they possessed were left by our army and picked up on the road by them.—They had been promised ten-dollars per month, but had received no pay as yet. Said they were badly fed and were tired of the business. They belonged to the 19th Virginia regiment. Since our last picket fight their pickets had been stationed half a mile back of the river.—They had no personal spite against us, and our boys hadn't anything in particular against them. Each party invited the other to cross over and partake of a soldier's hospitality. Secesh would come over, but had no boat, and some of our boys pushed out to go to them, but were stopped by our officers. The very sensible question was asked, but not satisfactorily answered: What are we fighting each other for? Would to God the people of all sections could thus have conversed with each other across the Potomac. Then would they have known each other better, and this unnatural war would have been avoided.[32]

Henry Taylor was among the Minnesotans who broke the monotony of picket duty by striking up an exchange with his opposite number: "I had quite a conversation with one of the Confederate pickets across the Potomac. He was gentlemanly in speech."[33] But the informal truces didn't always hold. Confederates upriver from Edwards' Ferry brazenly jeered and harassed the men of the Forty-second New York, or "Tammany," Regiment, knowing that their smoothbore muskets rendered them incapable of retaliation. The Minnesotans were invited to help even the odds one morning. "At a favorable moment our boys opened upon them with the 'deadly Minnie musket,' " "Raisins" wrote, "and as often as a head showed itself one or more eunical sensationists would fall in that vicinity. Some left their covers and ran away, some crawled away, and some stood their ground bravely. Such was the effect of this firing that a battery of artillery situated further back, opened with shot and shell upon the boys, and under cover of which the enemy ran down and carried away their killed and wounded. Three bodies were seen being carried away, and according to rebel authority, ten were killed and several wounded."[34]

Bassett described the incident more succinctly: "The Rebs shot among [the New Yorkers] and made Paddy Say 'och, murder,' he say. Some of our boys went up there and shot across, makeing the Rebs sing Paddy's song, they took to their heels, crying out, 'there are them Dam Blue Bellies again.' "[35]

Fifteen-year-old Charley Goddard rejoined the regiment several weeks after it arrived at Edwards' Ferry. Illness had confined him to a Washington hospital and had kept him from Bull Run, and the experience had nearly ended his army career. "I was laying on the bed with my cloths on & there was a doctor come in one that did not belong to my ward," Goddard wrote his mother. "He asked me how old I was   I supposed he only wanted to know to satisfy himself so I told him I was 17 years   he did not say any thing but continued to make his rounds from room to room and the first thing I knew he handed me a discharge   I took it and saw what it was   I said nothing but maid for the Regiment and told Capt H C Lester I did not want a discharge   he told me I need not take it unless I wanted to   this is the way the thing was arranged."[36]

The weather that greeted Goddard when he arrived at Edwards' Ferry and that continued during September was close to perfect. The subtle hues of the first foliage underscored the splendor of the surroundings. Life settled into a pleasant routine for the Minnesotans: daily drilling when not on picket duty and plenty of free time and pocket change to pursue whatever diversions were available. "The condition of the regiment seems to be in many respects better than it ever was before," Stebbins told his readers. "Many peddlers come into camp every day, bringing in for sale vegetables, butter, pies, cakes, family bread, etc. I have gained eight pounds since payday." There were only occasional and small disappointments. "I have just bought a pie," Bassett recorded, "an apple pie as they said, but alas, it was a seccesh pie as I found out when I cut it open. There was not more than a spoonful of apple under the lid."[37]

If anything intruded on the tranquillity at Camp Stone it was whiskey. The enlisted men deeply resented Gorman's order prohibiting them from purchasing liquor from the sutler—Oscar King had followed the regiment up the Potomac—while the officers were under no such injunction. The men were nonetheless able to get it "by surreptitious devices," according to Searles, either in villages close by or from enterprising slaves on surrounding farms. "You cannot buy much of anything [in nearby Darnstown] but whiskey, which is forbidden to soldiers," Bassett wrote. "Our Regt. is pretty temperate as a whole, and playing for money is forbidden to soldiers. This is nothing that will effect me, I am glad of it."[38]

Not everyone shared Bassett's temperance, certainly not William Bates, a private in Company H. One night Bates got drunk and "snapped his gun" at "John," a black cook, killing him. Claiming he thought the gun was unloaded, Bates was fined twelve dollars and sentenced to fifteen days in the guardhouse. The Union army may have gone to war with slaveholders, but it was not yet prepared to weigh a black life on the same scale as a white one. Shortly after this incident Gorman caught three slaves selling whiskey to his men. In an effort to settle on an appropriate punishment, he sought the views of the slaves' master, who suggested that the "black rascals" be whipped by the men who had bought the whiskey. Gorman agreed, and although he had General Stone's approval for the flogging, the episode would inspire yet another controversy around the colonel in the coming months and jeopardize his military career. "The whipping was not severe," Thomas Pressnell would say years later in Gorman's defense, "but it stopped the traffic, and there was no further attempt to remove the lid in Gorman's brigade."[39]

For most of the men the stay at Camp Stone was their first sustained exposure to blacks and the institution of slavery. "The Corps d'Afrique is represented in camp by two ladies and ten 'gemmen ob color,'" "Raisins" wrote. "They are employed as cooks for the officers, and are generally good-natured, industrious and obliging. The two wenches have a sufficiency of lovers, and from indications a wedding will soon come off, in which an officer's man Mose will figure extensively."[40]

"We are camped in the midst of a slave holding people," Bassett recorded in August, shortly after he arrived. "Nearly every farmer has from one to one dozen, blacks, as they call them, to do the work. They are a small penurious people, in general, of course there are exceptions." Three months later he was absolutely certain of one thing: "The war will never end until we end slavery. There is no alternative but to fight."[41]

Bassett's may have been the prevailing view of slavery, but it was by no means the only view in the regiment. "I can get a rite smart *Negro* clear from blemish & in prime of life about *$1,000* a *Female* of same quality for *$600*," Mathew Marvin joked to his brother. "I reckon I will confiscate 2 of them at that price & bring home." More serious were the thoughts of Thomas Pressnell as he remembered them years later: "We have not come to meddle in the domestic affairs of other communities. We ask no questions as to slavery or emancipation, it is none of our business. We do not wish to interfere with the private rights of the people. We come not to destroy, but to protect. But we strike for the Union and Constitution and the old flag." Sergeant William Lochren probably reflected more accurately the views of his fellow soldiers on the question of slavery in 1861 when he noted the "constant recrimination and abuse passing between the haughty, arrogant representatives of the Southern slave-holders and the meddlesome Abolitionists of the North, each hating the other, and equally willing to disrupt the union which bound them together."[42]

By September the regiment numbered only about six hundred men, down from the more than a thousand who had left Minnesota a few months earlier. Illness and Bull Run had taken their toll, and replacements were needed. The regiment undertook a new recruiting drive in the state but, like veteran regiments elsewhere, discovered that filling the ranks was more difficult than it had been in the spring. The enthusiasm and fervor of the early days had waned, tempered by the disaster at Bull Run and especially, in the case of the First, by the high number of casualties suffered in that battle. Moreover, many potential recruits believed that their chances for promotion were greater in new regiments, where they would at least be on an equal footing with other newcomers, whereas in veteran units they would surely be at the bottom of the seniority ladder.

Nonetheless, some 150 new recruits were found for the First during its time at Camp Stone, and among them was Isaac Lyman Taylor. Isaac had special reason, of course, to join the regiment—his favorite brother, Henry, was already a member of Company E. By mid-August Isaac could no longer resist the call of adventure and patriotism. He and his cousin Edward Taylor followed the road that Henry had taken from Belle Prairie down the Mississippi to Fort Snelling only three months earlier. They were both mustered in on 21 August; Isaac joined the First Minnesota, Company E, and Edward joined Company C.

"There are now twenty one of us mustered in for the 1st Reg.," Isaac wrote his sister Mary from Fort Snelling. "We drill four hours each day. We are under command of Commissary Sergeant Overton of the 2d. Reg. He is going to St. Paul today & has appointed me Sergeant pro tem with orders to put the '1st. Reg.' through drill squad today. I didn't expect to be promoted to the command of the 1st. Reg. so soon. I suppose my promotion is due to 'meritorious conduct' at the battle of Manassas. There! the bugle sounds to drill call & I must start for the parade ground with my Reg."[43]

Like his brother, Isaac was a promising young man—twenty-four years old when he enlisted, a year older than Henry. He would exhibit a curiosity about virtually everything he encountered, from the geology of rock formations to the headstones in Virginia cemeteries. Fortunately, beginning on 1 January 1862, he too recorded most of what he saw and did in a diary that revealed much about the experience of the First Minnesota that was not included in any official record.

Another new recruit was Thomas Pressnell, who had actually enlisted earlier, when the regiment was at Fort Snelling, but who was forced by illness to remain in Minnesota. Spurning offers to join other Minnesota regiments, he responded eagerly when Lt. Samuel Raguet of the First returned to St. Paul on a recruiting drive. With ten other recruits he went to Fort Snelling, but the mustering officer, on learning that Pressnell was only eighteen, insisted that he produce written permission from his parents or guardian. He explained that his father was dead, his mother was in England, and he had no guardian, all to no avail.

Returning to St. Paul with Raguet, crushed but still determined to join the First, he hatched a scheme to have Raguet's father, a St. Paul businessman, named as his guardian. Over the next two days he persuaded the senior Raguet and a local probate judge to go along with the idea, and he returned to Fort Snelling with valid guardianship papers and a letter from his new "guardian" granting him permission to enlist. Pressnell recalled that he "signed the master roll, and was once more a 'sure enough' soldier."

The new recruits headed east on the same route the regiment had taken just a few months earlier, and their experience was much the same. "There was general cheering from every station as we passed along and at two towns in Ohio came huzzas for the First Minnesota," Pressnell wrote. He found Washington a "dirty and, except the Capitol and public bldgs., decidedly uninteresting city. If it had not been for the military activity one could easily have imagined himself treading the portals of the graves in Hamlet's burying ground." The highlight of the brief visit was catching a glimpse of "old Abe in the flesh," and then it was up the Potomac to Camp Stone, where Pressnell said he "was unprepared for the cordial and affectionate greetings" of his new comrades.[44]

"Isaac comes to camp today," Henry recorded in his diary on 19 September. "I now have three brothers enlisted."

Despite his propensity for controversy, it had been rumored for weeks that Gorman was due to be promoted. The official announcement came on 1 October: Gorman was appointed brigadier general of volunteers and given command of a brigade in Stone's division. He still had to be confirmed by the Senate, however, and the flogging incident would not help him there.

Named to replace Gorman as the new colonel of the First Minnesota was Napoleon Jackson Tecumseh Dana. Anyone with a name like that, it was said, had no choice but to pursue a military career. Like his predecessor, Dana was a West Point graduate with strong Minnesota ties. He had served in the U.S. Army for fifteen years and achieved a distinguished record in the Mexican War before he was wounded. In 1852 he was appointed quartermaster at Fort Snelling, a post that permitted him to choose the sites for two of Minnesota's three frontier forts, Ridgely and Ripley. He actually supervised the construction of Fort Ripley. In 1855 he resigned his commission to become a St. Paul banker and a leading figure in the community. When war broke out in 1861 Dana helped enlist recruits for the First Minnesota, and it was widely speculated from the outset that he would eventually succeed Gorman as colonel of the regiment.

Lochren described Dana as a "model officer. Always calm, temperate and gentlemanly in demeanor, and having a fine, soldierly presence, he enforced the strictest discipline, without causing any friction or complaint, or giving rise to any dissatisfaction. His long, daily drills, with packed knapsacks, made the regiment perfect in the execution of all battalion movements, and developed the muscle, so needful in its subsequent service. The men became devotedly attached to him." Jasper Searles recalled that Dana "soon found where the discipline of the regiment could be improved," and praised his "personal supervision" of the full range of regimental activities. "He proved to be a strict disciplinarian," Pressnell agreed, "but he was so calm and gentle in his demeanor as to prevent friction or dissatisfaction."[46]

Almost anyone would have looked good after Gorman, but Dana was also seen as fair: one of his first orders prohibited not only enlisted men but officers from purchasing liquor. "Our Colonal Napoleon J.T. Dana is liked real well," Bassett wrote shortly after Dana's arrival. "He is temperance, and death on whiskey, and on the watch to detect some one selling something that will make 'drunken swine' as the Indian said."[47] Needless to say, the regimental officers did not receive the order with the same enthusiasm. Lochren's assessment of Dana notwithstanding, for them it caused more than a little "friction and complaint."

If the Minnesotans as a whole responded positively to Dana, he reciprocated. "The regiment is a very fine one and the officers & men are all willing to submit to discipline," he wrote a friend. "They will obey orders and can undoubtly be depended on—if they cannot then our cause is lost for they are the best troops in the field."[48]

The Union army also got new leadership after Bull Run. Lincoln, in search of a general who would bring him victories, jettisoned the luckless McDowell and sent for George B. McClellan, the only Northern general who had yet achieved one. Having risen rapidly in both military and civilian life without experiencing even the slightest adversity, McClellan, at thirty-five, had acquired a high opinion of his abilities and worth. The honor and deference he was accorded in Washington after responding to Lincoln's call only reinforced those inclinations, and he soon concluded that it was his destiny to save the nation. "By some strange operation of magic I seem to have become *the* power of the land," he wrote his wife shortly after arriving in the capital.[49]

It was probably inevitable that this messianic view of his role in the war—he even assumed a Napoleonic pose when photographed—would soon have grievous consequences, but in the meantime McClellan did what he did best: he turned scores of independent, inexperienced, and undisciplined regiments into an army. He ordered stragglers hanging about in Washington saloons arrested and returned to their units. He set up examining boards to oust incompetent officers. And he drilled the men hard, very hard. The soldiers understood what he was doing for them, and they responded with affection and respect for the man everyone called "the young Napoleon," an appellation to which he offered no objection. In creating the Army of the Potomac, McClellan also created a lasting bond with its men, including those in the First Minnesota. "McClellan is a working the thing about rite," Mathew Marvin wrote in late September. "We feel now that we have got a Gen at the helm that will take us through all rite."[50]

The new Union commander concluded by mid-October that it was time to clear the Confederates from the Virginia bank of the Potomac and, if possible, to force their withdrawal from nearby Leesburg, an important rail center, where a brigade of infantry and three troops of cavalry were headquartered. Unfortunately, the effort would reveal a tentativeness in McClellan that would prove costly to the Union cause over the next year and would drive Lincoln to distraction.

Receiving intelligence reports that the Southerners were planning to abandon the area for the greater security of Manassas, McClellan sent a division across the Potomac and up the Virginia side of the river to Dranesville, approximately ten miles from Leesburg, to hasten the rebel withdrawal. At the same time he ordered General Stone to make a "slight demonstration" on the Maryland side to reinforce the impression that a major offensive was imminent.[51] McClellan intended Stone's movements to divert attention from the main operation across the river, but Stone chose to interpret his orders broadly.

On 20 October he divided his force, sending Gorman's brigade, with its Minnesotans, to Edwards' Ferry to make a "display of force" and ordering the balance of the division four miles upriver to Harrison's Island, near Conrad's Ferry.[52] To attract Confederate fire and thereby assess enemy strength, Gorman ordered his regiments to show themselves, but when they did there was no fire from the opposite shore. He then ordered an artillery bombardment, and when there was still no response he sent two companies from the Minnesota regiment across the river in flatboats to reconnoiter the area. The troops flushed out several rebel pickets and drove them off, but after about fifteen minutes they returned to the Maryland side.

It was Isaac Taylor's first foray into enemy territory, and he was eager to tell of the experience. "I have just returned from an expedition into the country of the Secesh," he wrote his sister Alvira that night. "Tonight just at sundown, Cos. E & K, 1st Minn. Reg. crossed the Potomac at Edwards Ferry & set their unhallowed feet upon the 'sacred soil of Ole Virginny.' There were one hundred of us. We crossed to make a reconnaisance. The Secesh pickets took to their heels. After looking around a little we recrossed & came back to camp. We are ordered to hold ourselves in readiness. We shall probably cross a large force tomorrow."[53]

The Minnesotans began the night back at Camp Stone, but they were awakened at half-past one in the morning, fed a cold breakfast, and marched back to Edwards' Ferry. Arriving at sunup with the Eighty-second New York, the men immediately began crossing the river in force, two companies at a time, in flatboats and commandeered canal boats. The expedition appeared to be the chance that John McEwen of Company A had been looking for three days earlier, when he wrote his cousins, "We have not had any fighting since the disastrous affair at Bull Run but we are living in hopes that we will have a chance soon to give them another trial. We are well prepared for them this time and I think there is no danger of a defeat."[54]

"The regiment crossed by boat loads as rapidly as possible," Dana recounted in his official report of the action, "and at about half-past eight o'clock it was formed in line of battle. . . . with . . . two companies deployed as skirmishers about four hundred yards in front. This position we continued to hold for three days, during a great portion of which it rained violently and was very cold."[55]

It would be two days before Gorman managed to get his entire force of several thousand men on the Virginia side, but the effort was all to little effect. Stone intended Gorman's move to mask the main crossing, upriver at Harrison's Island, but Gorman found few Confederates to engage. When news of the action upriver arrived, he ordered the soldiers to dig rifle pits and entrenchments in expectation of an attack. It never came, but what little fighting occurred involved the Minnesotans. "There was a man shot by one of our sharpshooters while we were across the river," according to Charley Goddard, "and in his pocket was found a letter wrote probly by some thoughtless young girl asking him to shoot a yankey and send her his scalp. But alas he was the one to fall."[56] The First lost one killed and one wounded in the engagement.

Daniel Hand, the new assistant surgeon, who was experiencing his first combat, told of how he missed an opportunity to treat a ranking officer: "A few skirmishes on our front brought a number of wounded men, among them the noted General [Frederick] Lander, who rode up to me a few minutes after he had received a bullet in the calf of his leg. An aide asked me to examine the general's wound, and I was about to do so, when, as I pulled the boot-strap out of the hole where it had been carried by the ball, he swore a blue streak, and vowed he would go on to the ferry before having anything done. I was rather glad to get him off my hands. He was restless and intractable at all times, and by his independent conduct after this wound brought on a septic fever from which he died."[57]

The principal action was indeed occurring upriver, but not in the way that Stone had planned. On the morning of the twenty-first, elements of the Fifteenth Massachusetts crossed the Potomac at Harrison's Island on Stone's order and marched up the steep bank of the opposite shore, known locally as Ball's Bluff. They proceeded almost to Leesburg before encountering hostile fire, which caused them to withdraw to a field near the river. The commander of the small force asked Stone for instructions, and the general responded by sending reinforcements led by Col. Edward A. Baker, a U.S. senator from Oregon and friend of Lincoln's. Told to use his own judgment as whether to fight or withdraw, Baker, who was eager for a fight, had one by the time he arrived in Virginia. The Confederates knew precisely what the Union forces were up to, at Edwards' Ferry as well as at Ball's Bluff, and they committed all their available resources at the latter position to overwhelm the Northerners. After a fierce firefight of several hours, during which Baker had great difficulty getting his troops and especially his artillery pieces across the river and up the steep bank, he was forced to withdraw to the bluffs overlooking the Potomac, which proved an untenable position. Disaster quickly followed. The river was the only means of escape, but in the ensuing panic, boats capsized, men drowned, and those left on shore were picked off by rebel riflemen above. It was by every measure a massacre. When it was all over the Union forces had lost more than nine hundred men, the vast majority as prisoners of war. Among the killed was Colonel Baker and among the wounded was a young Massachusetts lieutenant named Oliver Wendell Holmes, Jr.

McClellan, meanwhile, had recalled his troops from Dranesville, but he had failed to inform Stone. The commanding general of the Union army arrived at Edwards' Ferry on the evening of the twenty-second and immediately became concerned that Gorman's forces, some of which had proceeded as far as a mile in from the river, were unnecessarily exposed. He ordered them to withdraw at once, and the First Minnesota, as the most experienced regiment on the scene, was directed to be the last to cross. Sergeant Lochren was detailed to Stone as his orderly and spent the night carrying orders to the various units. The removal of the troops back across the Potomac was orderly and uneventful—"With great labor and in perfect silence this trying task was fully and satisfactorily accomplished," Dana recorded—but the weather was not helpful. "The wind is blowing very hard," Bassett recorded. "It was hard to get many men across, because of the rough water."[58]

Lochren reported that Stone was the last to leave the Virginia side, but the claim was disputed by Cpl. M. F. Taylor, who had been ordered to stay back and look for stragglers. Finding none, he returned to the river and was about to embark when, he said, "hearing a call, I recognized Thos. Galvin of Company H, running down the bank of Goose Creek, followed by two or three rebel cavalrymen, but they abandoned the pursuit and Galvin was brought back safely."[59]

The regiment returned to Camp Stone and the routine it had established before Ball's Bluff. Jasper Searles recalled the daily bugle calls: "Reveille at sunrise; camp police immediately thereafter; coffee, half an hour after sunrise; drill, 7 A.M.; breakfast, 8 A.M.; sick-call, 8.30 A.M.; guard mount, 9 A.M.; general police, 9.30 A.M.; drill, 10 A.M.; adjutant's call, 12 M.; dinner, 1 P.M.; drill and parade, 4 P.M.; supper, 6 P.M.; retreat, sunset; tattoo, 8.30 P.M.; taps, 9 P.M."[60] Every day, weather permitting, the men could count on five hours of drill; since they were already proficient in the various maneuvers, many concluded that drill was really a pretext for exercise. Countless parades and inspections were an integral part of the routine, as was, of course, regular picket duty.

"We now have one drill in each day in 'Heavy marching order,' which means, with knapsacks packed, and haversacks, canteens, &c, or everything we have to carry on a march," "Raisins" reported in early November. "The object is, I presume, to accustom the men to carrying their 'Kit,' so that they will not be so easily fatigued when there is marching to be done. Every one is pleased with this order of things."[61]

As before, the men frequently broke up the boredom of long hours on the riverbank by conversing with their counterparts across the Potomac. The operating assumption, which invariably proved correct, was that an enemy sitting around your camp fire was an enemy unlikely to attack. But the practice was not officially condoned, as Henry Taylor noted: "A lieutenant and two privates are arrested for crossing the Potomac and conversing with Secesh pickets." Nor was it always so friendly, as Isaac Taylor reported: "Picket warfare on the river continues. I had three shots at the scamps to day. They commenced the game & if they would come within good range they would soon be game themselves."[62] Isaac was beginning to have a good time playing with words.

As cold weather approached, the men built what they called "California fireplaces" to heat their tents. "Raisins" explained how they worked: "A ditch is dug through the centre of the tent, about a foot deep and from fifteen to twenty inches in width. One end of this ditch is left open, the remainder is covered with flat stones, and the stones are covered in turn with clay. A chimney is built over the outer end of the ditch at a distance of from two to six feet from the tent, sometimes of stone work, but usually by placing two barrels, one upon the other, and plastering them on the inside to prevent their taking fire. A small quantity of wood in a fireplace of this description will keep a tent well warmed in the coldest weather."[63]

The barrel chimneys did manage to catch fire, however, and more than one tent was hastily evacuated in the middle of the night. The tents, moreover, were not always as warm as "Raisins" maintained, and as autumn turned to winter the men began cutting trees to make log-and-mud houses. Isaac Taylor wrote his aunt the first week in January that he and about thirty of his comrades "are comfortably housed in a log camp 20 by 26, with a double row of berths on each side and a generous fire in the center. We are to have three such buildings to accommodate the whole Co. but the other two are not quite finished yet." Some six weeks later he amended his appraisal of the structure: "Rain and hail the entire day," he wrote in his diary. "Our shanties a little too leaky for comfort, but who cares for that as long as rebelion was drying up." "Raisins" reported in December that the men had also cut logs to construct "a hospital, sutler's store, teamster's huts, stables, etc. . . . . It now begins to look as though we were soon to go into winter quarters— if, indeed, we are not already in them."[64]

"The Reg't has nothing to complain of in the world," Jasper Searles wrote in late September, "good victual and good clothes." George H. Woods, the unit's quartermaster, had reported to the state adjutant general at the end of July that army regulations permitted each man the following daily ration: "three-quarters of a pound of pork or bacon or one and one-quarter pounds of fresh or salt beef; one pound and two ounces of flour or bread or twelve ounces of hard bread; and at the rate, to one hundred rations, of eight quarts of peas or beans, or in lieu thereof, ten pounds of rice, ten pounds of coffee; fifteen pounds of sugar; four quarts of vinegar, one and one-half pounds candles, four pounds soap and two quarts salt." Since first arriving in Washington, he added, the regiment had always received "the full amount" of the rations.[65]

The "hard bread" was hardtack, a flour and water cracker the soldiers sometimes referred to as "teeth dullers." The men would do almost anything to make them more palatable. "I can relish my cup of coffy and hard crackers fried in greas," Charley Goddard wrote his mother. Others chose to pulverize them in coffee or soup or to toast them over a fire. Sometimes the crackers were stale or moldy or even infested with worms, but for all the grumbling and joking about hardtack, the men came to rely on its nutritional value and many actually came to like it. When the regiment was in camp, however, it had fresh bread every morning, according to Woods. "The bakery here is now in full blast," "Raisins" wrote in October, "turning out about five hundred supposed-to-be-twenty-two-ounce loaves daily.—The bakers are kept going day and night. Company B has made an oven also, for our cooks, And we now have hot buscuits or corn cake each night in addition to other rations."[66]

The quality of the pork and beef also sometimes left a good deal to be desired. It was often salt pork, or "sowbelly," as the men came to call it, and while it was most commonly broiled it was also fried, baked, or mixed in a stew. When the men were on the move and unable to cook, they would sometimes eat it raw in a hardtack sandwich. In camp, however, the Minnesotans usually were issued fresh beef twice a week.

Coffee was an especially prized item, and many of those who didn't drink it before entering the army soon acquired a taste for it. The longer a man was in uniform, it was said, the stronger he liked his coffee. The first thing the men would do after a long march would be to build a fire and cook some coffee.

Beans too played an important role in their diet. Charley Goddard reported one of the inventive ways to make them tasty: "Take as many beans as you want for a mess and par boil or partly boil them then take a spade and dig a hole large aneugh for the pot you are going to cook the beans in and build a fire in it and get it as warm as you can, then take the pot of beans and put a piece of meat in the center of the pot then cover the pot over and put it in the hole covering the pot with the coals that are in the hole and shovel earth on top of them and in twenty four hours you have a soldiers dish of baked beans."[67] These were men who seldom cooked before entering the army, let alone planned their meals a day in advance.

In the early days of the war the supply of food to the troops was at best irregular, but the system gradually improved. By the time the Minnesotans had settled in at Camp Stone, the quality of the food had improved as well. Lochren reported that the availability of soft flour "instead of hardtack, and purchasing meal at a neighboring mill, soon very much improved their fare; and, being well fed, well cared for and well exercised, [they] became more efficient and contented than ever before." Others confirmed that assessment, including Bassett: "We had a good oyster stew in the eve," he noted on Thanksgiving Day. "There are seven of us in the tent, and we had all the stew that we could eat." By January Isaac Taylor had been in camp long enough to see how much the food had improved: "We have better now in the eating line than when we first came here. A loaf of bread (the size of a bakers 5 cent loaf) is furnished to each soldier every day. Then we have beans, beef, pork, rice, hard bread, coffee, tea."[68]

The men organized themselves into messes to divide up the work of preparing meals. Isaac Taylor's log hut, housing some thirty men, for example, contained two messes. The men in each mess built separate cook houses and ovens and took turns cutting firewood, cooking, and cleaning up. The system worked reasonably well, especially when fresh meat and soft flour were available, as at Camp Stone. But, as Sam Stebbins pointed out to his readers in Winona, it could have its difficulties also. "Still, there are some things about camp life that are not quite so pleasant," he wrote in late August, after telling how morale generally had improved. "We are not allowed to choose our messmates, and there is a grumbler in almost every tent. These grumblers are the most disagreeable class of men to be found. They make things appear a great deal worse than they really are. They commence in the morning, and growl and complain because they have to get up; then they growl because they have the drill three hours a day, which they think is outrageous; then at night they complain because they have to go to bed and put the lights out at 9 o'clock. Such men as these are a nuisance in the world wherever they are."[69]

For variety and especially for sweets there were the ever-present sutlers, with their pies and cakes. Occasionally the men would splurge on a meal in town. "Went to Poolville and made some purchases," Isaac Taylor recorded in early February. "Had a first-rate dinner at Lamb's eating house for which I paid a first-rate price—37½ cents. Had coffee *as is coffee*."[70]

Being well fed and well exercised did not appear to keep the Minnesotans from getting sick. Illness was the hidden enemy in the Civil War, taking four lives for every one lost in combat. More men died of dysentery and diarrhea alone than were killed on the battlefield. Disease was especially prevalent early in the war, before basic sanitation, personal hygiene, and immunization practices were instituted, but even later the lack of discipline in enforcing them caused needless suffering.

For some reason the First Minnesota experienced less illness than most other regiments did during the fall and winter of 1861. "Our Regt is as healthy as it could possibly be while the Michigan Regt over here a little way is sickly," Goddard wrote. In mid-September Chaplain Neill was able to report, "By the kindness of Providence, the skill of our surgeons has, thus far, resulted in saving the lives of all those who have been inmates of the Regimental Hospital, and thus the chaplain has been spared the pain of conducting the solemn service of a soldier's funeral. . . . Probably not a regiment in the service has been so exempt from mortality by disease."[71]

A measles epidemic soon swept through the First Minnesota and surrounding regiments, however, immobilizing Goddard and numerous others. "I have been pretty sick with the measels for several days," Bassett wrote home, "but am alright now, only very weak." "I know that it is rather out of place for a person of my age to have the measels, especially when I had them once when I was a boy," Joseph Spencer wrote his sister, "but there is always something new written under the sun. I don't know but what I had them just as nice as though I was young." Not everyone recovered as well as Bassett and Spencer. "Chas. Woodworth of Company D died of typhoid after having the measles," Henry Taylor noted in his diary in late September. Two months later he spent Thanksgiving Day "in attending Isaac, ill with bilious fever." The widespread nature of the disease puzzled Dr. Hand. "It was astonishing to find so many grown-up men who had never had measles," he wrote, "and by comparing notes [with other surgeons] we found the number of such candidates was much greater in the country regiments than in those raised in cities. . . . In many other ways we found the city-raised soldiers had an early advantage over their country comrades. They had caught everything that was going while children, they were used to being up and out late at night, and they were prompt to take care of themselves, while the lads from the country had been coddled by their mothers, kept out of harm's way, and were slow to act."[72]

Although three Minnesotans had died of disease by December, a medical report in early February indicated that of 960 men then assigned to the regiment, including a number of newly arrived recruits, only 32 were sick, and most of those not seriously. Among the sick was Thomas Pressnell, who after much procrastination, was persuaded that his illness required proper medical attention. Years later he recalled that the regimental doctor performed a cursory examination, wrote out a "prescription," and told the nurse to have it filled. "In a few moments the nurse was back with a good sized package," Pressnell said, "the Dr. drew a cork-screw from his pocket, called for a tin cup and some water, unrolled the cover from the package, pulled the cork from a pint bottle of brandy, poured a lot of the stuff into the cup, added a small quantity of water, handed the mixture to me with orders to 'take that.' I managed to get the dose down—(it was the first time in my life that I had tasted brandy)—and in a short time I was feeling fairly well."[73]

The men did manage to inflict a good deal of injury on themselves. "Raisins" told of a "melancholy accident" that occurred in bayonet practice:

> During the drill the hammer of Helmer's musket caught in his clothing, and being loaded it was discharged, the ball passing through the right breast of Sergeant Cummings, near the collar bone and coming out between the shoulder blade and the spinal column. He lies in a precarious condition, but being of a strong constitution the surgeons think he will ultimately recover. Immediately after Helmer had seen the result of his carelessness (in drilling with a loaded gun) he ran to the Captain's tent, and cried, "O, Captain, for God's sake shoot me; I don't want to live a minute, I've killed poor Cummings." He was taken to the guard tent where he is now confined awaiting an examination. Cummings received two wounds in the Bull Run battle, one in the left breast and one in the hand. He had left the hospital but a few weeks. At the same battle Helmer received a severe wound in the thigh from which he had just recovered.

Despite the surgeons' confidence, Cummings died a month later. "His father arrived here a few hours before his death," "Raisins" wrote, "and was with him when he breathed his last. . . . Good bye—gallant, patriotic, but ill-fated Cummings."[74]

Dr. Hand reported that his first surgical case was "a face burned with creasote in an awkward attempt to cure the toothache." There were inevitably other accidents with firearms. "I remember well one poor fellow who was . . . shot through the body, being watched with much anxiety by all of us," the surgeon recalled. "One day he said, 'Doctor, will you stop those fellows from playing that tune?' and then I learned that our band, which had a shady nook back of the hospital, where they went for practice, had been tooting away on the 'Dead March' ever since the man was wounded. They thought it was to be their first chance for a military funeral."[75]

Lochren praised Hand for his "great skill, genial character and gentle manners," and he was apparently a popular figure in the regiment.[76] He was also unintimidated by authority. When he first joined the Minnesotans in Washington, before their march up the Potomac, he decided that he needed a horse because "above all things [I] disliked to walk." Having no money to buy one, he decided to go straight to the top of the army chain of command. He called on the headquarters of Gen. in Chief Winfield Scott, who, amazingly, saw him. "He was alone in a contracted office on Pennsylvania Avenue," Hand recalled later, "and even to my young eyes it was plain he was losing his grasp on affairs. Instead of resenting my intrusion, he received me kindly, and on hearing my statement gave me a card to the quartermaster." The doctor said he was saddened by the encounter, but he nonetheless came away from it with a "fine trotting mare" for the march to Edwards' Ferry.[77]

Hand and his colleague in the First, Dr. John H. Murphy, constantly had to deal with malingerers, whom Hand had begun to see after the demoralization of Bull Run. As time went on, the doctors became more creative in dealing with those trying to avoid duty. Murphy was "especially successful in his treatment of the few men who were disposed to shirk details for laborious or unpleasant duties on pretense of sickness," according to Lochren. "He was usually accurate in his diagnosis of such cases, and would feign to discover very serious illness, and would describe to the man such symptoms as for the time would convince him that his case was alarming, when he would be treated by blistering, or such nauseating medicines that he would pause before applying for sick-leave again."[78]

The men had plenty of time at Camp Stone for recreation and amusement, some of it organized but much of it deriving from their own ingenuity. Regiments competed with one another in drilling and sharpshooting contests, among other pursuits, as much to build unit pride as to test military proficiency. Regimental rivalries could get carried too far, however, as when Gorman learned that the chaplain of the Fifteenth Massachusetts had recently baptized three men from his unit, one of them a corporal. Determined to do better, Gorman ordered his adjutant to "detail a sergeant and four men to be baptised."[79]

Most of the men naturally preferred the activities they organized themselves. "The boys of K company are enjoying themselves," Bassett recorded. "They have 2 violins, a triangle and a bass instrument, and are danceing." "In co. E," Isaac Taylor wrote, "all excitement centered on wood-chopping race between L.U. Dow & John Harrington. Bet, five dollars, J. Haboot ¼ cord ahead." The men who had been printers in civilian life organized themselves into an association and decided to celebrate Faust's birthday "in honor of . . . the Father of the art of printing." Having no idea when Faust's birthday fell, they declared it to be "two days after payday" and managed to put together a magnificent dinner on November 22.[80]

Some of the men formed a lyceum in which the more serious-minded could discuss the large issues of the day. Still others organized ethnic clubs. Among these was the Turners' Association, begun by a group of German-Americans interested in physical prowess. "Spring-boards, swings, balancing poles, vaulting apparatus, etc., have been or are being put up," according to "Raisins." "Soon we will have a home institution among us—the Germans can't be beat when it comes to the genuine development of the muscle, and for good soldiers, better material does not exist, for they are orderly, economical, and never flinch when the real work comes."

"Raisins" also reported the formation of a secret society: "A Lodge of the I.O. of Q.D. has, it is said, been organized in this regiment. Not only is there a mystery as to what objects they have in view, but as to when, where and how they meet. Much curiosity is the result, and many a 'knowing one,' when talking on the subject, intimates, with the shake of the head, and a shrug of the shoulders, that he 'knows a thing or two if he chose to tell.' What makes the matter more a subject of doubt, is the rumor that [officer's] shoulder-straps disqualify a man from membership. What does it all mean?"[81]

The men spent much of their private time reading, and they especially coveted weekly newspapers from home. "Raisins" reported that on one day in October the regiment received 231 papers in addition to 728 letters.[82] The men had a voracious appetite for news, particularly war news, and publications such as *Harper's Weekly* and the *National Republican* were in great demand. On picket duty the men would sometimes arrange trades with their Confederate counterparts— Northern coffee for Southern newspapers. But their reading wasn't confined to the news. Chaplain Neill urged Colonel Dana to provide the men with "libraries of sound and elevating literature"; otherwise, he warned, "they will seek those pestiferous books, defiled with the scent of the groggery and brothel, which filthy and sneaky peddlers, 'foaming out their own shame,' hawk around the camp."[83]

But the books didn't please everyone's taste. "There are those who feed their minds on excitement—the froth cakes and vanity puddings of literature—and to such, books of real information are distasteful," "D" wrote in November. "The books are the best, in my humble judgment, that could have been bought for the money; but they don't supply us with sufficient reading matter, as it could not be expected they would.—There are minds in Company G, who want standard books of a miscellaneous character, which even this selection does not offer. If we go into winter quarters soon, we shall be sadly in need of something to relieve the tedium of the winter evenings."[84]

An entirely wholesome diversion appeared when a Minnesotan named Charley Robinson set up a photography studio, or "likeness shop," as it was known, near Camp Stone. "He is a first-rate fellow, and takes a good picture," "Raisins" wrote. "When the girls get pictures of their 'fellers' now, they will know they are good because they are taken by a Minnesota artist. Capt. Pell of company I, is having his company taken in groups, 'for future reference.' "[85]

"Played my first game of chess," Isaac Taylor recorded one day, and "Attended prayer meeting in cabin of Co. F this evening," a few days later. Bassett also attended services: "The boys have all gone into the grove to hear the Chaplin preach. He is quite interesting, in his discourse, and it seems like the camp meetings at home, until you look around and see all the men in uniform, with their swords, pistols and knives hanging at their sides." In addition to regular Sunday services Chaplain Neill conducted "brief daily prayer" at evening parade but he discontinued the practice "owing to the chilliness of the atmosphere at the hour of sunset and the fatigue of the men after a long drill." He commandeered a hospital tent for lectures two evenings a week but he was sufficiently displeased with the accommodations that he asked Colonel Dana "that an appropriate chapel of logs be constructed." His rationale was simple: "Experience has demonstrated that there is but little profit or consolation in listening to the words of the preacher, while the soldiers are obliged to stand in the open air on frozen earth."[86]

"D" gave an account of one of the sermons Neill delivered at a service in the woods:

> The cold winds brought the dead leaves down in showers, and swept them in heaps. The Chaplain could scarcely raise his voice above the rustling of the leaves; but we heard him say that Death was essential to Life and prosperity. It was so in the natural world. We could see around us that these trees, late densely covered with verdure, was now sapless and naked. But after the storms of the coming winter of death, a renewed friend of life would clothe with brighter verdure, these same trees. So it would be with our nation. Dangers and difficulties must be met. A long period of stormy adversity must be passed through to prepare the nation for greater excellency. Nations must be baptised in blood, and subjected to defeat, before sufficient strength of purpose and character is obtained to ensure permanent prosperity.[87]

The effect of this dispiriting message on the men is unrecorded.

Like soldiers everywhere, the men occasionally needed the release of pulling pranks. Dr. Hand told of one such "comical thing" that he observed shortly after he joined the Minnesotans: "A violent rain-storm came up, and while most of us were holding our tent-flaps a wild yell arose, and looking out we saw nearly the whole regiment turned out in a state of nature and in double file, running up and down the parade ground in the rain. Colonel Gorman was scandalized, and from the front of his tent shook his fist and shouted to them to go back. It was some time before clothing and peace were restored."[88]

If Chaplain Neill was scandalized by anything he saw, he failed to mention it when reporting to the people of Minnesota on the moral condition of the regiment: "The morals of the camp, without doubt, are susceptible of improvement, but never have I seen a village of a thousand male adults, exposed to fewer temptations, conducted with the same propriety. The vice of profanity, which Washington so frequently censured in decided language, has been rife, but it is not now so perceptible. The men, when allowed to visit the neighborhood, generally maintain their self-respect, and conduct themselves as becoming citizens of Minnesota and of the United States. The fact that eighteen hundred letters have been forwarded in one week by the soldiers to their friends, indicates the intelligence of the regiment."[89]

The Minnesotans did indeed spend a large part of their off-duty time—and countless hours while on picket duty as well—writing letters to family and friends, an activity that was officially encouraged. "The conveniences for writing in or near every tent," "D" told his readers, "is evidence that each man of our regiment considers himself a 'special corrspondent,' as no doubt do certain mothers, wives, sisters, and lovers, up in Minnesota."[90] Although their grammar and particularly their spelling were often flawed, the men managed to convey information and sentiments effectively. Besides reassuring loved ones that they were well, writing letters had two practical effects: it occupied their time and it ensured they would get letters in return. Most letters ended with "write soon" or a similar appeal, and, while the men could never receive enough correspondence, they were seldom disappointed by the lack of a response. "There is nothing does me so much good as a letter from some friend," John McEwen wrote his cousins in October.[91]

Young Charley Goddard expressed the same sentiment to his mother: "It has not ben long since I wrote to you but I have a good chance to write here now so I drop a line often and I would like to have you write as often as posable for it dose me a great deal of good to get a letter from home." Goddard did indeed write home often. He usually began by indicating when he last wrote, acknowledging his mother's most recent letter, and inquiring after the well-being of his younger brother, Orren. Much of his writing concerned money—he sent most of his army pay home—and attempts to reassure his widowed mother on whatever concerns she had expressed in her last letter: "When I am discharged (if I am ever) I will have one hundred dollars besides my last payment which will help us along considerable but will not begin to build us a hous. never mind Mother we will get along some how. all I ask is for you to keep good spirits." Although he had just turned sixteen, Goddard came to regard himself as the man of the house and freely offered his mother advice on a range of subjects. "I consider myself milatary General of our family and I wont allow you to make such a rash move as that," he said responding to her suggestion that she join his regiment as a nurse.[92]

Most of the men wrote of events in the camp, war news from other theaters, and, of course, the weather. They invariably told their correspondents that they were in good health and well provided for. Many were homesick, however, and didn't go to great lengths to disguise the fact. "I wish that you would one of these days, go & see my family & write to me as many particulars as you can," Jacob Marty implored a friend while the regiment was still camped in Alexandria.[93] "I should like to be at Home and take Dinner," James Ghostley confided to his diary one Sunday. "Cannot think the reason I do not hear from Home or Minneapolis."[94]

Much of what they saw suggested home. "As I passed along the road, it reminded me of Minn.," Bassett wrote in October after a visit to Poolesville. "The corn is ripe and cut up. The woods have begun to shed their foliage, and everything is tinted with the golden hue of autumn. I think, often of the happy days I have spent in the woods of Minnesota. I cannot say, I would like to be there unless the country is enjoying peace within its own borders." On another occasion he sent his father a sample of Maryland wheat: "It is a bald headed variety, and I think, a handsome wheat. Flour is $8.00 per BBL. Butter 25c per LB. Cheese 20 cents per lb. Potatoes $1.00 per bu. What did your reaper cost? How does the old mare work on it."[95]

Several of the Minnesotans, including Bassett, Mathew Marvin, and the Taylor brothers, didn't confine their writing to letters but also kept diaries. Some were purely factual, like that of Amos A. Berry, whose sparse account of his more than two years with the regiment filled just a few pages. The entire entry for 25 December 1861 reads, "Soup for Christmas Dinner."[96] Most diaries were more revealing than Berry's, however, and occasionally they contained thoughts, experiences, and emotions that went otherwise unexpressed. "A regular Indian summer day," read Isaac Taylor's first entry, on 1 January 1862. "The New Year smiles so bewitchingly & bounds so gleefully into the arena of time, that I suspect he has not yet heard of our civil dissension nor seen the black clouds that hang over the political prospects of the country which he visits."[97]

Acutely conscious of their mortality and aware of the "souvenir" scavenging by both sides, the diarists worried about what would become of their works if they were killed in battle. Having little choice, they invariably placed their trust in the enemy's better instincts. The first page of Isaac Taylor's diary read:

TO WHOM IT MAY CONCERN.

MR. SECESH;

　　Please forward this diary to J. H. Taylor, Prairie City, McDonough Co., Illinois. By so doing you will exhibit your magnanimity, accomodativeness & divers other virtues, besides conferring no small favor on A defunct individual.

Yours truly,

I. L. Taylor

High Private of Co. E

1st Reg. Minn. Vol[98]

Whiskey continued to represent a diversion for some of the Minnesotans. "Lt. Davids is officer of the guard, and is drunk, as usual," Bassett recorded in January. At about the same time, Isaac Taylor noted, "Officers of Van Allen's cavalry & Min. 1st., having a spree tonight. A number in the condition expressed by 'tight.' Officers are *commonly* supposed to set an *example* for the privates."[99] So much for Colonel Dana's order extending the prohibition on drinking to officers.

Things apparently got so out of hand on New Year's Day that Amos Berry felt compelled to make one of his lengthier diary entries: "Boys confiscate whiskey & got tight & have a regular spree." Isaac Taylor's letter to his aunt the next day from Edwards' Ferry was more revealing: "Last night I & four others came down to take the place of some fellows who, being placed on guard over some whiskey which Uncle Sam had 'confiscated,' allowed some of their comrads to steal a box of it and get 'tight.' Those guards and some of their 'fellow sogers' have been arrested & are now in the guard-house at Camp Stone. A few of us temperate boys now take turns in guarding Uncle Sam's liquor. Corporal P. H. Taylor has taken charge of one of our picket posts to relieve a sergeant who is under arrest for getting—as Artimus Ward would have it—'tightly slight' on contraband whiskey."[100]

Those who were determined to get their hands on spirits usually didn't have to steal it; there was almost always a sutler willing to run the risk of getting caught. Sometimes they did get caught, and Bassett witnessed the ceremony in which the Thirty-fourth New York's sutler was drummed out of camp by Gorman: "The whole Brigade was drawn up in line. He was marched the whole length of it, with seven or eight bif bottles strung around his neck, the Fifers and Drummers played the

Rogues march. They took him outside the lines and warned him not to appear among us again."[101]

Selling liquor wasn't the only misdeed that required disciplinary measures. Isaac Taylor told of a dress parade in early February at which the findings of a court martial were read: "Several of Co. F sentenced to forfeit one month's pay and perform guard duty from 8 to thirty days. Crimes, stealing sutler stores & allowing others to take stores over which they were standing sentry." He failed to note the irony of sentencing men to perform the very responsibility they had failed to perform. The next day Isaac noted a more serious offense: "About a dozen deserters from N.Y. [8]2d. in our g'd-house. Sixty or seventy of N.Y. [8]2d. have deserted within two weeks. It is a natural sequence to their conduct during the retreat from Va. in Oct. Brave soldiers! Illustrious patriots! Their pictures (with the orogonal) ought to be hung in some conspicuous place." Sometimes transgressors were shot, a fate which befell a man from the 3rd Vermont "for sleeping on post while on picket," according to Bassett.[102]

There is no indication of men deserting from the First Minnesota, but it would be surprising if there were none. The combination of homesickness, hardship, regimentation, and mortal danger impelled more than a few Union soldiers to abandon a life they hadn't bargained for. Charley Goddard's mother, opposed to his enlistment from the beginning, apparently suggested in her letters that he should come home. "Jest think how I would be received by friends if I *deserted* and not only that but it would disgrace the name of Goddard," he wrote back. "I don't think you would know me now I have grown so and am much diferent."[103]

When the officers weren't drinking they were frequently jockeying for promotion. The system was highly political and the officers and would-be officers were usually ambitious, a combination that guaranteed that much time and energy would be devoted to the pursuit of higher rank. Although the governor had authority to appoint company as well as regimental officers, the practice still called for the men of each unit to elect their own officers. The elections were increasingly viewed as advisory, however, and Governor Ramsey did not hesitate to ignore them if he was confronted with a more compelling political imperative. Still, men and officers frequently sent Ramsey and other state officials petitions registering either support for or opposition to a particular candidate. Forty-nine men from Company H wrote James Baker, Minnesota's secretary of state, opposing Private Francis Baasen's efforts to be made first lieutenant, because, they said, "he is exceedingly obnoxious to most of the company."[104]

The men grudgingly accepted the diminution of their "rights," particularly when strict seniority came to play such a controlling part in determining promotion, but they strongly resisted the appointment of officers over them from other companies. Dana wrote a letter in November that revealed just how sensitive these matters were and how much of a commander's time and attention they consumed. "Ramsey's late appointments do not appear to give much satisfaction," he told Rufus Peckham, a friend in Minnesota. "Even if it were necessary for Ramsey to apply the peculiar idiosyncrasy of his geographico political rules to the case there is no propriety in taking a Lieutenant from a company and make him a Lt. Col. over the head of his Captain who to say the least is as good an officer and lives in the same town. Three officers have tendered their resignations on account of those appointments; one of them—Lieut. Holtzborn probably the best soldier in the regt. his resignation however is denied in consequence of my disapproval."[105]

At least one other officer felt compelled to offer his resignation when he was passed over, not by Ramsey but by his own men. "Raisins" explained: "Lieut. Hollister of Company E, tendered his resignation . . . and, to his surprise, it *was* accepted. He was First Lieutenant and suited his boys so well that when they voted for a captain . . . they concluded to keep him where he was, and therefore selected Second Lieutenant Pomeroy over his head. He tendered his resignation, as he 'couldn't see the joke'—or 'any other man.' "[106]

Dana had to contend with friends back in Minnesota who bombarded him with pleas for advice and assistance in their quest for a commission. Peckham, a lawyer, was among the more persistent. He wanted not just any commission, apparently, but one commensurate with his opinion of his worth. Dana handled him deftly: "I have written a note to Ramsey on the subject but I have no faith in his paying any regard to anything I may say—you can never reckon on him. . . . If you go in as major or Lt. Col. you may make up your mind to go to

Kentucky or Missouri for the theatre of war is apparently about to move in that direction."[107] In fact, Ramsey paid a great deal of "regard" to Dana's views on promotions, much more than he had paid to Gorman's.

Occasionally, incompetent officers were compelled to resign as a result of the fitness reviews instituted by McClellan. A board consisting of Gorman and two other brigadiers examined the qualifications of the Minnesota officers in November, testing their knowledge not so much of relevant military doctrine, apparently, as of just about everything else. Second Lt. Henry Hoover of Company H later recounted his agony before the board:

> I thought they would examine me only in company movements (and I had been reading them for a week) but they didn't say a word. They took me in the regimental movements—away *up there* among the Colonels—and I was lost. They asked me when Napoleon conquered Sweden, and by George, I couldn't recollect. Then they asked me how Alabama was bounded, and I knew if I tried I would only get stuck, so I owned up at once and told them I could not. Next they asked me what Arithmetic was, and I told them "figgerin"—they laughed some—I don't know what at. . . . Then they asked me how many parts of speech there were, and I told them five. One of them said, "Well, what are they?" and to save my life, I couldn't think of but four; but since I've reckoned up seven—nouns, pronouns, adjective, verb, interogation, adverb and gender. When [they] got through, I tole them I was a carpenter and joiner when I was at home, and if they wanted me to draft a plan for a house, or anything of that kind, I could do it.

The board asked Hoover to resign his commission, the only Minnesotan so requested.[108]

The stakes were higher and the politics more complicated at the regimental level, where Ramsey took his appointive powers very seriously indeed. When Maj. William Dike resigned to seek the governorship of Minnesota, the regimental officers met to recommend his successor. Ten of the fifteen votes favored Capt. Mark Downie of Company B, and the nomination was quickly made unanimous. "Gen. Gorman, in a note to Gov. Ramsey on the subject, endorses in strong language the action of the officers," "Raisins" reported. "That Gov. Ramsey will grant the daughter of the regiment the position to which he has been recommended, is considered certain here by all parties—certain it is that he is the choice of the men as well as the officers, and that none deserves better at the hands of our State officials than he." Downie may have been the regiment's choice, but Capt. George Morgan of Company E was Ramsey's. "He is doubtless well qualified," "Raisins" wrote when the news arrived from St. Paul, "and I know him to be a first-rate fellow, but it seems to me the wishes of the officers of the regiment as expressed in a meeting, held by them, and the rejoicings of the men when they heard the result of such meeting should have received more weight than they did. But it may be Morgan was promised the office before the Governor learned of the meeting, and was appointed because he was the senior captain in the regiment."[109]

Ramsey managed to get himself into more serious trouble when he was compelled to choose a successor for Gorman. It was widely assumed, no doubt correctly, that the colonelcy of the First was Stephen Miller's for the asking. Miller was, after all, the regiment's number two officer already, he was popular with the men because of his performance at Bull Run, and he was a close political ally of the governor's. He couldn't make up his mind, however, whether to succeed Gorman, accept a commission in the regular army, or take command of the Third Minnesota Regiment, about to be formed. He finally decided on the last of these courses and urged Ramsey, as did Gorman, to appoint Dana. Knowing that Dana too would probably soon be made a brigadier, Ramsey made the appointment in early September. When he visited the regiment later that month, however, he was distressed to learn that the officers had just voted to recommend Miller for the position. Deeply chagrined, he indicated he would accede to the officers' preference. He wired Dana in St. Paul to offer the colonelcy of the Third Minnesota, but Dana was already on his way east and never saw the telegram. The governor, convinced that "mischief is impending on the Potomac," changed his mind again and gave command of the First to Dana and that of the Third to Miller, who was soon taken so seriously ill that he was unable to assume it.[110]

The officer who ultimately headed the Third did, however, come from the First. He was Henry Lester of Winona, captain of Company K, and his appointment would have tragic consequences: succumbing to a classic loss of nerve, he would unnecessarily surrender his regiment to an inferior Confederate force in Tennessee. His appointment revealed the flawed promotional system but it also showed how difficult it was for fellow officers, including experienced professionals, to assess leadership qualities in their colleagues. Dana, for example, was strongly supportive of Lester. Lester's friend and adviser while with the First was Dr. Hand, who saw him as "a gentle, scholarly man, thoroughly conscientious in performing his duty, and withal not ambitious" but who ultimately regretted the counsel he gave Lester. "When news came of his appointment as colonel of the Third Regiment he was surprised and stunned," Hand recounted. "He hesitated what to do, and it was only on my urgent advice that he decided to accept. I have been sorry since that I gave it. He knew himself better than I did,—knew the fatal indecision that was his, and so came disaster. He was never a coward, but when the supreme moment of his life came was not prepared for it."[111]

Shortly after Dana joined the First it was widely rumored that he too was likely to be promoted. There were not enough West Point–trained, combat-tested officers in the Union army, and those who held regimental commands during the early months of the war soon moved up. "Raisins" hoped that the rumor was false, "for we know that colonels such as he, 'like angel's visits,' are 'few and far between.'" Isaac Taylor agreed. "It is rumored that Col. Dana has received, or is about to receive, the appointment of brigadier general," he wrote his aunt the first week in January. "We dislike to loose him for we consider him as good a Col. as there is in the army of the Potomac. We will be particularly satisfied if we get into his brigade. He seems to know the duty of a Col & 'knowing dares to do it.'"[112]

The Minnesotans were genuinely sorry to see him go; he had been with them for only a few months, but he had earned their respect. "If we cant brag of our conels name I do not know who can," Goddard wrote.[113] The men collected $220 and bought him a saddle, bridle, gold-plated spurs, and a brace of Colt revolvers. When word arrived that he had been confirmed by the Senate, the regiment turned out in force to honor him. "Raisins" reported that the news "spread like wildfire from tent to tent—enthusiasm ran high—happiness was in every heart, and joy was visible in every eye. Soon the Regimental Band came out on the parade ground, and serenaded the— General. A vast crowd

The officers of the First Minnesota Volunteer Regiment and their ladies in front of the commandant's house at Fort Snelling in May 1861, one month after the regiment was formed. (Minnesota Historical Society)

Camp Stone, where the regiment spent six mostly peaceful months while on picket duty at Edwards' Ferry on the Potomac during the autumn and winter of 1861–62. (Minnesota Historical Society)

The "Grapevine Bridge" built by the Minnesotans over the Chickahominy River in Virginia. It was the only bridge to withstand the raging floodwaters of May 1862, and it permitted General Sumner's Second Corps to reach Fair Oaks in time to avert defeat. (Library of Congress)

Members of the First Minnesota following the battle at Fair Oaks, June 1862. (Minnesota Historical Society)

Union sick and wounded, including members of the First Minnesota, following the battle at Savage Station, Virginia, on the Peninsula. They were among the twenty-five hundred Federal troops taken prisoner when General McClellan continued his retreat to the James River. (Minnesota Historical Society)

Belle Isle, the Confederate prison located on a small island in the James River near Richmond, where Isaac and Henry Taylor spent six weeks in the late summer of 1862. The prisoners called the barren island "Camp Starvation." (Library of Congress)

ABOVE: *Oil on canvas (ca. 1905) by Rufus Zugbaum of the First Minnesota's charge at Gettysburg on July 2, 1863. The original hangs in the Minnesota State Capitol, St. Paul.* (Minnesota Historical Society)

FACING PAGE, TOP RIGHT: *The only known wartime photograph of Patrick Henry Taylor (left) and Isaac Lyman Taylor. It was probably taken in a "likeness shop" at Camp Stone shortly after Henry received his corporal stripes in December 1861.* (Courtesy William Frassanito)

FACING PAGE, CENTER: *Willis Arnold Gorman, the controversial first colonel of the regiment.* (Library of Congress)

LEFT: *Napoleon Jackson Tecumseh Dana, who commanded the regiment following Gorman's promotion to brigadier general. Though colonel of the First Minnesota only briefly, he won the affection and respect of the men. This photograph was taken by Matthew Brady in Washington in 1862. (Minnesota Historical Society)*

Alfred Sully, the third and last regular army officer to lead the Minnesotans, was credited with sparing the regiment from needless slaughter at Fredericksburg. (Minnesota Historical Society)

Stephen Miller, a political ally of Governor Alexander Ramsey, became the regiment's first lieutenant colonel and distinguished himself at Bull Run. He succeeded Ramsey as governor of Minnesota. (Minnesota Historical Society)

LEFT: *William Colvill III, the former lawyer and newspaper publisher from Red Wing who led the First Minnesota in its climactic moment at Gettysburg. (Library of Congress)*

Charley Goddard, the fifteen-year-old from Winona who ignored his worried mother's pleas to desert. Like many of the men, he was a prodigious letter writer. (Minnesota Historical Society)

Thomas H. Presnell, the audacious teenager who talked his way into the White House to meet Abraham Lincoln. He was one of the few members of the regiment who held General McClellan in low regard. (Minnesota Historical Society)

Pvt. Marshall Sherman with the colors of the Twenty-eighth Virginia, which he captured during General Pickett's charge at Gettysburg. He was awarded the Medal of Honor for the feat. (Minnesota Historical Society)

BOTTOM, LEFT: Josias R. King, of St. Paul, claimed to be the first man to enlist for the Union cause. The city of St. Paul built a monument to him despite the claim never fully being proved. He rose to the position of regimental adjutant. (Courtesy Wayne Jorgenson)

BOTTOM, RIGHT: Edward Bassett, the farm boy and diarist from Rice County in southern Minnesota, photographed at Fort Snelling in the spring of 1861.

gathered around, and during the intervals between the pieces, cheer upon cheer was given for Gen. Dana. It was by far the most exciting time the regiment had witnessed since its organization—Bull Run only excepted.[114]

They had bestowed no such honors on Gorman when he departed a few months earlier. According to Mathew Marvin, Dana told the men assembled in front of his tent that "we would be better off in our tents by the fire than out their in the damp chilly air of eavning And that we war acquainted with his strick manor of disciplin which is very easy he said that his commishion would be no source of pleasure to him if he wer sepperated from the *minnesota men* he said dont let us talk of what we can do but wate until we get in the field The band played an appropriate air & adjourned."[115]

As soon as it was learned that Dana would command a brigade in Stone's division, the men as well as the officers asked that the regiment be transferred from Gorman's brigade to Dana's. Twenty-four officers signed the request and delivered it to Gorman while the enlisted men were circulating a petition of their own. Already upset that Dana had received Senate confirmation while he was still waiting for his and no doubt irritated too by the regiment's demonstrable affection for Dana, Gorman became infuriated by the petitions. He had "made" the regiment, he declared, and he would keep it.[116] And so he did. General Stone had already written the U.S. Army chief of staff urging that Gorman be given command of a brigade of which the Minnesotans were a part: "I shall be somewhat uneasy about the condition of the First Minnesota Regiment should General Gorman be immediately detached."[117]

Gorman had presumably done his homework with Stone, but his more serious problem was with the Senate, where his nomination as brigadier was bogged down amidst accusations of misconduct. Not only was he compelled to defend the whipping of the whiskey-selling blacks but he had to fight the more serious and inaccurate charges appearing mysteriously in the *New York Tribune* that he had returned fugitive slaves to their owners.

"A member of our regiment, who for some cause had a great dislike for Gorman wrote a highly colored account of this whipping incident to the New York *Tribune*, which paper, vigorously denounced Gorman for flogging the slaves," Thomas Pressnell recalled. "The same soldier then wrote a communication to the *Tribune*, purporting to come from a friend of the General, advancing flimsy excuses but admitting the facts, as charged, and kept this up, managing both sides of the bogus controversy, to the detriment of Gorman's reputation, by bringing out several editorials, written in the vigorous style, if not by, Horace Greeley, which inflamed the abolitionists against him."[118]

This was grist for the radical Republican mill in the Senate, where Gorman, a Democrat, had few friends. In late December he made his case plainly to Senator Henry Wilson in an effort to fend off the same political forces that were then descending on Stone for the disaster at Ball's Bluff:

> The occurence of flogging Negroes for selling whiskey to soldiers took place more than *three months since* under direct orders from my superior officers, after conviction. . . . As to fugitive slaves, I never returned one while Col of the 1st Minnesota Regt nor in any capacity since. Nor did I ever know any to be returned, by my men, or officers, at any time, or under any circumstances, nor would I return one, or help to do so, or catch them, or let any body else under my control do it. I should not be displeased to see the whole slave population run away. I am for suppressing the wicked rebellion, if in its effects and consequences, the whole institution should be uprooted, and destroyed in every southern state on this Continent. I am for weakening the enemy in any, and every way that is possible, without any sort of tender regard to the "peculiar" institution. The *Tribune* has been *imposed* upon by some person or persons (not in the Army) who prefer to gratify personal spleen rather than manfully to shoulder their musket and defend the Government. I have sustained the Administration faithfully, I have not violated any military order of the Government, or of my superior officers, in relation to Slaves of rebels, or on any other point. I was appointed Brig Genl without asking it, but on the direct application to the President by high military authority as I am informed. Wherefore the Gov't & the Senate may rest assured that if rebels or any body else ever get a Slave returned to their master during the rebellion, they will have to find some other instrument to perform the work than myself. While I command any portion of the army I will have good discipline at any hazard to myself. Every fugitive slave that has come to my Brigade, has been fed & clothed and cared for, as we understand the order of the War Dept.[119]

The men of the First naturally followed the controversy with great interest. Mathew Marvin no doubt spoke for many of his comrades when he expressed a wish "that they would give us another gen in his place." He went on to articulate a curious understanding of the government he was defending but a firm belief that the army should be allowed to do its job: "I dont think congress has any business to interfear with the army & just so shure as they go to investigating the affairs of the army they will run it into the ground & I hope that Gen McClellan will send a regt of soldiers their & make them *desist* as Napolion did in france. The army regulations provides a remedy for all such things. And if they keep on they will be the means of another Bull Run. I reckon they have for got the old motto *Put your trust in your Gen & keep your powder dry.*"[120]

Gorman's defense was evidently persuasive, but it would still take the Senate another two months to confirm his nomination. Meanwhile, with Miller still recuperating from injuries to his kidneys and back caused by a fall from his horse, there was no logical candidate already with the regiment to succeed Dana. "We do not know who will be a Conel to us," Goddard wrote; "if we only could get a nother one like Dana." The officers agreed. They had served under two regular army men thus far with satisfactory results, and they asked Dana to recommend that Ramsey appoint another professional. He made two recommendations to the governor, both of them regular army, and of them Ramsey in late February selected Capt. Alfred Sully, commander of the Second U.S. Infantry.[121]

It may have been a beautiful autumn in Maryland in 1861, but it was a wretched winter. The rains were relentless, causing the river to rise to its highest level in twenty years. "The high water of the Potomac has done considerable damage to property," Bassett noted in late November. "It covered the canal and washed out the banks." But the mud was what made life miserable. By January he reported that the river had risen twelve feet and that the mud was "about knee deep. . . . It is none of your Minn. mud. It is about like that which you would get under the two top feet of Minn. soil. Charming indeed to wade through. We are armed with good heavy boots which we bought after our last pay."[122]

The mud disrupted everything, including daily drilling, and it quickly got on everyone's nerves. "This morning we could not get coffe for breakfast on account of the water being so muddy," Searles wrote. The only relief came when temperatures were cold enough to freeze it solid. In mid-January Joseph Spencer wrote his sister that "the Potomac is now frozen over, and the pickets at Edwards Ferry have ventured to cross over to the pickets on the other side and shake hands with each other, exchanged coat Buttons &c. and came back, none the wiser." But the thaw inevitably came, and with it more mud. "Robert I am heartily sick of this old camp," John McEwen wrote his cousin. "It is nothing but mud-mud-mud from morning till night and from night until morning. We had some snow last week but that is all gone now. We have had rain for three successive days so you can imagine just how we are situated. A little touch of Canadian winter would be a great blessing but we will grin and bear it; till we whip old Seccesh."[123]

The weather became such a consuming preoccupation in the boredom of the winter camp that it inspired some of the men to put it to verse. Joseph Spencer sent his sister this doggerel:

> First twas foggy, then it blew, then twas cloudy, then it Snew, then it friz, and then it thew, then it rained till all was blue, then the way the Mud did flew, or Slip into our low top't shoe. Then for a change more foggy grew, More Mud, More rain the winter through— Which made us wish we only knew, when this fighting would be through and We out this *"Rebel Stew."* When Uncle Sam would pay whats due, not in hard bread no one can chew, but real chink tho paper'll do, of which we'll have an *"Awful Slew."* then the next thing we would do, we'd start for *"hum"* and put it through, Until we found Fan, Em, Liz, Kate, or Sue, either *"on a pinch"* Would do, if she could bake, & wash, & Stew, then tell her if she thinks We'll *"du,"* We'll Stick to her like *"Spauldings Glue."*[124]

Those who had been much taken with the glorious Maryland autumn began to lose their enthusiasm for the place. "I never could be persuaded to live in the East," Goddard wrote in early December. "I do not like it   the West is the place for me."[125]

The men's unfavorable opinion of "old Seccesh," tempered somewhat during recent months by friendly exchanges on picket duty, was reinforced by stories of Confederate misconduct. "In nearly every paper," Bassett recorded, "we see accounts of the Rebs entering the homes of good Union people and takeing all the food their is. The is little doubt of recklessnes of some of them."[126] Their view of the enemy worsened when comrades who had been captured at Bull Run were released from a Richmond prison and returned to the regiment. "Many of our strong hearted men shed tears as they pressed the hands of our brave fellows," McEwen wrote of the emotional reunion.

> The tales of their capture and captivity we listened to with deep interest by all and were I not acquainted with the men and know them to be men of their word I would hardly credit some of their stories. The newspaper stories of the manner in which our men are abused are not exaggerated in the least. Five hundred of our Bull Run prisoners were confined in one small tobacco warehouse and if any of them ventured near windows they were sure to be fired at by the sentinels. Fifteen of our men were killed in this brutal manner and the perpetrators of these infamous acts were never once brought to justice. Sometimes their officers would question them about it but invariably their guns went off *accidentally,* and there it would end. This is southern chivalry![127]

Immobilized by the mud, the Minnesotans spent much of their idle time swapping rumors and speculating about the length of the war. They were no longer as optimistic as Bassett had been in September when he wrote, "We think that peace will be declaired in six months. . . . We have heard that the Rebs have sued for peace for sixty days." Now, after Ball's Bluff, they were simply guessing how soon they would be leaving Camp Stone. Isaac Taylor, one of those who had not yet seen real combat, wrote in January, "There are rumors in camp that we are to make an advance very soon but we give no credence to such reports for we have heard them too often. We can know what we shall do only when we are ordered to do it. When we are ordered to 'go in' we will 'go in' & do the best we can." The veteran Mathew Marvin, however, was prepared to stay put. "I am as contented as a pig on ice," he wrote his brother. "This business is just lazy enough to suit me for a while."[128]

Meanwhile Henry Taylor, himself a seasoned veteran, who had recently received a promotion to corporal, was more concerned with his present circumstances than he was with a future encounter with the enemy: "Fair weather; snow melts a little. Ike and I conclude to go down to the river and fire at the 'Secesh' at Ball Bluff. They fired first and the 15th Mass. replied—poor plan to fire at pickets. My bread is all gone and we yet have three nights to stay here. A soldier is not supposed to murmur at hardships, but I would like a little bread for my stomach's sake. Patriotism means lying out in a snow storm without bread."[129]

A few days later word finally came that the regiment was to move out. "At 1 p.m. we received orders to be ready to march at a moment's warning," Henry recorded on 23 February. The next day he was ready to go: "It is almost midnight. We have everything packed. Orders are to march at 8 a.m. tomorrow for Adamstown, Md., and take the cars—but for what place? is the question. This log house has paid for itself. Good-bye Bunk No. 2! You have patiently borne your part in this war. Camp Stone, farewell."[130]

The "place" to which the cars would take them was Harpers Ferry. General McClellan had decided to reopen the Baltimore and Ohio Railroad, connecting Washington with Pittsburgh and the West, and that meant not only rebuilding bridges near Harpers Ferry that had been destroyed by Stonewall Jackson's forces but also occupying neighboring Winchester and Strasburg in the Shenandoah Valley.

Dana having left and Sully having not yet arrived, the Minnesotans were led by Lieutenant Colonel Miller, who had recovered sufficiently to rejoin the regiment. The men broke camp on the morning of 25 February and began the march up the Potomac, leaving behind the relative comforts of Camp Stone and the serenity of Edwards' Ferry. Henry was still saying goodbye to his home of six months: "Cabin No. 1, you have sheltered us from many a storm and we would only leave to unfurl the good old flag and shield our beloved nation from the storm of traitors. (The storm is on!)"[131]

"The wind & cold put a 'quietus' on the mud last night making it fine marching this morning, with the exception of a little roughness of the roads," Isaac wrote. "A most delightful morning." The regiment spent the first night in a freezing bivouac near the Monocacy River, where Henry "paid 25c for a cake worth 10c."[132] They marched the next day to Adamstown, a station on the Baltimore and Ohio, where they boarded cars for Sandy Hook, just across the Potomac from Harpers Ferry.

As they crossed the river on a pontoon bridge, the Minnesotans could see the stone foundations and burned remains of the once great railroad bridge. They could also see that nearly all of Harpers Ferry's five thousand citizens had fled. Aside from the fact that it was the largest city they had seen since leaving Washington six months earlier, the men were fascinated by its commanding setting as well as its recent history. Lochren saw it as "a srikingly picturesque place. Maryland and Loudon Heights on either side, looking down on the chasm which the waters of the Potomac and Shenandoah, here uniting, had rent through the Blue Ridge. Solid piers of blackened masonry showed where had stood the costly bridges, destroyed by the Confederates; and the ruins of the armory buildings and other structures consumed with them gave an air of utter desolation to the deserted town, in which but few, and those the poorest of the population, remained."[133]

Isaac saw something else when he "took a stroll about town" his first full day in Harpers Ferry:

> Whatever blessing may attend rebelion elsewhere, it certainly does not pay in Harper's Ferry. The town is almost totally deserted. Churches, hotels, drug stores, groceries, dry goods establishments, public buildings and private residences abandoned. In my rambles I have seen but five citizens—two old men and three women. The sin of Secession had brought with it a curse almost equal to that which afflicted Babylon The gloominess of the cemetery that caps the summit of the hill is in perfect harmony with the desolation of the town beneath. Harper's Ferry is a striking illustration of the truth of "The way of the transgressor is hard." If Harper's Ferry is a fair example of what Secession has done for Va., God help her! for she is past help from any human source.

Mathew Marvin agreed with the assessment but put it differently: "It was a splendid place some time but it is played out now."[134]

The Minnesotans spent their first night in Harpers Ferry, according to Lochren, "in the partially destroyed buildings in which John Brown and his partisans had attempted defense" in 1859, following Brown's unsuccessful attempt to raid the U.S. arsenal and incite a slave insurrection. They were fascinated by his daring and "examined with curiosity the marks of his struggle still remaining." Bassett "took a walk up town and saw the house and cell where John Brown was confined," while Isaac Taylor visited the engine house where he was captured and "recd. an account of the whole affair from the lips of an old man, an eye witness."[135]

There was little to do during the week the regiment stayed at Harpers Ferry besides sightseeing, and the more curious took advantage of the opportunity. Among them, naturally, was Isaac, who reported visiting " 'Jefferson's Rock' on the bank of the Shenandoah, where he is said to have made a speech. It is supported by four red (granite) stone pillars to prevent its falling." Some men were more than curious, apparently, as Isaac's entry for 6 March revealed: "A patrol of ten men from Min. 1st sent out yesterday & to day to arrest stragglers without a pass. They brought in ten yesterday and five to day. They report being well recd. by the citizens & that the cider & 'old rye' was freely proffered &, of course, accepted. The rovers caught belonged to Co. A, of N.Y. 34th." Others were content simply to be mustered for pay, which, according to Bassett, "dident add any gloom to the atmosphere."[136]

Mathew Marvin also surveyed the town, which had already changed hands several times, and observed the debilitating effects: "The rebels have taken everything from the union men & now the federals are taking from the secesh & together it skins the country."[137]

On 7 March Gen. Nathaniel Banks, commander of the Fifth Corps and in charge of the Shenandoah Valley campaign, led his forces, including the Minnesotans, into the valley toward Winchester in search of Stonewall Jackson. They marched ten miles to Charlestown and discovered for the first time the splendor of the Shenandoah. "This is a fine country," Bassett recorded, "the best in Virginia that I have seen."[138]

They camped for three days on the outskirts of the town, and Isaac "saw the court house where old Ossawattami [John] Brown was tried & also the place where he was executed." Isaac was becoming an authority on the radical abolitionist's final days. Two days later he attended services conducted by Chaplain Neill at the local Presbyterian church: "Audience principly soldiers of Min. A few citizens present. A fine organ discoursed sweet music. The first sermon I have heard for three months. The church is a fine brick building with gallery & fixtures for lighting it with gas. The Min. 1st run the whole institution, organ & all.

The service awakes pleasant recolections." Marvin recorded the high points of Neill's sermon: "In the winding up of his remarks he said that everybody said we wer the best Regt on the Potomac for we allways paid our debts & no man could say we wer sheep or chicken theaves which could not be said of other Regts. The fact is they dont catch us for their was a pelt in front of my tent & next below the ground war covered with feathers." The service was more pleasant than the weather that followed, according to Henry: "Camped near town; a cool stormy night with no tents. . . . Night not congenial to my feeling—couldn't sleep—got up and run around to keep warm."[139]

On the tenth the regiment headed for Berryville "on a macadamized turnpike, which, wet with falling rain, played havoc with the soles of our army shoes," Lochren recounted.[140] The town, twelve miles away, was reported to be infested with rebels, and the First put two companies forward as skirmishers before rushing into it. Word of their presence in the area preceded them, however, and the Confederates had already fled. At the court house the Minnesotans nonetheless got the satisfaction of lowering the Confederate flag and raising the regiment's Stars and Stripes. Lt. Myron Shepard claimed to be the first man to enter Berryville and thus to have earned the honor of raising the colors, but he reported that his "glory was short-lived, for General Gorman rode up and took my flag from me, flourished it, and placed it . . . here. I thought it robbery after my great effort to be distinguished."[141]

The printers in the regiment discovered the offices of the Berryville *Conservator* and in them a half-completed edition of that week's newspaper. They worked through the night to fill the other half with what Lochren described as "a rollicking mixture of humor and patriotism, jibes upon the runaway editor of the *Conservator,* and the fleeing 'secesh,' and good advice to the inhabitants, which they were unlikely to profit by."[142] Calling themselves "The Typographic Fraternity of the First Minnesota Regiment," the men renamed the four-page paper *The First Minnesota* and sold copies at five cents apiece. The Minnesota readers undoubtedly learned more from the original side of the paper than from their own. They discovered the bitterness some Virginians felt toward the North, and toward Lincoln in particular, when they read an advertisement offering $20,000 for the president's head: "He has done more harm than any other man since the Creation. He has, with a fiendish malignity unsurpassed by savage or barbarian, brought a calamity upon a happy country and a mighty people, amounting to universal destruction. Talk of [Benedict] Arnold or Judas; why, they were white men compared to this scoundrel."[143] Bassett, an otherwise frugal diarist, was so fascinated by the ads that he filled several pages copying them, including two offering rewards for the return of runaway slaves.

Isaac Taylor, ever curious about the surroundings, told of a close call he experienced: "Strolled about town to take a view of things generally. Came very near being arrested but finally succeeded in eluding the patrol. . . . Secesh in this town are very meek & 'studiously refrain' from exhibiting Secession proclivities." At about the same time Bassett reported an incident that begged for more detail: "There was a row in the New York [8]2nd at night. Gen. Gorman arrested one Company and took their guns from them."[144] It was invariably New Yorkers, it seemed, whose conduct got the attention of the Minnesotans, and usually in an unfavorable way.

Marvin too witnessed an event that found its way into his diary: "Our pickets brot in 3 or 4 secesh this morning then 12 or 15 contrabands gave themselves up to the Marshalls   their master came soon after & looked in at the window   the nigars saw him & the guard would not let him in & while he was looking after the Marshall they broke for the back window & left for parts unknown   they said they would not go back alive they left their bundles and stachels   The Lieut gave me orders to search the bundles & if I found any paper to give them to the Marshall & do what I was a mind to with the rest   their was lots of clothing & $25 in silver that belonged to the preacher   I gave it to a contraband that lived their to give to his wife or his friends which he promised to do."[145]

Jackson was now reported to be at Winchester, ten miles to the west, and on the morning of 13 March, Gen. Nathaniel Banks's division headed in that direction. Before the Minnesotans got under way, however, they "observed a strange officer well along in years, with an abundant gray beard, on a handsome gray horse, ride to the centre of the line, followed by a black servant on another horse, and, after addressing Lieutenant Colonel Miller and the other officers with him, turned to the battalion, and, in a full, round, orotund voice, with charming military accent, distinctly heard along the entire line, issued the necessary commands to put the regiment in its place in the marching column."[146]

Thus, according to Jasper Searles's account, did Col. Alfred Sully assume command of the First. The son of the painter Thomas Sully, probably the most highly regarded American portrait artist of his time, the new colonel was a West Point graduate, he had seen active service in the Seminole campaign as well as the Mexican War, and, not incidentally, he had spent time on active duty in Minnesota at Fort Ridgely. Having actively sought the colonelcy of the regiment, he had ridden into the Shenandoah with the Union forces awaiting official word of his assignment. Although over time he would grow distant from the men and even the officers, one of his first orders made him instantly popular with the enlisted ranks. That night he discontinued the practice of posting sentries around the regiment's camp to keep the men from wandering off, using the sensible rationale that "men wouldn't go far in an enemy's country." "By this and other considerate acts," Searles said, "the men soon realized that they were commanded by an officer who would make no unnecessary demand on their strength or valor, and there resulted therefrom a mutual confidence never afterwards impaired."[147]

Isaac Taylor confirmed the verdict. "The boys are all jubilant over the arrival of our Col.," he wrote the day Sully arrived. "Now we are ready for a fight, having an officer in whom *we can have confidence. . . .* No guard tents pitched to night & hence have to lie around the fire & glean what comfort we can from that true friend of the soldier. It seems to be, now, beyond a doubt that the Secesh have left their famed strong hold at Centerville & Manassas. 'Things is working.' " "Raisins" too had a favorable impression of the new colonel. "He is evidently a fine officer, has a good voice, and is well liked. My opinion is that he will wear well," he predicted. The correspondent reported a week later that the men were already much taken with Sully: "The Colonel is so well liked by the boys that he has been dubbed 'a second Dana'—a title very few are deserving of; there is no 'grandmother' about him."[148]

Two miles short of Winchester the regiment received orders to reverse course and return to Harpers Ferry. Chasing the elusive Jackson, it appeared, would have to wait. Clearly the high command had other objectives in mind, but it chose not to reveal them to any Union troops in the Shenandoah Valley that day. The Minnesotans returned to Harpers Ferry to spend a cold and wet week in camp on Bolivar Heights. "Much speculation in our Regt. as to our next field of operations," Isaac wrote on 16 March. The general impression, he said, was that they were going to reinforce Gen. Ambrose Burnside, who was then commanding the Union forces in North Carolina. Six days later the regiment crossed the Potomac to Sandy Hook and boarded the B & O cars for Washington. "Considerable enthusiasm manifested on the route, especially by the ladies," Isaac recorded. "Between Pt. of Rocks & Anapolis Junction wheatfields exhibit a carpet of green. Rather cool riding in cars without any fire."[149]

The regiment reached the capital near midnight, spent the night at the Soldier's Retreat, which was intended for such untimely arrivals, and the next day returned to its familiar campground on Capitol Hill. Over the next few days, according to Searles, Colonel Sully "took great pleasure in exercising the regiment on parade for the benefit of his numerous friends in the regular army and acquaintances in the city." One day when they weren't parading, Bassett and the Taylors visited the Senate and House of Representatives, where, as Isaac put it, they "listened to the legislative wisdom of the country. How changed the aspect of affairs since Mass. & South Carolina, through their illustrious sons, Webster & Hayne, in that same Hall, emulated each other in expressions of devotion to the *Union* & the *Constitution*. Listened to a part of a speech of Sen. David of Kentucky on a proposition to abolish slavery in Dist. of Columbia. In Senate Chamber saw Lord Lyons English Minister to Washington. He is quite bald and dignified— a regular 'Johny Bull.' " Determined to see as much of Washington as possible before the unit was ordered out, Isaac visited the Patent Office and saw a model of an ironclad gunboat "pattented" just a week before. He then visited the Navy Yard "but was denied admission, having no pass," so he returned to the House of Representatives to watch a debate on a tax bill. Henry told of hearing "Sen Saulsbury of Delaware and others speak on the question, whether the Government ought to free the slaves in the U.S. by paying for them. He was against it."[150]

On 26 March the regiment was ordered to "rig up" for a "grand review" by President Lincoln, but, according to Isaac Taylor, "Gen. Gorman interferes & the thing is 'quashed' after keeping us waiting till most night & thus preventing me from getting a view of certain 'lions' of this city. Precious time wasted in idleness to give officers a chance to quarrel about a review." Later that day the men were marched over the Long Bridge across the Potomac and then, still unaware of their destination, onto cars that took them to Alexandria, where they arrived about 2:00 a.m. "Various halts and a 'right about, march' is followed by 'break ranks' & every fellow hunts his own sleeping ground—many 'locate' on brick side walk," Isaac wrote. "This individual & P.H.T. take 'military possession' of a covered wagon, 'make down' our bed & take passage for the land of dreams."[151]

Lochren recalled an ordeal that must have occurred earlier: "Through some blunder, we were left standing on the street, in a drenching rain, until morning, and then were taken to the ground on which we had camped before Bull Run. The men, wet and shivering, quickly resurrected the barrel of sutler's whisky, which they had buried the year before, and its contents, fairly distributed, were probably beneficial in counter-acting the effects of the exposure."[152] Happily for the First Minnesota that night, it was still a small war.

4

THE PENINSULA

"The boys implored us to stay."

The Taylor brothers awoke the morning of 27 March to discover that their regiment had left without them. Apparently unconcerned, they took advantage of the unexpected chance to do some sight-seeing in Alexandria. They visited the Marshall House, where, in the first days of the war, Elmer Ellsworth, a friend of Lincoln's and the colonel of the New York Fire Zouaves, achieved national renown and something approaching martyrdom by tearing down a Confederate flag, only to be shot and killed by the hotel's owner, becoming the Union's first casualty. They also went by Christ Church, George Washington's place of worship, "& thence proceeded to camp of 1st Min. N. of town about one mile, where we found hot coffee and hardbread awaiting our arrival. Troops visible in every direction."[1]

Edward A. Walker, a twenty-two-year-old corporal in Company D, who had been a machinist in Clearwater after coming west from Massachusetts, was already there, and he was also impressed by the Union numbers. "In the morning we were marched to our Old Camping Ground, the very one that we had when we first went to Alexandria. The face of the country had changed considerable since we were there, west all of the wood had been cut away, and Regts after Regts lay camped all around us   when we were there before there was but few Soldiers Camped around then. Couldn't help thinking how the army had increased and improved since then."[2]

The army had indeed increased. Nearly a hundred thousand men were camped in and around Alexandria, preparing to board ships of all

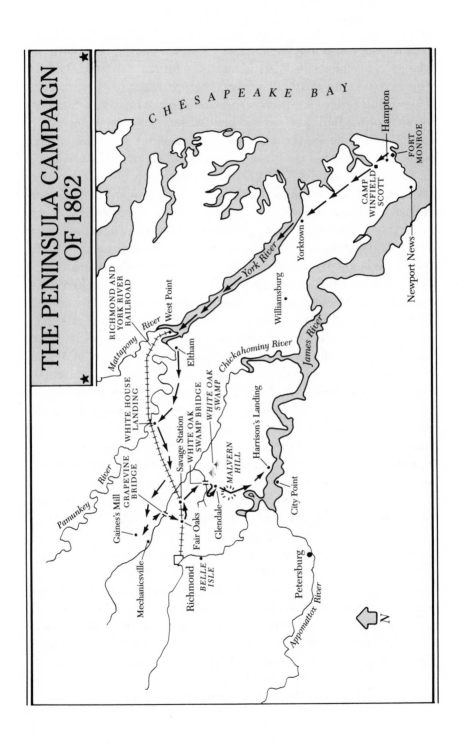

THE PENINSULA CAMPAIGN OF 1862

CHESAPEAKE BAY

Hampton

FORT MONROE

CAMP WINFIELD SCOTT

Yorktown

Newport News

Williamsburg

RICHMOND AND YORK RIVER RAILROAD

Mattapony River

West Point

Eltham

York River

Chickahominy River

James River

WHITE HOUSE LANDING

WHITE OAK SWAMP BRIDGE

WHITE OAK SWAMP

Harrison's Landing

Pamunkey River

GRAPEVINE BRIDGE

Savage Station

MALVERN HILL

Gaines's Mill

Fair Oaks

Glendale

City Point

Mechanicsville

Richmond

BELLE ISLE

Petersburg

Appomattox River

N

kinds for the trip down the Potomac, destination as yet unknown. An enlarged army meant an enlarged and more formal structure. The First Minnesota was still a part of Gorman's brigade, which was in turn a part of Gen. John Sedgwick's division and now a part of Gen. E. V. Sumner's Second Corps. "Bull" Sumner had been in the regular army since 1819, and at sixty-five he was the oldest corps commander in the Union army. While never regarded as a great general, he was admired by his men, if for no other reason than in battle he was invariably on the front lines waving his hat and encouraging them on. According to Mathew Marvin, Colonel Sully told "a good joke" on Sumner, which explained how he came to be known as "Bull": "While Sumner was a col in the regular service & being on the frontier one time in a brisk skirmish with the Indians he being in the hotest of the fite when a bullet struck him on the forehead & when picked up it was flat as a cent he was hence forward called Bullhead Sumner by the boys in his command."[3]

The Minnesotans were ordered to be ready to embark at 1:00 p.m. on 27 March, but, for reasons not explained, the order was canceled. Isaac Taylor naturally saw an opportunity to take in yet more of Alexandria's attractions, and he did so "without a pass—once out of camp & fellow is all right here." He visited Fort Ellsworth, where he saw Union soldiers recently paroled from Southern prisons and where he "had a delightful view of Washington, Alexandria & 'pomp & circumstance of glorious war.' " In the afternoon he "went down to the river to witness embarkation of troops; also had the much coveted privilege of viewing the interior of the church in which the Father of his Country used to worship." It was a warm and pleasant day, he reported, and the only discordant note was the state of his brother's health: "P.H. has aguechill this morning followed by considerable fever. Many of our boys are hoarse with colds since the bivouac on brick side-walk in Alexandria."[4]

The regiment finally embarked on the evening of 29 March, but without Henry Taylor. "I am quite sick in camp and [tomorrow] our regiment goes down the Potomac and I am sent to general hospital," Henry recorded on 28 March. "P.H. passes a restless night," Isaac wrote the next day. "Went with him to hospital on Washington Street. The Methodist church is used as a hospital—it is large, neat & has but few patients—a very good place for a sick man."[5] Leaving Henry at the church, Isaac walked through a snowstorm to the pier, where he boarded the small steamer *Golden Gate,* which, together with the *Jenny Lind* and several smaller craft, would carry the Minnesotans down the river.

The small armada got under way at six-thirty the next morning, passing Fort Washington on the Maryland side of the river an hour later and then Mount Vernon on the Virginia side. Conditions aboard the vessels left a good deal to be desired, according to Isaac: "Boat crowded Hot coffee scarce—places to sleep, 'ditto.' " He nonetheless found the Potomac "a broad & noble river . . . thickly dotted with crafts of various kinds—an occasional U.S. gunboat." Walker, who noted that the army "had chartered all the odds and ends to carry troups in," fared better "on a barge towed by a tug boat. . . . We were pretty crowded but 4 of us got the use of the pilot house, and as there was a stove and plenty of coal we got along better than we might have done."[6] Neither Isaac Taylor nor Edward Walker knew yet where the First Minnesota was headed, but they had to know that wherever it was, it was certain to demand more of them than Edwards' Ferry and the Shenandoah.

In fact, they were headed for the Peninsula, a fifty-mile stretch of land jutting east from Richmond into the Chesapeake Bay, bounded on the north by the York River and on the south by the James. It was George B. McClellan's decision to take his Army of the Potomac there. President Lincoln, while harboring serious doubts about the wisdom of the move, chose not to overrule his commander. Throughout the fall and winter Lincoln and his cabinet—indeed, all of Washington and much of the country's press—had urged McClellan to move against Gen. Joseph E. Johnston's forces at Manassas and Centreville and then south toward Richmond. But McClellan was never quite ready. He exaggerated the strength of Johnston's army and insisted that he needed more troops before he could proceed. Cautious to the core, he simply refused to risk his army and his reputation on a single great battle about which he had grave reservations, some of them legitimate.

Casting about for an alternative path to Richmond—like most of the country, he was obsessed with taking the enemy's capital instead of defeating its army—he became interested in the water route. After he was forced by Johnston's withdrawal from Manassas to abandon an initial plan, he finally settled on the Peninsula. Convinced that the York and the James offered secure supply lines to his army as it moved toward the rebel capital, he envisioned a decisive battle at the gates of Richmond that would end the war. Lincoln was concerned that Washington would be left exposed to a Confederate attack, and he insisted McClellan leave a significant force behind to protect the capital. But whatever his reservations, he allowed his commanding general to proceed with the plan because most of all, after months of procrastination, he wanted McClellan to act.

Their second day out of Alexandria the Minnesotans were on the Chesapeake Bay headed south. Unaccustomed to the open water, many became seasick; those who didn't were relieved to be simply cramped and uncomfortable. "A little before sunset, hove in sight of quite a large fleet of various craft lying in and at mouth of James River," Isaac wrote. "Lay down to sleep on a water barrell."

The next morning, 1 April, he found his steamer "surrounded by a forest of masts & near by the 'Yankee cheesebox on a raft,' known as the Monitor." The Union ironclad of revolutionary design had fought its famous battle with the *Merrimac* to a standoff only weeks before, and it fascinated the Minnesotans. "It lay quietly among a crowd of vessels," Lochren remembered, "—so small and unlike anything ever before imagined as a water-craft, and yet so powerful and impregnable. We could not study it enough." Writing a friend, Edward Walker described it as Isaac Taylor had, and indeed as much of the country had come to know it: "It certainly did look more like a cheese box on a raft than like a powerful battery. But this little craft has done Uncle Sam good service." As he got closer to the *Monitor* Walker "could plainly see the dent in the iron plate where the shot from the Merrimac struck, but they couldn't go through. It is worth seeing."[7]

The regiment disembarked that day at Hampton, near the tip of the Peninsula. There, Dr. Hand recalled, "our troubles began." The men set up camp about a mile from the town, in what Lochren described as "a low, wet field, without wood or good water." The brackish water and the dampness made many of the men sick and the rest miserable. Nor were matters helped by the lack of official foresight: "Here we had no tents having left them by orders," Walker wrote, "we now have to use our rubber blankets for tents, they do better than none, but when the sun shines they draw the heat." Some of the men, however, found relief in the discovery of the Chesapeake's delicacies—oysters and crabs—which they soon learned how to retrieve. Ever curious, Isaac Taylor toured Fortress Monroe and then the local cemetery, where he noted a tombstone engraved, "Capt. Willis Wilson, died 1701, aged 128 years."[8]

Three days after landing, the regiment broke camp and began its march up the Peninsula toward Richmond, nearly seventy-five miles away. Blocking its path, however, was the heavily fortified Confederate position at Yorktown, the site ten miles up the York River where Lord Cornwallis had surrendered to Gen. George Washington eighty-one years earlier. The rebels had in fact built earthworks across the full width of the Peninsula, taking full advantage of the marshy and wooded terrain.

It was clear at the outset that this would not be easy going, especially for those unacclimated to the oppressive heat and humidity. "If the spirit was strong the flesh was weak," "Raisins" reported, "and after a few miles travel, one by one they stopped to lighten their loads, by throwing away dress coats, blankets, overcoats, blouses, extra pants, shirts, boots, etc.—each one parting with what he thought he could best spare—and for the remainder of the journey the road was strewn with divers articles of good wearing apparel." But despite the discomfort, morale was high because at long last the men were on the move; they were as confident as they could be that defeat was behind them and that victory lay ahead up the Peninsula. "With what high hopes we started on that campaign!" Hand recalled later. "I think no one except our commander [McClellan] doubted our ability to march straight to Richmond. I remember . . . the feeling of despair that came over me one day when on a narrow bridge an obstreperous mule crushed my knee against the side of my horse, and I felt I should not be able to go into Richmond with the advance."[9]

As the regiment marched the ten miles to Big Bethel the first day on the road, the Confederates decided to fight elsewhere and withdrew from their earthworks and winter quarters. The next day it rained heavily and the march on to Yorktown was slowed by mud-filled roads. At one point, according to Lochren, McClellan and his entourage went by the Minnesotans: "When passing Col. Sully, with the formal salute came the familiar greeting of old comrades: 'How are you, Alf?' 'How do you do, George?' " McClellan later credited his interest in pursuing a military career to the time when Sully, a fellow student at a Philadelphia academy, received an appointment to West Point. "McClellan appeared strong, well-knit, a splendid horseman, and the picture of ruddy health," Lochren added. "His well-fitting uniform was perfectly neat and entirely plain—much plainer than the uniforms of his staff. He was already popular with the army, and heartily cheered as he passed along." Thomas Pressnell recalled years later, however, that the cheering for McClellan was not unanimous among the Minnesotans. "The boys of Company E observed that one of their number was not enthusing at all and asked his reason for not joining with them, said 'Better wait and see what he *does,* before you holler.' This recalcitrant was Ernest R. Jefferson, who to this day enjoys the distinction of never having cheered for McClellan."[10]

As they trudged through the mud, the Minnesotans encountered growing evidence that they were nearing the enemy. "We passed through more abandoned breastworks and shanties where the rebels had wintered," Walker wrote, "and when within a few miles of Yorktown we heard heavy guns, and knew that our advance was engaged." Lochren told of "cannonading and skirmishing in front" of the column and said the march "was varied by long halts and occasional movements at double-quick, giving the impression that an engagement was likely to occur at any moment; but the enemy retired sullenly, and we came within a couple of miles of the Confederate works in front of Yorktown." Isaac Taylor evidently had things other than the enemy to worry about that day. He was arrested by Lt. Josias R. King of Company A "for not being in ranks at taking of arms. 'Putting on style,' I think, Mr. King."[11]

The regiment established camp in a muddy lowland area opposite the Confederate works. "From the constant discomfort," Lochren said, "the boys named the place Camp Misery." "Rained all last night," Isaac recorded on 8 April. "Awoke this morning and found my sleeping place inundated—blankets wet—built a fire to warm my bones. Rained all day except interval of few hours in middle of day. Raining at night."[12] It took only a few days of this to persuade the officers to move the regiment to higher ground and to renew the demand for shelter tents, or "dog tents," as the men called them, which soon arrived.

The Minnesotans would spend nearly a month in Camp Winfield Scott, about a mile from the enemy lines. When they weren't on picket duty, the men occupied their days cutting down trees and using the logs to build roads to keep the artillery pieces and heavy wagons from getting mired in the mud. "The roads in this section are awful," "Raisins" wrote, "and new roads, of what is called the corduroy pattern, are being made in every direction, through swamps, marsh and woods. The 34th New York built a piece the other day, and on the day following our boys were sent to make it over. Gen. McClellan was down to inspect the work, and pronounced it 'the best piece of work he had seen for many a day—it could not be beaten.' Since then our regiment has had its hands full and 'corduroy' had become a byword. Yesterday afternoon the boys travelled three miles through the mud, cut a road through thick woods four miles in length, and timber enough to corduroy it, and returned to camp before tattoo singing 'Dixie.' Today they are at it again."[13]

A week later "Raisins" sent his last dispatch to the Stillwater *Messenger*. Although during the previous ten months he had offended most of the officers above him, he made it clear he was not leaving because he was "tired out." Rather, he said, "I have been summoned to report myself to Little Mac's Head-Quarters, and I must obey the call." Whether he or one of the offended officers arranged for the transfer is not known, but he was determined to be combative to the end. "I have made many enemies by telling the truth," he said; "such I would not lift a finger to conciliate—their enmity is preferable to their friendship." His editor, like any good editor, backed him fully while lamenting his departure to become McClellan's printer: "No man in the First Minnesota has been more abused and persecuted—no one has been more applauded than Edward A. Stevens. His vindication is now complete—having been called to a higher and more responsible position. . . . He has been a terror to incompetent and selfish mercenaries over him, and the stay and comfort of men like himself—in the ranks."[14]

By any measure it was not the regiment's best month. "The life before Yorktown was not pleasant," Dr. Hand recalled years later. "We were annoyed by the delay, and the daily firing on the picket-line, the frequent long-roll in the night, and the sight of comrades falling fruitlessly, made us heartsick." Lochren had a similar recollection: "We spent the month in constant and hard duty, either on picket or building fortifications or corduroy roads, and aroused nearly every night by musketry on the picket lines, and marched to threatened points; and were most of the time wet to the skin with the continued rains."[15]

By mid-April, according to Isaac, the shelling and skirmishing had settled into a routine, but not the predictable and pleasant routine of Edwards' Ferry. Here the Confederates were firing in earnest, as

Marvin learned one day when his company was sent out as skirmishers. Nonetheless, the men still displayed some of the reckless bravado of the early months: "We deployed through an open field then a narrow strip of woods that we advanced through cautiously to the open field in front of the fort Which was about 150 yds from the left flank of the company   we had just got to the edge of the woods when the rebels sent some grape shot at us that sounded like hale only moore so   We soon made them hunt their holes   we hallowed to them to come out & take a round but nary reply except *Zip Zip* against the trees   they durst not come out."[16]

The tedium of the routine was broken one day when a reconnaissance balloon carrying Gen. Fitz-John Porter appeared over the Minnesotans' camp. Sent aloft to observe the Confederate positions while tethered to the ground, the balloon, Lochren reported, "parted its lines, and for a little while was an object of exciting interest, as it sailed over the Confederate works; but a fortunate current brought it backward, and the aeronaut landed it in our division camp." The incident of course caught Isaac's attention as well: "Great excitement & big rush around the aerial voyager who was, no doubt, delighted to find himself among friends."[17]

Relief also came in another form: "Our sutler has arrived with butter, cheese, cakes & tobacco which can be obtained at enormous prices. The boys regard his arrival as a *sure* forerunner of the *Paymaster*." As predicted, the regiment was "paid off" a few days later. "Poker playing commences again in earnest," according to Isaac. "322 dollars worth of Postage Stamps sold in camp of Min. 1st to day."[18]

Walker observed in late April that it was taking "some time for McClellan to get ready," and indeed it was. "The 'Siege of York Town' is getting to be rather monotonous," Isaac complained. "We begin to long for the time when the racket of war shall commence in earnest."[19] No one wanted the racket of war to commence in earnest more than President Lincoln. McClellan was always preparing to fight the Confederates, in the president's view, but the preparation was never quite complete. "McClellan now had about 75,000 men present for duty," Pressnell recalled, "but was so persistently calling for more that many of the soldiers gave him the nom du plume of 'Oliver Twist II.' " Anticipating more procrastination, Lincoln had warned his general nine days after the Army of the Potomac reached the Peninsula, "The country will not fail to note—is now noting—that the present hesitation to move upon an entrenched enemy, is but the story of Manassas repeated. . . . [Y]ou *must act.*"[20]

But McClellan did not act. He was convinced that he was facing a superior Confederate force behind the Yorktown entrenchments, and he was strengthened in that view by the visible evidence of numerous rebel regiments constantly marching to new positions. What he didn't know was that the opposing forces were not in fact numerous—they were barely fifteen thousand to the Union's more than ninety thousand—but the imaginative Southern commander, a former actor, was staging a performance for McClellan's benefit by parading a few units continuously to give the impression of many. The Federals undoubtedly could have broken through the rebel lines at any time with relative ease, but the charade was all it took to persuade McClellan that the prudent course of action was to undertake a siege of Yorktown. A siege called for earthworks to be constructed and the big mortars to be brought forward, and it all took time. In these conditions, it took a great deal of time.

But while McClellan's strategy frustrated Lincoln, it had supporters among the Minnesotans, who were grateful they weren't being asked to assault the Yorktown fortifications. "I see by the papers now & then Slurs thrown out on McClellan which in my opinion is radically wrong & uncalled for & if the likes of them was hear in the army they would receive their just deserts at the hands of the soldiers," Mathew Marvin wrote. "Washington & [Winfield] Scott had their enemys at one time & now Mc is having his but they will find him sound as a nut & true as steel in the end. I can soldier as long as I can see plans at work to save the lives of the soldiers.   he *could* of had two thirds of us killed by this time had he been so disposed."[21]

Finally, at the beginning of May, McClellan was ready to act, and the men of the First knew it. "Much speculation among the boys as to what this unusually early start means," Isaac wrote on 2 May. "General opinion is that the 'ball is going to open this morning.' At 3 A.M. Col. Sully appears and orders all hands under arms. The camp guard (except sentinels on post), *sick* & everybody able to carry a gun join the Regt. There are two opinions as to what is going to 'turn up'; one is that an attack is apprehended from the rebels; the other that Mack will 'pounce on *them*' this morning. At 5 A.M. we stack arms, break ranks & I sit down to write an acount of last night's doings."[22]

Neither forecast proved correct. The Confederates had better intelligence of McClellan's intentions than McClellan had of theirs. Having achieved their purpose of delaying the Federal advance for a month so reinforcements could be brought to the Peninsula, they withdrew from Yorktown on 4 May, a day before the Union attack was scheduled to begin.

The Minnesotans went out on picket duty as usual that morning, but their plans were soon changed. "Gen. Gorman said that Gen. Dana had taken posession of the rebel works on our right," Mathew Marvin wrote, "& that he wanted Co. K to go out as Skirmishers & attack one of the fortifications in front & said their was *nobody their but* if their was we must attack & drive at the point of the bayonet everything before us Which we wer confident we could do with the backing that we had   Dana's brigade was first to plant their collors on the fortification & our next. The rebels evidently left in a hurry."[23]

" 'All hands' immediately ordered back to camp to prepare for immediate march, Secesh having evacuated their works," Isaac reported in his diary that night.

> As we move into the open field we see the Flag of the Union waving over the abandoned earth works. We march through them & halt about a mile beyond their works in front of a large deserted encampment. The enemy's camp fires still burning & meal, flour, bacon, cooking utensils, tents, &c. scattered in profusion throughout the late Secesh camp. The rebel fortifications we passed through are quite formidable earth works, embrasured & surmounted with sand-bags. . . . Secesh barracks in works considerably battered by our shell. Secesh ham and pan cakes made of Secesh flour & meal are very thankfully recd. by the stomachs of the "veteran 1st." To night we are protected from the rain and cool night air by the tents so magnanimously left behind by our retiring friends.

"We lived quite well at their expense," a comrade from Company B confirmed.[24]

Marvin was more effusive than ever in his praise of McClellan for having taken Yorktown "without the loss of a man in battle. The greatest strategy on reckerd And McClellan is the sole proprieter."[25]

The Minnesotans may have been grateful for the food and shelter the Confederates had left behind, but they were less appreciative of the land mines, or torpedoes, usually in the form of eight- or ten-inch mortar shells, that the rebels had implanted in the ground with their percussion caps pointed up so they would explode when impacted. One of the ensuing accidents made an impression on Marvin: "I was in one of the forts & saw a shell buried down just eaven with the ground. I thought to hit it a kick but for some reason I let it alone & lucky for me for within 3 hours after in the same place their was one man killed & 8 wounded by the infernal masheanes." Isaac had nothing but contempt for those who would resort to such a tactic: "Our *chivalrous* & *christian* friends in their haste to give us possession of these forts forgot to take with them their torpedoes & a number of Union soldiers have been killed & wounded by these concealed relics of a '*Higher Civilization.*' "[26]

The next day the men could hear the sounds of the battle of Williamsburg some twelve miles to the west as they left Yorktown in pursuit of the Confederates, but this plan too would go awry. "We marched a little over one-fourth of a mile from our camp," a member of Company K wrote, "and there waited—being a reserve, or to protect that part of our army that would be engaged, and if need be, go in ourselves. You have often fixed up for some journey or excursion, and after getting all ready to start have the time changed, and kept delaying from hour to hour. How long the time would seem; one would almost wish they had not promised to go. Well, this is something of the feeling we had to undergo, and from which we were relieved this morning. After standing in line for a long time the order would be given to rest; but would perhaps only get seated when we would hear sharper firing, and have to fall in again. This waiting and expecting a fight is harder than the engagement itself."[27]

Isaac's account of the ordeal almost certainly reflected the anger and frustration of his comrades: "Road so blocked up with troops that, after being out in the rain nearly all night the Min. 1st succeeds in advancing about *one mile* & are then 'about faced' & marched back to camp where we arrive at 3 A.M. of Tues. May 6th. & are soon stowed away in the Secesh tents which we pitched the preceeding P.M. I am willing to do *anything* calculated to put a quietus on this infernal rebellion, but such bungling & worse than useless movements as last night's ought to con-

sign some of our generals to a country in which there is but one zone, &
that *torrid.*" As bad as the day was, there were consolations for Isaac. He
saw "the spot where the sword of Corwallis was delivered up Oct. 19th,
1781," and he welcomed recruits newly arrived from Minnesota.[28]

Back in Alexandria, meanwhile, Henry Taylor spent the month of
April in the hospital recovering from his illness, the nature of which
was unclear. Frustrated because he knew his comrades were nearing
action—"I had rather be in two battles than in one hospital," he wrote
on the twelfth—he was finally told on 2 May to report to the provost
marshal for return to his regiment. After an uncomfortable night—
" 'My bones are sore; slept on the floor' "—he boarded the steamer
Commerce in the morning "and started down river." The next day he
saw a "forest of masts and smokestacks on Chesapeake Bay. The rebels
are evacuating Yorktown and we are kept on board to await further
orders. I don't feel very well and the spoiled bacon and hard bread we
have to eat in the open sun and rain makes one think he is serving his
country. Orders came at dark to go to York River and we steamed out
one-half mile into the Poquasin River and cast anchor." The next morning the steamer continued on to Yorktown, where Henry disembarked
to look for his comrades. "I found our regiment a mile from Yorktown,"
he wrote that night.[29]

After " 'Secesh' beans for breakfast and 'Secesh' tents to sleep in," as
Henry put it, the regiment proceeded up the York River on the steamer
Long Branch. Isaac described the short trip: "Transports loaded with
troops, & Uncle Sam's black sided gunboats, with the 'dogs of war' protruding from their sides moving up this noble stream bordered with the
green foliage of the forest interspersed with green plantation fields,
form a scene worth looking at." The destination was West Point, where
the Pamunkey River comes together with the Mattapony to form the
York. "At 11 A.M. it is announced that the fight has commenced on
shore & we are debarked as rapidly as possible & formed in rear of the
advance," Isaac wrote. "The artillery & infantry open pretty briskly &
our gun boats take position on our left & open on the enemy. Wounded
men are being brought in quite fast. At 1-10 P.M. a portion of our line
drive the Secesh back at the point of the bayonet, after which everything remains quiet." Ever the historian, Isaac was able to remember
that West Point "is where John Smith was captured by the Indians."[30]

Although the Minnesotans were not directly engaged in the fighting at West Point, at least one of them was eager—too eager as it turned out—to get into the action. "I obtained permission from the officer in our immediate command to go forward about 20 yards and climb up in a lone mulberry tree," Thomas Pressnell said later, "thinking that from that perch I could do some effective work. I had gotten pretty well up near the top of this tree when zip, zip, zip came 8 or 10 bullets in close proximity to my head and body, one of them cutting off a small branch for which I was just reaching. I concluded that this position was a little too hot for me, so, without having fired a shot I descended to mother earth and returned to the line feeling very much like a chicken looks when seeking shelter from a sudden summer shower."[31]

West Point could not accommodate all the Union troops pouring in, and after two days Sedgwick's division marched two miles up the Pamunkey to Eltham, where the Minnesotans spent a quiet week catching eels and playing poker when they weren't on picket duty. Isaac missed his newspapers: "It is aggravating to be deprived of 3 days news in these stirring times & be compelled to content ourselves with the little incidents of our own camp & the lying rumors from other parts of the Peninsula."[32]

Two incidents on 11 May revealed the scorn Isaac was beginning to develop for his officers: "Sentinels are nearly roasting beneath the broiling sun with uniform coats on to gratify the fancy of the gentlemen with shoulder-straps. They are either great fools or great villians. There's a time coming when eagles & bars can't rob men of health & comfort. *God speed the day!*" Later that day the sutler arrived in camp and Isaac reported "a grand rush for his 'eatables' notwithstanding enormous prices. Our Col., in order to disperse the crowd about the sutlers tent before which the sutler's supply of good things is fast vanishing orders the bugler to sound 'attention' & then 'wades in' for his 'regular butter and cheese.' " Isaac may not have seen serious combat yet, but he was unmistakably a veteran in the time-honored army tradition of grousing and well on his way to raising the practice to an art form. The next day he showed that his sympathies were with the enlisted men even when they were rebels: "Six Secesh prisoners brought into camp—two of them mere boys. Poor fellows! they look rather disconsolate."[33]

Henry, meanwhile, told of another Gorman incident, this one involving a "row in the 34th N.Y. Regiment—some of the companies refuse to change position in the regiment and are arrested. Gen. Gorman threatens to shoot them if they cheer again—line of battle formed around them, guns loaded!" Two days later Henry's diary revealed Gorman's no-nonsense resolution of the insurrection in his brigade: "The captain and first lieutenant of Company A of the 34th N.Y. are arrested and sent to Yorktown—the company returned to duty."[34]

On 15 May the Minnesotans broke camp and began a slow, wet, and largely miserable stop-and-go march in the direction of Richmond. "We moved on sometimes, thru the rain and mud, it was heavy going at times," Edward Bassett recorded. "We had marched about 8 miles in a Teriable & unseacing rain," Marvin noted. "The mud was about as thick as a hasty pudding. . . . it was Ancle deep all of the way & to our knees part of the time." Over the next ten days the regiment moved up the Pamunkey to the point where it intersected the Richmond and York River Railroad and then followed the railroad due west toward the Confederate capital, sometimes covering only a few miles a day. If the men weren't drenched by the rain, they were scorched by the sun; either way they were unhappy, but Marvin at least managed to cope. "Brush the mud off our clothes," he wrote on the sixteenth. "Charley & I are half dead laughing at some of them grumbling about spilt milk or for what cant be helped."[35]

Isaac's entries during the period show how he took his mind off the disagreeable conditions:

May 16. Spend a portion of the day in reading "Lectures on Rhetoric & Belles Lettres by Hugh Blair, D.D.F.R.S. Prof. of Rhet. in Uni'y of Edinburgh." . . . May 18. By the road-side at West end of town [New Kent] are a pair of twin (white) oaks of gigantic size & wide-spreading branches clothed in the fresh foliage of spring. I never saw anything of the tree kind that equals it.—Nature seems to have excelled Herself. . . . May 19. Reading Blair & playing chess with [cousin] Ed. Taylor. N.Y. Herald of 16th and Balt. Clipper of 17th. contain a proclamation purporting to come from Gen. Hunter, declaring slaves of S.C., Ga. & Fa. *free*. What are you up to Mr. Hunter? Who told you to do that? . . . May 20. Blair's lectures are a source of much enjoyment while lying in camp. . . . May 21.

The boys throw away overcoats, blankets &c. I manage to keep my baggage all aboard. . . . We find here good water and plenty of blackberry blossoms. . . . May 22. Heat is oppressive till 1 P.M. when we get a magnificent thunder-shower. . . . To day we get the Proclamation of Pres. Lincoln declaring Gen. Hunter's emancipation order "unauthorized" & that it was issued (if genuine) without the knowledge of the Government. . . . May 23. Passed several fine plantations with apple & peach orchards headed with young fruit. Both negroes & whites along the road are engaged in tilling the soil. The people of this locality show their good sense by remaining at home tending to their business instead of abandoning their property like many in the lower part of the Peninsula. . . . I leave my great coat in camp—guess I sh'an't need it any more.[36]

Inexplicably, the usually attentive historian failed to make note of passing White House, Martha Custis's home when she married George Washington, or St. Peter's Church, where the couple were wed.

"The talk now is, as it has been for some weeks past, 'on to Richmond,' but we do not get on very fast," reported "Shingles," the new "occasional correspondent" for the Stillwater *Messenger*. "The present indications are that we are to have one great battle before reaching Richmond, the rebels having fallen back beyond the Chickahominy River where they are entrenching themselves. It remains to be seen whether they will be allowed to remain unmolested, or whether they will be 'pushed to the wall.' "[37] As it happened, that was the right question.

Chaplain Neill, meanwhile, was beginning to get on the men's nerves, although they couldn't explain just what it was about him that bothered them. Before he left the regiment, "Raisins" indicated how little impressed he was with the professional demands made of the chaplain. Back at Yorktown he had written that Neill "got here a day or two ago—the first time he has been in camp, I believe, since we left Bolivar. As I have not seen him to-day, I presume 'he has gone to Philadelphia.' With the exception of drawing the pay of a captain of cavalry, and keeping close custody of the Hospital Fund, what is a chaplain for? Who wouldn't (and, as far as the duties are concerned, who couldn't) be a chaplain?" Thomas Pressnell confirmed the uneasiness toward Neill and added another dimension underlying it: "They liked him as a *preacher,* but disliked his austere manners. Well knowing this feeling toward him he took occasion during his sermon on the bright and beautiful Sabbath we spent at Eltham to unmercifully lamboost and roast the boys. He called them a pack of liars and black-legs—and used other choice epitaphs in his denunciations, which were rather to amuse than enrage his audience, which was composed of more than half the regiment. In this the chaplain not only lost his temper but somewhat compromised his dignity. Still his onslaught was not without some reason."[38]

A milestone of sorts was reached on 22 May, when the regiment, as Bassett noted, "Received whiskey rations for the first time." Evidently the army concluded that men exposed to malaria or misery or both required medicinal fortification, and the men did not disagree. Three days later, however, General Gorman demonstrated again that he had not lost his talent for generating controversy. "Order issued to night by Gen. Gorman requiring whiskey rations to be dealt out to each man at brigade commissary & *drank there,* instead of being issued to each Regt. as formerly," Isaac wrote. "Minn. unanimously resolved that Gorman can keep his whiskey." The brigade commander quickly got the message from his former regiment. "Gen. Gorman permits the 1st. Min. to draw their whiskey as formerly," Isaac indicated the next day. Henry, still not fully recovered from his illness three weeks after leaving the hospital, recorded he "took a dose of whiskey" but could not keep it down.[39]

When the regiment reached the Chickahominy River, which runs southeasterly down the Peninsula until it meets the James halfway to the Chesapeake, it followed the river as far north as Cold Harbor before reversing course and making camp on the north bank, about ten miles from Richmond. "The Chickahominy is a very small stream at this point," Isaac noted, and indeed it was only about forty feet across.[40] It swelled during heavy rains, however, frequently flooding the swampy lowlands on both sides. As the Confederates had moved back up the Peninsula they had destroyed nearly all the bridges, and now McClellan's army, which straddled the river, was in effect split in two. Bridges would have to be constructed quickly, and the First was given the task of building one.

Supervised by army engineers, the Minnesotans spent all of 27 May cutting trees and laying them across the river. "It was built of logs," Lochren remembered, "cut near the banks by the men, and was completed before sunset, excepting a part of the corduroy approach on the north side, which was constructed by another regiment on the following day. As grapevines, which grew plentifully on the banks, were used instead of withes about its construction, it was called by some the 'Grapevine Bridge.' " Marvin recorded that "about 3 companys had to work in the watter waste deep all day. . . . We built what has since been called Sumners uper Bridge or Sullys Bridge." As they worked through the day, the men could readily hear cannon and musketry to the east, and suspected they would be using the bridge soon to get to the fighting. Bassett remained in camp to guard commissary stores and didn't regret missing the bridge building. "Those left had a fine time," he noted.[41]

That night Isaac was not so exhausted from the day's work that he failed to record an unusual ceremony: "Capt. Wm L. Oswell Co. A 34th N.Y. has his sword broken & buttons cut from his coat in presence of the Division, pursuant to sentence of court martial. He is also to be imprisoned one year at Washington D.C. His offense is 'mutinous conduct' on the 12th inst."[42]

Gen. Joseph Johnston, the Confederate commander, was persuaded to move against McClellan while the Union forces were still divided, and he decided to attack the lesser part of the army below the Chickahominy on 31 May. Unusually heavy rains in the preceding days washed out nearly all the recently constructed Union bridges, imperiling McClellan's position. The Minnesotans' grapevine bridge held, but barely. "On Saturday, May 31st, about 1 P.M. we were suddenly aroused by very heavy firing of artillery and musketry, indicating a hard fought battle on the south side of the Chickahominy," Lochren recalled. Johnston's attack was under way, and Sumner was ordered to take his Second Corps across the river at once to aid Heintzelman's corps, which was receiving the brunt of the rebel assault. "Left camp about 3-30 P.M. in 'light marching order' with one day's rations," Isaac Taylor wrote.[43]

The Minnesotans found the river greatly swollen, and most doubted whether the bridge would continue to stand up under the force of the rushing water. One observer wrote that "the rough logs forming the corduroy approaches over the swamp were mostly afloat and only kept from drifting off by the stumps of trees to which they were fastened. The portion over the body of the stream was suspended from the trunks of trees by ropes, on the strength of which depended the possibility of passage."[44] Even General Sumner doubted the bridge would hold, but he had no choice but to order his men across. It swayed back and forth as the first men passed over, but as it received greater weight the primitive span settled down and became more secure. "As the bridge was approached it was seen to be surrounded by swift water," Chaplain Neill wrote later. "The soldiers waded up to their wastes, reached it, and crossed. Then followed Kirby's Battery [formerly Ricketts's battery and still brigaded with the First], the drivers lashing their horses, the nozzles of the guns immersed, and as they plunged on the log bridge it trembled, undulated, and was ready to float away."[45] Dr. Hand recalled that "the logs would bob up and down under the horses' feet in a startling manner."[46] The bridge held long enough to get Sedgwick's division and two other brigades across, a great point of pride to the men who built it. Soon thereafter it collapsed and disappeared in pieces down the roaring river.

The First Minnesota led Gorman's brigade "to the nearest sound of the conflict,—through mud knee deep part of the way," according to Lochren. "The condition of the air or direction of the wind made the sound of musketry seem nearer than it was in fact." The regiment was headed for Fair Oaks Station on the Richmond and York River Railroad, but before they got there they encountered retreating Union soldiers, some of them wounded, who told tales of a disaster on the battlefield they had just fled. Ignoring what Lochren called these "fleeing stragglers and cowards, who reported utter and irretrievable defeat," the Minnesotans marched the three miles to Fair Oaks, where they discovered the Federal forces, like the bridge they had just crossed, in a precarious state.[47]

Arriving on the field, Colonel Sully found that one Union division had already been "repulsed" and another, Darius Couch's, was "hard-pressed by an overwhelming force of the rebels" while attempting to take up a new position. "As the enemy are threatening our right flank, Gen. Sumner orders Min. 1st. to the extreme right," Isaac recorded that night.[48] One of Couch's staff officers galloped to the head of the

Union relief column, detached the First Minnesota, and led it to a position to the immediate right of Couch's division while the remainder of Gorman's brigade—the Fifteenth Massachusetts and the Thirty-fourth and Eighty-second New York, plus Lt. Edmund Kirby's battery—was placed to the left. The First was the most experienced of the advancing regiments, and the field commanders evidently decided to position it in the place of greatest immediate need.

Sully said later that he moved his regiment "rapidly to the right about a quarter of a mile, formed my regiment in line of battle, wheeled them to the right, and charging across the field, took my position in an oblique direction, my right resting on a farm house, my left on the edge of a woods. The enemy opened on us, but fired too high." The Minnesotans quickly deployed themselves behind a rail fence in a wheat field belonging to a farmer named Courtney, whose farmhouse anchored the regiment's right. "Our Brigade was in to line in the twinkling of an Eye," according to Mathew Marvin.[49]

Chaplain Neill later offered his description of the events:

> Colonel Sully rode into a field near the Courtenay house with his staff, and dismounted to make observations. Stooping down and looking into the belt of woods in front, instantly, with expletives forcible but not at all polite, I heard him call out to Adjutant Chase, "Hurry the regiment into place!" Standing by my horse holding the bridle, I noticed that his ears were bent back, and that he was very restless. He was not like his rider, slow to hear. It was evident that something was coming. There was a chicken-coop in front made of very frail slats, and, foolish fellow that I was, I wondered if it would be expedient to lie behind it. Deliberations of the subject were stopped by a swift blowing and leaves falling from the adjoining trees. The enemy had aimed to high, and no one was injuried.[50]

The men took up their positions "just in time," according to Lochren, "for the disposition was hardly complete when a heavy attack came." The "fierce roar of musketry" made the earth tremble, Henry Taylor said. Dr. Hand, meanwhile, was receiving his baptism by fire: "Almost before the men realized what was coming bullets were whistling about us, horses were excited and some running away, and all around smoke and flying splinters. General Gorman had advanced his brigade behind the fences and out-buildings of a large farm-house, and the splinters from the picket-fence flew in every direction. I was never more excited in my life, for it was really my first battle. I forgot all about the wounded and the hospitals, and with the rest of the staff went in to encourage the men and keep them well up."[51]

Infantrymen in Confederate gray poured out of the woods opposite the Minnesotans and, screeching the now familiar rebel yell, advanced across the open field toward the Union line. Fortunately for the men of the First, the Confederate left extended only far enough across the Union right to engage three of the regiment's ten companies. Mathew Marvin told how he watched the Confederates coming out of the woods and across the field. "When they got within about 20 or 30 paces we gave them the best we had," he wrote in his diary that night. "They could not see our line, it being posted at the edge of the woods & behind a fence. The rebels saw our support drawn up about 200 yards behind us in another peace of woods. The rebs fired at them & they broke & ran like sheep but wer soon rallied by their officers. . . . Their wer only 3 companys of our regt that done any fireing the rest layed low in the grass for a better chance. Our company averaged about 12 rounds each. We had a crossfire on the rebels & I think gave them fitz." A few days later he wrote his brother of the action: "Wall now their is no man that can discribe the like. Nothing but personal experance could teach anybody the *regularity* the *accuracy* & the *execution* of our firing."[52]

By this time three of Kirby's artillery pieces had also come into position, on a hill in front of a peach orchard—the remaining three guns were mired in the mud on the road from the Chickahominy—and their shelling combined with rifle fire to take a devastating toll on the Southerners. The skill of the artillerymen quickly attracted notice, according to Neill: "The rapidity of the loading and firing of Kirby's guns sounded like the incessant pounding in some great steam-boiler shop, and excited the attention and admiration of General Sumner and the division commanders." Dr. Hand also observed the way Lieutenant Kirby and Lieutenant James Woodruff handled their twelve-pound guns and concluded it "was beautiful. They fired grape and shrapnel into that grove so fast the advance was stopped."[53]

The firepower of the defending force was simply too much for the attackers to withstand, just as it had been nearly a year before at Bull Run, when the roles, however, were reversed, and the Union soldiers were the attackers. "The enemy were here slaughtered in great numbers within a very few yards of our line," Sully reported three days later.[54] Ironically, among the Confederate regiments receiving the Minnesotans' enfilading fire were the Fourth Alabama and the Second Mississippi, which in the earlier battle had delivered precisely the same kind of destruction on the First.

Union casualties at this point were few, but among them—sort of—was Dr. Hand. While watching the artillerymen, he recounted later, "I received the only wound that came to me during the war, but as the bullet hit me in the rear I said little about it. A round ball passed through the cupper of my saddle and lodged against the end of my spine. It was easily extracted, and I kept it as a souvenir. The wound did not disable me, and soon after I joined the other surgeons in caring for the wounded in and about the farm-house."[55]

The Confederates were forced to withdraw, but not for long. They came again at the Union lines, and specifically at Kirby's battery, only this time they were met on the field by advancing Federals. Gorman was ordered to throw all his regiments but the First, which was still separated from the brigade by Couch's division, into the fray. The other three regiments advanced and fired alternately until they were only fifty yards from the enemy, when General Sumner shouted to the brigade commander, "Charge 'em with the bayonet, General Gorman." The Thirty-fourth and Eighty-second New York, "now in battle for the first time, fought like veterans," according to Lochren. Supported by five other regiments and Kirby's now complete battery, they did as they were ordered and drove the Confederates back. Only a single South Carolina unit remained in place to receive the charge, but when the Thirty-fourth New York got within ten paces, it too turned and fled. "34th. & [8]2d. New York behave nobly, surpassing all our expectations," Isaac wrote that night.[56]

Lochren summed up the day for the Minnesotans: "The victory on our part of the field was complete and decisive that night. The Confederates were driven at all points, and with very heavy loss."[57] The regiment took a number of prisoners, including a North Carolina colonel who had served in Sully's company in the prewar army. Its own casualties had been low considering the extent and ferocity of the fighting: two killed and several wounded.

All in all, things had gone well. If the grapevine bridge hadn't held, reinforcements wouldn't have reached Fair Oaks in time to prevent a total collapse of Couch's division, which could easily have led to defeat up and down the Union line. (As it was, the Confederates got the better of an engagement that same day a few miles away at Seven Pines.) In addition, the First was sufficiently fast and steady to help anchor the defensive line in the face of a fierce and determined attack. Finally, it was the first time the regiment had taken part in a significant Union victory. For all of that, there appears to have been no great joy expressed that evening either in diaries or elsewhere, no doubt owing to exhaustion and the expectation of renewed hostilities in the morning.

Sully said in his official report that the regiment "behaved with great coolness, under as heavy a fire as I have ever seen." Gorman, who of course knew the unit well, reported that the Minnesotans were "under a severe fire, which they received and returned with great coolness and gallantry." General Sedgwick said their actions were "marked by admirable coolness and judgment."[58] Word was getting around about the regiment's "coolness."

"The battle did not cease until the shades of night had fallen," Neill recounted later. "Then the woods seemed to be alive with huge lightning-bugs; but they were the soldiers of the blue and gray with lanterns searching for dead comrades, and, observing the amenities of humanity, did not molest each other while engaged in their sad work." It was a long night for those on picket duty, who couldn't help the wounded. "We could plainly hear the groans of the wounded," Marvin wrote; "it sounded most horriable to the weary pickets that owing to their duty could render no assistance whatever & the thought of leaving them thus for 12 long hours." Expecting another attack in the morning, some of the Minnesotans felled trees and covered them with earth in front of the Courtney house. "We slept in the field, on our arms," Bassett wrote. "All quiet, except for the groaning of the wounded."[59]

Early the next morning Chaplain Neill set out to find his brother, a colonel in another brigade, who, he had been told "with well-meant kindness but poor judgment," had been killed. "At the battle of Bull Run, having heard many wild rumors that failed to be confirmed, I did not feel that his death was certain, although the announcement in the midst of the conflict was not soothing." He walked over the battlefield until he found Sumner and Couch sitting on an artillery carriage; neither had seen his brother. As the fighting resumed, his attention was drawn to a group of ambulances, where, instead of finding his brother, he was pressed into assisting in the amputation of a general's arm. "The surgeon's operating table was a novelty," he said. "It was a barrel on its side, placed against a tree in front of a farmhouse. I was expected to keep the barrel steady by placing my feet under it, and then held the patient against the tree while the surgeon used the knife." After two hours of this, the surgeon "needed rest" and Neill returned to the Courtney house, where at midday he was delivered a message from an officer in Couch's division: "I have the pleasure to inform you that Colonel Neill is alive and uninjured."[60]

The next morning the Confederates did indeed try again, but too far away for the Minnesotans to become directly engaged. Isaac described his view of what happened: "At 7-45 A.M. the Secesh renew the attack a little further to our left than where the main fight occured after our arrival yesterday. (Early this moring our left is thrown forward considerably.) At 9-15 A.M. a brigade in rear of right is ordered (double quick) to the left where our line is being hotly pressed. Shortly after a tremendous roar of musketry tells that they have opened on the enemy. At 9-45 the firing ceases the enemy having retired."

Only fifteen minutes later General McClellan appeared and, according to Isaac, "is recd. with enthusiastic cheers. A few minutes before 11 A.M. he visits our position, accompanied by his staff. Min. 1st. gives him six cheers & two 'tigers.' He acknowledges the compliment by raising his hat; after which he rides through our line between Cos. E & B & says 'Well, lads, are you prepared for everything that comes? I trust this point to you.' Some of our boys answer 'We will try to hold it,' to which McClellan replies, 'You *will do it*, then,' & adds, 'All goes well everywhere.' "[61]

Some of the men may have cheered McClellan enthusiastically, but Thomas Pressnell was not among them. "McClellan came along in our front," he wrote, "halted and gave us some palavar. We were ordered to cheer him, but the response was not as hearty or fullsome as at Big Bethel." Charley Goddard disagreed: "You can plainly see [McClellan] dont go in to the field and get half his men killed off. . . . How very plain to be seen General McClellan is a General that econimizes life   Mother you mark my word General Mc will be recorded in history one of the greatest Generals that ever lived not excepting Napolion Bonipart."[62]

The Minnesotans didn't have to "try to hold it." The Confederates had had enough, and the serious fighting at Fair Oaks was over. But Dr. Hand's work at the hospital set up in the Courtney house was far from over. "The wounded were constantly being brought in and laid on the grass about the yard," he recounted later. "All that afternoon the surgeon's knife flashed lively, and arms and legs and thighs were sacrificed, but not without thoughtful care. Whenever there was a possible chance to save a limb a council of all of us was called to decide; and as surgeon in charge of the hospital I was held responsible for what was done. This was the most anxious part of my duty." Like many other army surgeons Hand agonized over whether to amputate. He had been troubled a month earlier at Yorktown when a Massachusetts officer lost his leg: "The sight of his thigh being amputated for an insignificant-looking bullet-wound in the knee made me study over again the literature of joint wounds. As we then looked at it, the question was between saving the life or the limb. Now I believe such a limb can be saved."

The surgeon described how his long day at Fair Oaks ended: "By night all was quiet in front and we were tired out. All tried to get some sleep. It was late in the night before my own cares allowed me to rest, and then, where should I lie down? A cold wind was blowing, and we shivered in our scanty clothing. Every foot of sheltered ground was covered with sleeping men, but near the operating table, which was under a tree in the house-yard, there lay a long row of dead soldiers. My faithful steward, Cyrus Brooks, a detailed man from the First Minnesota, suggested we make a wind-break by piling them up against the remnants of a fence. We did so, and then lying down behind them, we slept soundly until morning."[63]

The next day the men witnessed the carnage of the engagement close up. Goddard said he "never saw such sights in my life   Rickets grape & canister done good execution   The most of them seemed to be shot in the head a very few in the breast." Bassett reported the same sights, as did Dr. Hand, who described them vividly:

> Soon after sunrise I rode over the field in front of us to make sure
> no wounded man had been overlooked, and only those who have

visited a battle-field on a hot summer day can imagine the horrors then presented. Rubens must have seen this, for he painted the colors of the dead just as I saw them that day. . . . [B]urial-parties were clearing the field. A pit was dug some one hundred feet long by twelve feet wide about half-way between Courtney's house and the woods out of which the enemy came, and at a depth of four or five feet they came to water. Into this wet hole our dead were laid in two rows, and one above the other, until they were within a foot of the surface. Then the dirt was piled on them, and I doubt if any record can now be found of who was laid there.[64]

When the bridge over the Chickahominy washed out, preventing supplies from reaching the field, feeding the wounded became a serious problem. The medical director called Hand "to one side, and . . . suggested that I have some horses quietly killed." The surgeon acquired two cavalry horses and "a detail of two-butcher-boys from the First Minnesota," one of whom was Edward Bassett. "We led the horses into a grove near the hospital," Hand said, "and in a very short time some beautiful beef was lying on the skins with the edges carefully turned under. Another detail of men carried it to the hospitals, and the cooks were soon making soup and broth. This was served to the wounded, and no doubt helped many of them to tide over that critical time." That afternoon the wounded were loaded onto boxcars at Fair Oaks Station and, with several Confederate surgeons who had "rendered us good service," according to Hand, were sent to White House. "Within a few hours the wounded were all gone and the hospital broken up."[65]

Still expecting another Confederate attack, the Union forces dug in where they were. When the attack didn't come, they gradually settled back into routine camp life, at least as routine as life could be at the front. Henry Taylor still had not fully recovered from his illness of April: "June 3—Several alarms today. I am not well. Storm. June 4—Companies E and D went on picket duty. I feel miserably. June 6—I have eaten nothin for four days. Last evening I paid 5 cents for two cold potatoes. June 7—Baked beans for breakfast. I feel better."[66] Evidently he soon recovered fully; he recorded no further indications of illness.

During the balance of June, according to Lochren, the Minnesotans were "kept on constant and severe duty, on picket and building corduroy roads, and felling the forest in front of our lines. Our pickets were attacked and shelled nearly every day, and scarcely a night passed that we were not in line once or oftener from some alarm, and we were required to keep our arms on, sleeping or waking, in readiness to fall into line at a moment's notice." A Rhode Island artillery battery was located nearby, and as it exchanged shells with enemy batteries, Pressnell wrote, "the men learned the art of dodging the fragments of bursting shell pretty well, so much so that but few, and those slight, casualties occurred."[67]

Pressnell, who had not been entirely cured of his eagerness to climb trees by the close call at White House, allowed himself to be coaxed into another one as an artillery spotter:

> One day several of the boys reminded me of my mulberry tree experience and dared me to go to the observatory in this tree during an exchange of shots between the batteries. I told them I would go if I could be of any service to the gunners of the battery, and could obtain permission from the officer in charge. Within a hour the rebel battery opened. I obtained the consent of the Lieut. in charge, who also let me have his powerful field glasses upon my promising to report the effect of his shells and up I went into the perch above. It was a bright day and as the rebels were then directing their shots to another part of our line I was enabled to so focus the glasses as to reduce the distance between us of about ¾ of a mile to what seemed to be a few rods. I could plainly see the rebel guns and gunners and called down to the Lieut. to "fire away," and he did, his first shell bursting in the air but close down and apparently directly over the center of the four guns of the Johnnies. I reported the result and suggested that he lower the aim and give them another shot. This he did, and his shell seemed to burst at the very muzzle of one of the rebel guns. I could plainly see the gun drop to the earth and one of its wheels fly up and sidewise for quite a distance, while the men were scattered in all directions. But within 3 minutes afterward I saw the white puff of another of their guns shoot in our direction and in less time than it takes me to tell it about 6 feet of the extreme top of the tree which I was in went whizzing past me to the ground. The way I scampered out of that tree and sought safety with the other boys close under our breastworks was a caution. Except when in search of cherries, peaches or other fruit, and doubly assured that no rebel cannon were in eruption within range, I have never climbed a tree since.[68]

Nearly a week after the regiment had been engaged, Isaac Taylor recorded these events: "About 9 A.M. one of Porter's batteries on our right open on Secesh. At 9-15 Secesh respond & artillery fire is very brisk till 10 A.M. when light musketry fire is opened & Secesh artillery fire ceases. Occasional artillery firing on both sides throughout the day. Our line of brest-works extended. Additional guns planted. Secesh shower the canister about our picket post. . . . At dusk a reconnaissance in small force from our side occasions a little musketry." And so it went through the month. The men were well dug in to protect themselves from the shelling, but sometimes not well enough. One day Neill was called to a log entrenchment, where he found a Minnesotan "leaning against the side towards the enemy. His face was placid, and there was no discoloration, but his heart did not beat. A round shot had struck the log where his head was, and although it did not penetrate, the concussion was sufficient to snap the thread of life."[69]

Apart from such occasional losses, heat and disease were the Minnesotans' chief adversaries that June; for most of the month the temperature was in the nineties when it wasn't raining. "The only water for drinking was surface water, as the ground was low, and malarial diseases and diarrhea were very prevalent," Lochren wrote. Not only was the surface water, connected as it was to the surrounding swamps and marshes, a source of malaria, it was also contaminated from the rotting corpses of men and horses. "The water is getting very bad, and the flies are a perfect torment," James Ghostley recorded in his diary. Unfortunately, the beneficial effects of boiling water had not yet been discovered. Hand, who knew something about the communication of disease, was contemptuous of McClellan's decision to leave his troops where they had fought: "Why it was necessary to put men into camp on a battle-field, and subject them to the risks not only of the fearful swamp fever, but also to be poisoned by the emanations from their fallen comrades, I never could understand."[70]

The surgeon's tent, according to Hand, was "within one hundred yards of the pit where our men were buried. Of the numerous horses killed . . . some were burned and some buried in shallow holes, and with the hot June sun pouring down, the smells engendered were overpowering. Our field hospitals were soon filled with the sick, and ambulances were kept constantly busy hauling the worst cases back to the general hospital at the White House. . . . After three weeks of this life I came down with a fever myself, and the large doses of quinine that were given me prevented my hearing anything for days." Ed Bassett got the fever as well: "I had an Ague chill; not very pleasant." There is no indication that either Isaac or Henry Taylor was afflicted, but Isaac took note of several who were. "Underwood . . . is in the hospital sick with the 'swamp fever,' " he wrote on 20 June, and the next day, "Nelson Card of Co. G buried to day. He died of fever."[71] General Gorman became so sick he had to be sent to the rear; Colonel Sully took over the brigade in his absence and Lieutenant Colonel Miller was once again given temporary command of the First Minnesota.

Meanwhile regimental life went on, and Isaac Taylor kept observing:

> June 4. Saw Gen. [Philip] Kearney; his left arm is gone. . . . June 5. McClellan names the battle of Sat. & Sun. "Fair Oaks" Dr. Hand, brigade surgeon, says the loss in Gorman's brigade is 201. . . . June 6. Reading Blair, writing & playing chess. . . . June 7. Whiskey is issued to Co. E to night for the first time since we crossed the Chickahominy. . . . June 10. Cannon shots exchanged & considerable picket firing. The Rebels are getting rather impudent; evidently anxious about what is going on in the Union camp. . . . June 12. Between 1 & 2 A.M. we are "turned out" by false alarm; our own pickets firing upon each other. . . . June 13. This morning rebels shell us quite extensively. Augustus Ellison, bugler of Co. I, killed. . . . June 18. McClellan passes along the lines & is recd. with much enthusiasm by the soldiers. . . . June 22. Sent a Sabre bayonet, taken at the battle of the "Seven Pines" or "Fair Oaks," to R.J. Taylor, Prairie City, McDonough Co. Ill. . . . June 23. There are indications that our generals are apprehensive of a row to night.

And so it went until 28 June, when it finally appeared the month at Fair Oaks was drawing to an end: "All sorts of speculation as to what is 'up.' "[72]

What was "up" was that Robert E. Lee had taken command of the Southern army, renamed it the Army of Northern Virginia, and put it immediately on the offensive. Replacing the wounded General Johnston, Lee was determined to strike a crushing blow at McClellan, and he sent Jeb Stuart's cavalry to scout for Union weaknesses. In four days Stuart rode completely around the Army of the Potomac and reported back to Lee that Fitz-John Porter's Fifth Corps was alone and exposed north of the Chickahominy.

McClellan, meanwhile, was close enough to Richmond that Charley Goddard could see the city's church spires from the top of a tree. Commanding a force larger than the Confederates', McClellan still managed to give Washington a seemingly endless list of reasons why he was not yet ready to move.

Lee was ready to move, however, and on 26 June he sent A. P. Hill's forces against Porter. The Taylor brothers witnessed the unfolding battle from a distance. "Cannonading begins about noon and we soon hear an almost continual roar of musketry and artillery," Henry noted. "We see the smoke of battle from a tree." "Heavy fighting this P.M. on left bank of Chickahominy up towards Mechanicsville," Isaac wrote that night. "Both cannon and musket firing very heavy. We listen with intense interest. Just before dark, man in the tree reports 'Enemy's line falling back.' Secesh opposite us cheer. In a few minutes [Gen. William 'Baldy'] Smiths Div. give similar vent to their feelings & the cheering spreads with the news that the enemy are being driven. Firing ceases about 9 P.M. . . . Rumor has it that Stonewall Jackson is engaged in this affair. Our bands play 'St. Patrick day in the Morning,' Dixie, Yankee Doodle &c."[73]

Isaac had it almost right. Jackson was supposed to be "engaged in this affair," but he was late getting his troops into position, leaving Hill to go forward with only a part of his force. As a result, Porter achieved a decisive victory at Mechanicsville, marking the beginning of what was to become known as the Seven Days. McClellan, convinced as always that he was badly outnumbered, refused to exploit the success and continued to think and act defensively. He sent Porter reinforcements, but not enough.

"Early this morning the ball opens again on the left bank of the Chickahominy," Isaac noted on 27 June. "Accounts of the results are conflicting. Secesh make demonstrations with artillery & infantry all along the line, probably with the design to prevent reinforcements being sent across the Chickahominy."[74] This time Isaac had it wrong. The Union line at Gaines's Mill had collapsed under the rebel charge, and a rout was narrowly averted. What's more, the "demonstrations" were not intended to prevent reinforcements so much as designed to persuade McClellan that he faced overwhelming numbers. The ploy worked; Lee knew the mind of his opposite number.

With the Confederates coming at him from the north, McClellan shifted his base of operations and supply line from the York to the

James River and, in doing so, abandoned any realistic hope of taking Richmond. Ordered to move south toward the James, the Army of the Potomac was engaged in an unacknowledged retreat.

The day after Gaines's Mill it was evident to Isaac, after an unnecessarily close call, that the Minnesotans were about to move out: "Lay on our arms all last night. On fatigue with axes. Our squad directed by an orderly to the wrong place in front of Smith's line where we are subjected to a perfect shower of shell—none of our squad hurt. Towards night ordered to pack up everything except tents. . . . As soon as it is dark we strike tents & lie down in open air." Henry's diary told the same story: "Great commotion on the left bank of the Chickahominy. . . . This has been an anxious day, and I see many long faces. It is said we will form a line on James River."[75]

Chaplain Neill rose early that day and went to the Courtney house, where he found General Sedgwick and Colonel Sully

> in silence, sitting on a rude bench in the yard—the former, as usual, modest and quiet, with none of the insignia of rank, without a coat, wearing only a simple blue flannel shirt. To the remark that the morning was sultry, Sully said, "Yesterday afternoon was bad for our troops." About six o'clock in the evening Surgeon Hand told me that Medical Director Hammond had been ordered to send off the sick and wounded in ambulances towards the James River, and asked me if I would accompany the train. It was not long before the procession of sufferers was moving. As I rode towards Fair Oaks station I noticed soldiers unscrewing the lids of cartridge boxes and throwing the contents into the vat of a tannery. At the railroad crossing a pile of cases of pilot-bread, twenty or thirty feet high, had been set on fire. There was no confusion. The only frightened person was a sutler who had hastened to be rich, and now was packing his wares in order that he might save his chattels and hasten out of danger.[76]

Dr. Hand discovered that the news of the regiment's imminent departure had a remarkable effect on his recuperative powers. A friend came to his tent,

> where I lay, sick and listless, and said the army was going to retreat, and I must go on ahead with the ambulances. That roused me, and in a few minutes I was on my horse and reporting at the division

headquarters. All was bustle and confusion then, but General Sedgwick sat silent and sad in a corner. As I went up to him he said, "Why doctor, I thought you were sick," and when I said, "General, this is no time to be sick," he took my hand and said, "You are right; it is serious work we now have to do." . . . I think that was the saddest night I passed during the war. All night we were quietly starting the regiments on their march, and about daylight we silently followed them. Before noon we could hear the enemy coming down the railroad, and we had to march lively . . . to get ahead of them.[77]

Isaac Taylor reflected on the disappointment and depression that settled on the withdrawing Union troops those two days in June: "From the time it was announced that we must fall back to James River, a general gloom pervaded the army, till it was dispelled by the roar of artillery and rattle of musketry as the enemy threw themselves upon our rear guard. Our Regt. formed a part of the rear guard. In the afternoon of Sat., the 28th of June, we were ordered to pack up everything except tents. Our tents were left standing till after dark so as not to reveal our purpose to the enemy. We lay on our arms all night, waiting for the trains, artillery, etc. to move off. That was a sad night. Instead of advancing on Richmond, we now must retire before the Confederate Army."[78]

Savage Station, three miles down the Richmond and York River Railroad line from Fair Oaks, was where the regiment was headed after it was ordered to get under way at 4:00 a.m. on Sunday. Late in the morning a skirmish took place at Allen's farm, sometimes known as the Peach Orchard, where the Minnesotans came under artillery fire but were not directly engaged by the enemy.

As Neill approached Savage Station, he was depressed by what he saw: "The saddest sight that day was sick soldiers, exhausted by the march, lying with closed eyes in the shade of trees, or tottering along with the aid of sticks. During the afternoon I found General Gorman sick on the porch of a farmhouse on an elevation overlooking White Oak Swamp. As I sat by him a cloud of white smoke arose in the direction of the railroad, and at a great height stood for a time. I thought of the pillar of cloud that by day preceded the army of Moses. It was caused by the blowing up of the bridge over the Chickahominy, the destruction of locomotives and other war material."[79]

Savage Station was filled with Federal supplies on their way to the James River, but it soon became evident that most would have to be destroyed or abandoned. Here, it was decided, was where the rear guard should stand and fight to give the main body more time to withdraw. "That 29th of June was one of the hottest days of the season," Hand recalled, "and when we reached the station, about five o'clock, many of the men were exhausted and fell down with sunstroke. While we were dragging them into the shade and pouring cold water over them an order came to form in line of battle." Lochren remembered that when the Minnesotans reached Savage Station they "were massed with a considerable body of the Second Corps near the road leading across White Oak swamp. The rest of the army had passed on, and large quantities of material were being destroyed. When the bridge, with engines and trains upon it, was blown up, an immense body of dense smoke arose, assuming perfectly symmetrical, and continually changing forms and colors, beautiful and grand to the view, in whatever form it took, like the changes in a kaleidoscope, and observed by all for several minutes before it was dissipated."[80]

Sully's and Gen. William Burns's brigades were bringing up the rear, and when they reached Savage Station they were placed in a clearing a half-mile long and a half-mile wide between the Williamsburg Road and the railroad line. At about 4:30 p.m. a Confederate railway car carrying a rifled cannon appeared and began shelling the Union forces with great effect. Soon rebel troops emerged and started the long march across the clearing toward the Federals. Burns led several of his regiments out to meet them, with the Minnesotans about 150 yards behind in support, but he quickly realized that he didn't have enough troops forward to match the advancing Confederates; unless he called up more regiments there would be a dangerous gap left in the line extending from the Williamsburg Road to the railroad. He ordered the First to move up on his left to prevent a flanking attack, and the regiment, under fire by now, quickly took up a position straddling the road.

The First Minnesota found itself in a position exactly reversed from that which it had occupied a month before at Fair Oaks. Instead of being able to fire at an oblique angle because there were no enemy forces charging directly opposite them, now they were receiving precisely that kind of enfilade because there still weren't enough forward

Union troops to reach across the field. The result was the same as it had been in the earlier engagement: the Minnesotans took a withering fire both head-on and diagonally from the left, and they started falling in alarming numbers. Suddenly a gap opened on the Minnesotans' right, between them and Burns's regiments, and for a while they fought as a wholly isolated unit.

"In order to reach Burns we were obliged to cross an open field on the double quick, being subjected to the fire of a battery of artillery," Thomas Pressnell remembered. "When about ½ the way across a shell burst in the immediate front of our company and knocked three of our number out—myself being of the number." The explosion threw gravel into the faces of his two comrades with such force "as to afterward give them the appearance of being pitted by smallpox. In coming down the opposite slope my well-filled bulging haversack had slipped from my hip and was dangling over my left groin. The butt-end of the shell struck the haversack squarely in the center, tearing it into shreds and scattering its contents in all directions, but knocked me so completely over, that when I came to realize what had happened I found myself stretched on my back with feet toward the top of the ridge while the other two boys were in a sitting posture rubbing their faces, eyes and heads—the regiment, in the meantime having gone on."[81]

Lieutenant Colonel Miller, now leading the regiment, acted quickly to prevent a collapse of his left: "In a few moments my left too was out-flanked, when I threw seven of my companies at nearly right angles with the line of battle, extending one to the left and advancing another to the front as skirmishers, and held the ground until the Vermont regiment advanced to our assistance. Here we remained, slightly changing our position as circumstances required, until dark."[82] The Vermonters apparently filled the gap just in time; the line held in the face of fierce fire, and the Confederates were compelled to retire.

Several months after the battle, Isaac Taylor summarized in a few lines the events he saw at Savage Station that day: "About an hour before sundown, the Secesh made their appearance, and opened on us with artillery. We were formed in an open field and ordered to advance on the enemy. The shells sounded wickedly as they passed over our heads, and plowed up the earth around us. Now and then, a man would reel from the ranks and be borne to the rear. Our artillery was planted on an eminence and fired over our heads. After advancing about half a mile, we met the rebel infantry, and the work commenced in good earnest. Besides the musket balls that filled the air, the Rebs sent grape and cannister about our ears in 'delightful profusion,' and the dead and wounded soon strewed the ground."[83]

Pressnell was one of those who "strewed the ground":

> Upon making an effort to turn over I found that my left groin was so sore that I could hardly move, the pain extending up and down, concluded that my left leg was shattered and that I was done for. By this time B[rack] and McD[onald] had discovered that they were not seriously hurt and came to my assistance and upon examination found that no bones were broken, but I was unable to stand, much less walk, from the intensity of the pain with which I was suffering, while the trickle of what I supposed was blood down my limb caused me to believe that either the piece of shell or something in my haversack [had] cut into my flesh and caused a gaping wound from which the blood was freely flowing. Throwing my arms around the necks of Billy on one side and Joe on the other we started for the rear and in the course of an hour reached the field hospital in charge of Dr. Morton, our regimental surgeon.[84]

Although the engagement lasted for only a brief time, it had been a much more demanding moment for the regiment than Fair Oaks. It was similar in its ferocity to Bull Run, which had been fought almost exactly a year earlier. One of the Minnesotans described their engagement this way: "On we went in the face of their fire, the shells frequently tearing through our ranks. One of them struck a German in Company A but a few feet from me, passing through him and tearing the shoulder off the man in his rear. . . . When we got near the rebels, they gave us canister, killing and wounding several. . . . Then the rebels advanced their infantry, and at it we went. The rebels, as well as our own men, fought with the utmost obstinacy; and, being often reinforced, made several desperate efforts to drive us from the position we had taken, but they were continually repulsed."[85]

The next day Burns told Miller, "Your regiment did nobly, sir," and Miller agreed, praising his men for the "coolness, courage and patience exhibited under the many trying circumstances through which we have just passed." Sully, although not with his regiment during the battle, said in his brigade report that his Minnesotans "did good service in protecting Burns' left flank and firmly held their ground against great odds. Their loss here was very heavy."[86] Indeed it was. Miller reported ninety casualties: six killed, forty-seven wounded, and thirty-seven missing. As more men were accounted for, the figures were revised downward, but only slightly.

Dr. Morton examined Thomas Pressnell at the field hospital and concluded that no bones had been broken. Nonetheless, Pressnell recalled, "my hip joint was so swollen that I could scarcely move while the pain was almost unbearable." The doctor judged him to be disabled, gave him a package of lint and water with which to bathe his wound, and told the eighteen-year-old to be prepared to fall into Confederate hands. But being left behind was not an idea that appealed much to Pressnell: "While he was talking my hand fell on a short Enfield rifle, the thought struck me that by putting the muzzle downward it would make a pretty good crutch so I said to him: 'Dr. if you will help me up I'll go on, as none of my bones are broken and I can stand any pain better than the thought of being taken prisoner.' He assisted me to my feet and helped me to adjust my improvised crutch, and bidding him good night and telling him that I would see him in the morning, I waddled out into the road along which our retreating troops were already on their way toward the White Oak Swamp bridge."[87]

"The fight was short but bloody," Dr. Hand recalled, "and many wounded from the First Minnesota then came on my hands." Among them was Henry Taylor. Isaac wrote that night: "C.G. Sherbrooke, H.C. Bradly, H.E. Scott, & Murdock Pattison & P.H. Taylor of Co. E wounded. Quite a number of others of our Re'gt. left wounded, Edward Taylor of Co. C mortally." In just a few hours he had a brother wounded and a cousin near death. "Cousin Edward Taylor, my particular friend," Isaac wrote several months later of the companion with whom he had grown up in Belle Prairie and with whom he had enlisted on the same day at Fort Snelling, "fell mortally wounded. He called us to bear witness that he fell with his face to the foe."[88]

"It seemed as though we might here hold our ground," Hand remembered, "but the burning piles of stores and the explosion of a trainload of ammunition which had been run out on the railroad bridge showed us we were in full retreat. Our sick and wounded in large numbers—I believe two thousand five hundred—were collected in tents about Savage Station, and a number of surgeons being detailed to remain with them, they were abandoned to the enemy."[89]

Certainly neither Isaac nor Henry had any intention of being abandoned to the enemy. The nature and extent of Henry's wound are not known, but it was not sufficiently serious to require him to remain behind. But as the brothers prepared to resume the retreat toward the James, the sudden and unexpected pleas of their wounded comrades persuaded them to reconsider. "Others and myself are wounded," Henry noted tersely that night. "Ike and I stay with the wounded." Isaac was equally succinct: "P.H. & I stay with the wounded Ed. Taylor dies about midnight experiencing but little pain."[90]

Later Isaac gave a more complete account of their decision:

> Henry and I remained with Edward, and the other wounded of our regiment, giving them water, etc. as long as we dared to, and were about to move on and join the Regt. when the man whom the Dr. had ordered to stay with the wounded "turned up" missing. The boys implored us to stay and not "leave them alone." We hesitated for we had no orders to stay. But the boys were suffering from thirst; they were lying on the ground in the open air, and it had already commenced to rain. Who would dress their wounds and take care of them on the morrow when the burning sun would pour his rays upon them? It took but a "jiffy" to twist Henry's gun into an unserviceable shape. I hated to destroy my gun which had been so true a friend, so I handed it over to a soldier who happened to be passing without one, and to work we went. We carried a portion of the wounded into a house nearby, and covered the rest with rubber blankets.[91]

Together with 2,500 other Union soldiers, whom McClellan felt compelled to leave behind, Isaac and Henry Taylor became prisoners of war.

That the Union forces were in "full retreat" was evident now to most of the men. Federal supplies were destroyed, Federal wounded were abandoned, and the direction of march was not toward Richmond but away from it. Savage Station was only one of several rear-guard actions that would be fought in the Seven Days before McClellan's army reached the James. The irony was that McClellan won almost all the engagements—including Savage Station—but that never kept him from ordering a withdrawal each time his troops bested the Confederates. So it was the night of 29 June, when, at ten o'clock, the First was ordered out of its position on the battlefield and into White Oak Swamp.

Already fatigued from marching and fighting since sunrise, the Minnesotans spent the night trudging through the marshes of the Peninsula until they reached the other side of the swamp near morning. "All night we marched over the narrow muddy road," Hand recalled, "the sombre quiet of the men being in marked contrast to the hilarity that prevailed as we marched up the Peninsula." Leading a mule train through a swamp at night was nothing any Minnesotan had ever attempted before, but one apparently was equal to the task. "But for the energetic and determined efforts of our brigade wagon-master Anson Northrup, . . . there would have been a mule panic," Pressnell wrote. "He managed to get his trains through with the loss of but about a dozen mules and two or three wagons."[92]

After bivouacking briefly the regiment marched another two miles only to be turned around and sent back to the swamp to meet a Confederate assault that never materialized. All the while they could hear artillery and musket fire ahead at Glendale, where the rebels, having gone around the swamp, hoped to cut off the Federal rear, which still included the Minnesotans. "Late in the afternoon we were hurriedly sent to Glendale," Lochren said, "moving for most of the distance at double-quick." Edward Bassett told how he got separated from his unit in the withdrawal: "June 30th very hot. Started early on the road to James River. I was left to help one of the wounded to an Ambulance. The Regiment left and I could not find it again all day."[93]

"We wer completely fagged out haveing no sleep for 3 nites & fore days & but very little poor watter," Marvin wrote. "Each man seemed to think that he could not live 15 minutes from the burning of the sun that was shineing & not a sign of any wind And doublequicking for nearly a half a mile. We passed Col Sulley who told us we had arrived just in time to save the day." Charley Goddard gave his own account of the ordeal: "Fighting day times and marching night almost killed the men. geting no sleep nor time to make a cup of coffee will naturely ware a man out."[94]

When they arrived on the battlefield at Glendale hot and exhausted, the men collapsed on the ground to catch their breath and, not incidentally, to avoid the hail of rebel minié balls whistling over their heads. Hand told later of spotting Sully "considerably in advance of his men, sitting alone and watching the fight." He approached the colonel to ask how the battle was going: "Shells were tearing up the dirt all about him, and the zip of flying bullets was incessant, but he turned and said, 'This is getting hot, and I am - - - - dry.' I pulled out a flask which had been retained for such occasions, and he took a long drink. Then he said, 'We will ride up to the general for orders.' As we reached General Sumner he was, in his usual way, swinging his spectacles in his hand, and just then a bullet broke one of the glasses. He was much annoyed, but quickly told Colonel Sully to bring up all the reserves."[95]

The Minnesotans were among the reserves called forward, and as they passed the general on their way to the front line, he told them, "Boys, I shall not see many of you again, but I know you will hold that line." General Dana, whose brigade was close by, offered to place his former regiment in line, but by the time they got there "the brunt of the battle had . . . passed," according to Lochren.[96] Once more the Union forces had staved off a Confederate advance, and once more the Federals withdrew.

The Minnesotans may have avoided the brunt of the battle at Glendale but they did not avoid casualties. The regiment suffered one killed and five wounded, and among the wounded was Capt. William Colvill of Company F. He took a bullet through his left breast but didn't tell his comrades. Lochren had nothing but admiration for the taciturn officer: "With that impertubability for which he was distinguished, he gave no sign of being hurt, and turned over his command to his lieutenant, as if for a few minutes absence, and no one knew that he was hurt until the next morning, when he was heard from as having walked to the field hospital at Malvern Hill." Dr. Hand found Colvill on his walk to the rear: "I slipped off his coat and found a ball had entered his chest two inches below the left collar-bone. It was a dangerous wound, and I told him he must keep quiet." Hand tended to the other wounded until Sully instructed him to join the march toward Malvern Hill. When the surgeon told Colvill that he must remain behind, "he just pulled his tall form from under the fence and said, 'No, he would not be left.' I did not think he could make the march, and we had no sort of conveyance; but Major Morgan, of the First Minnesota, came round hunting for his men, and offered to let the captain ride his horse. Captain Colvill would not accept that, but took a firm grip of the horses tail, and off they started. Three days later I found the captain on a transport at Harrison's Landing."[97]

Unlike Colvill, the wounded Pressnell had no compunctions about accepting a ride, and he finally managed to get one on a wagon loaded with oats, "which made a comparatively comfortable bed." After two hours, however, he "was dumped out at Malvern Hill":

> I hobbled toward a house over which a hospital flag was floating but, coming across a mossy banked spring determined to halt and ascertain what was the cause of my intense pain, and proceeded to an examination by pressing my wound with my fingers small pieces of glass appeared on the surface, and at the same time I noticed that my left trousers pocket was damp from an oily substance, and that there was quite a large hole in the bottom. I pulled out the bottle of oil which I had put in my pocket at Fair Oaks the morning before when I discovered that a portion of the neck had been cut off clean and broken into small pieces which had penetrated my flesh. By the use of my pocket knife I extracted as many as twenty pieces in size from a pin-head to a small pea. A surgeon came along and inquired what I was up to. I told him I was taking my first lesson in surgery, but I needed some help. He made a minute examination and with his lance extracted a piece of glass fully an 8th of an inch in circumfrance, and my pain immediately lessened.[98]

One of the reasons McClellan was so eager to reach the James was to bring the firepower of the Union gunboats to bear on the advancing Confederates. He succeeded as the rebels approached Malvern Hill. "During the latter part of this afternoon," Neill recalled, "immense shells from the gunboats passed over our heads into the woods, where the enemy was. A Confederate soldier is reported to have said that his regiment was doing very well until great cooking-stoves began to fly through the air and break into pieces in their midst."[99]

The next morning the rest of the regiment—minus Bassett, who still couldn't find it—headed for Malvern Hill as well, and when they got there, according to Lochren, they "found the whole army being posted in position for battle, some thirty or forty rods in front of the crest of the hill, on which the heavy siege artillery was placed."

It was a good battlefield, having about half or three-fourths of a mile of gently sloping clear ground in our front. Our position at first was near the centre of our line, where, about 8 o'clock, the enemy opened up on us a heavy artillery fire, slightly wounding several of our men with pieces of shell, but none severely. Our position was changed slightly several times, and toward noon we were moved to the rear and marched considerably to the right, off the elevated plateau, and stationed in an oat-field, on lower ground, and well to the right of the line of battle. There we remained without attack during the entire day, listening to the sound of the terrific conflict on the left, and expecting an attack at any moment. At times the volume of musketry and roar of artillery exceeded anything we had before listened to, and with the novel, unearthly shrieking of the immense shells thrown from gunboats passed the wildest conceptions of the terrible in battle. Gen McClellan came along our line in the afternoon, infusing that enthusiasm which his presence always brought on a battlefield. The conflict on the left continued through the entire day, and for some time after dark.[100]

When daylight faded into darkness, Neill recalled, "it was an awful sight to see bursting shells, like angry, fiery meteors, rushing through the air." He too commented favorably on McClellan's presence. "There was reason," he said, "why I looked upon him with some interest. He was born in the same city as myself. Our fathers were physicians. We were prepared for college by the same teachers. Before the war he had successfully wooed a graceful, delicate daughter of an army officer, living with her parents on Summit Avenue in St. Paul, and she and her mother were communicants of the church to which I ministered. While his headquarters were in Washington I had been called from the field to his house, and in the presence of a few relatives and some of his staff officers had officiated at the dedication of his firstborn, and offered a prayer that the infant become 'Christ's faithful soldier.' "[101]

The battle of Malvern Hill, during most of which the Minnesotans were out of harm's way in Binford's oat field, was the most decisive Union victory yet on the Peninsula. Lee, believing his opponents too exhausted and demoralized to put up much of a fight, sent his divisions across an open field and up a hill in a frontal attack on the well-placed Federals. Union artillery and musket fire cut them down like blades of grass, and the fight soon became a slaughter. At the end of the day,

5,500 rebels lay dead and wounded on the field, twice as many casualties as McClellan's forces had suffered.

Hand recalled joining Sully and a half dozen generals at Sumner's headquarters that night. It was the consensus of the group that, after the day's success, the Union should hold its position. "But while they talked a peremptory order came to continue the retreat to Harrison's Landing. . . . As usual we got started about 10 o'clock, but had to move slowly on account of the darkness and the crowded road. Towards morning it came on to rain, and for hours it just poured down. Somewhere near noon, on July 2, we reached Harrison's Landing, wet and hungry." Lochren said the Minnesotans "wallowed, rather than marched" the remaining seven miles to the river landing, named for the family of Benjamin Harrison, a signer of the Declaration of Independence, whose son and great-grandson would become presidents of the United States. Arriving there, Lochren said, the men "were massed for camp in a field of finely ripened wheat . . . on the rich bottom land near the river. . . . But with the mass of men who covered it, and the rain still pouring, within an hour there was not a sign of wheat—merely a black field of mud, upon which the soldiers set up their dog tents, and supplied them with bedding from large stack yards, where from some cause, the crops of previous years still stood unthreshed." Bassett, meanwhile, still couldn't locate his comrades: "I went down river five miles, but not finding the Regt. I returned to the Landing." The next day he was happy to find them at last, but not their conditions: "It was very muddy."[102]

The wounded Pressnell, too, found the regiment. After visiting a hospital to have "four more bits of glass" removed and his wounds treated, he said, "I threw away my crutch, procured a haversack, filled it with hospital rations, picked up a gun, a well-filled cartridge box and accuterments, limped off in search of my regiment and company, which I found within a couple of hours, and took my place in the ranks ready for duty. I had escaped a rebel prison, and demonstrated to my own satisfaction the power of mind and will over matter and pain." A few days later he and two other men discovered that their fates at Savage Station had been less than accurately reported: "By the first New York papers received at Harrison's Landing we learned that all three of us had been mortally wounded. The St. Paul papers announced that we

were all killed outright, while from a Stillwater paper, which had singled me out for special mention, I learned what a really good little boy
I had always been. Knowing that I had always, and rightly, too, been
regarded as one of the harumscarums of the town, this last 'notice' was,
to me, very amusing."[103] Pressnell was apparently the only member of
the regiment given the opportunity to read his own obituary.

The Minnesotans found enough to eat at Harrison's Landing but dry
land was harder to come by. "When we had arrived at Harrisons Landing," Goddard wrote six months later, "we wer very tired hungry cold
and wet seting around on sticks and any thing we could get to set on."
The rains continued unabated, causing the men's straw flooring to float
away and their tent pegs to come loose. Sleeping in pools of water
under collapsed tents for a few days was sufficient incentive for them to
find higher ground. "We moved into the country about a mile and
camped in a cornfield near a creek," Bassett recorded. "I took off my
shoes last nite to sleep for the first time in 33 days," Marvin wrote.[104]

The Union forces were still only twenty miles from Richmond, but for
all the threat they posed to the Confederate capital they might as well
have been back in Washington. Once McClellan decided not to follow
up on his victory at Malvern Hill, defeat hung in the air. The commander would never admit that his entire Peninsula campaign could not still
be a success, of course, and thus he was immobilized. The result for the
Minnesotans and the rest of the Army of the Potomac was five more
weeks of camp routine, albeit easier than normal, according to Mathew
Marvin: "The fatigue details are a great deal lighter than they have been.
We drill 2 hours a day & have a dress parade at nite." As usual they
adjusted to their new circumstances—they had little choice—and put
the past behind them. "The men were not so much depressed by this
retreat as might have been expected," Hand recalled, "and very soon
they were fixed comfortably and enjoying a rest."[105] They enjoyed less
the return of the "swamp fever" and other illnesses that had plagued
them since they set foot on the Peninsula, and once again hundreds of
Union soldiers were laid low by sickness.

On 9 July President Lincoln arrived to confer with his commanding
general and to review his army. "Honest Old Abe was up to see us yesterday," Charley Goddard wrote; "passed along our lines   cannon wer
fired & the troops cheered him evry place he went. . . . There was only

one person that was ahead of little Mc and that was the honest rail spliter This is the first time I ever saw the President." "[W]e all remember the kindly face he turned toward us as he rode along the lines with General McClellan," Hand recalled.[106]

The next day Neill left the regiment to become a hospital chaplain in Philadelphia. According to Goddard, the men were not sorry to see him go: "He was not the kind of man we wanted."[107] By the end of the month Hand too was gone, ordered to take charge of a hospital in Newport News.

On 22 July McClellan reviewed the Second Corps, and Sumner used the occasion to single out the First Minnesota as one of two model regiments in his command. Marvin used the occasion to do a little boasting: "Their was several hed McLellan say to Sumner that Sulley had the best *regt* in *Army*. We do put on Stile & no mistake. You can see your face in the Leather after blacking. The Brass shine like Silver & the guns are brite as they ever. No matter how lazy the man he must be clean or go to the guard house. Why is it . . . that when we have camped rite along side of another Regt when they would die like sheep & in our Regt their would be but 2 or 3 in the hospital & as many more in each company would go to sick call & get Pills or powder & go on duty. I believe We have not had more than 5 die from any desese in the regt since we have been in the servace (most 18 months). Some regt have lost hundreds by desease aloan."[108]

Sedgwick's division and the Minnesotans were sent back to Malvern Hill on a reconnaissance mission on 6 August. "We started at 6 P.M. with two days rations, and marched all night," Bassett wrote. "On the 6th we lay in front of the Malvern House and slept there all night. There was some fighting there the next morning, but the Rebs fled, leaving their camps and everything. Four companies of the Minn. 1st went forward as skirmishers and pickets. Considerable fireing, but no one hurt on our side."[109]

Marvin wrote his brother of the grisly scene the men encountered: "The Old Battle ground looked natureal as life but the rebells buried our dead miserably. their wer in several graves Arms & leggs & eavon heads above ground." According to Lochren, the regiment bivouacked where the heaviest fighting had taken place on 1 July. "The pits where the dead had been buried in cords had sunk," he said, "and bones were protruding." He added that he hoped this first major movement of the army in more than a month "was the beginning of a new advance along the James upon Richmond."[110] But it was not to be. The troops returned to their camp at Harrison's Landing.

The day after Marvin wrote of the horrible scene he had witnessed at Malvern Hill was a day he would long remember, but for another reason altogether. He was sitting on the edge of his bunk after a nap "when a Minie ball of 57 cal struck my thigh near the groin came out on the inside coming very close to the Ardery but without injury to it or the bone. It was done by some careless scallawag in the 5th N H regt whose camp is about 800 yards from here. . . . the ball passed through 4 tents in our Regt." Marvin's tentmates carried him to the hospital, where he would remain for the next month. "Had my wound dresed today," he wrote two days later; "it is doing first rate but it is a tender companion."[111]

President Lincoln's new general in chief, Henry Halleck, came to Harrison's Landing to determine whether McClellan had any real intention of advancing on Richmond. Halleck was worried that with John Pope's army outside Washington and McClellan's still on the Peninsula, Lee could easily take advantage of the split by concentrating all his forces on each of the Federal armies separately. When McClellan gave his usual response—he needed more men, more material, more time—Halleck concluded McClellan would not soon move on Richmond, and he ordered the Army of the Potomac to return to Washington. McClellan complained vigorously but to no avail. He prepared to remove his army from Virginia, although he would do so on his own schedule, which is to say, slowly.

After a series of false starts, the First Minnesota began its march back down the Peninsula on 16 August. An account of just how tedious the trek was came from a member of Company B, who sent the following description of the march to the Stillwater *Messenger* under the pen name "Saint Croix." It could have described almost any march any time:

> Our first orders came to be ready to move in light marching order on Monday, August 11, but owing to change of programme, or some other cause, we were kept in camp constantly on the *qui vive* until Saturday the 16th, when we finally got under way and dragged our slow length along out of the fortifications and over about four

miles of road, and encampt for the night within a mile or two of
Charles City Court House. In civil life we do not regard a walk of
ten or twenty miles in one day as anything very arduous. A good
traveler will make his forty miles a day without any great effort. But
a march of an army is quite a different affair. An unskilled general
will manage to make a march of five miles in one day by an army
corps a very exhausting day's work for the men. The reveille will
sound at half past two in the morning, and every man must get his
coffee and gird on his armor. One hour later the bugles sound
"attention" and the men fall in, all strapped up and loaded down.
Here they wait under arms right in their tracks one hour and a
half—this a moderate statement—when the welcome "forward" is
sounded, and your regiment marches off promptly for ten or twenty
rods and halts to let by a long column of cavalry, or infantry, or a
wagon train. This occupies from fifteen minutes to three hours,
according to the brilliancy and magnitude of the movement. By this
time the sun is high and the heat is great. Dust ditto. Finally the
regiment will get out of sight of camp, and it is time to take a lunch.
No sooner has the whole corps got stretched out on the road, than
the hateful, but inevitable order comes to "closeup," and the poor
devils toward the rear are compelled to take up a sort of double
quick step until some obstruction delays the head of the column,
and they come slap up against their file leaders. Then a long halt
and another weary stand-up ensues, to be followed by another double quick to make up for the accumulated time and distance lost by
all the men and trains in front. And thus we march and stand. No
matter how great the heat, how thick the dust, or how heavy the
loads on our shoulders. . . . By this style of marching, when five
miles are made, the men are very much fatigued, while a march of
ten or twelve miles is a serious affair.[112]

Edward Walker gave a friend another version of the march, together
with some questions: "Our greatest enemy was dust and you can imagine what thick clouds of dust we had to travel through. On our march we
passed through Williamsburg and through the works at Yorktown, here
we got another sight at our labors last spring, and now we were leaving
the Peninsula, and what had we accomplished, after leaving about one-
third of our army behind, the thought was anything but pleasant, and we
wondered—what next?—We continued on march to Newport News
and camped there waiting our turn to go on board transports."

Walker found Newport News "a splendid place to camp in, fine sea breeze all the time and the beach is a fine place to bathe. While we were there hundreds of the boys were out in the roads raking oysters with their hands, and when stewed they didn't go bad. We stopped here several days and got some of the dust washed off. As we had no change of clothes we would wash our shirts and wait for them to dry. A very fine thing this being your own clothes line."[113]

The day before his regiment reached Newport News, prisoner of war Isaac Taylor read in a Richmond newspaper that "McClellan has evacuated his position on the James River."[114] Isaac and Henry by now were well into their second month of captivity and their fourth week on Belle Isle, a small island off Richmond in the James River, which the Confederates were using as a prison for enlisted men. It had not been a pleasant experience for either of them recently, and certainly a long way from the early moments after they had come into rebel hands.

Isaac's diary entry for 30 June summarized his first day after the rear guard of the Second Corps had pulled out of Savage Station, leaving behind its wounded: "Rained a little last night. We get a portion of the Min. boys into the house. We have with us a surgeon of the 7th Ga. Regt. General Jackson's advance passes us in the A.M. I suppose we are considered prisoners of war. Got a good view of old Stonewall Jackson. We are treated very kindly by the Confederates. Paid one dime for 'Richmond Dispatch' printed on half sheet. . . . George L. Smith, Co. C., 1st. Min. died this A.M. . . . Heavy firing in the P.M. . . . We have a few wounded Confederates."[115]

Isaac didn't say so, but, by another account, Henry not only saw Jackson but exchanged a few good-humored words with him. The legendary general approached Henry near the swamp road, according to this account, and asked which direction his Union comrades had taken. "I don't know, General," Henry replied, "but no doubt you will find them soon enough." Jackson is reported to have smiled at this remark and then to have given Henry a pass to allow him through the lines to retrieve water for the wounded.[116]

The next day the Taylor brothers buried their cousin Edward Taylor and at least one other Minnesotan. Even though McClellan's forces were in retreat, Isaac was still confident: "The Confederates talk as though they have routed McClellan's army & that the war is soon to close in their favor. You're very much mistaken gentlemen." Word arrived of the fierce fighting at Glendale and Malvern Hill. "Ambulances passing with wounded all day. We are having a rough time of it with the wounded. . . . Confds, bring in several small guards of Union prisoners."[117]

The disabled Union prisoners were soon moved to improvised hospitals in and around Savage Station. On 4 July Isaac and Henry found themselves "in an old barn with 60 sick and wounded soldiers. We celebrate the Anniversary of our National Independence by dressing the wounds of soldiers who fell while maintaining that Independence. We hear that Gen. Dana was killed in the fight of the 29th ult. [the report was incorrect] P.H.T. put in charge of this branch of h's't'l."

Several months later Isaac said that during this period he and Henry "were constantly at work over the sick and wounded. Our patients appeared very grateful for services rendered. One young fellow of Baxter's Zouaves said he was going to have our names written in their family Bible. . . . Among the wounded that we had the care of were several Confederates. One young man from South Carolina Henry gave his canteen, which he seemed to prize very highly. We were obliged to work day and night, and then could only half take care of the wounded."[118]

Over the next week the Taylors fought off illness, scrounged for food, and did what they could to comfort the wounded:

> July 5th. A fine day. Our commissareit is quite poor & scanty. Somewhat wearied with constant care of wounded. The boys are highly elated by a rumor that the wounded are to be paroled in a few days & sent North. . . . Mon. 7th The boys are, generally, getting along well. . . . Tues. 8th A little unwell—threatened with fever—& take a dose of quinine. We get Richmond papers occasionally. Bread is brought from Richmond & sold at prices ranging from 10 to 25 cents per loaf. Very warm. Confeds. take away a good portion of our ice & leave us "minus." Wed. July 9th. Went a mile & a half into the country to get milk & eggs for the wounded. Refreshing to get out into the country A number—said to be 200—of Union prisoners came down on the cars from Richmond to assist in caring for the wounded. . . . Thur. 10th. Our wounded boys sing the national airs with a great deal of spirit.[119]

And so it went until 14 July, when the wounded were loaded on trains. Anticipating the move, Isaac and Henry had brought Hugh Cassidy, a sergeant in Company E who had suffered a severe leg wound, to their own hospital the day before "so as to take him along with us." The train left in the afternoon and reached Richmond about 6:00 p.m. Although a number of the wounded were left on the cars overnight, Isaac reported that he was "up nearly all night unloading wounded & taking care of Sergt. Hugh Cassidy. Cassidy died at 8-30 A.M. This A.M. got the remaining wounded into ware houses on 'James Canal.' Sick & tired."[120]

Not for the first time, and certainly not for the last, the prisoners' hopes of being released were raised by some report, usually untrue, only to be solidly dashed: "We hear that [Union] Gen. Dix is in Richmond arranging for an exchange of prisoners."[121] Gen. John Dix wasn't then in Richmond, but he would be within a few days to work out an agreement that would permit the two sides to exchange prisoners.

Meanwhile, life in the warehouse was going from bad to worse:

Wed. 16. Lint all gone, bandages few & no medicine. We have seen nothing of our doctor since yesterday morning. Towards night we are removed to tobacco factory a little distance up street. Every time they move us they put us in a worse place. This hospital is very filthy. Thur. July 17. Passed a miserable night in the heat & stench of this infernal prison. Got our squad of wounded soldiers together on 2d. floor & things a little systematized. Secesh give us nothing to eat till about 1 P.M. when we get ¼ loaf of bread & about 1 pint of rice soup each. . . . Three or 4 Union Drs. called late last night & promised to come again tomorrow. . . . Fri. 18. Heat not quite so oppressive today. . . . About noon we get our (beef) soup again. The boys would be "hard up" for food had they not a little money with which to buy bread. Sold my watch to day to get money to buy bread The Richmond Examiner of this morning says "it has been determined to parole 2500 of the worst wounded Yankees, immediately." Each of the boys are anxious to know if *they* will be included on the list. . . . Get bread & soup again to night. Sat. July 19. Two meals today. Most of the boys are getting along well. The Confederates call around every day to exchange Confederate notes for U.S. Treas. notes. Mon. 21. Secesh papers state that to day is to be "celebrated" as the anniversary of the battle of Bull Run.[122]

Not only were the prisoners hot, sick, hungry, and generally miserable, but they had to be reminded of their first defeat.

The sick and wounded were crowded together in squalid conditions, Isaac recalled later:

> Most of them lay upon a hard floor with nothing but a single blanket under them. There, a great many died that might have lived could they have had proper care. The despondence of some, I think, asisted materially in carrying them off. I believe that many died not from wounds or sickness, but simply because their spirits drooped. We tried to revive their spirits in every possible way. They frequently asked us to read the Richmond papers to them and were particularly interested in anything that related to the "Yankee prisoners." . . . Occasionally a woman with a well filled basket of delicacies would visit our loathsome prison and distribute them to the most feeble. We also found some very kind friends among the Confederate soldiery, and should they ever fall into our hands, we shall be happy to return their kindness. Among them is Sergeant Hussey of the 2nd Miss. Regt. He would buy milk, berries, etc., and bring to those who were most severely wounded. That man should never want for anything without reach should he fall into our hands.[123]

This hellhole confining the Taylors was the infamous Libby Prison, and the Confederates decided they had to get the men out of there. Beginning on 22 July they distributed them to different points, and some were paroled: "A number of the worst wounded in this hospital sent North via Petersburgh & City Point. The train took five hundred in all. The boys selected to go were wonderfully elated; some disappointed ones, very much depressed in spirit. Wed. July 23. A woman sends chicken soup to the wounded & sick at this hospital. Thur. 24. The boys are wild with joy when the Dr. tells them to be ready to start for *home* at 5 A.M. tomorrow. Fri. 25. Sick & wounded leave Hosp. No. 1 this A.M. We help remove those remaining at Hosp. No. 2, to Prison No. 1. Prison No. 1 is much cleaner than No. 2. 97 of us are placed in the upper story & relieved from the arduous duties of attendance on the sick & wounded."[124]

Isaac and Henry were not to be among those sent "home." Instead, they and the other "nurses" were sent the next day to Belle Isle, where the alternating heat and rains combined with barely edible food and no shelter to keep them in a state of nearly constant misery. They quickly learned to fend for themselves: "Sun. July 27. Henry & I construct a tent of our blankets. Our rations consist of mouldy bread & boiled beef. We are confined in rather close quarters & there are many inconveniences that in my opinion should be remidied. Mon. 28. We have a very good chance to bathe in James River. Some of our boys buy a barrell of flour at the Confederate Commissary for twenty dollars. Our boys make pancakes & sell them to their comrads for twenty five cents apiece. Our rations are ½ loaf of bread & a small piece of meat (sometimes soup) per day, and one spoonful salt per week. . . . Tues. 29. Get two 'unleavened' pancakes for a quarter of a dollar. Wed. 30. We pay one dollar for a lb. of sugar at Secesh Commissary."

One day all prisoners except the sick were assembled and counted. Isaac reported the number as 3,471, all crowding one another on just a few acres of sand. It was not surprising that men living under these conditions sometimes resorted to desperate measures or that those in a position to charge hungry men extortionate prices for food would do so: "Thur. 31. Stop thief! who stole both our canteens last night? . . . A number of sick & wounded removed from the Island. Only *six dollars* per gallon for molasses at C S Commissary! Walk up, all that you have money, & purchase before it takes another rise. . . . Sat. 2d. A Confederate gives me one dollar and fifty cents, in Va. Treas. note & Richmond scrip, for a gold dollar."[125]

As July turned to August, increasing numbers of Union prisoners left the island to board trains for the Federal lines, but not Isaac and Henry.

Sun. 3d. It seems that arrangements for a general exchange of prisoners have been made. We have rather dull times cooped up on one corner of "Belle-Isle." We have nothing to read and are not allowed to purchase the Richmond papers. The "visual line that girts us round" is, to us, "the World's extreme." Mon. Aug. 4. Another squad of "citizens" taken from the Island. Names of all persons on the island registered this evening. They say we shall be released from this bondage tomorrow. Just as soon as you can make it convenient, Mr. Secesh. We take a game or two of chess to day. Tues. 5. 2500 prisoners march from Belle-Isle to James River. P.H. & I are unfortunately left behind in this miserable hole of secession. I sell my over coat & rubber blanket to sentry for a Confederate one dollar note. Henry & I move into one of the vacated tents. We "build" a "minute" pudding for supper. Wed. 6. Henry & I busy ourselves with chess. We make pancakes for supper. Thur. Aug. 7. Hot day. Reading the Bible & playing chess. Crust coffee for breakfast & supper. Fri. Aug. 8. A scorching day—nearly wilted. . . . Sun. Aug. 10. Soup & meat for breakfast. Nothing but hard-bread & water for supper. We sigh for the "flesh pots" of the Army of the Potomac.[126]

As men departed the island others arrived to take their place. One day more than five hundred prisoners were transferred from Lynchburg. A few days later they were joined by "between 4 & 5 hundred of the 1st. Md. Regt." and several hundred men from General Banks's army in the Shenandoah. The faces of the prisoners changed, but conditions stayed the same. It had been seven weeks since the Taylors had been taken prisoner. They had learned to cope with their adversity, but now, as the unforgiving sun of August bore down, they wondered whether they would ever leave this miserable island. "Sun. 17. . . . Finished reading the book of Exodus. I'd like to know when we are going to make *our* exodus from this Godless, saltless Confederacy. We get no supper."[127]

5

ANTIETAM

"The dead were piled up against each other."

While Isaac and Henry Taylor were wondering whether they would ever get off Belle Isle, their regiment was on the steamer *Mississippi* heading back up the Chesapeake. To Edward Walker, conditions on board were almost as oppressive as those of a prison: "We were packed pretty snug, most of the brigade was on this boat. . . . When men are stowed on deck so thick they can't lay down it is about time to growl a little, but this is a fact, we had to stand the pressure two days and three nights, and I will warrant that Jonah in the whales belly wasnt more uncomfortable than we were." James Ghostley agreed: "Crowded almost to suffocation and it is almost impossible to get any fresh air. had to eat my meat raw because I could get no chance to cook it. hope we shall soon land again."[1]

The Minnesotans arrived at Alexandria the morning of 28 August and marched three miles toward Fairfax Court House, where, Lochren said, they "heard first news of disaster to Pope's army."[2] Seizing the moment before McClellan's forces, returning from the Peninsula, could join Pope outside Washington, Lee had boldly divided his own army to catch the Union commander off balance. While James Longstreet occupied Pope's attention in front, Lee sent Jackson to Manassas Junction on one of his infamous marches to hit the Federals from the rear. The result was another Union disaster at Bull Run; as the First Minnesota and Sumner's Second Corps rushed to help Pope, his army was already in full retreat.

"We heard the firing at the second battle of Bull Run when we were at Chain Bridge," Walker recalled. "We marched night and day, when

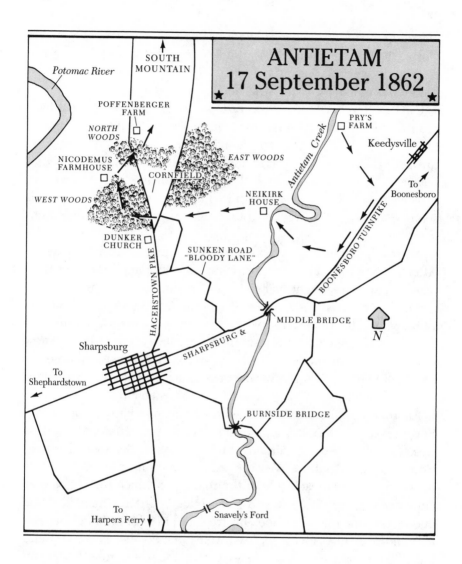

POTOMAC RIVER

SOUTH MOUNTAIN

ANTIETAM
17 September 1862

POFFENBERGER FARM

PRY'S FARM

NORTH WOODS

Keedysville

NICODEMUS FARMHOUSE

EAST WOODS

CORNFIELD

To Boonesboro

WEST WOODS

NEIKIRK HOUSE

DUNKER CHURCH

SUNKEN ROAD "BLOODY LANE"

ANTIETAM CREEK

BOONESBORO TURNPIKE

HAGERSTOWN PIKE

MIDDLE BRIDGE

N

Sharpsburg

SHARPSBURG &

To Shephardstown

BURNSIDE BRIDGE

To Harpers Ferry

Snavely's Ford

we got into Centerville we had with us about one quarter of Sumners Corps, the rest had given out on the way and what was left of us wasnt fit to go into action that day—fortunately we were not called on, and before morning most of the stragglers had come up with us."[3]

On 1 September Sumner was ordered to cover Pope's retreat back toward the Potomac, with the First, according to Lochren, "becoming the rear guard on the road to Vienna, following the army after dark, through deep mud, and reaching a position near Chantilly at dawn. . . . Here we halted for the day, seeing the army move off, exhausted and dispirited, and with them were sent such of our men as seemed unfit for duty, reducing the regiment to less than three hundred men."[4]

No one had to tell Walker what role the Minnesotans were playing. After passing abandoned wagons and burning commissary stores all day, he said the regiment "halted till all the other army corps passed us, did not all get past till most sudden as the last train was passing the Rebs, who all the time had kept watch on our movements, commenced shelling us. Did no damage, just hurried up the wagons. We knew now that we were to be the rear guard, the rear of all rears was composed of our Regiment. . . . We knew what rear guard meant and we knew if there was any fighting going on we would have a hand in."[5]

Another Minnesotan who learned what rear guard meant was Myron Shepard who, with another sergeant from Company B, volunteered for what he called "extra hazardous duty": "It was understood that [we] were to be sacrificed. . . . We were ordered to skirmish about 150 yards to the rear, one on each side of the road upon which the enemy was approaching. Our firing was to give notice to the regiment that the enemy was upon us. Each took his tree, and in a few minutes his cavalry and a battery appeared. Two well directed shots confused and halted them for a moment, while we took to the rear. A rebel battery on our right and cavalry on our left, and Sully's skirmishers on his rear made our escape doubtful. But we made it and found the regiment. . . . We were welcomed and congratulated by our comrades who had thought us lost."[6]

The pursuing Confederates kept up the pressure. The First Minnesota and two Rhode Island artillery pieces attached to it "were carefully scanned during the afternoon by the enemy's videttes, who increased to large numbers before night, and for some time kept up a continuous fire upon us at long range," according to Lochren. "Near sunset our pickets were driven in, and as all the rest of the army had been gone a considerable time, our regiment retired some distance to the cover of a wood, followed by a strong line of skirmishers. Suddenly a heavy body of cavalry formed line near us, and a full battery came into position near enough to sweep our line with grape and canister."[7]

It was clear to Colonel Sully that, between the rebel artillery and the cavalry, his regiment was in great danger, and he decided on a bold move. Holding the Confederates in place with the Minnesotans, he ordered the Rhode Islanders and their guns up the road a half mile to a position on Flint Hill. When they were in place he hurried his men back at the "double-quick" to "form on them as the centre," Lochren said.

> In the darkness which had come on, this was done with celerity and in silence. The two guns stood in the middle of the road near the top of the hill, and the wings of the regiment were, on either side, thrown forward, forming the letter V, so as to partly envelop the approaching foe. Silently we waited, but not long, for the rebel cavalry and artillery, finding the road clear, hurried on in pursuit, not discovering us until the advance was nearly at the muzzles of our guns. Sully's challenge, "Who comes there?" and the surprised response, "Who the devil are you?" and a pistol-shot from the rebel leader directed at Sully, brought a volley of canister from the two pieces and musketry from the First Minnesota, which must have done fearful execution, judging from the cries, groans, curses and commands, as those who were able dashed madly to the rear, hastened by a second volley from the guns and the regiment.[8]

"If our volley of musketry broke them up the artillery finished the job," Walker wrote, "and those that did not get killed went over the hill completely routed. We could plainly hear them yelling, and the officers trying to rally them, and such a mixture of . . . confusion generally, you never heard, but the sounds grew fainter in the distance, and we soon kept on our road. . . . This checked the Rebs so they troubled us no more that night. But our good luck was almost spoiled before morning."[9]

More accurately, the regiment's good luck turned to bad luck almost immediately. The Minnesotans fell victim to friendly fire when the

Ninth New York Cavalry, believing them to be Confederates, charged through their ranks. "It came from the front (not the rear) and we knew at once that 'some one had blundered,'" Myron Shepard said later. "We of course thought we had run into a nest of 'Guerrillas' and some of our men returned the fire," Walker wrote. "It was all over in no time, and we soon discovered that all belonged to our army, and that there was no Secesh near. The way the thing started as near as can be ascertained is as follows. One of the cavalry men going to one of the caissons dropped a cap which exploded, this created a panic among the teams and scared the horses, which in turn alarmed the cavalry and dashed off down the road through our ranks. . . . We lost some killed in the scrape, one man in our company wounded, had to have his leg amputated (has since died). This isn't the first confounded row that has happened on the road in the night."[10]

It was a costly night for the First Minnesota. The regiment lost four killed and five wounded in the two encounters. The survivors were exhausted and dirty from marching sixty-five miles day and night through scorching heat and enemy fire since they had landed at Alexandria a few days before. They wanted desperately to rest, but the next morning they pushed on to the Chain Bridge and crossed into Maryland. "We have been without clean shirts for 4 weeks and had not time to wash those we have on," Goddard wrote. "You may bet we are used up soldiers."[11] By the time they got to Tennallytown on 4 September there were fewer than five hundred men in the ranks fit for duty.

They were in Maryland because that's where the Federal command feared that Lee was headed, perhaps on his way toward Washington. Taking full advantage of Union disarray after routing Pope at Bull Run, Lee decided to take the offensive and invade the North. Once again the national capital appeared to be in danger, and Lincoln concluded he had no choice but to recall McClellan, who had been left effectively without a command since his Peninsula divisions had been sent to Pope as soon as they disembarked. Lincoln dispatched Pope to Minnesota to put down the Sioux uprising, and McClellan once again led the army he had created. Now all he had to do was to find and defeat Lee.

On 5 September Lee led the Army of Northern Virginia across the Potomac into Maryland. The next day, to block a Confederate advance on Washington, Sumner and his Second Corps headed up the river on the same road the Minnesotans had taken a year earlier. "By this time we began to think that we were going to Edwards Ferry again and perhaps picket duty this winter," Ed Walker wrote, "but waiting awhile the movements of Secesh, we were marched to Frederick City. Here the inhabitants had had a good look at Secesh, and probably concluded that they didn't want to be 'liberated' by Jackson, at any rate they welcomed us with enthusiasm, flags hung from most every house, sidewalks covered with women and children—the fact is Maryland will *blow* about sympathizing with Secesh, but when they come to have war on Maryland, they had rather be excused."[12]

Lee had left Frederick just before the Federals arrived and was pursuing another bold stroke. He again divided his army, sending Jackson to take Harpers Ferry and D. H. Hill to stop McClellan at South Mountain, while leaving the rest of his command at Hagerstown, near the Pennsylvania border. By sheer luck McClellan learned the details of Lee's plan—a Union soldier found a copy of Lee's order—and realized that he had an opportunity to destroy the Southern army piece by piece. As a first step, he decided to engage Hill's forces and to push through the gap at South Mountain. After a march of seventeen miles, the Minnesotans got there as the fighting was winding down.

"The next day we kept on," Walker continued.

> Sesech retreating till we came in sight of South Mountain, could see the smoke of our artillery and that of the Rebs contesting the pass through the mountains. Saturday in the afternoon we made a short halt, barely time to eat, when we were hurried on towards the firing as night came on we could see flashes of musketry and artillery, but the distance was so great we could not hear any report. We knew there must be quite a fight going on. . . . On we marched dark as pitch, over all sorts of places, till late at night we reached the field, met ambulances and stretchers carrying off the wounded. . . . Our Brigade was put to the front on picket and we expected to begin the fight in the morning. Our men had had a hard fight but had drove them and we held the field.[13]

Pvt. Charles A. Berry of Company E told later how he spent that night on the battlefield at South Mountain: "We camped there all night with the dead and dying all around us. The next morning I looked over the ground on our front and it was covered with the dead bodies of our enemies. There I saw a rebel sitting on a rock with a woman's picture in his hand as though he were looking at it, but he was dead."[14]

There would be no resumption of the fighting that day as Walker had expected there to be. Instead, he wrote,

> one of our companies was sent out skirmishing and found that in the night Secesh had skedadled. Our cavalry and flying artillery started after them and we followed on over the mountain. The Rebs had a good position here but was outnumbered and fairly whipped by our troops. As we marched along the road we saw any quantity of knapsacks and clothes left by Secesh. We made a halt on the road where there was a squad of about fifty prisoners, part of them taken in the fight, and some of them stragglers. I had a long talk with some of them, they had various ideas about the war. Some were forced in and was willing to take the oath of allegience, and some wanted Europe to interfere. Others were Secesh and would argue the best they knew how, but they all wanted the war to end, and were sick of it.[15]

The regiment crossed over South Mountain, passed through Boonesborough, and bivouacked that night near Shepardstown. "In the early morning of the 16th," Lochren recorded, "we marched through Keedysville, and halted on high ground overlooking the Antietam."[16]

The Antietam Creek, which Lochren saw from the regiment's camp less than a half mile away, flowed gently on a winding, unhurried twenty-mile course through the pastoral beauty of northern Maryland until it entered the Potomac seven miles above Harpers Ferry. It was shallow enough to ford in many places, but its banks were tall and steep almost everywhere. Two miles west of the creek was the village of Sharpsburg, and two miles beyond that flowed the Potomac. With the mountains now at their back, the Minnesotans looked out on a rolling countryside spotted with farmhouses, cornfields, and small woods, as serene and bucolic a picture as any they had seen since leaving the Shenandoah earlier that year.

But it would not remain serene for long, because both the Union and Confederate armies were assembling. Lee had learned that McClellan was aware that the Confederates had divided their forces, and, with the Union army about to pour across South Mountain, his first instinct was to withdraw to the Shenandoah. But he soon recognized the awkwardness of returning to Virginia from his northern invasion without having fought a major battle. Besides, the ease with which Jackson was taking Harpers Ferry reinforced Lee's notion that the Northerners were demoralized and wouldn't put up a stiff resistance. Directing Jackson and his other commanders to gather immediately near Sharpsburg, Lee decided to stand and fight.

McClellan also was preparing to fight but, as usual, at his own pace. By 16 September he had some sixty thousand troops on hand east of Antietam Creek and another fifteen thousand close by, while Lee had fewer that thirty thousand in positions between the creek and Sharpsburg. But instead of probing to determine Lee's strength, McClellan concluded once again that he was outnumbered. He decided to wait until his full force was in place the next day before launching an attack. It was another missed opportunity. What he didn't know but should have guessed was that Jackson, having captured twelve thousand Federals at Harpers Ferry with barely a fight, was moving his large force north to Sharpsburg as rapidly as possible. When it arrived, the opposing armies would be close to even in numbers.

The battle opened early the next morning when Joseph Hooker's First Corps led the Union assault on rebel positions in the woods and the cornfield east of the Hagerstown Pike and north of the Dunker Church. Hooker's men, followed shortly by those from Joseph Mansfield's Twelfth Corps, charged from the north into a withering fire from Confederates hidden in small clumps of trees and protected by stone walls and natural depressions in the earth. The Minnesotans, who had risen at four to be ready to march at sunrise, watched the unfolding battle with intense interest from their vantage point on Pry's farm about a mile to the east, knowing that their turn at the rebels would come soon. Many climbed trees and haystacks to get a better view, letting out cheers whenever the Federals advanced.

At 7:00 a.m. Sumner was ordered to take his Second Corps onto the field to follow up on the work of the First and the Twelfth, whose ranks had been decimated in the cornfield and what would be known later as the West Woods. After wading through the knee-deep water of the Antietam at previously selected and prepared positions, the five thousand men of Sedgwick's division formed three lines, with one brigade in each line. Gorman's brigade was placed in the front line, Dana's in a line fifty yards behind it, and Gen. Oliver Howard's about fifty yards behind that. The Minnesotans anchored the extreme right of Gorman's line. They numbered 435 men that morning, Company I having been assigned to provost guard duty.

It was cloudy and cool as the massed force began to march toward the west. Many of the men were pleased that at least they wouldn't have to fight again in sweltering heat. As they moved up a light slope from the creek, they entered a thinly wooded stand of trees, the East Woods. "We began the advance upon the enemy at a rapid pace," Gorman reported several days later. "Before we had advanced 50 yards, the enemy opened a rapid and well-directed fire upon us from one or more batteries. . . . Passing through a strip of timber, we entered a large, open field, which was strewn with the enemy's dead and wounded."[17]

They were now in the cornfield, and it was a scene few of them would forget. "As we advanced across the ploughed field towards the woods, their batteries pouring the shell into us," Walker wrote a few weeks later. "We advanced over the ground gained by Hooker, he had just been taken off the field wounded, and his men were exhausted. As we moved on the dead and wounded lay thick, and fragments of regiments cheered us as we passed. Our men and Secesh lay as they fell, many begging us for a drink of water, others telling us not to tread on them and it *was* difficult to march over the ground without stepping on some man."[18]

The three lines of Sedgwick's division, each stretching five hundred yards across the field, moved steadily, one behind the other, the three-quarters of a mile to the Hagerstown Pike and the West Woods, beyond where the Confederates lay waiting. The line of march was designed to meet an enemy force directly in front of the advance; a counterthrust from any other direction would impede mobility, with potentially disastrous consequences. The rebels had yet to level rifle fire at the oncoming Federals, but artillery shells from Jeb Stuart's batteries were starting to take their toll.

"We passed a spot where Secesh had their line of battle and the dead lay in rows in a line as they fell," Walker said. "I never could have believed [it] had I not seen it. Here we passed fragments of regiments that had been in the fight in the morning, they cheered us as we passed. We now crossed the turnpike, had to climb two fences, this was the place they were last drove from, the fences are perfectly riddled with bullets. Our men lay thick here, it was a hard place to carry. After climbing the fences and crossing the road we came into a piece of woods and advancing through it we found Secesh waiting for us."[19]

At the second fence Sgt. Sam Bloomer, twenty-three, of Company B, the First Minnesota's color-bearer, took a musket ball through the knee and went down. Unable to walk, he pulled himself into the West Woods in back of the Dunker Church and sought shelter behind an oak tree, but not before tearing the colors from their staff and stuffing them in his shirt to prevent their capture.

The regiment was now in the West Woods, and the advancing troops suddenly found themselves marching through a devastating artillery barrage. Those shells that didn't hit the Minnesotans and others in the front rank were almost certain to hit those behind them in the second and third ranks. The men were massed so closely that the Confederate artillerymen could hardly miss. Impervious to this danger, General Sumner was riding with the Minnesotans in the first line when he noticed that the regimental colors were still in their jacket. "In God's name, what are you fighting for?" he shouted. "Unfurl those colors!"[20]

When the men had made their way well into the woods, according to Gorman, "the enemy's heavy lines of infantry first came into view, the front of which retired in considerable disorder before our advance. We pursued them until we passed the strip of woods and emerged into the edge of a field. . . . Instantly my whole brigade became hotly engaged, giving and receiving the most deadly fire it has ever been my lot to witness. Although the firing was not so rapid, it was most deadly, and at very close range. We also had to stand the most terrific fire of grape and canister, which told fearfully on the three right regiments of the brigade."[21] The rebel infantry included some of the same Mississippi, Alabama, and North Carolina regiments that had faced Gorman's brigade at Fair Oaks. They were exhausted, short of ammunition, and badly in need of reinforcements.

Walker described the scene as he saw it at the edge of the woods:

> Our regiment was close to a rail fence and a corn field between us and the enemies battery. This battery was on a hill about 700 yards to our right—directly in front of us was their infantry, about 300 yards distant at the commencement of the fight. As soon as we got

into the proper position both sides commenced peppering one another. Our company fired a few shots at the artillerymen, but as the distance was so great we directed most of our shots at the rebel colors, they came down several times, but the men stuck to them well, a piece of the staff found after the fight had several ball marks on it and had been cut away two or three times. We kept firing at what we considered the best marks, every man firing at will, we could see their wounded hobbling to the rear and some that *wasn't* wounded, but they seemed to have plenty of reenforcements.[22]

Lochren wrote that "the musketry fire here was very heavy and long sustained, our men firing about fifty rounds, and the enemy's artillery using grape and canister." A soldier did well to load and fire a round a minute, so firing fifty rounds took almost an hour. It was a long and dangerous time for the Minnesotans, but, as Lochren noted, not as dangerous as it was for those behind them: "Although our loss here was heavy, it is a curious fact that the brigade which formed the second line, seventy-five paces in our rear, and did not fire a shot, sustained a heavier loss than our brigade in the front line."[23]

The Thirty-fourth New York, which had anchored the left end of the front line while the Minnesotans were anchoring the right, had inadvertently become detached from the brigade while crossing the Hagerstown Turnpike and had stopped near the Dunker Church. Worse, the other two divisions from Sumner's Second Corps, which were supposed to be following, drifted off to the south and never made it to the West Woods. Sedgwick's left was therefore entirely unsupported and highly vulnerable to a flanking attack from the south, which was precisely what hit them.

From his vantage point in the front line, Walker saw the battle change course: "About this time the shot was coming into us pretty thick, several had been wounded in our company, among them our captain, the man next to me on the right had left, wounded in the leg, and the next minute the man next to me on my left was hit in the side. Shot seemed to be coming in a new direction, and looking to our left we saw the line give way and the place that was occupied by our men was now full of Secesh and they pouring a fire into us *lengthwise*. It seems that Secesh had found the place where our division failed to connect and had made a break and got through."[24]

Walker had it exactly right. Gen. Lafayette McLaws's Confederate division, barely pausing to catch its breath after a hurried march from Harpers Ferry, suddenly appeared at the south edge of the West Woods, where Sedgwick's left flank lay dangerously exposed. Joining forces with another brigade, the Confederates, with piercing rebel yells, directed their fury at the unsuspecting Federals. "By some error," Lochren said with understatement, "the left of our brigade failed to connect with the right of [Gen. Israel B.] Richardson's Division, leaving a considerable space unoccupied, through which, after while, a strong force of Confederates poured."[25]

Within minutes Sedgwick's entire division was thrown into nearly hopeless confusion. With the three brigade lines massed and facing west as the attack came from the south, the Northerners couldn't return the rebel fire without shooting through their own lines. Scattered and well protected by trees and rocks, the Confederates, on the other hand, had an open field of fire, which permitted them to hit a Federal virtually every time they fired. Even more ominous, they were positioned to roll around the Union left and virtually isolate the division.

The recognition of this impending disaster began to spread panic through the far left of the Union lines, particularly the second and third lines of Dana's and Howard's brigades. General Sumner, with Gorman's lead brigade a quarter of a mile north of the attack, was slow to learn of the events unfolding on his left. Once he understood what was happening, however, he immediately grasped its significance and took action. He rode through the rear two ranks, waving his hat and shouting as he went, in an effort to move Dana's and Howard's units out of danger. "Back, boys, for God's sake, move back!" he cried as he rode. "You are in a bad fix!"[26] Although Dana and Howard tried desperately, it was all but impossible, in the growing chaos, to maneuver their brigades to face the attack. Dana was wounded for his efforts but refused to leave the field. Sedgwick was struck three times and was carried to the rear. Indifferent to the danger that was by now widespread, Sumner continued to rally his men. It seemed he was everywhere, doing his best to calm and steady the frightened troops, but the task was largely futile. The regiments on Dana's and Howard's far left began to break and run, and as they streamed north they overran still other regiments, not only preventing them from firing but inflicting on them their own contagious panic.

Gorman's brigade fared better than the other two, but it, too, soon felt the impact of the assault. "It became evident that [the enemy] was moving in large force on our left, where his firing became terrific," Gorman reported. "In five minutes the enemy's fire came pouring hotly on our left flank and rear. Being in front, and without orders of any kind from any one, and finding that the two rear lines were changing position and had already moved from their original place, I gave an order, which reached no one but Colonel Sully, to move quietly by the right flank so as to unmask the second and third lines, to enable them to direct their fire to check the rapid advance of the enemy on my rear, and to enable them to fire without endangering my left regiment."[27]

At the northwest corner of the Union force, the Minnesotans were the farthest removed from McLaws's initial attack, but they quickly felt its force. "The enemy soon appeared in force on the left of the brigade, opened a very severe fire of musketry on us, while some of their artillery in front of us also opened on us," Sully reported. "Our loss here was very heavy, yet the men bravely held their position, and did not leave it until the two brigades in rear had fallen back and the left regiments were moving, when they received the order to retire." William Smith, a twenty-six-year-old corporal in Company K, "was shot in the head by a musket ball and killed instantly," according to Charley Goddard. "He was acting as file closer and it seemed as if the ball went right through the ranks and struck him in the rear   he had not time to say anything."[28] Sgt. D. B. Dudley, twenty-five, also of Company K, was struck close by and fell, but he was able to stay with the regiment.

Gorman's order to "move quietly by the right flank" was in reality an order for his brigade to withdraw to the north.

> The attack of the enemy on the flank was so sudden and in such overwhelming force that I had no time to lose for my command could have been completely enveloped and probably captured, as the enemy was moving not only upon my left flank but also forcing a column toward my right, the two rear lines having both moved from their position before either of my three right regiments changed theirs. Perceiving this, after moving a short distance, my

command faced about again toward the enemy and gave him another fire, which to some extent checked his advance. After moving a short distance farther, his forces were perceived moving to our right, when the First Minnesota faced toward him and delivered another fire, which again checked his movement.[29]

The panic had been moving rapidly north through the nearly wrecked division, but it did not reach the Minnesotans. "The order had been given to fall back," Walker wrote, "but we being on the extreme right did not get or understand the order till the rest of the line had fallen back, as it was we came near being flanked. We were now ordered by the colonel to fall back and we slowly retired through the wood, this was done in pretty good order considering the circumstances. Some *Slinks* of course run but the men generally behaved better than they ever did in any fight before. We did not go out over the same ground that we came in on."[30]

"No one seems to know how it was done," Pressnell remembered, "but in falling back our massed division somehow so disentangled itself as to form in a comparatively straight line, division front by the time we reached the edge of the woods, but as the rebels followed us closely and rapidly our broken lines soon gave way and 'confusion worse confounded' reigned in our now depleted ranks until we reached a position on higher ground a short distance north of the church and west of the Hagerstown pike where portions of a couple of our batteries had taken position and by a liberal and effective use of grape and canister compelled the enemy to fall back after they had been uncovered by our retreating troops."[31]

With regiments all about them either destroyed or confused, the Minnesotans did their best to maintain an orderly withdrawal, fighting smoke and chaos as well as Confederates on three sides. "Owing to the cool head of Sully," Pressnell wrote, "the 1st Minnesota was the only regiment in the division which maintained anything like organization, and when we were about half way up the slight rise of ground over which we were retreating the Colonel gave the order to face and fire, with the result that a solid volley from about 300 muskets poured into the following enemy and caused a quite appreciable check to their oncoming." Pressnell mistakenly concluded that the order to turn and fire was an order to stand and fight. As a result, he reloaded and fired a second round before he "discovered that the rest of the boys were several rods in my rear hastily retreating." Sully was so impressed that he later promoted him to corporal over the objections of Pressnell's company commander. "Had I realized that the boys turned back after they fired their volley, I would have been with them, and in the lead," he later confessed. "So that it was a very foolish act of mine, under excitement, but misconstrued by Sully as bravery, that gave me my start in the line of promotion."[32]

"Retiring in line of battle," Sully himself wrote, "we halted again outside the woods, to hold the enemy in check while the rest were retiring. . . . We were soon again engaged with the enemy, but, seeing that the enemy were turning my right, I ordered the line to fall back in line of battle. The regiment here also suffered greatly in killed and wounded."[33] One of those killed was Capt. Gustavus A. Holtzborn of Company K, formerly an officer in the Prussian army, whom Dana had called "probably the best soldier in the regiment" a year before, when Holtzborn had tried to resign his commission in protest over one of Governor Ramsey's political appointments. Also mortally wounded was Pvt. John McEwen, who had tried to get a revolver as a souvenir for his cousin during the lull at Bull Run and who had complained of "mud-mud-mud" at Camp Stone.

Sam Bloomer, having sought safety in the woods after being hit in the knee, fared better. As the Confederates came upon Bloomer's position near the Dunker Church, Sgt. W. H. Andrews of the First Georgia Regulars saw his predicament, and, with several others, piled cordwood around him to protect him from stray bullets. It was a kindness, needless to say, that Bloomer would remember. A short while later a Confederate officer stripped him of his sword and revolver, to be followed by Stonewall Jackson himself, who reportedly had kind words for the wounded soldier.[34]

Charles Berry, who had slept among Confederate corpses at South Mountain, told of his own narrow escape from death and of being taken prisoner. He was "shot through the left side" as the regiment was falling back, but he could still walk.

> I went back to some wheat stacks and tried to find out how bad I was wounded, and then I saw that if I stayed there I would be taken prisoner. I tried to climb the high fence but could not. Nei-

ther could I crawl through, so I went behind the wheat stacks for shelter from the bullets that were flying thickly from both sides. There were fifteen or twenty other soldiers there and I tried to get them to go to the rear, but they would not go, and soon a rebel officer came in between the stacks. He ordered us to surrender, in not very pleasant terms. At the same time a rebel soldier came around the stack to my left and put the muzzle of his gun within six feet of me and fired. The only thing that saved my life was the fact that he was scared. I had broken my gun so it could be of no use to the enemy. For some distance we had to go lengthwise of their line and we were under the fire of our own men. It seemed to me as though the air was thick with bullets. The shells were coming in a steady stream about three feet apart and about three feet from the ground. The rebels were lying in a plowed field and I asked why they did not stand up like men. They said it was too hot for them. We went back into some timber and stopped. Pretty soon some twenty-lb. shells from our own battery on the hill commenced to burst about us. We moved further back, but the shells followed us.[35]

Berry's regiment, meanwhile, was still moving north. "We again made a stand near some farm-house [Nicodemus's] for a short time," according to Sully, "and there took up a strong position about 100 yards back, behind a stone fence, when a section of artillery [Kirby's, with which the First Minnesota was brigaded] was sent to assist us. We kept the enemy in check till they brought a battery of artillery on our flank, which compelled me to order the regiments back to join our line of battle."[36] One of the Confederate artillerymen firing at the withdrawing Minnesotans was a seventeen-year-old private, Robert E. Lee, Jr., whose father was not far away that day.

According to Walker, the Minnesotans "kept down the road after making another stand at a stonewall, the rebs not coming any further on account of our artillery, which now poured into them with fury, making up for lost time, they went back in a hurry and our brigade was ordered to another position, fresh troops taking our places."[37] The regiment eventually withdrew further to the Poffenberger farm and the North Woods, almost two miles north of the Dunker Church, where Hooker's men had camped the night before. Here, at last, with the help of fresh artillery and the First Corps, the Union retreat came to a halt. Except for what Walker called "cannonading at intervals," the battle was over for the Minnesotans. The fighting was moving south, first to the Sunken Road—which that day earned a new name, "Bloody Lane"—and then to the Stone Bridge spanning the Antietam, which Gen. Ambrose Burnside's men eventually crossed to take the heights opposite and bring the day's fighting to a close.

Now a prisoner, Charles Berry was moving farther to the Confederate rear: "When we were about 3 miles away we stopped where a rebel was baking bread in a Dutch oven. One of the shells came over and burst high in the air. After that I thought it was all over. I heard a piece of the shell coming down. It landed in the fire where the Johnnie was baking his bread. He swore because the Yankees had spoiled his fire. . . . General Stonewall Jackson was lying under a tree, asleep. He got up, rubbed his eyes and complained of the noise. He got on his horse and rode away." Meanwhile, several miles away, Sam Bloomer had his leg amputated in David Hoffman's barn. He would survive the ordeal, return to Stillwater, and during the balance of the war maintain a lively correspondence with his friend and cousin in Company B, Jacob Marty. He also, of course, sent back to the regiment the state flag that had been entrusted to his care and that he had hidden in his shirt when he was wounded.

The seventeenth of September was—and remains—the bloodiest day in American military history. The Union lost more than twelve thousand men, and the Confederacy almost as many. In his diary that night James Ghostley of Company H, who was given to brevity, called the battle simply a "Terrible Fight."[39] McClellan had stopped Lee's invasion of the North, but he had failed to destroy Lee's army. It was a Union victory, but with bolder leadership it could have ended the war.

The Minnesotans had reason to consider themselves fortunate, but only in a relative sense. Speaking of the remainder of Gorman's brigade, Walker said that "the other regiments loss was heavier than ours on account of the position they held, we being on the right put us in sort of a hollow, this protected us somewhat from the fire of their artillery, the 15th [Massachusetts] on the contrary was on high ground and a fine mark for their grape and cannister, they lost heavily as also did the 34th [New York], at any rate *nearly half of the brigade was lost in that fight.*" Walker was correct, but the more important reason the Minnesotans suffered only half the casualties of the other regiments in the brigade was that their position on the extreme right spared them the fury of the sudden Confederate assault. Walker's own company was less fortunate than most others in the First: "Our Co. D has always been very lucky till this time we *catched* it, went into action with 35 men, came out with about 20."[40]

The regiment had again demonstrated the steadiness and reliability under heavy fire—*coolness* was still the favored term in the official reports—that it had shown at Bull Run and on the Peninsula. "The officers and men of the regiment behaved nobly," Sully said of his Minnesotans, "and it was with some difficulty I got some of them to obey the order to fall back."[41] He reported a total of 118 casualties: 15 killed, 79 wounded, and 24 missing.

The Minnesotans camped that night in Poffenberger's fields, unable to retrieve their dead and wounded from the battlefield since it was now in enemy hands. "We slept on our arms that night expecting to renew the fight in the morning," Walker wrote, "but the day wore away neither side showing any disposition to attack." McClellan certainly was not disposed to attack, believing as always that he faced a superior force. In fact Lee's army was in no condition to resist a determined Union offensive, and McClellan let still another opportunity slip by. "Sept. 18th was pleasant and we lay on the battlefield this morning," Edward Bassett wrote in his diary.[42]

"That night our regiment was out on picket," Walker said, "all night we heard artillery and wagons moving. Sure signs of a retreat, in the morning we were ordered to advance and found the Rebs had left, crossed the [Potomac] river in the night, nothing left but a few stragglers." McClellan was in no hurry to follow. "We remained on the battlefield, engaged in burying the dead, and in picket duty and reconnaissances, for four days after the battle," Lochren wrote.[43]

Henry B. Whipple, the eminent Episcopal bishop of Minnesota, who had declined Ramsey's offer to become the regiment's first chaplain, appeared in the camp and delivered an address to the men. Pressnell wrote years later that Whipple "lauded McClellan to the skies. Upon returning to our camp from this address I made the remark that the Bishop was entitled to his opinion of McClellan, but as for me, I consider him either a very poor General or else a d–d traitor. No sooner had the last word escaped my lips than Jerry Collins, our company cook, and who had so befriended me when recovering from the measels, . . . hit me a whack upon my forehead which knocked me senseless. Upon coming to my senses I found Jerry over me crying and begging all the Saints known to his theology to lend their assistance in bringing me back to life. I told him that I was all right but that he would think as I did some day. And he did."[44]

Charley Goddard, who hadn't had much of a chance to write in recent days, took advantage of the lull to sum up the bloody day for his mother: "If the horrors of war cannot be seen on this battlefield they cant be seen any whare. The Rebbles fought well—I will give them credit for that." Bassett also conveyed his impressions to his parents: "The Rebs have crossed the Potomac, and are heading south. They are very poorly clothed, They stripped many of the dead of their good shoes, and left them barefoot. This seems hard, but it is true. There are hundreds of the citizens of Penn doing all they can for the wounded. Our regiment lost something over 100 men. It was a terrible sight. The dead were piled up against each other in many places. This was the battle of Antietam."[45]

At first light on 22 September the men broke camp, and Goddard, for one, was ready to go: "The stench was geting to be very bad and unhealthy." The Minnesotans soon saw for the first time the town by whose name the Confederates would know the epic battle they had fought nearby. "We marched through the town of Sharpsburg and almost every house bore the marks of our shell," according to Walker. They continued south for ten miles until they reached Harpers Ferry, where they forded the Potomac and returned to their old campsite on Bolivar Heights.[46]

While his former comrades were once again occupying Harpers Ferry, Charles Berry was heading south with the Army of Northern Virginia. After fording the Potomac he passed through Shepardstown and Winchester, where the Confederates spent a day resting and where Berry again revealed the bravado of a nineteen-year-old: "There were about 400 prisoners and the people we met were very curious and asked us many questions. We told them that we were the 44th Nova Scotia division. . . . We had no blankets and there was frost on the ground. We had no fire either and lived on green corn which we ate raw. I found two or three moldy pieces of hardtack where our cavalry had camped some months before. It tasted good. Marching every day proved to be too much for me, with a two ounce ball through my side, and I collapsed. I could not use my leg and had to walk between two of my comrades, leaning on them. We reached Stanton, where we took the cars for Richmond."[47]

As the First Minnesota approached Antietam Creek, Isaac and Henry Taylor were still languishing on Belle Isle, with no sign that they would soon be paroled or exchanged. The prisoners had renamed the place Camp Starvation: "We get a little 'bean water' this morning, but no bread," Isaac wrote in his diary on 18 August. "About 2 P.M. we get ¼ loaf of bread." It was even a crime for locals to sell food to hungry Yankees: "A woman is *dragged* to the guard house for selling pies to starving prisoners. . . . Get no supper."

Isaac and his comrades sought diversion from their predicament. "Time drags heavily," he wrote a few days later. "I learn to play eucre. . . . The dice box rattles in all parts of camp." And over the next few days: "Having a good time playing chess with Corporal John Calvin Brandon, Co. K, 1st Pa. R.C. . . . Get 'Napoleon's Maxims of War' to read. . . . We borrow Grimshaw's Hist. of U. States."

A decidedly unwelcome diversion arrived in the form of marauding bounty jumpers, who terrorized their fellow prisoners: "A mob of rowdies, thieves and cut-throats go about camp & steal all the flour, cakes, apples, pies &c. that they can lay their hands on, under the *pretense* of stopping exhorbitant prices. Probably the man that stole my cap is a worthy member of that *honor*able organization." Unfortunately for the men, the extortion worked. "First fruits of yesterday's mob—*four* loaves of bread for a dollar instead of *five*, as formerly," Isaac recorded the next day. He told of another diversion he could have done without: "A company of ladies & gents from the city come over to see the 'Yankee prisoners.' Among them are traitors that deserve the gallows."[48]

But whatever the diversion of the moment, the prisoners' attention always returned to food. Two months later Isaac looked back on this time and tried to describe it to his cousin:

> I never knew what it was to suffer the pangs of hunger till I was a prisoner of war. We managed to get bread enough to keep body and soul together by selling our watches and other available property, and stealing what we could from the Secesh commissary. When we first went on the Island, our ration of salt was one spoonful per week and very soon after, we could get none except on doctor's orders. We got hold of a paper containing the Dr's signature and

with a little practice, Henry got so he could manufacture salt orders just as good as the original. This device probably saved us from sickness, and certainly rendered our food somewhat palatable. You see what great crime hunger will drive a person to—theft and forgery. But some how, I don't feel much compunction of conscience. I suppose it is on account of the "demoralizing effects of the enemy."[49]

The hunger for war news was almost as great as that for food:

> Richmond papers say that McClellan has evacuated his position on James River. . . . Secesh papers state that Pope is retiring before Jackson. . . . Another squad of prisoners arrive. They report that McClellan has joined Pope & that they are retiring towards Manassas. I hope that our combined forces are sufficient to meet the Confederates when the proper moment arrives. *God send that moment as soon as possible.* . . . To day's Richmond Dispatch contains Jeff Davis' Message to Confed. Congress, in which he says that the Confederate army has defeated, upon the plains of Manassas, the combined forces of Pope, McClellan, Burnside and Hunter. . . . We get but meager accounts of the great battle of Sat. last & the position of the contending armies. Secesh claim a great victory but we cling to the hope that it is not so brilliant after all. The climax of misery: to be wasting away on Belle Isle in times like these. . . . Secesh papers say Confed. forces have crossed the Potomac into Md.[50]

The prisoners finally decided to do something about the marauding "mob": " 'Charging' active to day," Isaac wrote in early September. "An anti 'charge' meeting held & 'Huntley' appointed 'Chief of Police' to tend to those illustrous 'chargers.' " The next day the collective action produced results: "The crowd arrest a thief & shave the left side of his head. Two fellows get their heads bruised O tempora! O mores!"

As more prisoners were released Isaac once again permitted his hopes to rise. When, on 7 September, about five hundred prisoners were removed for exchange, he even took to verse:

> You leave this God-forsaken isle
> Ruled o'er by robers, traitors vile,
> To go where *Loyalty* hold sway
> And bask in *Union's* peerless ray.[51]

Five days later it became official, at least for Henry: "Wrote a letter to send home, but toward evening the glorious news that Squad No. 1 was to be paroled reached our ears and we were paroled about 10 p.m. 'We the undersigned employees of the United States of America do hereby solemnly pledge ourselves that we will not take up arms against the Confederate States of America or be found in any way aiding or abetting her enemies by information or otherwise until regularly exchanged or released, so help me God!' The Confederates took our age, complexion, color of eye and hair, and our occupation. Each man signed the oath of parole." The same day Isaac noted, " 'Northern money' in great demand since paroling commenced. Secesh scrip at a discount. Trade brisk on 'Broadway.' "⁵²

The thirteenth was to be Henry's lucky day, but not Isaac's. "About 1,000 paroled Union soldiers leave Belle Isle prison this morning," Henry wrote, "and as fortune favored me, I will not forget the ill-fated ones who are still left on the island, among them my brother, Isaac. The thought of soon being able to hear from my friends and of once more seeing the banner of freedom floating in the breeze, almost makes me too happy for this world of pain and sorrow. We marched down the left bank of the James River about 15 miles to A.H. Aikens landing. Cheer after cheer rent the air as we came in sight of the Stars & Stripes and some shed tears of joy. Happy day! Transferred from a state of hunger, misery, captivity and wretchedness to a land teeming plenty. A land of Liberty, and Land of Friends, and Hope. We hear that the remaining prisoners are to be sent north tomorrow."⁵³

Isaac, meanwhile, did his best to be patient: "Paroling finished in A.M. and prisoners ordered out of camp by squads. While buying some 'grub' for the journey our squad marches out of camp and leaves me a disconsolate prisoner on Belle-Isle. Capt. Montgomery & others 'whack' the crowed smartly with their swords to repress their eagerness to leave for that 'better land.' About 1050 men left on the island All the boys in our tent except Wheeler & myself get off. I rejoice in their deliverance but have a poor opinion of 'Ike' for not attending to 'so great salvation' instead of peaches." The next day, a Sunday, Isaac at last experienced his own deliverance. "All prisoners of war leave Belle-Isle this morning & are marched through Manchester & Richmond & down the Charles City road (about 12 mi) to Varina on James River where four U.S. transports receive us on board. . . . I get weary & lame, but, cheered by the prospect of *Liberty,* trudge along. Finaly get aboard one of Jeff's wagons & ride two or three miles. Once more the Stars & Stripes cheer our vision. I get aboard the *Coharbor* (U.S. Mail). We steam down the river about 1½ hour & at sunset anchor in stream. Uncle Samuel gives us a good supper of bread bacon & coffee. I am happy to night."[54]

Henry's steamer was already making its way down the river: "Good-bye 'Seceshers.' If we take you prisoner, we will not starve you." The vessel passed City Point and Jamestown, and Henry once more saw the famous *Monitor* before heading up the Chesapeake. Isaac followed the same course the next day; along the way he heard that "McClellan has gained a great victory in Md." They were both on their way to Camp Parole, a processing and instructional center in Annapolis for recently released prisoners of war. Henry arrived first, on 15 September. The next day he wrote, "Remainder of prisoners from Belle Isle arrive and I find Ike among them."[55]

They made the most of their time in Annapolis regaining their strength and catching up on the news. Friends from the Twelfth Illinois Cavalry gave each of them a clean shirt, and although they had no tents, they found nothing in their new liberty to complain about. Isaac witnessed, however, a scene reminiscent of Belle Isle: "This morning the boys 'charge' on a sutler shop, carry off three or four thousand dollars worth of goods, tear down his building & carry off the boards. *Alleged* cause, insult to *private* soldiers. *Real* cause, propensity for plunder. Pres. Lincoln emancipation procl*amation*."[56]

A few days later they were on a small steamer headed back down the Chesapeake for the mouth of the Potomac and then up the broad river toward Washington. They passed the now familiar sights of Mount Vernon and Fort Washington before arriving, on 28 September, back at Alexandria, whence their Peninsula adventure had begun six months before. Over the next week they found their Minnesota comrades and gradually readjusted to camp life:

> Mon. 29. Slept in the open last night. We have had the same kind of tent ever since we were released from Richmond. . . . We find Davis & Jackins of Co. E in Convnt camp. Peddlers are plenty— some "charging." Recd. a tent this evening. Tues. Sept. 30. A Dutch Col. assumed command of all paroled men. He makes a

speech in which he says we shall have plenty to eat if he has 'to steal it.' A rumor is afloat that Secesh have proposed terms of peace to our Government. I judge it is a hoax. A Shaw, Co. K, 1st Min. starts for Washington to visit his uncle, armed with a *citizens suit*. No passes are allowed to *soldiers*. Wed. Oct 1st. Hurry up Uncle Sam & get us some clothing & money. . . . Thur. Oct. 2. Twelve of us Minnesotans occupy one Sibly tent. . . . Sat. 4. I draw a new suit of cloths from Uncle Sam, wash up, put it on & feel like a new man.[57]

Prison had given Isaac plenty of time to reflect on the Union cause and the military effort to sustain it. In a 2 October letter to a cousin, all his bitterness and frustration poured out:

That great and proud army which set out for the Confederate Capitol last spring with high hopes, finds itself, after a six months campaign, back again upon the Potomac at its place of starting.

The spring campaign opened favorably and our country's sky was hopeful. Much blood and treasure had been expended and today, notwithstanding recent partial successes, the rebellion seems as far from being crushed as ever. If we had been, like the rebels, earnest from the beginning, something might have been accomplished. The task of crushing the rebellion had proved greater than the country anticipated. The Union sentiment of the South was "to overwhelm" the traitors as soon as the presence of our armies rendered such an enterprise safe, is "played out." The South is a unit and has her whole soul in this struggle. Her armies are large and made up of fighting men, fully impressed with the idea that they are contending for the right. They have fewer army supplies, and fewer grumblers than we have, and if they have not fewer rascals and plunderers, God help them! So far as I have observed, the Confederates (private soldiers), their standard of morals is higher than in our own army.

I wish you could look at this world through the army glass. One view would be sufficient to fill you with wonder at the levity of an Overruling Providence in withholding from it the fate of Sodom and Gomorrah. There, that will do on that point.

There is no way left for our Government but to subdue the rebels, utterly subdue them by force of arms. The day of honied words has passed, and the time for heavy blows (not newspaper blows) has arrived.

I am sick of this eternal prating about "magnificent plans" and "brilliant strategy." The strategy of superior numbers and hard fought battles is the only strategy that wins this war. We can't march our armies into an enemy's country and meet him with equal numbers—that too is "played out." I look for this fall's campaign to decide the failure or success of our army.

We expect to join our Regt. at Harper's Ferry in a few days.[58]

Three days later the brothers were drawn back to a place each had visited at least twice before. "Henry & I attend 'Washington's Church' (Protestant E.) in the city of Alexandria," Isaac wrote. "The first sermon I have heard since we were encamped at Eltham, on the Peninsula, in May last. The church service awakens recollections of home. Thanks to a sentinel of 33d. Regt. Mas. Vols. who allowed us to enter the city without a pass. Fine day."

On 7 October they took the short trip up the Potomac to Washington, where the next day they found Sgt. Myron Shepard of Company B. "Pay a visit to the capitol grounds & take a view of the 'Godess of Liberty' (bronze) which is to be placed upon the dome of the Capitol. Its heighth is 19½ feet. Her right hand grasps a sword, the left, a shield & olive branch. Quite a number of men at work upon the steps on the East front of the Capitol."[59]

That night they boarded the railroad cars for Harpers Ferry. Arriving about noon the next day, after what Henry called "a tiresome march," they decided to wait another day before joining their regiment. "Being weary and a little 'under the weather,' " Isaac wrote, "Henry and I 'make down' our bed upon the grass between Camp Hill & Bolivar Heighths." They located the First Minnesota's camp early the next morning. "Find a good many familiar faces but many are absent," Isaac noted. "The diminutive size of our Regt. tells a sad story of this summer's campaign. Less than three hundred on dress parade. . . . I receive six months' pay minus twelve dollars stoppage for extra clothing drawn up to July 1st 1862. Have a feast of good things."[60]

Henry's sparse account of the reunion stuck, as usual, to the basic facts: "Get up early and go into camp where I find many familiar faces. I get eight months pay, $104, from our paymaster."[61] Although neither of them said so, they were both glad to be back.

6

FREDERICKSBURG

"I was not going to murder my men."

N
amed in 1825 for the Great Liberator, then fighting for national independence several thousand miles to the south, Bolivar Heights was a ridge running roughly north and south about two miles west of Harpers Ferry and three hundred feet above it. Approximately a mile long, it offered an imposing view to the east of the three river gorges that intersected before the town—the Potomac, flowing down from the north, with Maryland Heights rising sharply on its left bank; the Shenandoah, coming up from the south, with the equally steep Loudoun Heights on its right bank; and, straight ahead, the point where the two rivers joined in the enlarged Potomac, rushing southeast over rapids toward the Catoctin Mountains on the horizon. The site obviously possessed a strategic value as well as a majestic view; whoever controlled Bolivar Heights controlled Harpers Ferry and communications for miles around, which was why it changed hands so many times during the war.

After the embarrassing surrender there of some twelve thousand troops to Stonewall Jackson before Antietam, the Union was determined not to lose it again. As a result, the Second Corps concentrated most of its energies on strengthening fortifications on all three heights. "Everything indicates that we will stop here for a *while* at least," Edward Walker wrote two weeks after the Minnesotans arrived. "Men are at work on Maryland and Loudon Heights clearing away the woods and fortifying, it is the intention to hold this place and there will probably be a large force winter here."[1]

The six weeks the regiment remained on Bolivar Heights were a welcome respite from the constant marching and fighting the men had experienced since returning from the Peninsula. Isaac Taylor wrote of having fresh oysters for supper, and Lochren recalled the simple joy of bathing: "Without opportunity for washing since leaving Harrison's Landing, a general bath in the Shenandoah and the boiling and washing of our clothing was a grateful task." Pressnell, too, remembered that most of their first full day at Bolivar the men were "engaged in washing and for good and sufficient reasons, unnecessary to state here, thoroughly *boiling* our tattered clothing."[2]

Once again they settled comfortably into the routine of camp life, although it was a bit confining. "We have an easy time here now," Bassett wrote. "Drill about two hours a day except Sat. and Sunday. We have looked over every book and paper in camp until they are worn out. Altho there are no guards to keep us in camp, if we go to Harper's Ferry we are apt to be picked up by the Provost Guard, and put to work on the brestworks with a shovel. If we go into the country we might run into the Patrol, and turned over to the Provost Guard."[3]

Charley Goddard may have been glad to get away from the "stench" of the battlefield at Antietam, but he couldn't get away from the suffering inflicted there. "Sergeant D.B. Dudly died on the 6th day of this month from wound received in the action of the 17th of Sept.," he wrote his mother of a fellow Winonan. "He seemed to be doing very well when we started to come up here, but the doctor says his wound comenced to discharge very freely and at first discharged out of the wound but for some reason or other it comenced to discharge inside and it brought on the fever and he died. Dudly was liked by all and was a good Soldier."[4]

On 16 October the regiment went on a reconnaissance mission to Charlestown, ten miles west, to locate Confederate positions. The experience did little to restore Isaac's confidence in his officers:

> When a short distance beyond Hall Town the 53d. Pa. & 1st. Minn. formed in line of battle on the left of the Charleston road. Several Secesh shells dropped in our vicinity one of which wounded Adjt. [Josias] King's horse. After an artillery "duel" of an hour or two's duration our skirmishers were thrown out & we advanced towards Charleston, sometimes in line of battle, sometimes in "column by division" & sometimes "by the right of companies to the front." We

occupied the town without resistance, remained in its vicinity till towards night when we were moved about two miles beyond, towards Winchester, & halted in a piece of woods. We couldn't exactly "see the point" of this move but rumor said it was designed to "draw the rebel cavalry into a trap." Co's E & G of 1st. Minn. sent on picket after dark. Thick clouds, lightning, thunder, rain & dark as Egypt. About 9 P.M. the pickets were called in & the Regt. ordered back to Charlestown. Fowler & I were "omitted" in the darkness & left on post "alone in our glory." A special expedition however succeeded in finding us & we rejoined the Regt. We start for Charlestown. After moving in divers directions it becomes evident that our "guide" is bewildered. Consultation held in which field & line officers and privates participate. Not much concord of sentiment as to the direction we ought to take but the opinion prevails quite generally that the "*veteran 1st*" stands a good chance to fall into the "trap" instead of the Secesh cavalry. We finally succeed in finding the Charlestown road & after wading through mud & water join our forces & encamp south of the town.[5]

Two uneventful days later the regiment returned to Bolivar with a "considerable amount of wheat & other forage," according to Isaac. The expedition had been led by Gen. Winfield Scott Hancock, a rising star in the Union army, whose path would intersect again—more fatefully—with that of the First Minnesota.

Several changes of command occurred while the regiment was on Bolivar Heights. The controversial Gorman, who had led the Minnesotans at either the regimental or brigade level from the beginning, was sent west to Arkansas and a new command. Like Gorman and Dana before him, Sully was promoted to general and placed in charge of the brigade. George Morgan, who had recently been named lieutenant colonel of the First, after serving as captain of Company E, became the regiment's colonel, its first who was not a regular army officer. He in turn was replaced by William Colvill, the major and third in command who, as the captain of Company F, had distinguished himself at Bull Run and been wounded on the Peninsula. Charles P. Adams, the captain of Company H, became the new major.

If a number of the regiment's officers were moving up, a larger number of its enlisted men were moving out. Enlistment practices permitted recruiters to entice men unhappy with their lot in the volunteer regiments to join regular army units without adding to their three-year commitments. Nearly a hundred Minnesotans left the First to pursue what they thought were more attractive opportunities elsewhere. For the most part these were in regular army artillery, cavalry, and signal corps units, whose glamour and reputed easier life appealed to more than a few volunteer infantrymen.

"You want to know what I think about the Cavalry branch of the service," Walker wrote an inquiring civilian friend several months later. "Well I cant speak from personal experience—quite a number of our boys have joined the cavalry and some say they like it better than infantry while others dislike it—I have about concluded that the easiest branch of the service is "Heavy Artillery" or the "Engineer Corps"—of the two I would prefer the *Heavy artillery*—they are of a necesity most always stationed in some Fort, and consequently do not see much hardship—and when there is fighting done the enemy have to *come to them,* they dont go about from place to place packing a knapsack and fighting their way as we poor soldiers do. But *service is service,* whatever branch you are in and a private or non-commissioned officers berth is not desireable by *me* for *more* than 3 *years* at any one time.[6]

The officers in command of the volunteer units naturally became alarmed at the depletion of their ranks and soon came under heavy pressure to put a stop to the raiding. "Gen. Gorman in 'hot water' this evening because a number of Minn. boys are attempting to enlist in the regular cavalry, pursuant to an order from the War Department," Isaac wrote in late October. The following day he noted that the brigadier had taken the kind of direct action for which he was known, not always favorably: "Gen. Gorman orders double guard to be placed arround our Regt. to prevent the boys from going down to the recruiting office. He also send out a patrol to catch the wayward soldiers of the 'veteran 1st.' and order that no passes be granted. Notwithstanding all this, the boys occasionally 'leak out.' Guards not *over vigilant.* A large number of our boys are at Sandy Hook waiting to be 'sworn in.' Combs of our company pays two dollars for a pass which takes him safely across the river to the recruiting office."[7]

The idea of the Army of the Potomac competing with itself for veteran soldiers was too much for General McClellan, and the next day, according to Isaac, he took steps to halt the practice: "Recruiting excitement continues. Some join the regular cavalry & others the 'Engineer Corps.' McClellan's order requiring those wishing to enlist in the Reg. army to give in their names to the Adjt. of the Regts., read on dress parade." The order apparently had the desired effect, as transfers dropped off dramatically. Three days later Isaac wrote that "Henry and I register our names as candidates for the U.S. Marines," but nothing came of it.

Isaac had been in the army for well over a year now, and during that time he had had little contact with civilians. He had had no contact whatsoever with young women of his own age, but one day toward the end of October he told how that suddenly changed: "A corporal & three privates, including myself, are detailed to guard the premises of a 'Union man.' When not on post we sit in the house by the fire conversing with the old gentleman's daughters & enjoying ourselves hugely. It is a long time since I was in a private house and as the 'gals' are quite sociable I enjoy this treat 'right smart.' They amuse us with a warm dinner & Secesh songs. It becomes our 'painful duty' to colar three of Baxter's Zouaves & forceably eject them from the domicile. Zouave oaths and women's screams commingle." The attractions apparently worked both ways, as Isaac noted the next day: "Sarah and Mary invite us to 'call again.' "[8]

Several hundred miles to the south, meanwhile, Charles Berry had less cause to enjoy his surroundings. Languishing in a Richmond prison and still not recovered from his Antietam wound, Berry, like Isaac and Henry a few months earlier, focused almost exclusively on food: "We received a loaf of bread about the size of two fists once a day and a pint of rice soup twice a day. It had very little rice in it and no salt. We had plenty of canal water to drink and the good hard floor to sleep on, and for exercise we picked gray-backs from our clothes. I got sick and could not eat for five days. Then a woman came in with milk which she sold at 40c a quart. I had fifty cents so I bought a quart. I ate five loaves of bread I had saved and drank the milk all at once. Then I felt better. There was a deserter from the Union army in the hospital. He died and the rebel officers wanted us to carry him out, but none of us would touch him."

Probably because of his wound, Berry was paroled after only nine days. With 1,600 other prisoners he was marched down the James

River to board a steamer for Fort Monroe. On the road they passed 2,600 returning Confederate prisoners, who had just gotten off the boat, and Berry spotted his "rebel friend that I had talked with at South Mountain. We talked a long time. He said, 'We'uns don't want to fight you uns.' He only wanted to fight the recruits that were doing guard duty over them at the fort where they were kept prisoners."

On reaching Fort Monroe Berry was sent to Chesapeake General Hospital "after going 26 days without any care for my wound":

> We had to bathe and change clothes at the river. We were given a pair of drawers and a pair of slippers and were told to throw away everything that we had. I was wounded the worst of all and could not change my clothes as fast as the others could. I washed my shoes, inside and out, and by that time the others had gone. I noticed a negro picking up discarded clothes. I thought I would make a trade with him. I traded my shirt, pants and drawers for a pair of clean pants and got him to wash my blouse. He was to give me a quart of milk. So I was better fixed than the others for clothing. Then I went into the hospital and they gave me a cot to sleep on. They told me that everyone that had the lead like I had died. I told them I was a tough case that would not die of it. I got my wound dressed for the first time. I stayed there one month.[9]

McClellan, under strong pressure from Lincoln since Antietam to pursue Lee, decided at last to move the Army of the Potomac south into Virginia. On 26 October the first units crossed the Potomac below Harpers Ferry, and four days later the Second Corps broke camp on Bolivar Heights and followed. The Minnesotans crossed the Shenandoah and moved into the Loudoun Valley, at the base of the Blue Ridge. It was an extremely hot day, according to Lochren, who recalled the effect of the heat on the Nineteenth Maine, a brand-new regiment recently brigaded with the Minnesotans and now marching just ahead of them. The men were "unused to marching with the heavy loads carried by soldiers, and having knapsacks stuffed with everything, provided by the thoughtful care of friends and relatives on leaving home, found their burdens too heavy, and, in general, lightened by throwing away their new overcoats, strapped on top, and most readily removed. As our regiment marched next behind, with light knapsacks, and were well seasoned to fatigue, the men picked up the overcoats, and before night were fully supplied, ready for the cold weather, which set in within a week afterward."[10]

That night the regiment camped in the woods near Hill Grove. "This is a narrow pleasant valley extending N.E. & S.W.," Isaac wrote. "The leaves lie thickly upon the ground making a fine mattress for the weary soldier."[11] Over the next several days the advancing army skirmished frequently with Jeb Stuart's cavalrymen at the Blue Ridge gaps, usually pushing them back into their Shenandoah Valley sanctuary. The Minnesotans were engaged at Snickers and Ashby gaps, but not seriously, as the Confederates chose each time to retire rather than fight.

Unlike other parts of Virginia they had seen, the hilly countryside of Loudoun County impressed the men. "This was a beautiful and fertile country," Lochren remembered, "divided into thrifty farms, and producing much fruit. It was dotted with pleasant villages, and had never been overrun by a hostile force, and fence rails were plenty for bivouac fires. The people were all disloyal; not adverse to selling their produce at good prices, but preferred Confederate money, and therefore got a good supply of counterfeit Confederate notes, with which an enterprising Philadelphia concern had just supplied our army." "The boys buy apples & poultry with Secesh mony of Phila. manufacture," Isaac noted.[12]

Although foraging was strictly forbidden, the abundance of plump livestock and poultry made it inevitable. "We are feasting on Secesh fowls, mutton and beef," Bassett wrote, "which we take whenever we can find it. The boys are picking two nice young turkeys now." Isaac told much the same story on 3 November: "The boys are hungry & the sheep, porkers & poultry have to suffer. I buy some milk and cornbread of a contraband." The next day he was on guard duty: "A nice pig generously introduces himself to the guard & is accepted as a martyr to the cause of the Union."[13]

Lochren told how a quick-thinking Minnesotan avoided getting caught red-handed:

> One of our men, an incorrigible forager, at the close of a day's march, with the assistance of two or three comrades, captured a fat sheep in the edge of a wood, and, while dresing it, a few men from a Maine regiment came up, and stood looking on and conversing. Glancing through the brush from his kneeling position he discov-

204 | THE LAST FULL MEASURE

ered a squad of the provost guard almost upon them, and speaking to his comrades, he said, quietly: "Boys, that other sheep we got is enough for us; let us give this one to these Maine boys." His comrades knew nothing of any other sheep, but, satisfied that he had some sufficient reason for his sudden generosity, assented, and followed him quickly into the wood, as the Maine men, just beginning to cut up the carcass, were pounced upon by the guard and marched off. Later in the day, passing division headquarters, he saw these men tied up to crossbars, and quietly asked how they relished the mutton.[14]

Meanwhile, Mathew Marvin returned to the regiment after recovering from the accidental gunshot wound he had suffered while sitting on his bunk at Harrison's Landing. He had spent the better part of the fall convalescing in a hospital at Craney Island, Virginia, and finally caught up with his Minnesota comrades in early November, as they were moving south through Virginia. "Just at dark we found our regt," he wrote. "Shook hands with all the boys took a drink of Whiskie eat a *harty* supper of H Tack & Fresh beef & Coffee."[15]

The regiment marched through Upperville to Paris, at Ashby's Gap, and on to Warrenton, where it arrived on 9 November. "Henry is sick & comes a part of the distance in ambulance," Isaac noted. Marvin wasn't doing so well either, the march having made it clear that his recovery was not yet complete. "My game leg is sorer than ever & the blisters nearly cover my feet but they are not as bad as my leg," he wrote a few days later. "Would give a Kingdom for a horse or a World for a mule or my life for an Ox   I want to rid[e] anyway but I wont ask for . . . sick leave as long as I can stand up   I will keep up or bust a trying."[16]

The Minnesotans learned that President Lincoln, frustrated at the army's slow pace and convinced that McClellan would not fight a decisive battle, had relieved him of command of the Army of the Potomac, replacing him with Ambrose Burnside. "Officers and men were stunned and exasperated almost to the point of mutiny," according to Lochren, an unrestrained admirer of "Little Mac," like most of his comrades. "Deepest sorrow and despondency prevailed on November 10th, when the army was drawn up to take leave of McClellan. Strong men shed tears. A majority of the line officers of the First Minnesota sent in their resignations, but, on the representation of Gen. Sully that such an act, in the face of the enemy, might subject them to disgraceful imputation, the resignations were recalled. The estimate of an army of the character and capacity of its commander, who has led it in many battles, is always accurate; and the confidence of this army, from its oldest corps commander to the men in the ranks, in McClellan was unbounded."[17]

Young Charley Goddard, demoralized by the event, displayed a good deal of prescience in predicting the consequences: "I hardly feel any interest in this war since General McClellans removed   it was a grand mistake and I think they will rue the day they took him from the command of the army of the Potomac. They will keep Gen Burnside in a little while and then the Editors of the papers through the Country will rais the cry, *he is doing nothing* and the people will take it up after them until the President thinks he had better put another one in and let old stone wall Jackson get after him and chase him back to Washington. Then they will begin to think there is no man in the world like little McClellan after all." Like many of the men, Goddard never wavered in his faith in McClellan, principally because he felt the general was looking out for the soldiers. "Little Mc made the Army of the Potomac what it is now," he wrote two months later, "and at Yorktown instead of chargeing on the enemys fortification and loosing thousands of lives he dug them out. and again when the officials at Washington refused to let McDowel cooperate with him at Fair Oaks little Mc was obliged to take the Army of the Potomac and fight his way to the James river. This retreat was conducted with so much military skill that the greater part of the Rebel Army acknowledged that they wer badly whiped evry place they came upon us."[18]

Thomas Pressnell held a quite different opinion of McClellan, and he maintained that many others did as well. "Lochren is to be excused," he wrote years later, "for, strange to say he was the most ardent admirer of the deposed General in the regiment." He added that it was a "very foolish thing" for the officers to offer their resignations in protest.[19]

But Isaac shared Lochren's unbounded confidence in the general who had turned these men into an army. "In A.M. the different Regts. of Couch's Corps form along the road in column by division, present arms & give McClellan three hearty cheers as he passes on his way to Washington Much indignation & "tall swearing" among the soldiers on account of McClellan's removal from the command of the Army of the Potomac. Why Little Mac is superceded & disgraced at this stage of the game is a mystery to the uninitiated. The army like Burnside well but Little Mac better. Let us see what results will be. At dress parade McClellan's Farewell address & Burnside's Inaugural is read."[20]

Curiously, few of McClellan's supporters blamed Lincoln for his removal. They preferred to believe that there was an anti-McClellan cabal in Washington against which Lincoln was helpless. Whoever forced McClellan's removal, Goddard wrote later, "was ignorant of his abilities to command We know that President Lincoln did not do it, but we do not blame him when there was so many that wanted him removed and they had such a great influence that he complied with there request. And in reality we can say that he did not do it."[21]

Only a few days after McClellan's departure—but after more than a year of putting up with his leisurely pace without complaint—Isaac was already out of patience with Burnside: "When will our new Gen. get ready to move against the enemy? This fine weather can't last always."[22] Burnside may or may not have felt his men's impatience, but there is little doubt he felt Lincoln's. Two days later, on 15 November, having spent more than a week reorganizing his command structure, he ordered the Army of the Potomac to Falmouth, on the northern bank of the Rappahannock River, opposite Fredericksburg, and thirty-five miles southeast of Warrenton. Burnside had mapped out his own road to Richmond.

His plan called for moving his army across the river before Lee had a chance to get his troops in place behind prepared defenses. He moved quickly, and within two days he had two corps ready to cross. "At 1 p.m. we encamp in the woods within 3 or 4 miles of Fredericksburg," Isaac wrote that night. "I hope that Burnside will hurry up this campaign as fast as prudence will allow."[23] But prudence would not allow a crossing that day or any day soon. Because of a miscommunication, the pontoons needed to bridge the river failed to arrive, and Burnside had no choice but to wait for them. The delay would prove one of the costliest of the war.

"We are camped near Falmouth on the river opposite Fredericksburg, where the Rebels are," Ed Bassett wrote on 23 November, in a passage that revealed how much soldierly cynicism could be acquired by an untraveled farm boy in little more than a year. "Things are going a lot different then I thought they would, but I suppose there had been enough done to make a few Major Gens., besides any number of Brigaders and Colonels. . . . Our Chaplain thinks this is a hard place to serve the Lord, but still takes courage when he thinks of the Paymaster and the Greenbacks that are forthcoming."[24]

Falmouth was not much to the men's liking. Writing to his mother at the beginning of December, Goddard called it "one of the most Godforsaken places I ever saw in my life": "The inhabitants that are around in the street standing or leaning up against the corners lookas if they had not a friend in the world and if you ask them how they like these visitors, 'Right smart,' will be ther answer and you cant get an other word out of them. The greater part of them do not know how to read and wright."[25]

Although everyone knew that armies don't fight in December but go into winter quarters until spring, it was understood by all that Burnside meant to cross the river and fight just as soon as he could get the bridges in place. Certainly that was Lee's assumption. The seventeen-day pontoon delay had permitted the Confederates to prepare defenses on Marye's Heights, a ridge about a mile behind Fredericksburg that offered a commanding view of anyone attempting to cross the sloping plain leading up from the town, a devastating field of fire. It was such a favorable piece of terrain for Lee that he believed no rational Union commander would send his troops into such certain death.

Isaac continued to wait, sustaining himself as usual with news from the outside world: "We get the President's message to day. He seems very earnest in the advocacy & confident of the adequateness of his emancipation plan for ending the struggle between North & South. We await Congressional proceedings with interest." He and his comrades busied themselves fending off winter, which had suddenly arrived. "Ground still white with yesterday's snow. We build a fire place of sticks & mud to our tent. Tis pleasant sitting by the fire this cool evening. Five of us have our 'shelter tents' pitched upon a base of pine logs about eighteen inches high."[26]

The regiment had marched to Falmouth without Pressnell, whose right eye was still inflamed from powder burns suffered at Flint Hill. He was confined to the hospital at Harpers Ferry but soon became frustrated at being separated from his comrades. When the doctor refused to release him even after the swelling and soreness had disappeared, he took matters into his own hands and plotted an escape. He would simply board a daily passenger train for Washington and make his way from there to the regiment at Falmouth.

"I went to my room," he later recounted, "packed up my duds and about 3 o'clock sneaked out of the building, descended the steep and rugged hill to the R.R. track, fell in with a dozen other soldiers and made my way to the R.R. station at the Ferry—having removed the bandage from my eye while going down the hill." He boarded the train and pleaded his case to a sympathetic officer, who secured quarters for him that night in Washington. The next day he barely avoided arrest for desertion before persuading a series of overbearing officers that it made more sense to return him to his regiment. He even managed to wrangle a pass from one of them, and, finding himself footloose in the nation's capital, he was determined to put his time to good use. After treating himself to a meal at "a swell looking restaurant up Pa. Ave.," he bought a ten-cent cigar "and started on up the Ave. In a few minutes I began to feel dizzy, and threw the cigar . . . away. It was about the 5th or 6th cigar that I had ever attempted to smoke." Then, he wrote:

> I loitered along up the Av. turning up 15th St., passed the Treasury Bldg. then up the Av. again, turning into the Circel-way between the White House and the enclosed Jackson monument. When opposite the White House steps the guard or orderly—for he only had his side arms on—on the porch blurted out "What are you loafing around here for, why don't you go to your regiment?" I had noticed this fellow as I came down the walk, and had also observed that he wore the Johnny-colored uniform of what was known . . . as the "Crack 7th New York Regiment," but whose service consisted of answering emergency calls by going to Washington and relieving troops on duty there who were in turn sent to the front, but was never itself ordered beyond Washington. For this reason that regiment became the butt-end of contemptuous ridicule by those of us to whom the front was home and the rear unknown. So to be imperiously accosted by one of these "critters" was irritating in the extreme. Endeavoring to reflect from my unbandaged eye, the contempt in which I held him I answered with the enquiry, "Are you speaking to me?" to which he replied "Yes, I am." "Well I came up

to see Abraham Lincoln" was my retort. Now up to the very instant that I here mentioned Lincoln's name, [it] had not entered my mind during the entire day. While the idea of trying to call upon him was the very remotest from my thoughts. But I had now said it, and to fail to at least make an effort would be ignominious retreat, so with quickened step I brushed past him to the very door, which stood slightly ajar, when to my utmost surprise who should step out but President Lincoln himself, and extending his hand said: "Well here I am, my man, what can I do for you?" at the same time giving my hand a squeeze which I felt for days afterward. "Oh: nothing in particular, only that I was on my way to my regiment at the front I would like to be able to tell the boys that I had had the pleasure of shaking hands with Abraham Lincoln." was my stammering answer, to which he said "Well, you can now do that, which is your regiment?" When I gave him the name he said "Why that is Gen. Gorman's old regiment" and complimented both the regiment and the General. He pulled the bandage down so that he could see my eye and remarked that you have had a very bad eye, be careful with it. He then gave me another but less tightened shake by the hand and went back saying "Good bye, God bless you." with what I intended to be a withering look at the orderly who was still standing at "Attention" I proceeded to retrace my steps down the Av. and toward the Soldier's Rest where I was due to take the train in about an hour. When about two-thirds of the way down I remembered that John G. Nicolay, the man who, ten years before had taught me to set type when he was the foreman and I was the miniature devil of the Pike County Free press, published at Pittsfield, Ill., and who was now the President's private secretary. Why didn't I enquire for and see him? But I had not thought of it in time and it was now too late to go back.[27]

Meanwhile, Burnside was finally ready to move. On the morning of 11 December the Union artillery massed on Stafford Heights, on the north bank of the Rappahannock, began shelling Fredericksburg, many of whose citizens had long since fled. At the same time Union engineers began laying the pontoon bridges, but rebel sharpshooters prevented their construction until several regiments crossed in boats and attempted to clear the city in house-to-house fighting. Soon the bridges were laid, and as dark fell the Union forces poured across. The Minnesotans, who had been awakened at 4:00 a.m. to be ready to move, marched two miles down the north bank of the river to the Lacy House, the imposing Georgian mansion directly opposite Fredericksburg that was the ancestral home of Lee's wife.

The First crossed the river at sundown, Pressnell recalled, and as it was "leaving the bridge on the Frk'g side, Col. Morgan noticed an old fellow, not in uniform, but fitted out with a gun, knapsack and cartridge box, trudging along by his side, and upon closer observation discovered that it was our new chaplain. 'What the devil are you doing there, Chaplain,' said Morgan. 'Well, answered [F. A.] Conwell, I suppose I ought to do something, and not knowing what else there was for me to do, I fixed myself up to fight.' 'Well throw away that gun and cartridge box and get the musicians of the regiment and as many others as you can get together and prepare to take care of the wounded, for if this movement continues you will have plenty to do' was Morgan's reply."[28]

"We followed after the Mich. boys and the bullets were flying pretty brisk when we crossed," Bassett said. "We had possession of the city by ten P.M." Later that night Union troops, including some Minnesotans, ransacked and pillaged the town. Inexplicably, the officers allowed it to go on, until clothes and furnishings from virtually every house under Union control had been pulled into the street. One Minnesotan, who chose to remain anonymous, gave an account several days later to the St. Paul *Pioneer:* "It was a rich scene. There was a dirty soldier dressed in the choicest silks, escorted by other soldiers dressed in long tail coats, and plug hats. Some were loaded down with tobacco, whisky, wines, silver and china ware, and the finest kind of bed clothing. One of the boys picked up a violin, and a soldier was soon found who could play it, so they took positions for a cotillon. Between setts the ladies would sit on the curb-stones and the gentlemen would do the honors. But I cannot do justice to the scene." Charley Goddard told his mother, "This is the first town I have saw pilaged since I have been in the service. I do wish you could have seen us   some had fidles playing them while others danced.   you could not of helped laughing.   we did have a fine time."[29]

Edward Walker gave his account of the incident: "Some of the 'Big Bugs' had splendid libraries, how I would like to have some of the books I saw there. There was not a house but what had ball holes in it, but the most damage was done by the soldiers. A squad from Co. D (myself included) happened into an old Secesh sheriffs house, and finding plenty of flour and the tools for mixing, we soon set down to a good plate full of 'Pancakes' which didnt go bad considering that we had been living on Hard Bread for several months. Another *benefit* the boys received was in getting plenty of *tobacco*—some of the boys laid in quite a stock, as the article is costly here it is quite an item to have a lot on hand."[30]

The next day the Union troops occupied the rest of the town, and the pillaging continued. Lochren told what happened when the Minnesotans moved to one of the main streets:

> Gen. Sully took possession of a handsome residence that chanced to be near the place occupied by the regiment, and, when it was invaded by a squad of the boys, told them to help themselves freely to everything they could find, as the place belonged to his brother-in-law, "a blamed rebel." The house had many portraits, by the general's father, Thomas Sully, the eminent painter, among them one of the general himself when a child of three or four years. Well did Sully know that his bluff invitation to plunder, coupled with the statement that the premises belonged to a relative of his, would secure the place from intrusion. The boys took nothing, and kept off all other marauders. The men were not allowed to quarter in the houses, but fences and outhouses were broken up for little fires in the street to boil coffee; the men sat around the fires on sofas and stuffed chairs.[31]

The town having changed hands, it now came under Confederate instead of Union artillery fire. "Nearly every house I have seen is pretty effectually 'gutted,'" Isaac wrote. "A few citizens remained in cellars during the bombardment. We are obliged to the Secesh for potatoes & fresh meat for dinner."[32] The regiment spent a cold night on picket duty on the western edge of Fredericksburg, near the grave and unfinished monument of George Washington's mother, Mary.

The next morning, 13 December, Burnside prepared to unleash his army. His original plan called for Gen. William B. Franklin's grand division to lead the main Union assault against Jackson's forces several miles below the town, where the Northerners wouldn't have to overcome the formidable obstacles on Marye's Heights. But that morning he changed his mind and directed Sumner and Hooker to lead their troops against Longstreet's entrenched Confederates behind Fredericksburg. He reasoned that Lee would not expect such a move, and he was right; Lee did not believe anyone could be so foolish.

As it was, Franklin nearly broke through on the Union left, but the principal action was on Marye's Heights. Wave after wave of bluecoats advanced over the open plain toward the heights only to be cut down by withering artillery and musket fire. The Confederate riflemen, standing four ranks deep in a sunken road and protected by a stone wall, fired and reloaded so quickly that they rained a nearly constant fire down on the approaching Northerners. Rebel artillery back on the hill added a deadly enfilading fire. The Union command ordered fourteen assaults on the Confederate positions. None got within twenty-five paces of the stone wall.

The First Minnesota, meanwhile, had been placed "upon the right of the brigade . . . in front and in support of Kirby's battery, upon an elevated ridge at the right of our line of battle," according to Colonel Morgan. "In this position the regiment was, for several hours, exposed to a tremendous cannonade of the enemy, who apparently concentrated their fire upon Kirby's guns and this regiment." When they weren't ducking Confederate shells, the Minnesotans were witnessing the massacre on Marye's Heights, less than a mile away, thinking all the while that their turn would surely come soon. "From our position we have a good view of the battlefield," Isaac wrote that night. "The fight continues with occasional lulls, till after dark. I judge that our loss has been greater than the Confederate's. They have much the advantage of position. . . . Our men have gained some ground but the enemy still holds the heighths." Henry had the same vantage point but was more precise in his estimates of the casualties: "Sumner's Grand Division tried to storm the heights but failed. Our troops fought gallantly. I had a good view of the fight. Our loss was about 10,000—the enemy's about 2,000."[33]

Years later the senseless assaults were still vivid to Lochren: "At noon the slaughter began, and we witnessed the sacrifice of [Gen. William H.] French's and [Gen. Winfield Scott] Hancock's divisions of our corps, as one, following the other, was led across the canal, swept by hundreds of cannon, and gallantly rushed against the stone wall at the foot of Marye's Heights, which sheltered as heavy a force of Confederate infantry as could operate behind it, while the face of the hill in the rear was terraced with lines of breastworks, manned by Longstreet's Veteran Corps, being able to fire from each line of works over the heads of the lines in front. It was murder to attempt such an assault. . . . But the orders were imperative, and were obeyed."[34]

The other two brigades in Howard's division were cut to pieces before the stone wall, but Sully's brigade with the Minnesotans never followed. "Our Regt. was ordered to charge," according to Bassett, "but it was countered, so we did not get into the hardest part of the fight." There is little doubt that Sully himself was responsible for keeping them from certain destruction. "The Second and Third brigades of our division came into this action, and suffered bravely," Lochren said, "but Sully, as judicious as brave, realizing the utter folly of also sacrificing his brigade, the very last in the corps, when there was no chance or possibility of achieving anything but its destruction, detailed it in a place of comparative safety, and his action, which saved the First Minnesota, was approved, or at least passed without question."[35]

"Our thanks to Gen Sully who dared to disobey orders & get us out of a job that is one of the impossibilities," Marvin wrote that night. "He ordered us to come back & keep out of sight behind a brick wall which we wer darned glad to do for the rebs wer shelling us like blazes." A soldier from Company B wrote his hometown newspaper of the battle and quoted Sully as saying, "They might court martial me and be d—d, I was not going to murder my men, and it would be nothing less than murder to have sent them there."[36]

Sully simply reported that he was ordered to charge, "but, after having taken position, this order was countermanded." Whatever actually happened, the impression that Sully opposed the entire operation was widespread. "I thin[k] Gen Sullys remark while in Fredericksburg on seeing a Brigade marche in to the fite is applicable to the army," Marvin wrote his brother after the battle. "Viz Their goes a lot of brave Soldiers to *hell* that is providing that is their destination He was opposed to the crossing."[37]

The Minnesotans spent that night sleeping on the sidewalks of Fredericksburg. The next day, according to Henry, things were "very quiet. Now and then a shell is thrown or a few shots fired by the pickets." Lochren witnessed skirmishing at the front, and constant firing of sharpshooters there from rifle-pits. While the Confederates evidently spared the buildings in the town, they sent shells down the streets leading toward Marye's Heights whenever any considerable number of soldiers appeared in them. This brought to my notice an instance of female pluck and nerve. . . . A rather young, and evidently modest, respectable and well-dressed lady (the only woman I remember seeing in that place) was walking along the sidewalk of one of these streets toward the river, when a body of our soldiers crossed it at a street crossing a few rods in front of her. Instantly a half dozen shells came ricochetting and bursting down the street past her, and the soldiers sought cover, but the woman kept her pace with perfect calmness, apparently giving the matter no heed whatever.[38]

That night, in "intense darkness," according to Lochren, the regiment was sent forward on picket duty to a place on the battlefield, "within a few rods of the enemy's rifle-pits," that had been the scene the day before of some of the fiercest fighting. "We hear spades & pick-axes busily at work in front of us," Isaac wrote. "No one appears to know whether they belong to our men or the Secesh. Corp'l Irvine, Co. D, sent out to reconnoiter is shot down by a Rebel picket. We hear his moans but can not go to his assistance and he is close to the Rebel lines. A few spades & shovels are procured & we dig some rifle pits."[39] Actually Corporal Irvine was captured and not wounded, but there was no way for Isaac to know that.

Pressnell recounted an incident that remained "fresh and vivid" in his memory for years afterward: "After three hours of steady hard work on the trenches I was relieved about 2 o'clock for a two hour's rest. In groping around for a place to lie down I came upon a man covered by a large double blanket. Considering that this blanket was large enough to cover two comfortably I crept in beside him and in two minutes was sound asleep. About 4 o'clock I was awakened by a subdued voice and ordered to 'fall-in.' Observing that my sleeping companion did not move I endeavored to awaken him, also, but there being no response to my kicks I passed my hand over his face and thus discovered that I had been sleeping with a dead man. With cold chills creeping all over me I sought my place in the ranks and tried to 'forget it.' "[40]

For the second day in a row the Minnesotans had reason to appreciate their leadership: when Colonel Morgan sent for tools and ordered his men to dig rifle pits, he spared them from being caught in the open at daybreak. "This precaution, doubtless, saved many men on the day following," Morgan said in his report, "when the enemy poured upon them a terrible fire, both from the front and enfilading from our right flank." The experience had a profound, and unexpected, effect on Mathew Marvin. "We layed under the fire of the rebs Shell all one day & the next," he wrote. "it was an incessant fire of Shot Shell & sharpshooters   their was not over 10 minutes at one time but what the missels of death wer whistleing their song close to our ears   if I ever dug a hole in the ground with my *nose* it was that day. Wen day broke that morning I saw our posishion & herd the bullets whistle & for the first time during this war I lost my appetite & did not eat a mouthful all day & erly in the morning I was hungry as a woolf. . . . I lost a chunk of my Patriotism as large as my foot. I would do most anything to get Shut of this most unjust & unGodly uncalled for war."[41]

"Hill, Goulding, Brower & myself occupy a rifle pit in front of our line of battle," Isaac recorded. "Secesh sharp-shooters keep blasting away all day but only get an occasional shot in return. In P.M. the enemy open upon us with artillery causing the Regt. on our right (said to be 127th Pa.) to skedaddle to the rear like a flock of sheep. The Secesh then opened with musketry but the rest of our line standing firm they didn't think it prudent to advance on us. As our indignation subsides we indulge in some merriment at the expense of the skedaddlers." Bassett saw it similarly from his rifle pit: "If a man showed his head he got a bullet after him. The Penn Regt. on our right pulled out and left our flank exposed, but the Rebs dident attack. It would have been pretty rough for us if they had. I was hit for the first time by a piece of shell, it was about spent and did no harm."[42]

Lochren reported that the "contagion" of the fleeing Pennsylvanians spread to two other regiments, endangering the First's right: "The regiment, however, stood firm, and by its conduct held the balance of the line in its place. Gen. Howard, with his brigade commanders, occupied a house in the rear, overlooking the line, and saw with alarm the retreat of the three regiments, one after another. Seeing our regiment stand fast, Howard exclaimed: 'Sully, your First Minnesota doesn't run!' Sully

... answered calmly, 'General, the First Minnesota never runs.' Gen. Howard was extremely gratfied at the conduct of the regiment ... and complimented it in general orders."[43]

The Minnesotans kept their heads down the rest of the day. "We all counted the sun down to Seconds to see how mutch longer we would have to stay in that horrible place of danger and stanch & our killed lying arround us yet unberried," Marvin wrote. "Gen Howard sent word by our Adjutant that he would give to our Regt what he never gave before   That was his heart felt thanks for the noble manor in which we held our ground when the 127th break   he thought ours would but Sully would bet his life that they would not a man of us stir untill overpowered by numbers."[44]

That night, under cover of darkness, the regiment withdrew back across the Rappahannock to its camp near Falmouth. All in all the Minnesotans were lucky, suffering fewer than fifteen wounded and missing while south of the river. Other Union regiments were virtually annihilated, together losing more than twelve thousand men. The engagement was an unmitigated Union disaster, attributable almost solely to bad judgment. When Burnside had been appointed to replace McClellan, he had protested that he was not competent to command an army, and he had proved it. The troops "have made another Brilliant advance, equaled only by the retreat that followed," Walker said. "Fredericksburg was a *very unhealthy* place for us, at least we found it so while we stopped there." Isaac too showed his bitterness: "Burnside has touched off his 'big thing' & lost twenty thousand men. 'Little Mac' used the *spade* at Yorktown Burnside '*stormed*' at Fredericksburg. . . . Gen. Howard sends us his 'tear felt thanks' for our good conduct to day."[45]

Two days after the regiment returned to Falmouth, Charles Berry and several others who had been captured at Antietam returned to their unit following an absence of three months. They found their comrades demoralized by the defeat, which they blamed squarely on Burnside. When Burnside reviewed the Second Corps a few days later, the men maintained a stony silence instead of offering the customary cheers while passing before their commander. Chagrined at the slight, Sumner felt compelled to order his men to cheer, which they did with little enthusiasm.

The men kept busy by preparing their quarters for winter—having been through one already, they overcame their difficulties more easily this time. "To live in Shelter tents was out of the question," Mathew Marvin wrote his brother. "So we all put in our best lick to build something better that is a house about 12 ft long 6 wide & 4 high shingled with 6 tents & a fire place in the side." "Our fireplace smokes awfully this evening," Isaac wrote on 21 December, but the next day all was well: "We remodel our chimney—it dont smoke this time."[46]

On Christmas day Isaac and Henry got passes and went to Falmouth, where they bought a dollar's worth of "soft bread" for their holiday meal. Isaac used the occasion to unleash a burst of allegoristic energy: "Upon this 'merry christmas' morn deep fog enshrouds the camp. Thick vapor doth the soldier's vision limit and dim the luster of the rising sun. If once assured this fog would always shroud the hills & valleys with its pale mantle, and shut forever from our view the radience of yon sun, 'how drear & desolate the earth.' But no; the fog must 'lift,' the vapory curtain rise, revealing Natures face more beautiful by contrast with the mist that marked its loveliness. Would 'twere as certain that the hellish fog of treason and the ghastly pall of war, red with burning cities and the crimson field, might vanish. May the peerless ray of Freedom's sun dispel the thickening gloom & bring us peace & unity."[47]

For his part, James Ghostley saw "nothing to put me in mind of its being Christmas except to be eating the cake Sister Emma sent." Mathew Marvin had difficulty getting into the holiday spirit as well. "Christmas but cant see it," he wrote. "No luxeries of any kind to be had."[48]

A week later, on New Year's Day, the Taylor brothers appear to have discussed the year just past and the direction of the war. Their diary entries for the day are nearly identical. Isaac: "A bright, clear day. This is almost precisely like the first day of 1862. The cause of the Union seems to have progressed little during the past year. The South is gaining & the North looseing confidence in its cause. A decisive victory may restore confidence. Let us hope for it." Henry: "A bright, clear day, similar to that of January 1, 1862. The Union cause has progressed very little during 1862, yet many thousands have been slain. Indeed, the South seems to be gaining confidence. President Lincoln signed a proclamation today freeing all the slaves of the states that are in arms against the United States."[49] On the same day Isaac and Henry wrote their parents of Henry's promotion to sergeant and the welcome fact that he would now earn seventeen dollars a month.

Camped close by the Rappahannock and within easy view of the Confederates on the opposite bank, the men resumed the routine of drill and picket duty. "Right across the River there is another army *most* if not *quite* as large as ours," Walker observed. "We can now plainly see the Rebel camps for *miles* and *miles* along the ridges back of the Rappahannock and on every pleasant day they come out to drill same as we do, we can see them go through all of the movements and of course they can see us equally as plain, for we are nearer the River than their army."[50]

As usual when they were in camp, their thoughts were never far from food. "Our rations come regular now," Bassett wrote in early January. "We get pork from Indiana, Pilot bread from New York, fresh beef once in a while. Rice and coffee are in abundance, with plenty of sugar and salt." Isaac recorded his New Year's Day fare: "For breakfast, baked beans & 'dunderfunk' [hard bread soaked in water and then fried in grease]. Dinner, fried pork, coffee & hardbread. Supper, rice & coffee."[51]

Isaac attended church and made a set of chessmen but mostly he read. "Would circumstances allow it I should feel myself the happiest of mortals, could I but resume my studies at school," he wrote his younger sisters in Illinois. "As it is, however, I content myself with the perusal of such books as I chance to get hold of in the country through which we march. I am now reading a book which I got in Fredericksburg."[52] While others were looting the town for tobacco and whiskey, Isaac was apparently picking up books, although how many he didn't say. During the next few weeks, however, he told of reading "Johnston's Lectures on Agriculture," "Relations of Science to Agriculture," the Book of Joshua, and the first ten chapters of Deuteronomy. One day when he tired of reading books he got a pass and went to the Falmouth cemetery to read tombstone inscriptions, the more interesting of which he recorded in his diary.

There were more reviews and parades, and after a year and a half they still managed to impress many of the men, such as Ed Bassett: "We had a grand Review yesterday, with several thousand troops drawn up in line. The bands were playing, and it was a very brillient sight. The commanding Gen. Burnside and staff, and Generls Sumner, Couch, Sedgewick, Howard, French and Sully. These Men all mounted, and with their staffs accompanying them rode along the lines. It was quite a sight." At the same review Isaac noted that Burnside "is large, full faced, bald headed, black whiskered, and rides a sorel bobtailed horse with three white feet. One Regt on review (said to be the 127th. Pa) has no colors. The colors of the 127th. were taken from them for bad conduct at Fredericksburg on Mon. Dec. 15th."[53]

Earlier in the month Horatio Seymour, the newly elected Democratic governor of New York, had created a furor throughout the North when he denounced emancipation in his inaugural address and suggested that the South be allowed to leave the Union with slavery intact. When word of his speech reached the Army of the Potomac, many of whose soldiers were fighting to rid the nation of slavery, it met with a predictable response. "I do not think I am going to protect the homes of such black hearted traitors as these are," Goddard told his mother. "I am for disloging any officer who dose not give the Presidents proclamation his entire support." Edward Walker agreed:

> All the generals in the army cant bring the war to a successful termination as long as such a party as *Seymours* is allowed to grow and bully the North into a disgraceful peace with the South. If the people of the North are *satisfied* that they cannot bring them to terms *then* let them *recognize* them, and let them that go and we will own up that we cant lick them—but as for hatching up any confounded peace arrangement where the South will as heretofore *Rule us,* I am decidedly opposed to it. Fighting is hard business but I dont see that we are whipped yet. If the North was only *united* the South never could gain their independence. I sincerely hope that we may finally come off Victorious notwithstanding the many drawbacks we *have* and *are* having.[54]

Morale throughout the army was near a new low following the disaster at Fredericksburg. Lack of confidence in the army's ability to win battles became pervasive. "In talking with some of the soldiers & eavon some of the officers they will remark that it is better to be a living Son b–h than a *dead* patriot," Mathew Marvin wrote his parents in mid-January. "Patriotism in the army is played out   they are counting the months they have to serve & the money that they have due them Theirs a screw looses somewhar for While McClellan was in command I believe I never herd a remark of the kind The people wer once arroused to the extent of the rebellion but Congress was in the dark then & they ar still unchanged Why dont the People wh[o] hold the reins of the north & the keys to the vast resources wharwith to put down the rebellion We ought to have a new army of at least 500,000 to stand any kind of a show of ending the war."[55]

Charley Goddard was one of those counting the money due him— his goal was to save enough to build a house for his mother after he was discharged—but he was convinced that the enlisted men "will be cheated out of our bounty. There is so many vilains at Washington that rap the cloak of patriotism around them and go in hand over hand robbing the helpless Soldier of what are his dues. It matters not to them how long the war lasts. They are growing rich by their thieving. I realy think if we wer to go as straight to Washington as we could and burn the City and some of those vilains with it we would be doing more good than to engage the enemy and whip him."[56]

The Army of the Potomac was just settling into what its men believed would be an uneventful winter when Burnside, determined to avenge his loss at Fredericksburg, ordered another crossing of the Rappahannock. He intended to lead a large force against Lee's flank seven miles above the town. This time he ran afoul not of Lee but of nature.

Isaac wanted to believe the new effort would lead to success, but he harbored serious doubts: "Gen. Burnside says that our late victories in N.C., Tenn. & Arkansas have 'weakened and divided the enemy on the Rappahannock' and that the 'auspicious moment' for striking a decisive blow, seems to have arrived. Hope we may achieve a decisive victory. I see some artillery moving up river this P.M. It is my opinion that Burnside will find the enemy *not very much* divided or weakened; however, I think we can whip them on a fair field if every soldier will do his duty & not go whining arround laying all the blame on the generals."[57]

Burnside directed Hooker and Franklin to march their grand divisions up the river several miles and, Walker wrote, "to cross there and attack them on the flank, leaving Sumners Grand Division to cross at, or near the same point we did before. Franklins troops had gone up the river with pontoons, artillery &c. *We* were under orders waiting the word to move when the whole thing was completely '*knocked in the head*' by a severe rain-storm, it rained two or three days and night, and stirred up Virginia mud so that it was impossible to move. The pontoons are now up the river 'stuck in the mud' and the artillery was got back by using thirty horses where six generally do the business. The troops returned to their old camps yesterday, and for a *few* days at least this army may be considered *stuck*. Secesh can take half of their army away and reenforce whatever point they choose as far as *we* are concerned."[58]

On 22 January Isaac heard that the roads had proved impassable and that the troops had been ordered to return: "Providence don't seem to favor us this time." The following day, still inclined to defend Burnside, he saw Franklin's bedraggled men pass the Minnesotans' camp on their return from what immediately became known as the "Mud March": "They have been out during the past three days & look rather the 'worse for wear.' Some of them threaten to 'sit up nights to curse Burnside' for taking them out in the mud & storm. I think, myself, that Burnside ought to be removed for allowing it to rain. If Burnside is not smart enough to out-wit the Lord in these matters, it is clear that he is not the man to handle the Army of the Potomac."[59]

A few days later Isaac heard that a soldier had asked Burnside, "When are you going to *butcher* again?" The Union commander, Walker noted with understatement, "appears to be out of luck, am sorry as I think he is a good general, though he does not at the present time enjoy the confidence of the majority of the army as does McClellan."[60] Nor did he any longer enjoy the confidence of President Lincoln, who soon replaced him with Joseph Hooker.

"Fighting Joe" Hooker had helped undermine confidence in Burnside in hopes of being given command of the army himself, and Lincoln knew it. He chose Hooker anyway, much to Burnside's chagrin, because he believed the general had not been given his nickname for nothing. Hooker immediately began to rebuild the Army of the Potomac and restore its morale. He eliminated Burnside's grand-division structure, instituted a furlough program based on performance, divided the cavalry into separate units, improved the quality of the food, got rid of corrupt quartermasters, and cleaned up the camps. All of this had a pronounced effect on morale, as absenteeism and desertion rates fell. "One of his earliest acts was to order the adoption of corps badges," Lochren recalled, "worn on the hat or cap of the soldiers or officers, and so born upon flags, as easily to identify corps, divisions and brigades on the march or battlefield. They were useful in many ways, and tended to strengthen the *esprit du corps* of the organizations."[61] The Minnesotans, as part of the Second Division of the Second Corps, wore a white trefoil, or cloverleaf.

They would remain in their camp near Falmouth for three more months, but according to Mathew Marvin they were not overburdened with official responsibilities. "The hardest duty to be performed at present is to turnout at Reveille," he wrote toward the end of March. "We have only drilled three times this month." When they weren't on picket duty, they spent their time and energies much as they had the winter before at Edward's Ferry, trying to keep warm, well fed, and, if at all possible, amused. The heavier than normal snowfall gave them a chance to relive Minnesota winters and to get into trouble in the process: "A number of the boys are arrested for throwing snowballs but are held in custody only a few minutes," Isaac recorded. One day he presided over an elaborate mathematical "trial," complete with isosceles triangles, to test the proposition, "Does it require more canvas to 'double-roof' than to 'single-roof' a shantie; the 'pitch' of the roof being the same in both cases?" After hearing the evidence of both sides, "the court rendereth Her verdict in favor of the Neg."[62]

Isaac faithfully recorded the usual disciplinary problems. In early February Sgt. Milton Bevans of Company F was stripped of his rank for refusing to "tie up" a soldier "who was under arrest for groaning for Burnside while on review." A week later Isaac told of a divisional provost guard's " 'drumming out' a man said to belong to the 20th. Mass. Vols. The prisoner had a board tied to his back labeled 'Coward.' "[63]

There was growing speculation that the First would be returned to Minnesota to help put down the Sioux uprising, which had taken the lives of hundreds of settlers in the southern part of the state and which had spread panic everywhere. There seemed to be some basis for the rumor, according to Isaac: "The 'Saint Paul Press' of the 21st ult. [February] contains a letter from Gov. Ramsey to Sec'y Stanton, asking that the 1st Minn. be sent back to the State to recruit and fight Indians;

also a Resolution of the State Legislature asking the same thing." Walker, however, dismissed the rumor, though he found the idea of fighting Indians preferable to the regiment's actual prospects: "They dont have any artillery and therefore can't scare people to death with shells." When Governor Ramsey, having just been elected to the U.S. Senate by the state legislature, visited the regiment in early April, the men hoped he would clarify whether the regiment would be returning to Minnesota. "The boys would greatly rejoyce at the change," Marvin wrote, "but I dont think that a majority would ask to be so releaved. They would stay until they are grey as rats first."[64]

Instead of clarifying their future, Ramsey presented the Minnesotans with a new state flag and lavishly praised them for their conduct. "The Governor's speech daubes us all over with glory," was how Isaac put it. Ramsey overdid it in the view of many of the men, who as a whole had never held him in high regard. They resented his attempt to exploit them, as well as his failure to address their concerns. Marvin character-ized his remarks as "soft soap."[65] In any case, fighting Indians may have been the priority in Minnesota, but fighting Confederates was the pri-ority in Washington, and the regiment stayed where it was.

Isaac craved news from Washington as well as from other theaters of the war. "The 'Conscription bill,' as amended by the House, has passed the Senate," he noted in early March. "I suppose 'Old Abe' will give it the finishing touch & then, Mr. Copperhead, you can have a chance to fight for your country." Nothing made him angrier than being denied access to newspapers, for whatever reason: "A news boy passes through camp but refuses to sell his papers to any except *officers*. Report says an order has been issued allowing but one news-paper vender to a divi-sion. No wonder that the army is 'demoralized' if they are to be deprived of all information respecting the progress of the cause in which they voluntarily peril their lives. Gentlemen of the Star frater-nity, you can take your hard-bread & welcome, but for God's sake do us the favor to let us read your old papers when you get through with them, if you can possibly work yourself up to so generous a pitch."[66]

Henry went to town and brought back copies of "Harper's Weekly, 'Nix Nax,' 'Budget of Fun,' 'Phunny Phellow' &c." Isaac sent away for "Geology of the Globe" in the middle of February and was reading it three weeks later. When he finished he sent for "Hitchcock's Elementary Geology" and "Websters Army & Navy Pocket Dictionary" and bought locally a copy of "Frost's Hist. of U.S." In the meantime he finished the Book of Isaiah and the report of the Committee on the Conduct of the War.[67]

When the brothers weren't reading they were writing, either entries in their diaries or letters home, most often to their older sister Sarah. One day Isaac was moved to send a sign of spring to his younger sister Mary Jane: "Inclosed I send you a peach blossom picked March 17, 1863." Few wrote as prolifically as the Taylors, but most of the men tried to write regularly, eager to relieve the anxiety of family members and friends. The writing tended to be remarkably legible, considering the difficult physical circumstances. "I am setting this evening on the ground, in my tent," Bassett recounted in January. "My bayonet is stuck in the ground, to hold the candle while I write this letter. There is a hard wind blowing."[68]

Walker was another regular writer. Every month or so he wrote his friend George Knight in Worcester, Massachusetts, telling him of the most recent events involving the regiment. He frequently urged him to come to Minnesota after the war, and he sometimes offered advice on joining the army: "You think some of enlisting at times—I should judge—Well, you can't be too careful about that same thing, for as much as I want the Rebellion put down and would like to see *most* anybody in the field, I cant advise all my friends to enlist. It is a hard life to live this soldiering, *especially carrying knapsack.*"[69]

Charley Goddard, still another regular writer, agreed with Walker that soldiering was a "hard life," but as usual he tried to respond to his mother's worries: "If you have been led to believe by my letters that I am very anncious to get home before the Rebellion is crushed, or that in the hasty letters I have written to you, I thought the soldiers life a hard one, it is something I never intended to do. I acknowledge we do have some hard times, and that if we would give way to the impulses of a moment, one would feel as if he could work for any boddy but Uncle Sam But when we get in camp and have time to get a cup of warm coffee and a slice of corn beef—called 'salt horse'—he feels as if he might stand it a very little while longer."[70]

Isaac and Henry took to a new game called baseball. "Playing ball is quite a common sport in our Regt. now-a-days," Isaac noted at the end of March. Walker told Knight that it had been "rather dull" in camp except for St. Patrick's Day, which featured "a big horse race" and several other contests. "The track was arranged with four hurdles (or fences) and four ditches to jump," he wrote.

> The racers took their places at the sound of the bugle, and at the second call started, the track was very muddy and when the horses came to jump the "hurdles" many a man got tumbled in the mud. On the first heat but two or three succeeded in getting in all right, twas fun for the lookers on, but excuse *me* from being tumbled into the mud as I saw some of them. Well the racing lasted till noon and most all the generals of the army of the Potomac were present, Hooker included. In the afternoon it was announced there would be a "bad" race, "climbing greased poles," catching "lubricated pigs" &c., but unfortunately for lookers on there had been a smart cannonading on our right—and the generals getting rather apprehensive of danger dismissed the crowd, and all hands returned to camp, thus St. Patrick's Day was brought to an untimely end—two horses were killed, several men wounded and any quantity of officers in a *fair way* of getting drunk.[71]

As at Edwards' Ferry the year before, some of the officers chose to pass the time and break up the monotony of winter camp with drink. "Yesterday several boxes of liquor for the officers of our Regt. arrived," Isaac noted on the first day of March, "& to day certain officers & privates are 'slightly inebriated.' " But most of the officers discovered furloughs to be a more appealing solution to the tedium of camp life. They left for Minnesota in ever-increasing numbers for fifteen days or longer at a time. "Capt. N.S. Messick Co. G of the 1st Regiment, returned home for a short visit on Saturday night last," the Faribault *Central Republican* reported in early February. "The Captain is looking well."[72] Sometimes so many were gone that the senior officer in charge of the regiment was a lieutenant. Needless to say, the enlisted men, for whom furloughs were considerably more difficult to obtain, resented the practice, particularly when it was abused.

Probably the most egregious abuse involved Capt. Mark Downie, who went on leave at Fair Oaks in June 1862 and failed to return to the regiment until the following February. His absence went unpunished, prompting one Minnesotan to write, "Of course it is all right, for he will undoubtedly draw pay to the tune of about eight hundred dollars for being away from the regiment during the battles of Savage's Station, Peach Orchard, Allen's Farm, Glendale, White Oak Bridge, Malvern, Antietam, Fredericksburg, and others of lesser importance. There are many others like him."[73]

Again, like the year before, there was the inevitable politicking for promotion. To fill three vacant second lieutenancies, the board of officers recommended the three most senior sergeants, William Lochren, Myron Shepard, and Charles Mason. Colonel Morgan then forwarded their names to Governor Ramsey. Lochren and Mason received commissions, according to Lochren, "but instead of one for Shepard came a long letter from the state adjutant general, urging that a former first lieutenant of the regiment—who, after obtaining a leave of absence to visit the state in the fall of 1861, had procured details for various duties at Fort Snelling, and remained there in spite of orders to return to the regiment, until forced to resign because of his continued absence— should be given this commission instead of Shepard, a most competent and deserving soldier, who had served in the field with credit the entire time. The regiment felt indignant at this action, and it drew forth a letter of warm remonstrance from Col. Morgan, which brought Shepard's commission without further delay."[74]

Race relations in the Army of the Potomac hadn't noticeably improved since Lincoln issued his Emancipation Proclamation, even though there was broad support for its intent. "A contraband dies in our regimental hospital from effect of gun-shot wound inflicted by a 'brave' Union soldier," Isaac noted in mid-January. "The negro refused to get off from his masters horse & deliver it over to a stranger. That soldier has immortalized himself by that *brave* act."[75]

The men were fascinated with the "contrabands" and the stories they had to tell. " 'Nigger Joe' comes into our tent this evening & gives us a history of his life & escape from slavery," Isaac wrote in mid-March. " 'Baptist Joe' is a smart lad." After issuing the Emancipation Proclamation, Lincoln authorized the formation of four Negro regiments, stirring great controversy as to whether blacks were capable of being effective soldiers. " 'Baptist Joe' calls on us this evening & relates his religious experience & gives his views of the 'Negro enlistment' programme. Joe thinks that the 'colored population' *will fight*."[76]

"What is your opinion about confiscating or arming negroes 'or other men' in order to put down the Rebellion?" Edward Walker asked Knight. "My sentiments are that the Government cant do enough to hurt the South as much as she deserves, and I go in for teaching negroes to fight, also for retaliation, if the Rebs undertake any Shikanery. I havent the least doubt but that the South can be whipped if the North are only united, confound such men as [Vallandigham], Seymour &c they prolong the war by giving the rebels comfort. Occasionally you may find a retired soldier who is favor of peace, but such slinks do not represent the majority of the army."[77]

Picket duty continued to occupy the regiment's on-duty time, although one Saturday in February Isaac reported that he was "building corduroy road at brigade commissary. At noon they give each man on detail, a ration of whiskey." Their regular picket assignment, according to Isaac, was just above Falmouth on the Rappahannock: "The river here is about 400 yards wide. A dam extends across the river at the head of the canal which supplies the city of Fredericksburg with water. Pickits converse across the river. . . . High bluffs on either side of the river. Circular grapevine swing."[78]

The unusually cold winter and heavy snow sometimes made for very unpleasant nights. "I was on picket the 4th inst.," Bassett wrote his parents. "About sundown it started to snow and some 6 inches fell. It was the worst night I have spent since I have been in the army." Isaac chafed under orders preventing the men from building fires within sight of the Confederates across the river. "On out post from five till twelve last night," he wrote in late February. "It being against orders to have fire on the out-post at night, we shiver with cold while the Secesh sit around cheerful fires toasting their shins." Ten days later the foolishness of the prohibition was too much for him: "Though we are stationed in plain sight of the enemy we are not allowed to have fires even in the day time. I suppose a fire would enable the Rebels to see across the river by day light & thus reveal our position to the enemy. What fertile brains our generals seem to possess!"[79]

As at Edwards' Ferry, the men were prohibited from conversing with the enemy pickets. But, as they had the year before, relations between Union and Confederate pickets warmed over time, and despite orders the opposing soldiers continually engaged one another in conversation, barter, and even games. "Their pickets along the river ask us to come over and see them," Bassett wrote in April. "They send us a Richmond paper occasionally. Since the fish commenced to run they are continually fishing. When we get orders to march, we are to take 8 days rations. The Rebs have found this out, and ask us when we are coming over with the grub."[80]

Virginia leaf tobacco was traded for Northern coffee, New York and Washington newspapers for those from Richmond and Charleston. Sometimes the exchanges were made on makeshift rafts and toy boats, which frequently went astray when wind calculations proved wrong. "They sent over a little sail boat with a Richmond paper in it, and we returned it with a cargo of coffee," Bassett wrote. "At post No. 6 the Scesh & our boys put one another through the manuel of arms, giving the orders across the river," Isaac noted in early March. "Thatcher 'pats' for Secesh 'John' to dance. Secesh sing 'Come, come away,' 'Old John Brown' &c."[81]

At about the same time Isaac encountered another, even more welcome diversion: "I am on post No. 1, opposite an island. A pair of Secesh damsels promenade up and down the island opposite our post. A little urchin who is with them says his name is Montgomery & that his father owns the entire island which comprises 'eighty acres of level land.' I call Sergt. Wakefield down to the river bank & he goes into ecstacies at the sight of the fair ones, & sighs 'oh this war.' " Presumably there were no further sightings of the "fair ones" until a month later, when Isaac was again on picket duty opposite the island: "The Misses Montgomery come down to the river bank & I 'present arms.' They acknowledge the salute by waving their handkerchiefs." The next day "just before we are relieved a Lieut. of 15th Mass. throws a note across to the girls & they in return throw back the 'Southern Illustrated News.' "[82]

In mid-March Isaac made a trip to Aquia Creek, the army's supply base on the Potomac, where he met a soldier from the Sixtieth New York who "was taken prisoner at the last Bull Run battle where he saw & talked with my cousin, Capt. Leonard Johnson of the Secesh army." A week later Isaac and Henry were visited by their brother Danforth, or Daff, and a friend from Prairie City, Illinois. Only five days later they decided to pay a return visit: "Henry & I get a pass for two days & visit the camp of the 12th Ill. Cavalry near Belle-Plain . . . where Daff, Chet Warren, Ike Painter &c. are on duty. We have a rich feast of fresh oysters for dinner & other agreeable incidents throughout the day. The Co. D boys are relieved at night & Lieut. Marsh invites us to ride up to camp on horseback. Some racing—my little grey pony comes out ahead."[83]

While Bassett may have thought the reviews and parades "quite a sight," as he wrote in January, Isaac was tiring of them by March. "In A.M. the 2d Army Corps is reviewed by Maj. Gen. Joseph Hooker, on the same ground where it was reviewed by Gen. Burnside on the 17th. of Jan. last. Gen. Hooker is a little more than medium size, gray haired light complexion, red faced &c. He had his face shaved smooth & rode a light-grey horse. The review had, at least, one redeeming feature; *there was no cheering.* I never wish to hurrah again till we *do something worth cheering for.* . . . The Corps was fifty five minutes passing 'Fighting Joe.'" Goddard echoed Isaac's view: "It does not pay [to cheer] until we know wheather the man is worth cheering for, and then he never fails to get as many as he wants."[84]

Walker was more impressed when President Lincoln visited the army: " 'Old Abe' his wife and little boy . . . made us a visit and we formed in review before them—was quite a *big thing*—would like to have you see the whole army of the Potomac on review, its a sight that *we soldiers even,* like to see, the fact is we couldnt see the *whole* army—there isnt level ground enough around here to put the whole army on." Bassett thought the President "looked rather careworn," and Isaac confirmed that that impression was shared by others.[85]

Many of the Minnesotans were approaching the second anniversary of their three-year enlistments, and it gave some of them reason to reflect on their experience as well as to look forward to the time one year hence when they would be discharged. "You want to know whether I intend going west after my time is out or go east," Walker wrote his friend in Massachusetts.

> Well I cant tell yet it will depend on circumstances, if the war ends *before* our Regts. time expires, we will probably all be sent to Fort Snelling and "Mustered out" there—but if the war continues longer than our time of service we may be discharged wherever we are. The troops whose time expires this spring are to have 30 days furlough and $50 bounty *if* they will reinlist. In most of the 9 months

Regts. and 2 year Regts. there are many 3 years men—they of course will have to serve their time out. Our Regt. was mustered into U.S. service on the 29th April 1861 and have one more year to serve, from the 29th of this month. But we have had between 3 and 4 hundred recruits at different times—and *they* were *each* sworn in for "three years or during" and if the government chooses, it can hold them for their *full 3 years*. But I hope this summer will wind up Secesh and then we can *all* go home (that is—what is left).

"I expect when I get out of this (if I ever do)," Walker continued, "that I shall be as fond of 'changing base' as ever, *indeed,* I can think of no better fun, than to go on some expedition (provided) there is no fighting to be done—for sometimes I think that I will turn Quaker or some other Harmless sort of animal and live at peace with all mankind (and woman too). But unfortunately (or otherwise) I am in for 'three years or during' and perhaps it will be best to be *beligerent* during that time."[86]

Isaac kept his thoughts on the future largely to himself, and at least once, following a huge storm, he reflected in poetry:

> The storm has past, ethereal blue
> Presents itself again to view
> And kindly glance of myriad stars
> Darts hope unto the son of Mars
> And tells him that beyond the storm
> He'll find the peerless, peaceful form
> Of Liberty and Law.[87]

In the months since Hooker had taken charge the morale of the army had demonstrably improved. "The health is excellent, and the army in good fighting trim," Bassett concluded. "We have the best rations that we have ever had." Goddard found the quantity of food wanting—"There is no danger of us Soldiers getting more eggs and ham than is good for us"—but agreed with Bassett that the regiment was in good health: "There was no person died to my knowledge since we have been in this camp."[88]

Hooker judged that with spring having arrived and his army in shape, it was time to act. The men sensed it too, and they were confident that "Fighting Joe" would not let them down. "It was reported that the rebs wer coming down in big force," Marvin wrote. "But I hardly think they will ever catch Old Jo asleep."[89]

Rumors as to the army's next move were constant and usually wrong. Most of the veterans knew how to deal with them, and as the first sergeant of his company Marvin had all of the veteran's instincts: "This morning about 3 oclock Jake the cook came & woke me saying that the other companys had orders to march at a moments notice with three days rations   I told him to go back to bed & waite till we got the order from the Capt. I would not wake the Co till I got the order rite so I went to sleep & when I turned out at reveillee I saw the [8]2nd N.Y. drawn up in line to support the pickets & the Battery all ready to move & this Regt was astir when we had turned out   I asked the Capt for orders he said he had none about rations   he said he would not disturb our rest for the order he got   Madam Rumor said their was a large force comeing in our rear & that the rest of the Army had been up all nite."[90]

Evidently Isaac's first sergeant did not respond to the rumors in the way Marvin had. "About 4 A.M. we are arroused to 'pack up' & be ready to march at a moments notice," he wrote on the same day. "Rumors are various. Our pickets that were relieved this morning heard cannonading up the river." But nothing happened for nearly two weeks, until 14 April: "We are ordered to be ready to march tomorrow morning with eight day's rations and sixty rounds of ammunition. Report says our cavalry are already across the river above here."[91]

"We have been expecting a move for some time," Walker wrote, "and now have orders to have five days rations of Hard Bread, Coffee, Sugar, &c. in our knapsacks—and three days additional in our haversacks, making in all Eight days provisions and we must throw clothing aside to make room for provisions." Bassett said the men "have packed all of our blankets and extra clothing in boxes to leave here. Last summer I had to throw away about $15.00 worth on the march."[92]

On the day the regiment received its orders, Henry, a veteran now of almost two years, took occasion to "note a few facts concerning soldiering":

> Carry as light a load as possible but be sure to have at least one blanket, one towel, one shirt, two pairs of socks, needle and thread,

and writing material in your knapsack. One or two small books will not come amiss. More fear is felt going into action than after you get in. Artillery is more frightful than destructive except at short range, where grape and cannister is thrown. Infantry are apt to fire too high. Cavalry can do nothing with Infantry, if they stand firm. Infantry seldom cross bayonets—one side or the other will give way in case of a charge before the parties meet. Always have water in your canteen when you go into action. Wounded men must have water. Use cold water in dressing a fresh wound. Treat prisoners of war kindly. Pickets should not fire on one another. Always be ready for battle when you are near the enemy. Letters from friends are a great source of enjoyment to the soldier. It pays to fix up a comfortable bed or shanty for a few days. As a general thing, soldiers are very profane—the influence of women is taken away to a great extent. War should never be resorted to, but as a last extremity. It costs but little to keep a brief diary.[93]

Whoever promoted Henry Taylor to sergeant knew what he was doing.

Walker was ready to get on with it: "Old Hooker intends pushing things and if we dont see some hard marching connected with *very* hard fighting this summer, then I shall be agreeably disappointed. The order was given several days ago, but it has rained severely since and has delayed our movements—as it now is—we may move at a few moments notice—and I *do* hope our movements will be successful."[94]

7

CHANCELLORSVILLE

"The fortunes of war often change, boys."

O ld Hooker," as Walker called him, had spent the last several
months planning an attack on the Confederates still dug in
across the Rappahannock behind Fredericksburg. To repeat
Burnside's assault on Marye's Heights would be sheer folly; Lee had
used the time to strengthen his defenses on the Heights and also to
extend them up and down the river. The answer, Hooker concluded,
lay in forcing Lee out from behind his fortifications and into the open,
where the Union's superior numbers could provide a decisive advantage. To force Lee to come out Hooker proposed sending the bulk of
his army, some seventy thousand men, far to the north, where they
would cross the Rappahannock and approach the Southerners from the
rear. He would leave a smaller force of about forty thousand to feign an
attack on Fredericksburg in hopes that Lee would leave most of his
army in place to meet it.

On 27 April Union troops began quietly moving out of camp, some
to the north and others to the south. The First Minnesota and the rest
of the division, now commanded by Gen. John Gibbon, stayed where
they were since their camp was in plain sight of the Confederates and
their departure would have been an obvious sign that a major movement was under way. "Troops are moving, hard to tell which way they
go—this forenoon we see troops filing to the right and this afternoon
they return and go to the left," Walker wrote on the twenty-eighth.
"Everything indicates a big row before many days," Isaac noted.[1]

"Some firing today both up and down the river," Walker observed
the following day. "Most of the troops have left (with the exception of

our division) makes the place look deserted and lonely."[2] Hooker's main force forded the river nine miles north of Fredericksburg, doubled back, and approached the crossroads called Chancellorsville from the west. At the same time two Union corps under Maj. Gen. John Sedgwick crossed the Rappahannock two miles south of Fredericksburg. It seemed to the Minnesotans that everyone in the Army of the Potomac was on the move except them.

"This afternoon & evening we see the flash of artillery just below Fredericksburg; the report is scarcely audible," Isaac wrote on the thirtieth. "We have orders to march tomorrow morning with eight day's rations. 'Fighting Joe' says that the enemy is in such a position that he will be compelled to make a hasty retreat or come out & fight us on our own ground. 'Joe,' we'll do the best we can for you." Walker reported that he "could see our troops below town and across the River—could also see the Rebs line of battle a short distance from ours. Reb pickets are not as thick along the River as usual, they have got other business to attend to."[3]

On the first of May one of the Minnesotans' companion regiments, instead of helping to put down a rebellion, engaged in one of its own. "About 100 of the 34th N.Y. Vols. claim that their term (2 years) expires today and they refuse to do duty," Henry noted. "Gens. Sully and Gibbons call out the remainder of the regiment, also the 15th Mass. and placed the mutineers under guard—guns loaded. Gen. Gibbons made a speech to them, telling them that they had better return to duty as the U.S. Government would not recognize their service until they were sworn into the U.S. Service. Gen. Gibbons told them he had authority from Gen. Hooker to shoot everyone if they did not return to duty. Then they gave three cheers for Gen. Gibbons and returned to duty."[4]

Walker understood that the officers of the Thirty-fourth "had got them in on a 'false muster' " and concluded, "No doubt there is 'Skull-dug' somewhere."[5] Skullduggery or not, there was nothing like loaded weapons to bring mutinous men to reason. The incident had an unhappy consequence for General Sully, who as brigade commander was immediately responsible for the conduct of his regiments. Apparently Sully was uncertain as to the degree of force he was authorized to use in putting down the insurrection, and his hesitation caused his division commander, John Gibbon, to relieve him of command. Sully asked a court of inquiry to clear him, which it ultimately did, but he failed to get his command back.

Isaac too witnessed the Thirty-fourth's unsuccessful protest, but he recorded what was for him a more alarming development: "The news boy reports 'no more papers allowed to come to this army till further orders.' Reading geology; pitching quoits &c."[6]

It was evident to the Minnesotans the next day that major actions were under way both up river and down, but it was impossible to get accurate news of either. Their chance to fight would come the day after. A call went out for twenty-five volunteers from each of the brigade's four regiments to undertake a hazardous mission as forward skirmishers before Sedgwick's advance. More than enough Minnesotans came forward, led by Lt. Hezekiah Bruce of Company F. One of the volunteers, C. W. Merritt, said the men had great confidence in Bruce, whom he called a "cool, level headed officer. His men knew him well and knew they could depend upon his cool judgment and courage which means much in a tight place." E. F. Grow, a member of the First but not one of the twenty-five volunteers, recalled Bruce's instructions: "Take his men, cross the river and lead the charge of the 6th Corps on the Confederate works. And I assure you it did not look like boys' play, for we could see cannon sticking out over the works behind."[7]

The regiment, under the command of Lieutenant Colonel Colvill since Colonel Morgan went on sick leave, was "routed out about midnight and marched to the bank of the river opposite Fredericksburg by 2 a.m.," according to Henry. "Then," C. W. Merritt recounted, "the pontoons were quickly laid and Bruce and his men charged across, capturing a number of prisoners that remained in the rifle pits." Gibbon's division and the rest of the Minnesotans followed, except for Isaac and a few others, who were on picket duty. "At 2-15 A.M. our pickets are entirely withdrawn & we are ordered back to camp where we arrive just at day-break & find our Regt. gone," he wrote that night. "At daylight heavy firing commences in the vicinity of Fredericksburg. At six A.M. our picket squad leave camp, march down to the Lacy House, cross the Rappahannock on a pontoon bridge at the precise point where we crossed on the 11th of Dec. last, and join our Regt. in the city."[8]

The crossing was made against little opposition; the Confederates appeared to have abandoned Fredericksburg for the heights behind it. "We marched up town and halted near the same house where one of our company was wounded at the last fight," Walker recalled. "The town is pretty well dug up with rifle pits—and we found new ones that had been dug since our last fight. After a short halt we marched to the lower end of town—another halt and then back again to 'Princess Ann St.' By this time the Rebs commenced to show themselves behind their works, and we find that there are a *few* left."[9]

The Union forces stormed the works, with Bruce and the other volunteers leading the assault. "We were a separate organization, acting as skirmishers and were in the front ranks with Sedgwick's men when Mary's Heights were carried and the enemy driven out at the point of the bayonet," Merritt remembered. Two waves of bluecoats charged across the same killing field before Marye's Heights with the same bloody result that had met the December attacks. But because so many of the defenders had been drawn to the main action at Chancellorsville, the line was thinner now, and the third Union assault, a bayonet charge, broke through. That night Henry put it this way: "They took the 'caps' off their guns and went in with 'cold' steel."[10]

The Minnesotans were again spared the brunt of the action. The regiment moved "up river across a level open field & halt just above Falmouth. During this movement seven of our Regt are wounded by shell from the enemies batteries on the Heighths," Isaac wrote. "It appears that we were to draw as many Rebs as possible away from the left of town in order to favor Sedgwick," reasoned Walker,

> So we kept moving slowly to the right, this soon brought us nearly out of range of their artillery. As we moved to the right, the Rebs moved also—distant from us about 400 yards—might have done considerable execution if they had fired on us—but they let us alone waiting for closer work which they soon expected. We saw two lines of Rebs—one line in the pits and another in the rear—those in the rear not sheltered by the pits, didnt like the idea of stopping to fight and we could see their officers flourish their swords and order them to stand fast. It was impossible for us to charge them on account of a canal between them and us—therefore the order was not given, and after marching as far to the right as possible we halted—and then Sedgwick attacking them on the

left carried the heights and we soon had the pleasure of seeing the Rebs in our front begin to break and in less than five minutes they had all 'Skedaddled' our men following and yelling.[11]

It had to have been an exhilarating moment for any Union soldier who had witnessed the carnage at the same place four and a half months earlier.

Bruce and his volunteers kept going, leading Sedgwick's drive west to link up with Hooker at Chancellorsville. "We were again deployed as skirmishers moving to the right towards the Rappahannock above the city," Merritt recounted. "In the rifle pits on the side of the hill were squads of 'Johnnies' who failed to get out in time. They surrendered and were sent to the rear. . . . We had a good scrap with about twenty men lodged in an old log barn. When we had them nearly surrounded, they attempted to get out, but our persuasive Springfield rifles dropped several of them and the rest surrendered. The wounded we were obliged to leave. They were cared for later."

Merritt also recounted a "funny" incident involving "the capture of a redout of earth work, with two embrasures from which pointed two guns of large calibre":

> Bruce maneuvered for its capture without getting directly in front of the guns, and then charged the works. The guns proved to be stove pipes mounted on old wagon wheels. There were several "Johnnies" inside, but they made no show of fight and were disarmed and sent back. A little further on we captured a sergeant and a number of men that had been left on the picket line in the bend of the river above town. From this we moved on up the river with now and then a lively scrimmage with the enemy who supposed the battle line was close behind. But in fact, the commander had lost us. We went back towards Chancellorsville some two miles picking up small squads of prisoners.[12]

Meanwhile the regiment, according to Walker, was moved to the left

> and marched up near the road we done picket duty on last fall— Rebs had filled *our* rifle pits but otherwise the place looked as natural as ever, we kept on till we had passed all of their works—saw many of our men killed and wounded along the road—Had been a hard fight—After passing their works we halted about ½ hour

Sedgwicks troops all the while advancing. The Heights being taken and Sedgwick having no further use for us, we were ordered back to town—passing by the famous stonewall of the Rebs and the scene of the hottest of the fight last fall—The buildings around here were completely peppered with bullets. Had the Rebs been here in full force—our chances would have been slim. As it is we have lost *enough* but have got something to *show for it.* The day so far has been very hot many suffering from sunstroke—had a slight touch of it myself—gives a severe headache.[13]

That afternoon the Minnesotans recrossed the Rappahannock on a bridge at the lower end of Fredericksburg in order to support two heavy batteries on the river flats. Bruce and his men—none of the volunteers had been lost during the day's action—joined them after dark, according to Merritt: "A drizzling rain had set in and wet, foot sore and weary we found the regiment about midnight and we were very glad to bunk down on a wet blanket."[14]

The First's good luck was holding. Not a single Minnesotan had been killed during the day, and the regiment had not even been seriously engaged. While that may have been welcome news to the men, it didn't necessarily read well in official reports. Lieutenant Colonel Colvill nonetheless made the most of it in his report five days later: "Although not placed in such a prominent position as has usually been its fortune in the engagements, my command—officers and men, all of them—displayed the same steadiness and alacrity in the performance of its duties as has distinguished it under former commanders, and, from the time the march commenced until the present moment, every member of it, except the wounded, has been constantly present for duty."[15]

The night he returned from Fredericksburg, Walker wrote that if Hooker's men "are doing as well on the right as Sedgwick has just done Rebs will get whipped. . . . Have pitched our tents and expect a good nights rest. Our chaplain reports that Hooker has gained a victory on the right—captured (8000) prisoners &c, &c, &c.—We all hope it is true—but cant rely on *reports.*" Isaac had evidently heard the same reports, and he was optimistic: "We are all in good spirits to night. Every thing appears favorable at this point & we hear that 'Fighting Joe' has been equally successful on the right."[16]

As it happened, "Fighting Joe" was not living up to his name. For reasons that perplexed even his immediate subordinates, Hooker had gone on the defensive as soon as he engaged Lee's forces rushing west from Fredericksburg. The Confederate commander gambled that the main Union threat came from upriver, and he guessed right. Leaving ten thousand men under Jubal Early to defend Fredericksburg—about a third of the number Sedgwick would mount against him—Lee stunned Hooker with his quick response and his decision to split his army, causing the Union commander to lose his nerve. On the night of 1 May Lee and Stonewall Jackson decided to divide the Confederate army *again* by sending Jackson on a twelve-mile march through the Wilderness, an almost impenetrable second-growth forest of scrub oak and underbrush, to launch a surprise assault on Hooker's exposed flank. The evening of 2 May Jackson's men stormed out of the woods against the surprised Yankees, sending them reeling back in confusion. Hooker, bewildered by the sudden turn of events, couldn't bring all his forces to bear and ordered a withdrawal to the north behind a defensive line. Lee's gamble had paid off; in perhaps the finest moment of generalship in the entire war, he had not only staved off an attack by a much superior force but had defeated that force—badly.

But the action was not yet over. Learning that Sedgwick had taken Marye's Heights and was coming overland to join forces with Hooker, Lee detached two divisions to meet him. Sedgwick repulsed the Confederate attack on 4 May but, informed that Hooker had withdrawn, decided to pull back as well. Meanwhile, the Southerners were reoccupying the fortifications above Fredericksburg from which Sedgwick had driven them the day before.

"We soon found that the Rebs were fileing into their works again from the left of the 'plank road,' Walker noted at midday. "As Sedgwick has gone on to join Hooker we did not have men enough to hold the works and after a sharp skirmish our men fell back to the first line of works. Our artillery on this side shelled them severely and we saw them break and run like sheep—but they would appear in other places and soon had possession of the works in full force. This is a *new wrinkle*— and we dont see the point—it may be all right *but* it looks as if Sedgwick had allowed the Rebs to get in his rear. However they can't hurt him much if he has joined Hooker." Except that Sedgwick had never joined Hooker.

The regiment was sent down to the river to dig rifle pits to protect the pontoons, Walker added. "Our ambulances have gone over after the wounded and everything looks as if we would again abandon the city of Fredericksburg. We are divided into relief and are digging pits along the bank of the river. More artillery has taken position on the bank—and instead of holding Fredericksburg we are to hold *this side of the river.*—'The fortunes of war often change, boys.' "[17]

According to Isaac, Companies B and E were detached from the regiment "to the lower bridge to arrest the tide of stragglers that begins to flow pretty freely across the river."

> Wagon train, wounded &c all taken across to the left bank of the river. A little skirmishing just back of the city during the day. At 5-30 P.M. our Regt. recross the river & the engineers "swing" the lower pontoon bridge. Soon after heavy musketry & artillery firing commences beyond the hills. We can see the flash of the guns very distinctly. I suppose Sedgwick is trying to retake the highths. Our batteries shell the enemy from the left bank of the river. The firing seems to recede indicating that Sedgwick is being driven. At sunset one half of our Regt go on picket & at 10 P.M. the remainder move up to the Lacy House & occupy the rifle pits at the two upper bridges.

The men still didn't know what had happened in the fighting at Chancellorsville. As Walker put it that night, "We hear nothing and know nothing."[18]

As word of the defeat up the river began to filter into camp, however, Mathew Marvin refused to believe it. "Rumor says our army is all on this side of the river again," he wrote his brother, "& that all but two or three of our Gens. have been killed or wounded but I dont believe it & shant ask you to believe it because I still think we are all right yet & that the rebs will be knocked into a kocked hat before this move is done."[19]

The next day Henry saw an ominous sign upriver and drew the correct conclusion: "Dust is rising on this side of the river above Falmouth, and it looks to me as though our right was recrossing the river. I fear the 'Grand Old Army of the Republic' is again defeated." Walker too sensed unease when rebel pickets came down to the river on the opposite bank to occupy rifle pits: "They appeared to feel first rate—said 'Good Morning' to us, and &c.—We heard their officers give the order not to fire on us, and to keep quiet."[20]

When the Confederates withdrew, according to Walker, "another diversion took place, in [the] shape of a deserter coming down toward the river—as he neared the bank we discovered him to be a 'contraband.' . . . He kept on to the river bank and flourishing an old bayonet gave us to understand that he wanted to come over, but couldnt swim—two of our men swam over and putting darky on a log brought *him* over. He appeared very glad to get on this side—said he was a slave to an Adjutant of a Mississippi Regt. . . . He was taken to headqrs."

Heavy rains that night flooded the flats where the regiment was camped, Walker reported: "Arrived on the flat at dark and found it covered with water—no tents pitched—and no disposition on the part of the 'bosses' to change position. This state of affairs was *'slightly* demoralizing'—part of the men pitched in the mud—but the greater part scattered, every man for himself. Many (myself included) went up to the old log camp on the hill [where they had spent the previous four months] and found it some better than laying out in the water. This morning we came down to the flat. Drew 2 days rations of hard bread, pork, sugar and coffee, weather continues very cold and windy with some rain."[21]

It soon became evident what had happened upriver, and the speculation ended: "I see long lines of our infantry coming in from the right," Henry noted. "We are whipped. The blame is laid on the 11th Corps." Isaac saw the same Union columns coming downriver: "It seems we have not *exactly* whipped the Secesh *this time.* The 11th Army Corps is said to have behaved badly. I suppose we will have to recruit up a little & 'try again.' "

Walker had still not fully grasped the truth by the next day: "We are in the dark about our movements—things look suspicious, and we begin to realize the unpleasant fact that another unsuccessful battle has been fought, of course it will take time to learn the results." Henry had moved beyond the results to the consequences: "Who can tell the number of tears that will be shed by fathers, mothers, brothers, and sisters and friends of those who have fallen in this long and bloody battle? This suffering after the battle is over is the most mournful feature of the war."[22]

Lincoln came down from Washington to get a firsthand account of the disaster, which gave him even more cause to appear "careworn."

The Confederates occupied Fredericksburg once again, and their new mood was both visible and disconcerting to the Yankees across the river. "Secesh appear to be quite jubilant," Isaac noted. "Rebs are now seen swarming about the city," Walker wrote.

> Most of them are quiet but now and then one breaks out and tracts on facts like the following—
>
> Wheres little Mac?
> laid on the shelf—
> Wheres Pope? ditto.
> Wheres Burnside? laid on the shelf also.
> Wheres fighting Joe? He'll lay on the shelf.
> Wheres Bob Lee?
> In Fredericksburg By G-d
> Wheres your nice rubber blankets?
> Rebs got em.
> Wheres your greenbacks?
> in our pockets.
> Wheres the boys that can whip you?
> There they stand.

"There is some truth in the above," Walker concluded, "but we live and *die* in hopes that the table will turn soon."[23]

Bassett had occasion to observe the civilians as well as the Confederate soldiers who reappeared in Fredericksburg once the fighting stopped: "The Rebs are prowling the city hunting for knapsacks, etc. that our men lost. . . . There are more families in the town that I thought. The women are nearly all Secesh, and look poison. One old lady said that she hopes that she would die before we would conquer the south. Our Lieut. said that he hoped that she would. One old lady has five sons in the Union army. She wants the Rebs whipped."[24]

The only thing left to do was to gather up the wounded and bury the dead. "Flags of truce cross & recross the river," Isaac wrote on 9 May. "Our men ferry ambulances across the river on a pontoon raft & bring in a portion of Sedgwick's wounded. About 200 of them still lie on the field of Monday's fight."[25]

Gradually things returned to normal. "For the month following the battle of Chancellorsville perfect quiet existed between the two armies," Lochren remembered. "Drills, reviews and picket duty occupied the time. Our division had encamped just below the Lacy House, near the river, and right under the hundreds of guns which bristled along Marye's Heights, less than a mile away, and Confederate infantry were in camp, in plain sight, and within musket shot of us, and under the guns on the heights behind us."[26]

Several days after the battle the Minnesotans received disconcerting news. "Gen. Sully is ordered to Minnesota to prosecute the war against the Indians," Isaac wrote. "In his farewell address to the '1st Brig.' Gen. Sully says, 'I have the satisfaction of knowing that in all the battles I have fought with you, you have done your duty & never yielded an inch of ground to the enemy. You are a body of men which I have always been proud to command.' "[27]

"We lost a good Gen when Sulley left us," Goddard told his mother. "We loved Gen. Sully," Henry wrote. Their sentiments were universally shared in the regiment: Sully had seen them through the ordeal of the Peninsula, saved them from being overtaken by Confederate cavalry after the second battle of Bull Run, helped them survive Antietam, and—his greatest gift to them—spared them the slaughter at Fredericksburg. About the same time, Colonel Morgan, who had been on leave because of illness, resigned. He was replaced by his second in command, William Colvill. Although Colvill's performances at Bull Run and on the Peninsula had proved that he was personally brave, the Minnesotans were unsure of his leadership abilities. Colonels of the First Minnesota were now judged by a new standard, that set by Sully, and it was hard for a civilian like Colvill, no matter how courageous, to measure up. No one would know what kind of leader he would be until he was tested in battle. Maj. Charles P. Adams was promoted to lieutenant colonel to replace Colvill, and Capt. Mark Downie, despite his unauthorized eight-month absence from the regiment, was named major.

Isaac reported that Hooker tried to put the best face on the Chancellorsville debacle: "At dress parade Fighting Joe's 'General Orders No 49' was read to us. He 'congratulates' the army on its 'achievements of the last seven days' & adds 'If it has not accomplished all that was expected, the reasons are well known to the army. It is sufficient to say they were of a character not to be foreseen or prevented by human sagacity or resources.'" A week later he wrote, "Ordered to draw fatigue caps so as to look 'putty,' on parade. The officers of this army appear to think that *show* is the *grand object* while fighting is *merely incidental*. I think we have played boy long enough & if we can't act like men we might as well go home & see 'ma.'"[28]

Picket duty resumed and, with it, friendly contact with Confederates across the river. "Talking . . . was expressly forbidden for fear of too great familiarity, but would nevertheless ocassionally break out in good-natured *badinage*," Lochren recalled. "The men on both sides were now seasoned soldiers; hardy, steady veterans, who would fight each other to the death in the line of duty in battle, but would not be guilty of assassination, and regarded each other with feelings of respect, unmixed with any rancor or ill will."[29]

Although the Confederates had won huge victories at Fredericksburg and Chancellorsville, the accidental death of Stonewall Jackson at the latter and a lack of food and supplies hurt their morale. "They send out a detail to fish and every day about a dozen of them are in the water up to their necks dragging a 'seine' or net," Walker wrote. "They come more than half way across the river, when the tide is out they can easily come across—as some have done already. The last time I was on picket—the man on the end of the 'seine' nearest to our shore quietly left and come out to us—our boys give him some clothes and he was taken up the Hd. Qrs. Quite a number of them have deserted since the fight. Today the cars took away 47 that had deserted—they were on their way north."[30]

Isaac, meanwhile, was getting his affairs in order. He sent the first two books of his diary to his cousin Dency E. Keyes in Prairie City, Illinois. He sent twenty dollars to his father and, evidently having found a photographer in Falmouth, he sent his "likeness" to his sister Sarah. He spent more and more of his time reading books on geology and studying rock samples and formations wherever he could. "Studying geology as usual," he wrote. "Doble takes a lump of rock salt down to the Chaplin's tent to get him to tell what kind of a rock it is. The preacher not being at home our investment yields a less per cent of fun than we anticipated." A few days later he sent a "specimen" to the Geological Society of Prairie City Academy, which he had attended.

From time to time an especially revealing scientific fact or rule would find its way into the diary: " 'The decrease of the mean temperature from the equator towards the poles is nearly in the proportion of the cosines of latitude.' Hitchcock's Geology, Pg. 306." Another day he wrote, "Henry & I make a geological exploration & find examples of clayey 'concretions' in sandstone. Yesterday while on 'fatigue' I explored about ¼ of a mile of upturned strata containing 'joints,' numerous 'veins of segregation' &c."

He also found time to read "Pollock's 'Course of Time' and a history of the 'Sioux War,' " and he sent to a bookstore in Washington for "Wood's Botany." He attended regular prayer meetings at the Lacy House, where his interest appeared to be secular as well as spiritual: "Three women at meeting at Lacy House this evening. Blessed relics of civilization!" About the same time he reported hearing "sacred songs ascending from prayer meetings on both sides of the Rappahannock."

One Sunday Isaac went to the Lacy House twice, the first time for "Sunday School" in the afternoon. "Each one read a verse of the 14th. Chap. of John & then Mrs. Harris proposed questions which were discussed. There were three ladies and one small girl present. I attend meeting at 'Lacy House' this evening & witness the administration of the 'Lord's Supper.' 'All who love the lord' whether connected with any church or not, are invited. A lieut. assists in passing the bread & wine."[31]

Henry pondered the age-old question of which side of the war God was on: "This is Sunday. Hear church bells in the city on opposite shore. Thus, enemies, the U.S.A. and C.S.A. worship God in plain sight of one another and each appeal to god for the rectitude of their purpose. Strange world!"[32]

Isaac and his comrades did much of their reading and socializing at night, in their tents, and staying up too late got some of them in trouble: "The wind blew so hard last night that the inmates of our tent did not hear 'taps,' " Henry wrote in mid-May, "and Lt. Bruce, officer of the guard, came around and arrested Sergt. Wakefield and Sergt. P. H. Taylor—others, including Ike, 'sloped out the back' end of the tent and escaped. This is the first time Wakefield or I have been arrested, save by the enemy. As soon as the officer of the guard ascertained we were sergeants, he sent us back to our tents, but we were still under arrest, and had to go to Lieutenant-Colonel Colville and explain. He says he 'did not apprehend any further trouble; that's all.' Good Joke." In his own account of the incident and his escape, Isaac said, "We do not like the idea of being arrested for such *light* offenses." Isaac's most serious offense appears to have occurred a few weeks later, when he wrote, "I am sent out of the ranks for not having my cap on it being packed in my knapsack ready for a march."[33]

One day in May Isaac was nearly rhapsodic in reporting the departure of the 127th Pennsylvania, the regiment that had "skedaddled" not just once but twice in engagements at Fredericksburg. He and a number of the Minnesotans went to the train depot to see it off: "As the train starts off the boys annoy them with such impudent questions as 'Who run at Fredericksburg?' " Goddard reported that the Minnesotans "groaned" at the Pennsylvanians, who were "noted for their cowardice . . . the officers fairly foamed at the mouth, but did not do them any good."[34]

It was a different story altogether, several weeks later, when it was time for the Thirty-fourth New York to leave. Brigaded with each other since Edwards' Ferry, the two regiments had been through much together and the Minnesotans had great affection and respect for the New Yorkers. The evening before leaving, the officers of the Thirty-fourth were boisterously entertained by fellow New Yorkers in the Eighty-second. "I should think by the noise they made that they had plenty of whiskey after supper and before," Henry noted. Isaac concurred: "On my return from meeting this evening I hear them advocating 'short speeches and big drinks.' "[35]

The next morning, according to Henry, the First "turned out at 7 a.m. and presented arms to and gave three cheers for the 34th N.Y. Volunteers. They have been with us in many battles and done good service. It is hard to part with them, for they seem like brothers." Bassett shared the sentiment: "They were a two year Regt. and one of the best. When the train started the band struck up Auld Lang Syne. The Minn. 1st and the N.Y. [8]2nd gave them three rousing cheers. They have lost a great many men in battle."[36]

Edward Walker also watched the departure of the regiment and reflected on what it would mean for those left behind: "The 2 year and 9 months Regts. are going home and will weaken the army somewhat. But as 'Old Abe' says, we must keep 'pegging away' and time will do the rest. If I live my time out I shall vote to continue the war as long as may be necessary to whip them out. We may have the good luck to whale them before our time is out."[37]

With no victories of their own to cheer, the men of the Army of the Potomac hungered for news of Union victory elsewhere, especially at Vicksburg, on the Mississippi River, where Gen. Ulysses S. Grant was undertaking a siege. Isaac's diary reflected his intense interest in the western war: "[May] 24 . . . We get the news that Gen. Grant's army has defeated the rebels in several engagements taking large numbers of cannon & prisoners & that Vicksburg is now closely invested by our troops. [May] 25 . . . Vicksburg is reported in our possession. The army of the Potomac ought to have sent the gallant western boys, notes of victory from the Rappahannock." It soon became apparent that the Army of the Potomac would be leaving the Rappahannock. "The general packing up that is going on indicates that we shall not stay here a great while," Isaac concluded on 13 June. The next day he returned from Falmouth to camp, "where I find everything packed up ready for a move. . . . I get Richardson of Co. K. 1st Minn. to transport my Botany & Geology in a baggage wagon so as to lighten my knapsack."[38]

The same day Henry recorded that the move was imminent: "Our forces have withdrawn from the right bank of the river and a pontoon train is seen moving back towards Aquia at reveille. By 7 a.m. everything of value is moved from the depot. See U.S. Cavalry moving towards Falmouth at 8 a.m. Our pickets will take all their effects with them this morning. At 10 a.m. the enemy tents on the opposite side of the river disappear. This division forms rear guard on this retreat. I suppose we will soon find ourselves in the vicinity of Washington, D.C. We know we are to march on the 'Telegraph Road,' but what telegraph road is the question. I presume we will go by Stafford C[ourt] H[ouse], Dumfries, and Occoquon. No mail goes out today, and none received."[39] Henry correctly predicted which "telegraph road" the army would take, but no Union soldier could guess its ultimate destination. That was up to Robert E. Lee, who at that moment was heading north.

Buoyed by his stunning victories on the Rappahannock but still under no illusions about the great odds facing his cause, Lee became convinced that the South's only hope of ultimate victory lay in a successful invasion of the North, his failed effort of the previous year notwithstanding. Only in the North, he argued, could he find the supplies and food he needed to sustain his army, and only there could he inflict the kind of decisive defeat that would shock the North into ending the war. At the very least, he believed, he would remove the immediate threat to Richmond and bolster support for those Democrats in the North who were urging peace. And he aimed to accomplish all this by marching through Maryland to an unmistakably Northern state, Pennsylvania, which up to this point had been spared the ravages of war. President Jefferson Davis and others in Richmond had their doubts about the wisdom of the plan, but after Chancellorsville, Lee's standing throughout the South was so great that they all deferred to him.

The Confederate commander used the month after Chancellorsville to reorganize and rebuild the Army of Northern Virginia. In early June he began moving northwest toward Culpepper and then into the Shenandoah Valley, using the Blue Ridge to screen his movements. Fear and panic spreading before them, his advance units passed unhindered into Pennsylvania. Hooker, meanwhile, saw Lee's departure from Fredericksburg as an opportunity to move on Richmond, but when that plan was vetoed in Washington he uprooted the Army of the Potomac and began to pursue Lee, being sure all the while to keep his army between the Confederates and Washington.

For the Minnesotans, at least, it was an inauspicious beginning. "Left camp last night at dark and after marching toward Stafford C[ourt] H[ouse] three miles, we 'bout faced' and marched to the river below our old camp," Henry wrote on 15 June. They set out again at daybreak on the same road, but this time under a scorching sun. "It has been very warm & many cases of 'sun-stroke' occur," Isaac said. "I don't recolect of ever seeing so many 'sun-struck' and 'fagged out' on a march. I stand the march 'first rate.' Among those 'fagged out' are many officers." Charley Goddard wrote his mother on 20 June, "Since I last wrote we have been doing some 'tall' marching. There has been no less than 70 men fell dead out of this Corps . . . caused by hard marching and excessive heat. There has been a great many disabled, also—about 1200 disabled and dead."[40] According to Sgt. James A. Wright of Company F, one of the Hamline University students who had enlisted in Red Wing, "It was one of the most heart-breaking marches of our experience and many men wilted in the scorching heat and dust like mown grass. . . . There were a number of cases of fatal sunstroke, and some dying almost as quickly as if struck by a bullet in a vital part. All of the ambulances were filled with helpless men and those left behind were coming in all of the first part of the night."[41]

Mathew Marvin was one of those wilting in the heat. "I came darned near going under two or three times," he wrote. "I thought sure I was a gone duck   I would get in the shad & sweat & rest a spell & then mull on as before."[42]

The men crossed Aquia Creek and the Occoquan River, and after two days they reached Sangster's Station, which they had last seen on their way to the first battle of Bull Run. They heard rumors that Lee's forces had reached Winchester and Harpers Ferry, then Hagerstown, and finally Pennsylvania. "Rebels are reported to be at Carlisle Pa.," Isaac wrote. "Our destination is said to be Harpers Ferry. I hope Gen. Hooker will be able to make the rebels feel the *united* strength of the army of the Potomac." Charley Goddard reported that his comrades were also eager to engage Lee: "We have heard here that the Rebs are up in Chambersburg, and most all of the boys rejoic at the news, saying that [they] will hunt out some of those skinks in Pennsylvania."[43]

Bringing up the army's rear, the Minnesotans were not moving at breakneck speed. The blistering heat was a factor, of course, but so was Hooker, who was overtaken by caution. Isaac found plenty of time to meander through cemeteries, making notes on headstones. He had his own cautious moment, apparently, and decided to send his geology and botany books to "C.C. Coggswell" in Washington, D.C.

"This morning I went over to a mud hole & washed as well as I could changed my closed & throwed the dirty ones away for the want of washing & transportation which I thought was played out," Marvin wrote. "I should have thrown them yesterday but the Lt insisted on carrying them himself. Tim, Keily & I layed under a big walnut tree all day Tim like myself is played out."[44]

On 19 June the regiment reached Centreville, which had served as McDowell's staging area before the first great battle of the war two years earlier. Goddard recalled that it was the regiment's third visit to the place: "The 1st time I was not able to fight, the 2d time I could jest fight and that was all, the 3d and last time, I believe I could fight pretty good, doubtful wheather we will get a chance." The men witnessed a dress parade of the 111th New York Volunteers, and to Isaac, at least, it was an incongruous sight for an army on its way to battle: "They are rigged up in fancy style with dress coats & white gloves. Four ladies visit our camp to see the 'sogers' cook supper"[45] The New Yorkers reported that five army corps had passed through Centreville in recent days.

Accompanied by a herd of two hundred beef cattle, the regiment moved out across the Bull Run battlefield the next day. Colonel Colvill and Sergeant Wright took time to reexamine the place where they had experienced their first combat two years earlier and where another battle had been fought more recently. Wright later recalled what they saw: "Many of the dead had not been buried for some days . . . and then [they were] covered where they lay; and even this had not been done with overmuch care, and we frequently saw partly exposed skeletons, where the washing of the rain or rooting of the hogs had uncovered them. On a recently cut stump some grim jester had set a skull, as if in mockery of a real sentry. Much of the skin was still on it—dried and shrunken—and a bullet had passed through it from the right temple to a point above the left ear. There was nothing to indicate the color of the uniform he had worn." Marvin also saw the skeletons and concluded "it was rather a hard sight especially at that time & hour of the nite for we expected a Battle within a few days at the most."[46]

The regiment soon neared Haymarket, which Isaac described as "once a small town but . . . now almost a 'pile without inhabitants.' It was burned by our forces in Nov. last." Two days later it paused at Thoroughfare Gap, where Isaac found time to pursue his interest in geology: "This P.M. I 'reconnoitre' . . . & find two old grist mills, a few dwelling houses, Broad Run, highly inclined strata, tortuous lamina, joints, cleavage planes, igneous rocks, bold 'crags & peaks' & much magnificent scenery. If I were a free man I should enjoy a whole day's ramble in this vicinity, but in these 'exciting times' a soldier does not venture very far from camp for fear that something may turn up that requires his presence."

As the regiment approached Haymarket on 25 June it ran into Jeb Stuart's cavalry, then in the process of circling the entire Union army on a reconnaissance mission for Lee. At noon, according to Isaac, "some cavalry appear on a bluff south of us & while the boys are ernestly arguing the question 'Are they our men?', a white puff of smoke and the unearthly screech of a shell closes the debate & a unanimous decision is rendered in the Neg. Shells fly about our ears pretty lively for a short time but our batterys soon get into position & succeed in quelling the disturbance."[47]

The brief encounter unexpectedly provided the men with some comic relief, according to Lochren: "A large number of non-combatants were with us, regarding the rear as the place of safety. The panic among them was ludicrous, and the men shouted with glee as the crowd of sutlers, surgeons, chaplains and negro servants broke and rushed, in terror and disorder, from the vicinity of the rapidly bursting shells. 'De'il tak the hindmost!' was evidently the guiding sentiment,' as, with all speed, they went ahead, ridding themselves of all incumbrances."[48] Lochren recalled being "greatly amused by the antics of my own colored boy Tobe, a . . . young contraband, who carried in a large basket, usually on his head, the provisions of Colvill, Heffelfinger, and my self":

> He was marching that morning in unusual pride, in a new pair of coarse cotton pants having up-and-down stripes of bright yellow, blue, and white. He started with the others at the first shot, but at the scream of every fresh shell would throw himself on the ground, grasping his load and running again after the explosion. A strong skirmish line soon drove off the artillery, and after going on three or four miles we found Tobe about the only darkey who had carried off his load. But his gaudy pants had given place to ragged blue. "Lieutenant," said he, "dem pants was too bright. De Rebs seed 'em, and didn't fire at nuffin else but just dem pants."[49]

Wright remembered that the "shells were sufficiently depressed to do damage and one of them struck the hind legs of Col. Colvill's horse, tumbling man and horse into the muddy road. Fortunately the colonel was able to clear his feet from the stirrups and quick-witted enough to roll out of the way of the struggling animal. He got to his feet without suffering any serious injury, but he was well-plastered with a coating of dull red, Virginia mud." Retrieving his personal effects, Colvill resumed "his place at the head of the regiment and continued the march on foot."[50]

Marching in the rain that afternoon, the regiment followed what Henry called a "zig-zag course" through Haymarket and Sudley Springs. By now the rough roads had taken their toll on the new shoes that had been issued in Falmouth, and many of the men were virtually barefoot. "We are obliged to halt frequently to allow the [baggage] train time to get out of the way," Isaac wrote. "Our march today has been through a beautiful plain with gently undulating surface. It seems to be better cultivated & better supplied with apple & peach orchards than most parts of Va. through which we have passed. The prevailing timber is oak." That night they bivouacked at Gum Spring, according to Henry: "Ike and I lay down in the rain without supper, but plenty of mud."[51]

"The drum beating Reveillee waked me up this morning & reminded me that I was a Soldier & suffering his comforts," Marvin wrote the next day. "My stockings wer soaking wet & my cloths wer nicely damp & as long as I lay still I was warm & all rite but when I would change position Oh cracky the cold chills would run all over me warm. . . . On starting out we thought that the nite had transfered us from Leight to heavy infantry our cloaths & knapsacks wer wet & hung down heavy." In the late morning Isaac came to the place where he had joined the regiment more than a year and a half before: "We come in sight of the 'old familiar hills' of 'My Maryland' & soon halt on the brow of a hill overlooking Edward's Ferry."[52]

The regiment kept coming back to the same places: Bull Run, Centreville, Harpers Ferry, Alexandria, Edwards' Ferry. Geographically, it was still a small war, at least for the Army of the Potomac. The men spent the rest of the day watching other troops cross the Potomac on pontoon bridges until it was their turn. Judging from the similarity of their diary entries, it is likely that the Taylor brothers were passing the time together counting pontoons. Isaac: "There are two pontoon bridges across the river, one above & the other below Goose Creek. Upper bridge is 1360 feet long & had 64 pontoons. Lower bridge, 66 pontoons." Henry: "There are two pontoon bridges here, one above and one below Goose Creek. The upper bridge is 1360 feet long and has 64 pontoon boats." They finally crossed the river at 10:00 p.m. and bivouacked a few miles from Edwards' Ferry. "Gen. Lee's main force is reported to be in Md. & Pa.," Isaac recorded that night. "We shall probably pay our respects to him one of these days."[53]

On 27 June the regiment passed through Poolesville and Barnsville before halting at 11:00 p.m. at the foot of Sugarloaf Mountain. "Just as we get fairly asleep we are roused up to go on picket," Isaac said. "The *mild* expressions that fall from the lips of the weary soldiers of the 'veteran 1st' show that they are in no amiable mood." Marvin, still feeling the effects of his wound, awoke in a similar mood: "It was awful hard work to get up for the bones hung to the ground like grim death to a dead Nigar."[54]

The following day, refreshed, the men passed through Urbana before camping on the Monocacy River within sight of Frederick, Maryland. "We had a delightful march through Maryland," Colvill would recall. "It was just before harvest—golden wheat fields beautiful as ever we saw; a rolling well watered rich country, dimpled with woods; the South Mountain range in the distance on the west, the people all of the Union, and crowding, to see us, in the highways."[55] Henry echoed Isaac's thought of two nights before: "I presume we will meet the enemy in battle ere long."[56]

President Lincoln, whose confidence in Hooker had been shaken by his performance at Chancellorsville and then shaken further when Hooker proposed to march on Richmond instead of pursuing Lee, became convinced that his commanding general would not conclusively engage the Confederate army. Hooker had allowed Lee's forces, strung out for miles on end, to cross the Potomac unmolested. What's more, he was starting to sound a lot like McClellan: he was badly outnumbered . . . he needed more troops before he could engage Lee . . . Washington didn't understand or support his needs. It was all too much for Lincoln, who decided to replace him, although it was evident that a major battle would likely be fought within a matter of days.

In Hooker's place Lincoln named George Gordon Meade, an irascible and short-tempered career officer who had displayed competence, if not brilliance, in earlier campaigns. While his specialty was military engineering—he had helped build the defenses around Washington in the early months of the war—he had steadily gained the confidence of his superiors as commander of a brigade on the Peninsula, a division at Antietam, and the Fifth Corps at Chancellorsville. Isaac's response to the news on 28 June was typical: "The intelligence that 'Fighting Joe' is superceded by Gen. Meade falls on us 'like a wet blanket.' "[57]

Lochren recalled that the report "caused a momentary depression" among the men, many of whom, like Isaac, knew that they had been badly led.[58] They believed they were doing their part to put down the rebellion, and all they wanted was competent and consistent leadership. Specifically they wanted McClellan back. McClellan had turned them into an army and had made them feel good about being one and about themselves. The wish soon turned to rumor, as reports swept the Army of the Potomac that Little Mac had been restored to command. Marvin thought it "to good news to be true that Mc was our commander again I did not see a man in any Regt but what wished it was so."[59] But it was not so.

The next day there was a new sense of urgency to the march as the regiment covered a full thirty-three miles, crossing the Monocacy River three times before making camp that night at Uniontown, near the Pennsylvania border. "The day was extremely hot," Lochren remembered, "the roads dusty, and at the halt the men were so exhausted that most of them dropped at once on their blankets, without attempt to make coffee or do more than nibble a little handtack and raw pork."

Lochren recounted an incident that day that led to the arrest and removal of the regiment's colonel, just as battle seemed imminent:

> About three hours on the road we came to a considerable creek, crossed by fording something more than knee-deep, and having a timber, hewn on top, crossing it . . . for pedestrians. To allow the men to cross these timbers would impede the march, and Col. Charles H. Morgan, the efficient inspector general of the corps, remained here, directing each regimental commander to march his command right through the water. The direction was given to Colvill as we approached, . . . [b]ut a few of the men and line officers skurried across on the timbers, losing no time, and saving themselves from scalding feet in the long day's march before them. Morgan became angry, and having some further trouble with the Fifteenth Massachusetts Regiment which followed next behind, and being groaned by that regiment when he passed our brigade at a halt shortly after, and believing that act of insubordination to come from our regiment, he caused Col. Colvill to be placed in arrest. This act produced a strong feeling of resentment in the men, who felt that their colonel was most unjustly dealt with.[60]

Henry Taylor, a veteran of two years and countless marches, didn't make it the distance: "My feet are so sore I had to fall out one and one-half miles from camp, and after getting 'sick leave,' several others and myself planted our weary bones under the boughs of a stately oak." Those who reached Uniontown that night, however, were rewarded. "The women brought out bread, milk, cakes and pies and gave to us, and very few would take any pay," Bassett wrote the next day. "They all gave freely. They had no warning of our approach, and were happy to see us as they had expected the Rebs."[61]

When they finally halted for the night, Lochren remembered, the men were "so weary that we dropped down for sleep without care for supper, Heffelfinger and I, as usual, doubling and sharing our blankets. We had just lain down when I heard my name called by the adjutant to go with the picket detail. It seemed impossible to move again, but there was no help for it; and I thought I could detect in Heffelfinger's profuse and sincere condolences an undertone of satisfaction that the lot had fallen on me rather than on him. I could not blame the feeling, and gathering the grumbling detail . . . we went about three miles farther and posted pickets. Morning was long in coming."[62]

Henry rejoined the regiment the next morning, the men were mustered for pay, and Isaac, tired of hardtack and raw pork, went off in search of something better: "I go 'out arround' to farm houses & get bread, butter, milk, eggs &c. A good Union lady gives me a quart of apple butter. We live on the 'top shelf' to day. The boys are enthusiastic in their admiration of Maryland generally & the nice bread and nice girls in particular." Mathew Marvin agreed: "Their is some fun in Soldiering in a country like this whare the citizens are about half humane."[63] The officers accepted an invitation to attend a dance in Uniontown that evening.

As they passed into Pennsylvania the next day some of the men noticed a different attitude among the people they encountered. John W. Plummer, a sergeant in Company D, wrote his brother that the area reminded him of "the poorer parts of Virginia, and the people like the Virginians, for they seemed perfectly indifferent to our army passing through." But he was struck by a group he believed to be "truly loyal," and "a very intelligent looking woman" in particular, who "said to us while passing, with much feeling, 'It gives us so much pleasure to see our good Union soldiers coming.' Many a fervent 'God bless you!' and 'Good for you!' were uttered by the tired and weary soldiers, And many, too, forgot their weariness and their loads, feeling that for such they could fight and endure any hardship without grumbling. One of our boys . . . said, 'Boys, who wouldn't fight for such as these?' Just that little expression, and the way it was expressed, seemed to put new life into all of us, and we resolved, if possible, to give them yet more pleasure by driving the invaders from their soil."[64]

On the morning of 1 July, according to Lochren, "the heavy sound of distant artillery soon put us on the march toward it." By late afternoon, he said, "we began to meet the crowd of cowards and camp followers, fleeing in terror, with their frightened tales of utter defeat and rout. As most of the soldiers wore the crescent badge of the Eleventh Corps, which was held in little respect since Chancellorsville, they received but taunts and jeers from the sturdy veterans of the Second Corps."[65]

Marvin recorded that the men "began to see teams & teamstirs Soldiers & Straglers mostly of the elevanth Corps they set all sorts of rumors afloat in the collume of Batteries taken & lost of whole Brigades lost & captured & that they had seen over sixty dead Cavalryman   all their rumors of hard fought battles went into one ear & out at the other.   The 2nd Corps has Soldiered to long to believe all they herd from the half moon [the insignia of the Eleventh Corps]." The sight of retreating bluecoats was followed by a report Isaac found just as foreboding: "The news that Gen. Meade has superceeded Gen. Hooker is confirmed. I shall hope for the best but I don't like the idea of changing commanders on the eve of a battle."[66]

By late afternoon the regiment learned for the first time the name of the place toward which it was headed. "At Taneytown we hear there has been fighting at Gettysburg to day," Isaac wrote. "At 8-45 P.M. we halt within a few miles of Gettysburg & bivouac for the night." The march from Fredericksburg had taken fourteen days, eleven of them actually on the road. The men had averaged more than fourteen miles a day, and they were exhausted. They were also jittery, especially the officers. Every time an order was issued, it seemed, it was quickly countermanded. "Three times we got permission to have fires & twice they wer put out," Marvin wrote; "four times we made coffee & three times we threw it away packed up and fell in."[67]

The Taylor brothers also made coffee and ate some hardtack before they finally spread their blankets and tried to sleep, but foreboding of what the next day could bring kept them awake. "We talked a few moments of the great battle that we expected in the morn," Henry recalled later. While Isaac was "indignant" at the conduct of the Eleventh Corps at Chancellorsville, Henry expressed confidence that "we could whip Lee if our forces were well handled, and our troops would fight."[68]

8

GETTYSBURG

"All I can give you is a soldier's grave."

Cut free from its supply line to Virginia, Lee's army split into three parts, which foraged their way leisurely through southern Pennsylvania. Longstreet's and A. P. Hill's corps were twenty-five miles northwest of Gettysburg, at Chambersburg; part of Richard Ewell's corps was an equal distance north of the city, at Carlisle; and the balance was farther to the east, at York. As usual, Lee was relying on Jeb Stuart's cavalry to tell him where the enemy was, and since he hadn't heard from Stuart, he assumed the Union army was nowhere in the vicinity and, doubtless, still south of the Potomac. He learned from a Confederate spy on 28 June, however, that the Northern forces, now commanded by Meade, were less than thirty miles away, at Frederick. Though Lee hadn't known where Meade was, Meade had a good idea where Lee was, and he was rushing north to engage him.

The Confederate commander became alarmed that his separated forces would be easy prey for the concentrated Army of the Potomac, and he sent couriers to Ewell's divisions at Carlisle and York with instructions to meet him at Cashtown, on the road from Chambersburg to Gettysburg. Waiting for the army to gather, one of A. P. Hill's divisions was ordered into Gettysburg to secure a supply of shoes that had been reported there, but on approaching the town on 1 July the Confederates ran into more than they had bargained for. The day before, Gen. John Buford, a savvy and experienced Union cavalryman, had arrived in the town with a division of horsemen and had immediately recognized its strategic value. Not only did roads converge on

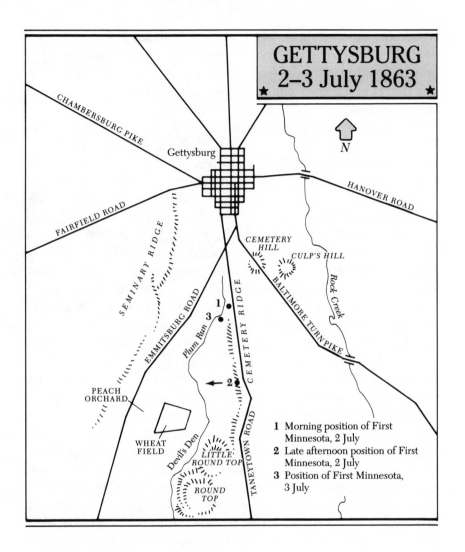

GETTYSBURG
2–3 July 1863

CHAMBERSBURG PIKE

Gettysburg

HANOVER ROAD

FAIRFIELD ROAD

N

SEMINARY RIDGE

EMMITSBURG ROAD

CEMETERY
HILL

CULP'S HILL

Rock Creek

BALTIMORE TURNPIKE

Plum Run

1

3

CEMETERY RIDGE

2

PEACH
ORCHARD

WHEAT
FIELD

Devil's Den

LITTLE
ROUND TOP

ROUND
TOP

TANEYTOWN ROAD

1 Morning position of First
   Minnesota, 2 July
2 Late afternoon position of First
   Minnesota, 2 July
3 Position of First Minnesota,
   3 July

Gettysburg from all directions but the hills behind it offered ideal defensive positions for the battle he and everyone knew was coming. If only he could hold off the Confederates until Meade occupied those hills, he reasoned, the Union might have an advantage similar to Lee's at Fredericksburg.

Buford's dismounted cavalrymen surprised Hill's men coming down the Chambersburg Road, just outside Gettysburg, and for two hours held back the much larger Confederate force with their new breech-loading carbines. Both sides called for reinforcements, and soon Union and Confederate forces began converging from all directions on this unlikely pastoral town of thirty-five hundred. Neither Lee nor Meade had planned to fight here, but once the fighting started, the town became a giant magnet, pulling both sides irresistibly toward it. Thus the largest battle ever fought on the North American continent, and the most important engagement of the Civil War, began—almost as an accident.

Buford got reinforcements from the First Corps in time to save his small force, but ultimately the greater Confederate numbers pushed the bluecoats back about a mile. At the end of the day it appeared to many of the Southerners that they were on the verge of another decisive victory. Their judgment was premature, however, because they underestimated the significance of Buford's achievement in keeping the heights behind Gettysburg out of Confederate hands.

On hearing news of the fighting, Meade dispatched Gen. Winfield Scott Hancock to Gettysburg to assess the situation and begin positioning the arriving Union troops for the continuation of the battle the next day. Now commander of the Second Corps, containing the First Minnesota, Hancock had become known throughout the army as "Hancock the Superb" after George McClellan, his friend since they were at West Point together, used the word to describe a brilliant maneuver Hancock had executed on the Peninsula as a brigade commander. McClellan gave him command of a division during the fighting at Antietam, and at Fredericksburg his men made it farther up Marye's Heights than any other Union troops. After his quick thinking at Chancellorsville helped prevent a defeat from turning into a rout, Lincoln gave him the Second Corps. He was smart and tough and a soldier from head to toe.

Like Buford, Hancock immediately recognized the strategic value of the hills around Gettysburg, and he laid out a defense line following their contours in the shape of an upside-down fishhook. The Union line would be anchored on the right by Culp's Hill, at the point of the hook, then it would swing west to Cemetery Hill, overlooking Gettysburg, before turning south for two miles along Cemetery Ridge to Little Round Top, a rocky hill that would anchor the left at the end of the fishhook's shaft. The plan was obviously the best use of the terrain because facing Cemetery Ridge a mile to the west was another ridge, roughly parallel to it and soon to be occupied by the Confederate army. To take the Union right, Lee's forces would have to scale two hills where the defenders would have enormous advantages; to take the center or left, they would have to cross open fields against massed artillery and musketry. Either way, Hancock figured, it was going to cost Lee more than he could afford to lose. Although he initially thought otherwise, Meade too became persuaded that this was where he should fight Lee, and he ordered the rest of the Union army to move forward during the night. When they were all in place, the Northern troops numbered eighty-five thousand. Gathering opposite them on Seminary Ridge and beyond were sixty-five thousand Confederates. There was little doubt but that the war would look very different after these two great armies clashed the next day.

Morning came early for the First Minnesota on 2 July, and if there was any doubt about what the day would hold, it was quickly dispelled. "Arroused at 3 A.M. & ordered to pack up & at 4 A.M. move towards the battle field where we arrive at 5-40 A.M.," Isaac wrote. "Order from Gen. Gibbon read to us in which he says this is to be the great battle of the war & that any soldier leaving the ranks without leave will be instantly put to death."[1]

It was a curious way to inspire men who had fought willingly and courageously for two years, but at least one Minnesotan thought the message as a whole was effective. "It was good," wrote Sgt. John Plummer of Company D, "and we all felt better after hearing it. . . . I have always thought it would do good to make these addresses to troops before going into action, to rouse their enthusiasm and make them fight much better. Napoleon used to and the Southerners do; but it is practiced little in our army. One thing our armies lack is enthusiasm, and no efforts are made to create it, when, in many cases, it would accomplish more than real bravery or bulldog courage; so I think at least."[2]

The morning was "foggy, sultry and murky," according to one of the men, who identified himself simply as "Sergeant" in an account for the St. Paul *Pioneer*.[3] The Second Corps was placed in a position on the ridge just south of the cemetery, but the Minnesotans were not put on the front line. "For some reason the . . . Regiment was not placed in this line," Lochren recalled, "but apparently in reserve, a short distance to the rear."[4] Confederate activity during the morning was relatively light, and it appeared that the Minnesotans' luck was holding. As the day wore on there was no sign of a major Confederate attack on Cemetery Ridge.

Colonel Colvill's superiors concluded that it made little sense to deprive the regiment of its commanding officer before a major battle, so he was released from arrest and returned to the First shortly after it arrived on the ridge. He later described the position of the regiment as "just behind the crest of the ridge, to the left of the cemetery; a few rods to the left, and in front of a small white building near the Baltimore Pike, having the appearance of a summer house, and which I understood was occupied a part of the day by General Meade. The artillery of the enemy commanded this position from the direction of Gettysburg, and from behind [Culp's Hill] and also from the low ground in front of Round Top, so that shells crossed each other over us, and we lost several men during the day from such as happened to drop in the ranks."[5]

Lochren, who was now serving as the regiment's adjutant, gave a similar account of the morning's action: "We lay quietly in a slight hollow, fairly secure from the enemy's shells, which came over us occasionally, killing one of our men and wounding another; and although there were some collisions of infantry in establishing positions, there was no protracted fighting during the forenoon." After the Confederate artillery opened on them, John Plummer wrote, "the way the ambulances, hospital men, stragglers and darkies did skedaddle for the rear, was amusing to those old fellows who had got used, somewhat, to such things as shells. . . . After laying there about two hours . . . we were ordered to get our things on and be ready to move, as the Third Corps on our left was going in, and we might be needed to help them."[6]

So much smoke lay over the field, according to Alfred Carpenter, a twenty-six-year-old sergeant in Company K, that it "shut the combatants from sight and we could only judge of the direction of the fight by the sound, but this was sufficient to tell who were retreating and who were advancing."[7] "Sergeant" described what he saw as the smoke lifted:

> Although obliged to keep low, to avoid the cannon balls and shells continually whistling and bursting above and around us, we now beheld a grand sight. Below and before us was the plain where the battle was raging. Every movement was discernable, and watched with the anxiety of spectators so deeply interested in the result; though but little of this could be seen in the faces of our boys, long accustomed to conceal their emotions on such occasions beneath the mask of reckless indifference. Presently the view was obscured, for, though the sun shone brightly, the air was damp, and the smoke lay heavily on the fight. Sometimes it formed a well-defined wall, following the lines of battle, and reaching from the ground straight up to the clouds. Through this the moving battalions—the forms of the combatants seeming gigantic in the haze—could be seen; but the positions of the batteries, more densely clouded, could only be discovered by the red flashes glaring through the darkness. Again the cause of all the turmoil, cheers and noise would be completely hidden, and none could tell how the battle was going. When, after such a moment, the wind would raise the veil, but few could repress a smile or an exclamation of delight, to see that "our flag was still there," and that our men were "crowding the fight."[8]

"The greater share of the 'Army of the Potomac' is here," Henry observed, and indeed it was.[9] Daniel Sickle's Third Corps, directly to the south of Hancock's Second, anchored the far left of the Union line near Little Round Top. Three other corps extended to the right and bent around Cemetery and Culp's hills. Still another corps was held in reserve, and one more was on its way, only a few miles distant. The previous day's delaying action and Meade's decisiveness—the latter an uncommon thing in the Army of the Potomac—made it possible for the Union now to have more than ninety thousand men at hand. What's more, they were in excellent defensive positions, which Lee would be compelled to attack.

Lee, whose forces had increased overnight to about seventy thousand men, believed he had no choice but to attack. After Chancellorsville he was supremely confident of his army's ability to defeat the hapless Northerners, and his men, their morale sky-high, shared that confidence. But James Longstreet, Lee's most trusted corps commander since Stonewall Jackson's death and a defensive fighter by instinct, disagreed. He urged Lee to move south around Meade's left flank, thereby getting between the Union army and Washington, then to take up a strong position and force the Union army to attack *them*. Lee would have none of it. Going on the defensive would destroy his men's morale, he believed, and the Union could not be relied on to repeat the folly of Fredericksburg. He had come North to fight a decisive battle with the Union forces, and he could do that successfully only if he had the freedom to outmaneuver and outwit his adversaries, as he had at Chancellorsville. He also believed that Union morale after two defeats on the Rappahannock was at an all-time low—a judgment not far from the truth—and that therefore the Northerners would likely break again under a vigorous assault.

Lee's plan called for Richard Ewell's corps to attack the Union right at Culp's Hill while Longstreet assaulted its left at the southern tip of Cemetery Ridge. The goal was to collapse one or both of the Union flanks, create confusion and panic in the rear area, and then roll up the Northerners toward the center of their lines. Lee had his hopes for success pinned on Longstreet's corps, and he urged his trusted lieutenant to get started as early in the day as possible. But the reason the Minnesotans witnessed so little activity, besides artillery fire, during most of the day was that Longstreet, for a variety of reasons, failed to get that early start. By the time he did get under way, about 4:00 p.m., he found the Union army where it wasn't supposed to be.

Gen. Daniel Sickles, commander of the Union Third Corps, at the southern tip of Cemetery Ridge, whose forces were to be the object of Longstreet's attack, was the only one of Meade's corps commanders who was not a professional military officer. Rather he was a flamboyant Tammany Hall Democrat who had scandalized Washington when, as a congressman, he became the first person to successfully plead insanity as a defense to a murder charge—in his case, for killing his wife's lover, son of Francis Scott Key. He embraced the Union cause once war broke out and, through assiduous cultivation of President and Mrs. Lincoln, became one of the North's most successful political generals.

Sickles's lack of military training and experience became evident on 2 July, however, when he concluded that he didn't much like the ground he had been ordered to defend and decided to do something about it. Because Cemetery Ridge virtually disappeared into flat farm-land as it ran south before meeting Little Round Top, it offered Sick-les's troops little, if any, natural protection against an attack from the west. A half mile directly ahead of him, however, Sickles spotted higher ground, which he believed would give him the advantage he lacked on the ridge. On his own authority he ordered his corps to advance to the new position. He assembled the center of his line in a peach orchard so that it formed a salient pointed straight at Seminary Ridge, while he affixed his left just to the west of Little Round Top in a labyrinth of boulders known as Devil's Den. Sickles had found the higher ground he was looking for, but in doing so he had left both of his flanks hang-ing in the air and thus dangerously exposed. He was a half mile in front of the rest of the Union line and effectively disconnected from it.

In the late afternoon Longstreet's forces hit Sickles's with an unyield-ing ferocity. "About 4 oclock the ball opened in earnest & such a racket is seldom herd in any battle," Mathew Marvin observed from the First's position, nearly a mile to the north; "it was huge in the extreme."[10] For the next few hours the fighting raged through the peach orchard, the wheat field, Devil's Den, and Little Round Top, often in hand-to-hand combat. Back and forth the tide of battle flowed; the wheat field alone changed hands six times. Sheer courage and a little luck enabled the Northerners to occupy and then hold Little Round Top, a rock-strewn hill that would have enabled the Confederates, if they had taken it, to rake nearly the entire Union line with artillery fire. But the Southerners finally broke through Sickles's line in the peach orchard, overpowering the Union salient with fire from three sides. Slowly at first, the Third Corps began to move back.

Seeing at once the danger created by Sickles's move forward, General Hancock had ordered parts of his own Second Corps to move a quarter of a mile to the left to fill the gap on Cemetery Ridge. According to "Sergeant," Hancock "in person moved our regiment, and posted it to the left of Battery A, Fourth United States Artillery, and behind the right division of the third corps." Lochren recalled that they "were sent to the centre of the line just vacated by Sickles' advance. . . . No other troops were then near us, and we stood by this battery, in full view of Sickles' battle in the peach orchard half a mile to the front, and witnessed with eager anxiety the varying fortunes of that sanguinary conflict."[11]

The regiment's position on Cemetery Ridge was now approximately midway between Cemetery Hill to the north and Little Round Top to the south. The ground sloped gently to the west some two hundred yards over pastureland until it reached Plum Run, in the midst of a swale, or marshy area. The creek bed, bordered on both sides by moss-covered rocks and clumps of brush and small trees, was dry that day. Beyond the run the ground began to rise again at the same gradual angle until it crossed the Emmitsburg Road and peaked at Seminary Ridge, three-quarters of a mile to the west. In the distance lay the Catoctin Mountains, running as far north and south as the eye could see.

The Minnesotans had a panoramic view of the vast field before them, but their attention was fixed on the peach orchard to the southwest, halfway between Plum Run and Seminary Ridge, where Sickles's men were engaged in a desperate struggle with Longstreet's corps. They were not reassured by what they saw. Plummer wrote that the men were

> ordered to lie down in front of the batteries, as the shot and shell were coming over pretty plentifully. From there we could look all over the field, seeing our lines, the rebs' lines and their batteries very plainly. As I saw our men fall back, rally, and fall back again, skedaddlers rushing to the rear in squads, I never felt so bad in my life. I thought sure the day was gone for us, and felt that I would prefer to die there, rather than live and suffer the disgrace and humiliation a defeat of our army there would entail on us; and if ever I offered a sincere prayer in my life, it was then, that we might be saved from defeat. We all felt bad, but resolved when our chance came to do our best to retrieve the fortunes of the day, hardly expecting to come out of the conflict unharmed."[12]

Finally the greater Confederate numbers and Sickles's exposed position tipped the battle to the South, and Longstreet's men began to push the bluecoats back down the slope toward the creek. The anonymous "Sergeant" saw the front line of Sickles's corps collapse:

> The second line met the attack gallantly and turned the enemy back. They charged again and for a while the contest was sharp and desperate—at this critical moment a fresh division of the enemy charged down—the Third Corps gave way and came to the rear in squads carrying back men, flags and wounded, and running over

our ranks in spite of all our attempts to rally them. The enemy's artillery poured grape and shrapnel into the retreating groups, and in return our Battery "A" opened upon the rebel infantry, who were advancing with loud cheers and pouring volley after volley into the broken lines of the Third. This turned their attention to the battery, and soon a dozen of their crimson battle flags, followed by as many regiments, were advancing towards it, its only support being our eight companies of the First Minnesota.[13]

Lochren recalled seeing the men of the Third Corps finally "broken and in utter disorder, rushing down the slope . . . across the low ground, up the slope on our side, and past our position to the rear, followed by a strong force—the large brigades of [Gen. Cadmus] Wilcox and [Gen. William] Barksdale—in regular lines, moving steadily in the flush of victory, and firing on the fugitives. They had reached the low ground, and in a few minutes would be at our position, on the rear of the left flank of our line, which they could roll up. . . . There was no organized force near to oppose them, except our handful of two hundred and sixty-two men."[14]

At that number the First Minnesota was considerably understrength, in part because three of its companies were on detached duty. Company C was provost guard at division headquarters, Company F was off skirmishing to the left, near Little Round Top, and Company L, a supernumerary unit of "sharpshooters" sometimes assigned to the regiment, was supporting an artillery battery on Cemetery Hill. If Sickles's men continued to pour through the First's ranks to the rear, it was apparent to everyone on the ridge at that moment that only these 262 Minnesotans stood between the advancing Confederate brigades and the Union rear. If the Southerners kept coming and managed to get over the ridge, they would split the entire Union line in two. They would then be in a position to create havoc by "rolling up" the Northern forces on the ridge all the way to Cemetery Hill and perhaps beyond, to Culp's Hill. It would be, in short, a Union disaster of immense proportions. Not only the day would be lost but almost certainly the battle as well. Lee would have the victory he had come north to seek.

"The stragglers came rushing through our lines, whom we in vain tried to stop and at last gave it up entirely, believing they were of more injury than help to us," wrote Alfred Carpenter.[15] General Hancock, who, among other things, had a talent for being wherever the greatest danger presented itself, appeared at this moment and, with Colonel Colvill's assistance, tried to stanch the panic of Sickles's men. When Sickles was wounded, Hancock had assumed command of the Third Corps as well as his own Second and had immediately begun sending reinforcements forward to bolster the beleaguered Third. But he was only able to slow, not stop, the Confederate advance.

"Gen. Hancock was with us," Colvill wrote, "and immediately dismounted and with all his energy sought to rally them. Our field and staff also dismounted and aided him. It was useless; they were perfectly demoralized. Then the rebel line, following, came in sight across the hollow, looming through the smoke, and pushed down the slope into the bottom, their left extended out on the terrace—we could not see how far. The last of Sickles' men had passed, and this skirmish line opened a scattering fire upon us. Then over the ridge came the rebels' first line and moved rapidly down into the hollow."[16]

Carpenter saw the Confederates coming "in two splendid lines, firing as they advanced, capturing one of our batteries, which they turned against us, and gained the cover of the ravine. The plain was strewed with dead and dying men. The Rebs had advanced their batteries and were hurling death and destruction into the ranks of the retreating men. They were nearing the hill, which if gained, the day was lost to us."[17]

Hancock had sent for reserves to plug the gap, but there was no way they could arrive before the Confederates reached Cemetery Ridge. He urgently needed to delay their advance for five minutes, or for however much longer it would take for reinforcements to appear. According to Colvill, Hancock looked at the 262 men of the First Minnesota and exclaimed, "My God! Are these all the men we have here?"[18] It was obvious that they were, and he then turned to the colonel and asked, "What regiment is this?" "First Minnesota," replied Colvill. "Charge those lines!" commanded Hancock, according to Lochren.* "Every man realized in an instant what that order meant—death or wounds to us all; the sacrifice of the regiment to gain a few minutes time and save the position, and probably the battlefield—and every man saw and accepted the necessity for the sacrifice."[19]

* Hancock remembered the wording of his order differently: " 'Colonel, do you see those colors?' Hancock asked, pointing to Wilcox's Confederates. When Colvill replied, Hancock spoke sharply, 'Then take them' " (Glenn Tucker, *Hancock the Superb* [Indianapolis: Bobbs-Merrill Co., 1960], 144).

There was no time for the men to reflect on the grim odds of surviving a charge against a vastly superior number of onrushing Confederates. According to Charles Muller, a twenty-nine-year-old French-born stonecutter from St. Paul, Colvill stepped in front of the regiment and asked the men, "will we go along . . . and we answered yes."[20] "I immediately gave the order, 'Forward, double-quick,' " Colvill said, "and under a galling fire from the enemy we advanced." Later he recalled that the men "started down the slopes in a beautiful line," which they tried hard to maintain as they quickened the pace.[21]

With bayonets fixed, officers and men were running downhill in a line extending nearly one hundred yards from end to end, although to call the incline a hill would be to exaggerate. It was an ever so gradual slope extending two hundred yards across two fields to the swale at the bottom, now heavy with smoke from Confederate firing. "In a moment," according to Lochren, the regiment was "sweeping down the slope directly upon the enemy's centre." The full force of Gen. Cadmus Wilcox's brigade of nearly 1,600 Alabamans was now focused on the 262 advancing Minnesotans, and artillery shelling combined with accurate musketry to deadly effect. "Bullets whistled past us," Carpenter said, "shells screached over us; canister and grape fell about us; comrade after comrade dropped from the ranks; but on the line went. No one took a second look at his fallen companion. 'We had no time to weep.' "[22]

One of those hit was Mathew Marvin: "We had not fired a musket & the rebs were fireing rappedly I droped to the ground with a wound some whar I picked my self up as quickly as possible when I saw blood on my shoe the heel of which was tore out I thought it a slight one & run to ketch up thinking that no rebel line could stand a charg of my Regt & if the Bayonet must be used I wanted a chance in as it was free to all I had just ketched up when I fell a second time to Faint to get up."[23]

"Sergeant" was acting as file closer for his company, bringing up the rear to keep stragglers from falling back:

> Now their cannon were pointed to us, and round shot, grape and shrapnel tore fearfully through our ranks, and the more deadly Enfield rifles were directed to us alone. Great heavens, how fast our men fell. . . . It seemed as if every step was over some fallen

comrade. Yet no man wavers; every gap is closed up—and bringing down their bayonets, the boys press shoulder to shoulder and disdaining the fictitious courage proceeding from noise and excitement, without a word or cheer, but with silent, desperate determination, step firmly forward in unbroken line. . . . Three times [our] colors are shot down—and, three times arising go forward as before. One fourth of the men have fallen, and yet no shot has been fired at the enemy, who paused a moment to look with awe upon that line of leveled bayonets, and then, panic-stricken, turned and run; but another line took their place—and poured murderous volleys into us, not thirty yards distant.[24]

"Silently, without orders, and, almost from the start," Lochren remembered, "double-quick had changed to utmost speed":

for in utmost speed lay the only hope that any of us would pass through that storm of lead and strike the enemy. "Charge!" shouted Colvill, as we neared their first line; and with leveled bayonets, at full speed, we rushed upon it; fortunately, as it was slightly disordered in crossing a dry brook at the foot of a slope. The men were never made who will stand against leveled bayonets coming with such momentum and evident desperation. The first line broke in our front as we reached it, and rushed back through the second line, stopping the whole advance. We then poured in our first fire, and availing ourselves of such shelter as the low banks of the dry brook afforded, held the entire force at bay for a considerable time.[25]

"We could not see our comrades fall," "Sergeant" recalled, "when every faculty was absorbed in the one thought of whipping the enemy in front. I know we reached the brink of the little run and gave them one volley which swept them from the earth; but a new line rises from the bed of the run at our feet, and a brigade advances down the hollow on our right; both open fire and our men fall, many pierced by balls, both from the right side and front, which crossed each other in their courses through the body. We fire away three, four, five irregular volleys, and but little ammunition is wasted when the muzzles of opposing guns almost meet. The enemy seemed to sink into the ground. They are checked and staggered."[26]

Sergeant Plummer's Company D was on the left of the Minnesota line, moving at a slower pace than those on the right. As Plummer recounted the charge later, the exasperation of his comrades was apparent:

> We went forward on a run, and with a yell, till about half way across the second field, when we were ordered, for some unaccountable reason to us, to halt, and the bullets were coming like hailstones, and whittling our boys like grain before the sickle. "Why don't they let us charge?" cried all of us. "Why do they stop us here to be murdered?" Everyone seemed anxious to go forward, and some run way out ahead and beckoned for us to come on. We have always believed that a determined charge would break any line, and that more would be accomplished and less life lost, than by lying down and firing two or three hours. We felt that we could check and force them to retreat, and we wanted to go against them with a vengeance and get over the deadly ground as soon as possible. We were halted again when across the second field, and though by this time few were left, we were just as anxious to go forward. We were almost together and the rebs had nearly flanked the right of the regiment. But what surprised me most was to see some of the rebs, not fifty yards from us, standing out openly and loading and firing as deliberately as though they were in no danger whatever. Oh! There is no mistake but what some of those rebs are just as brave as it is possible for human beings to be. I expected they would turn and run when they see us coming so determinedly, and I believe they would, had we went right on.[27]

Almost as soon as the regiment reached the swale, it lost its colonel. "I was immediately behind the colors," Colvill remembered.

> Owing to the blinding smoke, we could see distinctly only at intervals. There was a gleam of light, in which my glance took in the slope on my left. I saw numbers of our men lying upon it as they had fallen. Then came a shock like a sledge hammer on my back bone between the shoulders. It turned me partly round and made me "see stars." I supposed it was a piece of shell. Just then I perceived Capt. Coates who said "Colonel, you are badly hurt." I said "I don't know; take care of the men." Just then I was putting my foot on the ground; there was a sharp pang through it; it gave way, and falling forward to

the ground I saw just beside me a gully not more than two feet wide and less in depth. As I struck the ground I rolled over into it, and listening among other things to the bullets "zipping" along the ground, and thought how fortunate for me was the fact of the gully.[28]

The regiment's number two officer was also disabled. Lt. Col. Charles Adams was struck five times before a ball hit him square in the chest and tore through his lungs and back, finally putting him out of action. The number three and four officers, too, were wounded, each of them twice, leaving the regiment without a single field officer. Command fell to Capt. Nathan Messick of Company G, who ordered the men to take cover in the shallow creek bed behind the boulders and to fire at will at the rebels, some of whom were only a few yards away. The Minnesotans were now fighting individually or in small groups; communication among them was all but impossible, and the rebels were at such close quarters that it was a matter of every man for himself.

"Had the enemy rallied quickly to a counter charge," Lochren concluded later, "its great numbers would have crushed us in a moment, and we would have made but slight pause in its advance. But the ferocity of our onset seemed to paralyze them for the time, and although they poured upon us a terrible and continuous fire from the front and enveloping flanks, they kept at a respectful distance from our bayonets."[29]

The Confederates had been stunned by the effect of this small but determined force descending on them as they struggled through the marshy bogs on both sides of Plum Run. Catching the rebels by surprise at a moment when they were partially disorganized was a stroke of luck for the Minnesotans, the only one they would see that day. The charge, all five minutes of it, had stopped the Confederate advance, which, of course, was Hancock's goal in ordering it. Thus, for the moment at least, the threat to the Union line on Cemetery Ridge was removed. "The bloody field was in our possession," Carpenter wrote, "but at what a cost! The ground was strewed with dead and dying, whose groans and prayers and cries for help and water rent the air."[30] Among those on the ground was young Charley Goddard, hit in both the leg and the shoulder.

Only about 150 men had made it the full distance from Cemetery Ridge to the swale; they were badly outnumbered, and when the

Confederates regained some degree of order the Minnesotans would be in danger of being overwhelmed. At dusk, the Southerners began to extend their line around the regiment's right, eventually subjecting it to enfilading as well as frontal fire. The creek bed was poor cover to begin with, but now, with fire coming from two directions, it was almost useless. Yet the men had to stay where they were to buy the precious minutes Hancock's reinforcements needed to come up. The minutes seemed like hours to them. It also seemed as if the entire war had descended on them, as indeed it had. Their return fire came more infrequently as the Confederates picked them off one by one, an easy task at short range. When Lt. Chris Heffelfinger, a house painter from Minneapolis, got to his feet to survey the field, he was hit immediately. Ernest Jefferson of Company E was struck in the leg. As the rebels fired, they gradually moved so far around the regiment's right that they endangered its rear.

"By the time the ditch or gully was reached," Colvill remembered, "[the enemy's] fire was delivered into the backs of the First. This fire was returned by one or two companies on our right, the remainder of the line firing on the rebels in front. It was flank fire which wrought ruin in the ranks of the Minnesota regiment. It continued for what seemed an endless time. Had it been daylight, not a man could have escaped death, wounds or capture."[31] But even in semidarkness the position was untenable, and about fifteen minutes after the regiment had reached the creek bed Colvill ordered Captain Coates to lead it back to the ridge line. As soon as the withdrawal began—and none too soon—the Eighty-second New York, the First's companion regiment, arrived on the right to relieve the pressure. At the same time a full brigade appeared on the left, and the Minnesotans were no longer alone.

Charles Muller fired his first round at the Alabamans as he reached the bottom of the slope. Then, he recalled, "I stood bihind a Brush and reloded my Gun and as I was redy to fire I just stapt to the right of the Brush when a [Confederate] coller sargent cam up on the other sid of the Brush and calld for the other to folow him and just as [he] dit so and move his flag I held my gun up to him and fired wen the pure man fell down   then I begin to see for my friends but the most of them have gone or wer shot down   then I started to run out of it to but wen I got out on the fild the enemis flanks had so mush advanzed that the[y] wer only about 50 yards apart and I had to go trouht ther and just as [I] went trought that point a man from my left dit rais his gun and point at me and fired and hit me in my right tigh but as it hapen did not Brok my boon so I Kupt on running up to the open fild in a ziksak way."[32] Muller eventually made it back to the ridge and was escorted to the hospital in the rear.

Marvin was also trying to make his way to the rear, but his foot wound made it extremely difficult. "I drank some watter & put some on my head & rists then I tried to walk to the rear   was to week for that so after resting again I tried the hands & knees," he wrote that night. "I got in the rear of our batteries when I divested myself of Gun & Equipment & Knapsack. When Charley North gave me a helping hand to the Hospital behind a big rock he was slightly wounded. . . . the ambulances came & took us to the rear. I have got about all the pain I can stand."[33]

Not everyone heard the order to retreat, and as a result the withdrawal was confused and sporadic. Company E had been especially hard hit, and Sgt. Henry Taylor found himself in a situation he had doubtless never anticipated: "Order to 'fall back' and about 50 of us rally on the colors amid a storm of shell and bullets, and I find that I am left in command of Company E."[34] Every other officer and sergeant in the company was either dead or wounded. The dead, of course, had to be left behind, and the wounded who were unable to walk had to fend for themselves. Some crawled back toward the ridge while others sought shelter behind boulders and small trees to avoid flying bullets as well as capture.

"We dreaded to go back for the danger of it, more than staying there," Plummer recalled, "and we felt though only obeying orders, that we were being disgraced to fall back when we knew we could hold our own. We fell back, and it was then I had the first feeling of fear during the fight. I felt almost sure I would be hit, and I saw many wounded going back. When we got back to the colors, where we rallied, scarce 25 men were to be found. Most who went in were killed, wounded, or helping off the wounded. The enemy advanced no further, and soon some of our boys who did not fall back when ordered, came in bringing in prisoners, and they said when we fell back the rebs were making for the rear as fast as possible. It was now about dark."[35] Once the Minnesotans were reinforced, Wilcox broke off the engagement and also withdrew. For the Minnesotans, the fighting of 2 July was over, but not the dying.

∎ ∎ ∎

"What Hancock had given us to do was done thoroughly," Lochren wrote. "The regiment had stopped the enemy, and held back its mighty force and saved the position. But at what sacrifice! Nearly every officer was dead or lay weltering with bloody wounds, our galant colonel and every field officer among them. Of the two hundred and sixty-two men who made the charge, two hundred and fifteen lay upon the field, stricken down by rebel bullets, forty-seven were still in line, and not a man was missing. The annals of war contain no parallel to this charge. In its desperate valor, complete execution, successful result, and in its sacrifice of men in proportion to the number engaged, authentic history has no record with which it can be compared."[36] The Minnesotans' casualties were extraordinarily heavy: 82 percent of those engaged, if Lochren's figures were accurate, the highest pecentage of casualties suffered by any Union regiment in a single engagement in the entire war.* But the losses in Wilcox's brigade were also heavy. Although not all its losses were due to the engagement with the First Minnesota, the Alabamans began the day with more than seventeen hundred men and ended it with fewer than a thousand.

All that remained was the care of the wounded and the burial of the dead. "A few of us went back to look for our wounded," Henry Taylor wrote, and of course he was looking for Isaac, who had not returned from the swale with the rest of Company E. Instead he found Colonel Colvill, who later recounted the experience of lying helpless where he had fallen: "I saw it grow dark; then it became quiet. I saw the stars shining out overhead. Presently I heard the voices of our men. The boys were then looking up the dead and wounded. I heard some of them talking with the wounded, in one case where their search had found a comrade, and they were taking his last words for his home and family."[37]

Henry feared the worst: "I help our colonel off the field but fail to find my brother who, I suppose, is killed. I rejoin the regiment and lie down in the moonlight, rather sorrowful. Where is Isaac?" Henry helped carry Colvill, with wounds to the left shoulder and the right

---

* Uncertainty remains both as to the precise number of Minnesotans engaged in the charge of 2 July 1863 as well as to the number of casualties. The research of Robert W. Meinhard of Winona State University led him to conclude that there were at most 179 killed and wounded, a casualty rate of 68 percent (Meinhard, letter to Tom Harrison, chief historian, Gettysburg National Military Park, 20 May 1982; Meinhard, letter to author, 10 Dec. 1990).

ankle, to a large stone barn being used as a hospital in the rear of the Union lines. Lieutenant Colonel Adams, also badly wounded, was taken to the same place. "Wm. Ramsey, Cal Jackson and myself went down unto the field to do what we could for the wounded," Edward Bassett wrote, "and as fast as the stretchers and ambulances could be got they were borne from the field to the hospitals."[38] Corp. Henry D. O'Brien found Ernest Jefferson, who had been hit in the leg, and helped him off the field. Jefferson would survive, but, like many others that day, he would lose his limb.

Alfred Carpenter too was among those looking for the wounded: "The sun had gone down and in the darkness we hurried, stumbled over the field in search of fallen companions, and when the living were cared for, laid ourselves down on the ground to gain a little rest, for the morrow bid faire for more stern and bloody work, the living sleeping side by side with the dead. Thousands had fallen, and on the morrow they would be followed to their long home by thousands more. Canister and shrapnel had made horrid gaps, and as the ranks were closed up we counted files, scarcely a hundred men were left out of the three hundred and more who were with us in the morning. Two out of every three had fallen."[39]

After the wounded had been gathered and sent back to hospitals, the regiment was ordered to return to the position it had occupied in the morning, about a quarter of a mile north on Cemetery Ridge. On the way John Plummer became convinced that the day would be lost yet: "As we were going to the right to join the brigade, musketry was heard very plain, seemingly scarce half a mile off, and completely in our rear; in fact, some of the bullets whistled over our heads. Now we were sure that the battle was gone for us, for the fighting continued fierce, and seemed growing nearer all the time. We made up our minds that we were whipped, and expected before morning to see the whole army routed, and flying for Baltimore. The prospect was gloomy and discouraging in the extreme. . . . The firing soon ceased on the right and what seemed our rear; the troops were got in their places, and put in position for the contest, whenever it should open again."[40]

"Leaving our boys to the tender mercies of doctors and hospital attendants, we moved our 'squad' to the designated point," "Sergeant" reported. "Tired and weary, we might not sleep, or even build fires to make coffee, but rested on our arms all the long, damp, drizzly night, in wakeful anticipation of an attack." Plummer had no difficulty sleeping: "I here say I never slept better and had more pleasant dreams in my life than I had on the battlefield at Gettysburg, with dead men and horses lying all around me; but the excitement and exhaustion had been so great that a man could sleep in any condition, and under any circumstances."[41]

Henry Taylor did not record how he slept, but it's likely he thought of little besides Isaac's fate. Early the next morning he received news:

> About 8:30, Mr. Snow of Company B tells me thinks he saw my brother, and I accompany him to the spot, and I find my dear brother dead! A shell struck him on the top of his head and passed out through his back, cutting his belt in two. The poor fellow did not know what hit him. I secured his pocketbook, watch, diary, knife, etc., and with Wm. E. Cundy and J.S. Brown buried him at 10 o'clock a.m., 350 paces west of a road which passes north and south by the house of Jacob Hummelbaugh and John Swisher (colored) and equi-distant from each, and by a stone wall where he fell, about a mile south of Gettysburg. I placed a board at his head on which I inscribed:
>
> > No useless coffin enclosed his breast,
> > Nor in sheet nor in shroud we bound him,
> > But he lay like a warrior taking his rest,
> > With his shelter tent around him.[42]

Henry gave the complete inscription on the headboard when he made the last entry in Isaac's diary, dated 4 July 1863: "The owner of this diary was killed by a shell about sunset July 2d 1863—his face was toward the enemy. . . . The following is inscribed on a board at his head:

> I. L. Taylor
> 1st Minn. Vols.
> Buried at 10 O'clock A.M. of July 3d, 1863
> By his brother
> Sergt P.H. Taylor
> Co. "E" 1st Min. Vols.[43]

It wasn't until three days after he buried Isaac that Henry notified his parents. Whether he wasn't able to write sooner or couldn't bring himself to the painful task he doesn't say, although the latter is more likely, since he found time each day to write in his diary.

>Two Taverns, five miles from Gettysburg, July 6, '63
>
>Dear Parents:
>
>I scarcely dare write you that my dear brother who has shared many privations with me on more than one battlefield has fallen. He was killed by a shell about sunset on the 2nd inst. on the field of 'Gettysburg,' and was buried by two of my comrades and myself at 10 o'clock A.M. 3rd inst. The shell took off the back part of his head, passed out his back cutting his belt in two—instantly killed. A few moments before, he, with the rest of our Reg., charged the enemy, and all of our Co. officers were lost, and I was left in command of the company.
>
>We were engaged again the 3rd inst., with loss. Our Reg. lost over two-thirds of its number during the two days' fight; but thanks be to God the victory is ours. I have Isaac's things and will send most of them home but I shall keep his watch with your permission. He wished Father to have his Diary, and expressed a desire that the one he sent to Russell should fall into Father's hands—this before he was injured.
>
>I will write more as soon as I can and give you all the particulars. . . . Isaac has not fallen in vain. What though one of your six soldiers has fallen on the altar of our country. 'Tis a glorious death; better die free than live slaves. Pleas make no arrangements for his funeral until you hear from me again, and I will write more fully. He wrote in his diary while on the field of battle before killed. I cannot express to you my sorrow at his loss. I feel as though I was all alone.
>
>Your and my country's,
>Henry[44]

It was nearly two weeks before Henry wrote the promised, more complete account, and when he did it was to his older sister Sarah, to whom both he and Isaac had been close since childhood:

>Camp near Snicker's Gap, Va. July 19, 1863
>
>My dear Sister:
>
>I wrote father of the death of our dear student brother, Isaac. I will now speak more fully of his death. After we crossed the

Potomac at Edward's Ferry, he seemed in excellent spirits and frequently spoke of the Maryland Campaign's being more pleasant than campaigning in Virginia. The citizens were pleasant and obliging, frequently giving food to the soldiers.

While we lay at Uniontown, June 30, Isaac went into the country and bought some bread, butter, pies, eggs, etc., and a young lady *gave* him a quart of apple butter. When he came in, a few of his comrades including myself, had a good feast (see his diary). We were that day 'Mustered for Pay' for the months of May and June. The First of July we bivouaced at 9 P.M. about four miles from the bloody fields of Gettysburg. He made coffee for both of us while I helped to build a barricade, and we then sat down on our knapsacks, ate some hard bread, drank our coffee, spread our blankets and rubbers, and using our knapsacks for pillows, lay down to rest. We talked a few moments of the great battle that we expected on the morn. He was confident we could whip Lee if our forces were well handled, and our troops would fight. He was very indignant at the conduct of the 11th Corps at Chancellorsville—thought Hooker a Good Genl., but said his troops did not stand by him. Little did I think this was the last time I would camp with Isaac, yet I was aware of the probabilities of loss in action.

July 2 we moved to the field early as you will see by Isaac's diary. On a half sheet of paper in his diary you will find a memorandum till four p.m. July 2nd. I wish you would copy that in this book when it arrives. It commences, aroused at . . . He speaks there of H. & I take a cup of coffee. . . . I made a cup for him and myself and this was the last we ate and drank together.

The enemy were then shelling us, and the Infantry was rather sharply engaged at times. We then moved one fourth of a mile to the left and front and shortly after were ordered by Gen. Hancock to charge the enemy who were making for our batteries. Hancock says the charge was made in gallant style. I saw several of our company fall before we fired a gun. We still pressed on at double quick. I thought I saw Isaac fall—no time to stop then—faltering might decide the battle against us—half of our regiment had fallen—the Col gave the order to "fall back." I repeated the order—our colors stood firm, and the men would not leave. "Fall back, fall back" was repeated along the line, and the color bearer (three had been shot and the fourth had the colors) turned and march slowly back, and the men obeyed the order, several being wounded in "falling back."

We rallied on the flag at the place we started from to make the charge. Col., Lt. Col, Major and Adjutant were all wounded besides many line officers. Company E went in with thirty-eight men, including the two commissioned officers, three Sergts., six corporals, and twenty-seven privates. After the "charge," we were one Sergt., two corporals (one of them slightly wounded) and five privates! How changed in fifteen minutes! I was now in command of the company. I was one of a small party who volunteered to return to the field where our brave had fallen—we found many of our comrades and assisted them off.

I looked for Isaac till about 9 P.M. but could not find him. Corporal Austin said he saw him after most of our Regt. had fallen back—he had just fired his gun and turned his head around with a kind of smile, and soon after he saw him falling back. I knew he was either killed or wounded, for had he been unharmed he would soon have been with the Regt.

Isaac was a brave soldier, and his calmness and coolness in action had been spoken of frequently by many of his comrades. I have always been proud of his conduct in battle. I rejoined the Regiment about 10 P.M. and lay down in line of battle. The enemy had been repulsed and we held our position. The dead and wounded were all around me but I must rest on arms and be ready for another battle. I slept a little. July third, half past eight, a man of Company G (Snow) was coming up with coffee for some of the officers, and saw Isaac lying dead—he told me he thought he saw my brother—killed. I went with him to the spot and found it to be too true, secured his things—knapsack, haversack, and canteen were gone, he probably threw them off when he went into action. I found a spade and took William E. Cundy and James L. Brown of Co. E and went and dug his grave. We laid him down with all his clothes on, as he fell, and spread a shelter tent over him. As we laid him down, I remarked, Well, Isaac, all I can give you is a soldier's grave. I then sat down on a stone while the two comrades buried him. I was the only one to weep over his grave—his Father, Mother, brothers and sisters were all ignorant of his death, but we must hurry back for an engagement is momentarily expected. It was ten o'clock when we finished burying. . . .

July 20, 1863 A.M.

You will see by Isaac's Diary where he was buried. Hummelbaugh has lived there 17 years and Fisher (colored) 12 years, I believe. I wish his remains could be taken up and buried in some burying ground near there, if not moved to Ill. Please keep everything in his Diary when you get it till I explain to you where he got many of the little things in it. He thought a great deal of his "blessed trio" as he called them, Mattie Keyes and two others. I took the case off, wrote Isaac L. Taylor, Co. E., 1st Minn. Vols. He has five brothers in the army, in it, and laid it on his brest when I buried him. I buried his accoutrements also. Isaac was always studying something and from his knowledge of military tactics, he was frequently called "Tactic" by the boys to distinguish him from the two other Taylors in the company. He sent a work on Geology and one on Botany to C.C. Coggswell, Washington, D.C., the 18th for safe keeping.

Hope you will have a funeral sermon preach for Isaac by some-one and give me a full account of it.

> Affectionately yours,
> P.H. Taylor[45]

Like the day before, 3 July began early for the Minnesotans. "Red and fiery through the morning mists at length arose the sun," "Sergeant" recalled. "The forenoon passed as did the previous one," which is to say with a minimum of activity. "Most of us," Plummer said, "got some coffee during the forenoon, by going one or two at a time back to the rear, where they were allowed fires and cooking, which, of course, greatly refreshed us. A man's appetite generally, during a battle, is not very voracious."[46]

During the night Company F had returned from its skirmishing assignment off to the left and rejoined the regiment. The "depressing news" of the regiment's fate had reached the company earlier, according to James Wright, the university student turned sergeant, who said it "at first almost stunned us, though we were expecting bad news." The reunion was filled with emotion: "Going down the line, past the weary, sleepy men, we found Capt. N.S. Messick, with the colors and what was left of the regiment—47 men, who had not been hit, and a few that had. We had not been separated far, or long, but the greetings were as sincere and earnest as if oceans had divided us and years had elapsed. There was a flood of inquiries about the missing ones, and the answers left no doubts in our minds of the awful calamity that [had] befallen the regiment."[47]

On what already promised to be a hot and humid day, the men took up positions on the slope of Cemetery Ridge facing west toward Seminary Ridge—and Lee's army—nearly a mile away. The Minnesotans were almost directly in the center of the Union defense line stretching down the ridge, and they spent much of the morning getting ready for the attack they were sure was coming. "We gathered rails, stones, sticks, brush, &c. which we piled in front of us," Wright remembered, "loosened the dirt with our bayonets and scooped it onto these with our tin plates and onto this we placed our knapsacks and blankets. Altogether it made a barricade from 18 inches to 2 feet high that would protect against rifle bullets. . . . After an examination of our rifles and ammunition, which each man was told to make and refill his box from the extra ones we carried, we laid down behind the little shelters we had made and went to sleep." Wright reported that one of his comrades in Company F "was hit by a sharpshooter, the ball passing through his shoulders, and making a remarkably loud noise so that some thought at first it was an explosive bullet, but an examination showed that the ball had passed through numerous folds of his rubber blanket."[48]

Company C, which had also missed the action of the previous day, was still detached as provost guard at division headquarters, where it was the custom to wear full dress uniform. Lt. William Harmon recounted being at the headquarters when General Meade, General Hancock, and General Gibbon, the division commander, arrived for lunch:

The mess chest was taken from the mess wagon and the generals sat down together to eat and discuss the battle. I was standing near by and heard all their conversation. In the course of it, Gen Meade said to the others:

"Lee has concentrated his 160 guns in his center, and will soon open fire on our center. Our arty. will answer, and for a while there will be a grand arty. duel. After it is over, Lee, having massed his inf., will attack our center in force. There will be close and desperate fighting, so desperate that every available man must be used. Gen. Gibbon, see that all your provost guards are sent to the front after the arty. ceases firing."

At the conclusion of this accurate prediction of what Lee would do, Gen. Gibbon turned to me and said: "Do you hear that, Harmon?" "Yes," I answered. "Well, see that your co. is there."

Almost at this moment Lee fired his two signal guns for the action to commence. One of the shells decapitated Gibbon's orderly, frightened the mess wagon horses so that they overturned the wagon; and the three generals scurried away from the spot where the fire was centered. In a minute it was a very center of death and destruction. We all lay low while the arty. duel lasted.[49]

Plummer and several of his comrades were on the regiment's forward position, listening to one of their lieutenants read accounts from a Baltimore newspaper of the day before, when a shell landed twenty yards away:

> That stopped the reading; each man took his place, laid down, and for the next two hours hugged the ground just about as close as human beings are generally in the habit of doing. The first gun was the signal for a hundred more to open, at less than half a mile distance, which till then their existence was perfectly unknown to us. Such an artillery fire has never been witnessed in this war. The air seemed to be filled with the hissing, screaming, bursting missiles, and all of them really seemed to be directed at us. They knew our exact position, for before we lay down they could with the naked eye plainly see us, but, fortunately, most of them just went far enough to clear us, while many struck in front of us and bounded over us. We lay behind a slight rise of ground, just enough, by laying close, to hide us from the view of the rebs. A good many shell and pieces struck mighty close to us, and among us, but strange to say, none of us were injured, while the troops that lay behind us had many killed and wounded. Our batteries replied, but for the first time in our experience, they were powerless to silence the rebs, and, in fact, many of our guns were silenced. So many of their horses and men were killed that they could not work their guns, and drew them off the field. Caisson after caisson blowed up, and still the rebels' fire was fierce and rapid as ever. I kept thinking surely they cannot fire much longer, their guns will get so hot they will have to stop, and they cannot afford, so far from their base, to waste so much ammunition. It was awful hot where we lay, with the sun shining down on us and we so close to the ground that not a breath of air could reach us. We kept wishing and hoping they would dry up, as much to get out of the heat as the danger, for the latter we thought little of.[50]

The ferocious two-hour artillery duel left an indelible impression on everyone who experienced it, including Lochren: "We had been in many battles, and thought ourselves familiar with the roar of artillery, and with the striking and bursting of its missiles, but nothing approaching this cannonade had ever greeted our ears." Wright said that he was not particularly surprised when the shelling began but was soon "astonished" by its intensity: "The enemy's guns formed an arc of nearly a quarter of a circle, the distance was from 1500 to 2000 yards; it quickly converged its fire on the ridge and principally on that portion of it held by the Second Corps and [Gen. Abner] Doubleday's division of the First. There was an incessant, discordant flight of shells, seemingly in and from all directions; howling, shrieking, exploding, tearing, smashing and destroying; producing a scene that words cannot present and was well nigh unbearable."[51]

"Many of their shot, fired from batteries to the west of us, passed clear over our 'horse shoe' and fell among their own men, facing us from the east," "Sergeant" wrote.

> Imagine our position in the center. Our artillery opened as vigorously in return, and now the scene became sublime. The roar was terrific and deafening, and cannon balls, bursting shell, grape, canister, shrapnel, railroad iron and Whitworth bolts from England, and even sledges, caisson bolts and spikes, and iron in every imaginable shape, was tearing up the ground and flying with horrible screeches, as of invisible demons, through the air, dismounting cannon, shattering limbers, mangling thousands of horses and men, tearing through trees and houses, and destroying everything, while ever and anon an ammunition caisson would explode, scattering destruction for yards around, carrying fragments of timber, wheels, clothing and bodies high into the air, and shooting up swift volumes of smoke, to join the dense white clouds rolling up to the sky from all parts of the field. The batteries and others whose duty it was, were, of course, exposed, but all other living things sought shelter from the terrible storm, and the scene brought before the imagination that great day when men shall call upon the mountains and rocks to fall upon and hide them.[52]

As awful as the shelling was, the veterans knew that what would follow would be worse. "As we lay there," Henry Taylor wrote, "we were talking of what was yet to come, for we knew that the Infantry would be sent forward as soon as shelling slackened, and then the men must fall. As it began to slacken, Gen. Gibbons who commanded our Division, walked along the line in front of us, seeming to say, Boys, this is the way to face danger. We all noticed it and many said, See there, see Gen. Gibbons."[53]

Many of the shells that "Sergeant" saw passing over landed in the hospital area just to the rear, where Mathew Marvin and his wounded comrades thought they would be safe. As Marvin described in his diary, that was far from the case:

> I thought that if the rebs had a shell for me that it could not kill me any younger & that they cant do it but once   For about an hour the shell came pretty thick & those that could crawl up near the Tre whare I was. A solled shot came & struck whare a man had just got up not more than ten ft from me   That made me think that I had just as leave be a thousand miles from here as not another shell went through the top of the apple tree over us   I was laying by the side of my capt who was wounded in the head the ball entering at the nose & came out back of the left ear in taking care of him I got pretty well covered with blood as he bled a goodeal   he wanted to go back to the front so I had to hold him most of the time   I had got over being faint & could crawl on my hands & knes   the Ambulances soon came & took us about 2 miles to the rear whar they had established the hospital in a hollow near a creek. . . . we wer all rite at last.[54]

Back on the ridge, Carpenter saw a shell tear the knapsack off a man as he lay prone. "There were over two hundred guns at work in this part of the line," he said. "firing as fast as men could load them."

> The noise it produced . . . is indescribable. I can think of no adjective and collection of adjectives that will describe it. It must be seen, heard, felt, to be understood. Now a wounded man attempts to go back to a hospital and perhaps is cut down before he can gain the rear of the ridge fifteen rods behind us. A case of sunstroke and his comrades start to carry him off; perhaps one of their number is looped off; perhaps all pass uninjured. By turning on our backs we can see our artillery, It is getting roughly handled. A dozen of our caissons have already exploded. Gun after gun is dismounted by the solid shots of the enemy. Here is a battery abandoned because there are not enough men left to work it or horses to take it off. There is a battery of Napoleons in the same situation, because the guns have become so heated that cartridges explode before they

can be rammed home. There goes a battery to the rear because they have no more ammunition. Our fire begins to slacken. "Have they silenced our Artillery?" is the anxious question that flashes through our minds.[55]

The Union artillery had not been silenced but the Northern generals wanted Lee to believe it had. Ammunition was running low on both sides; Lee's goal was to force Meade to use his up, while Meade was determined to save as much as possible for the infantry attack that he had predicted would come at his center. "At length our artillery ceased to reply," Lochren wrote:

> We were surprised at this, thinking that we excelled the enemy in this arm. The Confederate fire appeared to increase in volume and rapidity for a few minutes, and then stopped at once. We well knew what was to follow, and we were all alert in a moment, every man straining his eyes toward the wood, three-fourths of a mile distant, from which the Confederate infantry began to emerge in heavy force, forming two strong lines, with a supporting force in rear of each flank. . . . Moving directly for our position, with firm step and in perfect order, our artillery soon opened upon them with terrible effect, but without causing any pause, and we could not repress feelings and expressions of admiration at the steady, resolute style in which they came on, breasting that storm of shell and grape, which was plainly thinning their ranks. When about sixty rods distant from our line our division opened with musketry, and the slaughter was very great; but instead of hesitating, the step was changed to double-quick, and they rushed to the charge.[56]

It was Gen. George Pickett's division of Longstreet's corps and two divisions of A. P. Hill's corps, fifteen thousand men in all, coming across the open field toward Cemetery Ridge. Pickett had arrived at Gettysburg late and had not seen action during the first two days of the battle. Worried that his Virginians would miss the chance altogether, he pleaded for an opportunity to fight on the third day, and he got it.

At the end of the previous day's fighting, Lee had concluded, as he had the day before, that he had nearly defeated the Northern forces and that with one more determined effort they would collapse. He still believed he was facing the same dispirited and badly led Army of the Potomac that he had overwhelmed on the Rappahannock. But most important, he had come north resolved to win a conclusive battle. Having attacked both the Union flanks on the second day, he believed that Meade must have moved troops from the center to bolster them, thus leaving the center thin. He proposed to send Ewell's corps against Meade's right flank and Jeb Stuart's cavalry into Meade's rear so they would be in position to exploit the success of the main Confederate assault against the center. Longstreet tried to dissuade Lee from going forward with the plan on the grounds that an assault of fifteen thousand men over nearly a mile of open field against artillery and protected infantry could not possibly succeed. But he failed to convince Lee, who ordered the attack to proceed.

The broad ranks of Confederate infantrymen moved inexorably toward the Union line, down the gradual slope of Seminary Ridge, across the floor of the shallow valley, and up the western slope of Cemetery Ridge, unimpeded by wheat fields, stone walls, rail fences, marshes, or a ravine. The aiming point for the Confederate attack was a clump of trees on the crest of Cemetery Ridge, approximately four hundred feet to the right of the Minnesotans' position. If the assault kept coming at the ridge in a straight line, nearly its full force would hit the First, which, with the return of Company F and others who had been detailed for special duty, now numbered about 150 men. Captain Messick was still in command.

"[W]e could see near the center of the advancing line," Wright remembered, "as they came down towards the Emmitsburg Road."

> It was a magnificent spectacle. A rising tide of armed men rolling toward us in steel crested billows. It was an intensely interesting sight, especially to us who must face it, brest it, break it—or be broken by it. The tense inaction of hours was ended and we hastily made preparations to meet this avalanche of bayonets that was being projected against us. The line was adjusted, advancing it a few paces for better position, then, front rank kneeling, we awaited their coming and the order to fire. Command was given not to fire until ordered—and then to fire at their feet. This was to correct, as far as possible, the tendency to overshoot.[57]

"Over the plain, still covered with the dead and wounded of yesterday—in three beautiful lines of battle, preceded by skirmishers, with their arms at right shoulder shift, and with double quick step—right gallantly they came on," said "Sergeant." "What was left of our artillery opened, but they never seemed to give it any attention. Calmly we awaited the onset, and when within two hundred yards we opened fire. Their front line went down like grass before the scythe, again and again we gave it to them."[58]

The Union artillery was concentrated heavily on its left, on the lower part of Cemetery Ridge and on Little Round Top, and its impact helped force the advancing Confederates toward the Union right. "From the Cemetery near the town to Little Round Top there was a mighty thunder of guns and shrieking chorus of flying shells," Wright said.

> The whole ridge was wreathed in smoke and flame, and the sulphurous vapor whirled in clouds around us. It was a deadly, and effective fire, too, but not enough to stop them or turn them back; but the right of their line did seem to shrink to its left, and its supports appeared to separate from it, as they got the full force of the fire. When they crossed the Emmitsburg Road . . . they were still 500 to 600 yards from the right of our division. At this time the right of Picketts division appeared to change its direction to the left, by a partial wheel or oblique movement exposing it to a flank fire. Gen. Hancock was quick to see this and prompt to take advantage of it by ordering the advance of [Gen. George J.] Stannard's brigade. By this movement they were able to get an effective enfilading fire on [Gen. James L.] Kemper's Confederate brigade, which was [to] the right of Pickett's division.[59]

When the men received the order to fire, according to Wright, they "sent a rolling fire to the right oblique, directed at their feet, which was about all we could see of them at the time, as all above their knees was covered with the smoke from their own guns. Then every man fired as rapidly as he could handle cartridges and adjust caps." As the Union muskets opened up, Carpenter recalled, "men stagger from their ranks by scores, hundreds, thousands; but on they come like an inrolling wave of the sea. They have gained a part of our line; the rest of their line is within a few rods of us; but torn, bleeding, decimated, they can come no farther, but are determined not to yield, for they halt, plant their colors, and wait for their reserve to come up. Time after time these colors fall, but are quickly caught up until scarcely a man is left around them. Their support advances but our artillery pour into them such a fire that they reel, turn and fly."[60]

"Well," Edward Walker wrote his friend George Knight after the battle, "we *mowed* them down—twas Fredericksburg reversed—the first line went down in no time and the others broke—many throwing down their arms and rushing for our lines—Perhaps we didnt feel good when we saw them scatter? It appears their officers had told them that the Militia was fighting them and would break and run at their approach—*but* they found it *somewhat* different. As one of their men gave himself up he says—'Militia be d- -'d—we've seen these flags before.' " Walker soon felt a bullet pass through his canteen, "making the water fly a little."[61]

As the surviving rebels hit the Union line near the clump of trees they had used as an aiming point—the spot would soon become known as the "high-water mark" of the rebellion—the First Minnesota and the other regiments in Harrow's brigade received orders to leave their positions and charge headlong into the Confederate flank. At this moment the men of Company C, still attired in full dress uniform from provost guard duty, were reunited with the regiment entirely by accident. "We had hardly begun to advance when [Captain Farrell] was killed," Lieutenant Harmon recalled. "Just as we were going into action, I caught sight of Heffelfinger, so it happened by chance that we fought near the rest of the First. Minn., though we had not been with them during the battle. I was struck in the belt by a bullet, but, in the excitement, didn't feel my hurt enough to keep still and, getting up, went into the melee with the rest of the co."[62]

The firing at close range couldn't help but be effective as the Northerners closed on the Confederates. "The fire from both sides, so near to each other, was most deadly while it lasted," Lochren recounted.

> Corp. Dehn, the last of our color guard, then carrying our tattered flag, was here shot through the hand, and the flagstaff cut in two. Corp. Henry D. O'Brien of Company E instantly seized the flag by the remnant of the staff. Whether the command to charge was given by any general officer I do not know. My impression then was that it came as a spontaneous outburst from the men, and instantly the line precipitated itself upon the enemy. O'Brien, who then had the broken staff and tatters of our battle flag, with his characteristic bravery and impetuosity sprang with it to the front at the first sound of the word charge, and rushed right up to the enemy's line, keeping it noticeably in advance of every other

color. My feeling at the instant blamed his rashness in so risking its capture. But the effect was electrical. Every man of the First Minnesota sprang to protect its flag, and the rest rushed with them upon the enemy. The bayonet was used for a few minutes, and cobble stones, with which the ground was well covered, filled the air, being thrown by those in the rear over the heads of their comrades.[63]

For his bravery in leading the Minnesotans into the fray, O'Brien would be awarded the Medal of Honor.

As the men charged the enemy's exposed flank, they threw every bit of energy they had into the assault. "It was a grand rush to get there in the quickest time," Wright wrote later, "without much regard to the manner of it—and we knew very well what we were there for—and proceeded to business without ceremony. Closing on them with a rush and a cheer; there was shooting stabbing and clubbing, for there was no time to reload. . . . We rushed for the low wall where the break had been made, and very quickly all who passed it were killed, captured or had fled."[64]

The fighting quickly became frenzied, according to Harmon: "If men ever become devils, that was one of the times. We were crazy with the excitement of the fight. We just rushed in like wild beasts. Men swore and cursed and struggled and fought, grappled in hand-to-hand fight, threw stones, clubbed their muskets, kicked, yelled and hurrahed. But it was over in no time. . . . When the line had passed, those who were not wounded threw down their arms. I remember that a Conf. officer . . . gathered himself up as our men swept by and cooly remarked, 'You have done it this time.' "[65]

Captain Messick was hit and fell dead, leaving the regiment leaderless for the second time in two days. General Hancock and General Gibbon were also struck down,* but, according to Plummer, the absence of commanders made little difference to the outcome in this kind of fighting. Each man "fought on his own hook," he said, and

---

* Hancock was hit by a minié ball that entered his groin after passing through his saddle and his right thigh, carrying with it pieces of wood and a bent nail, probably from the saddle. After removing the nail from his wound by himself, he told those around him, "They must be hard up for ammunition when they throw such shot as that" (Tucker, 155–56).

"acted as though he felt what was at stake in the contest, and did all in their power to drive the enemy, without regard to officers, or whether there was any or not." "Sergeant" agreed: "Orders were unnecessary. The fight had become a perfect melee. . . . The enemy had halted and were firing on us from behind some bushes. We pushed on; they fired till we reached the muzzles of their guns, but they could not stand the bayonet, and broke before the cold steel, in disorder and dismay."[66]

The men were exhilarated by their involvement in the battle, as well as by the direction it was taking. "Our boys felt bully during all the fight," Plummer wrote, "and no one thought of running or of the danger. . . . We took revenge for what they had done to our poor fellows the day before, and never had had such a chance before. Most of us fired over twenty [rounds], and at close range enough to do splendid execution; and if we didn't kill some secesh in that battle we never did, and I fear never will during the war."[67]

"For two hours we had fought desperately," Carpenter wrote a few weeks later. "Our muskets became so heated we could no longer handle them. We dropped them and picked up those of the wounded. Our cartridges gave out. We rifled the boxes of the dead. Artillerymen from the disabled pieces in our rear sprang forward, and seizing guns and cartridges of the wounded, fought by our side as infantrymen. Many of the men became deaf, and did not recover their hearing for a day or two. It was a grand and terrible scene."[68]

The Minnesotans had plunged into the midst of the Twenty-eighth Virginia, and during the pandemonium that followed Pvt. Marshall Sherman of Company C captured the regimental colors, an act for which he too would win the Medal of Honor. (Daniel Bond of Company F would later maintain that the flag bearer of the Virginia regiment had leaned his colors against a tree before surrendering and that Sherman, closer to the flag than Bond, had beaten him to it.[69]) At almost the same time, Corporal O'Brien was hit, and a new bearer, Corporal Irvine, retrieved the colors and kept the men moving.

It was apparent now that Pickett's division was spent and had no choice but to fall back. "As soon as the smoke lifted sufficiently to permit us to see," Wright recalled, "all that could be seen of the mighty force . . . was scattered and running to the rear."

That is—all that were able to run. The bodies of many unfortunate victims marked the course of the assault. Some of these lay still, where they had fallen, and others were trying to find some safer place. It is very encouraging, at a time like that, when you have done your best, and know it, to see the backs of your enemies, and the space between you and them widening. It was so satisfactory that our fellows could not refrain from cheering as we ceased firing and realized the situation. It was an occasion worthy of cheers—if ever—despite the fact that many were dead and dying.[70]

Some of the men did not realize the fighting was over, according to Lieutenant Harmon:

When the rebs were throwing down their arms and surrendering by the thousands, Gen. [Joseph] Hays rode along the line swearing like a pirate, as the best of men sometimes will in battle. He was trailing a Conf. flag in the dust behind his horse and was shouting "Stop firing, you - - - - fools; don't you know enough to stop firing; it's all over—stop! stop! stop!" Then our company was ordered to the front to pick up the straggling prisoners. We advanced clear to the Emmitsburg Road, gathering up the defeated men and sending them to the rear. I remember that one Confederate private tried to get me to overlook a slightly wounded officer. A little later a straggler lying in a fence corner drew a bead on me, and was about to shoot, when I covered him with my revolver and told him to drop his gun. He did, too, and it was all I could do to keep the boys from killing him.[71]

The Minnesotans would be credited with capturing five hundred prisoners.

Suddenly it was all over. The men collapsed, physically and emotionally drained. "For about 65 hours we had been under almost constant physical or mental strain—or both—and had pretty nearly reached the limit of both, and, as soon as the need for further exercise of muscles or will ceased to be imperative, most of the men realized that they were bordering upon a condition of collapse," Wright recounted. "Those who have not had the experience cannot easily understand how the intense energies necessary to carry men through days of action and excitement, and worked to the utmost in such struggle, use up the vital forces; but those who have 'been there' do not need to be shown."

Wright did not realize until later that his neck and face were bleeding. He had been hit in the shoulder and breast "with shreds of lead and splinters of wood, and several of the latter were driven into the side of my face and neck. . . . A more careful inspection showed that the splinters were of seasoned walnut. They must have come from a gunstock and the lead from a bullet that struck something harder at the same time, but I never knew whose gun or more about it."[72] His experience was nearly identical to that of Henry Taylor two years earlier, at Bull Run.

The battlefield, strewn with the dead and wounded, was a scene that shocked even the most hardened veterans. "The sights on the field were horrible; by far the worst of any field we have seen," Plummer said. The Minnesotans, now under the command of Capt. H. C. Coates of Company A, were marched back to their original position on the ridge. "The field is ours," Carpenter wrote his family, neglecting to tell them that he had been wounded twice. "Can we not go and care for the wounded? No, another attack is expected, and every man must be in his place. Hospital attendants must take care of the wounded till darkness closes down about us. Then we go supperless to sleep; our bed, Mother Earth; our covering, the broad canopy of the starry decked Heavens; the unburied dead sleeping around us."[73]

Bassett had the sad duty of seeing to Capt. Nathan Messick, a close family friend from Rice County. "I helped carry his body from the field perhaps a half hour after the Rebs were driven back," he wrote his parents of the man who had led the First Minnesota into battle that day.

We took him back to the Field Hospital where his cook took charge, staying with him until an ambulance took him to the Generel hospital. His sword and pocket book were taken from him within fifteen minutes after he fell. Who took them, I dont know. There was perhaps $15.00 in it. There was a gold watch in his pocket, that belonged to Col. Adams, who was wounded the day before. It was returned to Col. Adams. I was not present when he was buried. My duty called me to the front, and I returned at once to my place. After we laid him down, I was looking at him for the last time, and thinking if there was anything more that I could do, that would do any good. I asked Mr. Williams, his cook, to take off his shoulder straps and send to his wife, which he did. I am sorry that we couldent save his sword, but in a battle like that there are lots of things one would like to do, but cannot. The Rebs were still shelling us with some long range rifled cannon on the side of the mountain. He died at his post, doing his duty. Thousands fell that day the same way. Capt. Messick died as he would wish to die, fighting for his country. . . . I do not wish to write or say anything that will cause Mrs. Messick any more sorrow. Please give my respects to Mrs. Messick. Tell her that we are trying to keep up the reputation of the Minn. 1st.[74]

In Company F, Sergeant Wright and his comrades managed to care for the dead and wounded before caring for themselves.

We now began to realize that we were getting hungry, and in the gathering darkness we built little fires and made coffee. None of us knew where we were likely to be, or what the morrow would bring for us to do, and as we drank our coffee we decided to bury Hamlin that night. Search was made for a spade and after some time a shovel was found. With this a shallow trench was dug beside a walnut tree, near which he had been killed, struck by four bullets. His blanket and tent-cloth were spread in it, he was then laid upon them and covered with the remaining portions. Then those present knelt in silence about him, with uncovered, bowed heads. I do not recall that a word was spoken; but it was a sincere and reverential service fitting the time and the situation. Then we covered him over with the dirt and stones we had thrown out of the trench and placed at his head a board, on which his name, company and regiment, had been marked.[75]

Philip Hamlin was twenty when he enlisted and twenty-three when he died. He had been the first sergeant of Company F, and Wright greatly admired him: "He was always and everywhere an honest, earnest, consistent, christian man; whose open, unostentatious, frank, manly and unobtrusive observance of what he considered his religion was well-known and respected by all who knew him. . . . Deprecating war, loving and praying for peace, he was fighting for his government as the performance of a sacred duty he owed to it and to God. He had the most implicit faith in an 'over-ruling Providence' and seemed to feel that, no matter what happened to him personally, all that he was fighting for was certain to be accomplished. The results were a splendid vindication of his sublime faith."

Soon there was nothing left to do but sleep. "Sancho Panza invoked a blessing on 'the man that *invented* sleep,' and it is a blessing," Wright reflected, "not only to the exhausted body but to the disturbed mind."

> It is true we were no longer the sensitive, sentimental youngsters we were when we left our northern homes. Mere sentiment had been knocked out of us by the actual experiences of years of active war; military training and everyday surroundings had tended to repress expressions of feeling and had changed us to seasoned soldiers; but no one, though but moderately endowed with common sense and no more than the ordinary amount of compassion in his make-up, could fail to sympathize, deeply, with the overwhelming amount of suffering that existed and which they were powerless to relieve. Tens of thousands were suffering from wounds, many were dying every hour; and many still living considered those already dead more fortunate than themselves. It was indeed a blessing, a gracious blessing, that our exhausted bodies and over-wrought minds could find respite and renewal in sleep.[76]

While the outcome of the battle was immediately apparent to everyone on both sides, the full extent of the human carnage was almost beyond comprehension. More than fifty-one thousand men—nearly one out of every three engaged—had been killed or wounded during the three days of fighting. Some twenty-eight thousand Southerners had fallen, and twenty-three thousand Northerners. After two years of a war that had already claimed thousands of young lives, the numbers would shock the nation—and the world—as nothing had before.

The enormity of what the Union army had accomplished was slow to dawn on the Minnesotans. The Confederates had thrown their best forces at them and they had held—they had defeated Lee! They had known nothing but defeat and frustration for so long they could hardly believe it. They had fought better than they had ever fought before, but they had paid an extraordinarily heavy price, the full extent of which stunned them. On 3 July the First Minnesota had suffered 55 additional casualties, 23 of them killed or mortally wounded. "Our loss of so many brave men is heartrending," Captain Coates wrote Governor Ramsey two days later in his official report, "and will carry mourning into all parts of the state. But they have fallen in a holy cause, and their memory will not soon perish. Our loss is 4 commissioned officers and 47 men killed; 13 officers and 162 men wounded, and 6 men missing— total 232—out of less than 330 men and officers engaged."[77] As staggering as these numbers were, Coates understated the fatalities. There were, in fact, at least 80 Minnesotans killed or mortally wounded during the two days and another 149 wounded. Seventy percent of those actually engaged in the fighting—229 men—had fallen.[78]

After three days of fighting in which many units had distinguished themselves, the contribution of the First Minnesota, especially on the second day, wasn't immediately apparent to those who hadn't actually witnessed it. General Hancock, having ordered the charge, was one of the few who had seen it, and in his report to Secretary of War Stanton he singled out the regiment for unusual praise: "Proceding along the line, I met a regiment of the enemy, the head of whose column was passing through an unprotected interval in our line. A fringe of undergrowth in front of the line offered facilities for it to approach very close to our lines without being observed. It was advancing, firing, and had already twice wounded my aide, Captain Miller. The First Minnesota Regiment coming up at this moment, charged the rebel regiment in handsome style, capturing its colors, and driving it back in disorder. I cannot speak too highly of this regiment and its commander in its attack, as well as in its subsequent advance against the enemy, in which it lost three-fourths of the officers and men engaged."[79] Although the report was incorrect in three respects—the Confederate unit was a brigade, not a regiment; the First was not "coming up" but already on the scene; and the Minnesotans did not capture the enemy's colors— Hancock never failed to acknowledge the regiment's performance and sacrifice.

He later told Senator Morton Wilkinson of Minnesota, "I had no alternative but to order the regiment in. We had no force on hand to meet the sudden emergency. Troops had been ordered up and were coming on the run, but I saw that in some way five minutes must be gained or we were lost. It was fortunate that I found there so grand a body of men as the First Minnesota. I knew they must lose heavily and it caused me pain to give the order for them to advance, but I would have done it if I had known every man would be killed. It was a sacrifice that must be made. The superb gallantry of those men saved our line from being broken. No soldiers, on any field, in this or any other country, ever displayed grander heroism."[80]

But the statement of Hancock's that helped immortalize the charge was simple and unequivocal: "There is no more gallant deed recorded in history."[81]

The night of 3 July 1863, the men of the First Minnesota were not thinking of history or of their role in it. They were thinking simply of victory and death, of coffee and sleep. Henry Taylor was thinking of Isaac: "I feel that I have partly avenged the death of my brother."[82]

EPILOGUE

T
he next morning, the Fourth of July, the men awoke fully expecting a resumption of the fighting. Hancock had, in fact, urged Meade to follow up the destruction of Pickett's force with an assault on Lee's weakened line, but Meade, content with what he had achieved and not eager to jeopardize it, decided to settle for his success of the day before. In the now well-established pattern of Union commanders in the eastern theater, Meade permitted another opportunity—one that could perhaps have ended the war right there—to slip away.

In a final homage to his brother, Henry Taylor placed stones around Isaac's grave before he and the rest of the Union army began to follow Lee south. Meade missed still one more opportunity when he allowed the Southerners to cross the Potomac unmolested. The two armies played the same cat-and-mouse game they had played a year earlier, after Antietam, with Lee masking his movement south on the western side of the Blue Ridge as the Union forces shadowed him from the other side, skirmishing at the gaps along the way.

Arriving back on the Rappahannock, the Minnesotans learned that they had been ordered to New York City to help maintain order while the new draft was being conducted. Rioting had disrupted the first attempt, a few weeks earlier, and, with military manpower needs no longer satisfied by volunteers, the administration was taking no chances on a recurrence. The Minnesotans believed they had been selected for the assignment largely as a reward for their heroic performance at

Gettysburg, and it was indeed a pleasant interlude for them. They spent two agreeable weeks in the city, where the draft was carried out without incident.

But the men's appearance showed the unmistakable evidence of their recent experience. As they were marching through Brooklyn on 28 August, a woman who had seen the regiment leave Fort Snelling more than two years earlier watched as the battered but proud unit passed by. She was moved to write the St. Paul *Press* of the effect the scene had on her:

> As I saw this little fragment of the once splendid Minnesota First march by me, carrying their stained and tattered flag, scarcely a shred of which is left, except the design close by the staff, and take their places in line of battle just as they stood on that bright morning more than two years ago at Fort Snelling, when so many of us were there and heard General Gorman's last directions and Mr. Neill's prayer previous to their breaking camp and embarking for the war, and their glorious destiny, I absolutely shivered with emotion. There the brave fellows stood, a grand shadow of the regiment which Fort Snelling knew. Their bronzed faces looked so composed and serious. There was a history written on every one of them. I never felt so much like falling down and doing reverence to any living men. The music of the band, as the men went steadily through the changes of the drill was very sweet, but it seemed to me all the while like a dirge for the fallen."[1]

The regiment returned to the Rappahannock in time to join the rest of the Union army in following another of Lee's thrusts north, this time a seeming race toward Washington. After several days on the march, A. P. Hill's Confederate corps tried to surprise the rear of the Union column but was itself surprised by the Minnesotans and the rest of the Second Corps at Bristoe Station. It was an unqualified Union victory. Hill's attack had been stopped cold, and Lee's entire offensive had been knocked off balance. The Federals had inflicted nearly 1,400 Confederate casualties and took an additional 450 prisoners; the First Minnesota was credited with capturing 322 of them. The regiment also seized five cannons and two sets of enemy colors. Their own casualties were comparatively light: 1 killed and 16 wounded. Again, the regiment had acquitted itself with the "coolness" for which it was renowned.

Lee was forced to abandon his offensive, and he sought safety once more below the Rapidan River. Now it was Meade's turn to go on the offensive. He led his army across the river in an unsuccessful attempt to catch Lee off guard. The Minnesotans spent a long, cold night at Mine Run waiting for the signal guns to announce the begining of a charge they believed few, if any, of them would survive. In the end Meade was persuaded that the assault would only lead to senseless slaughter, and another Fredericksburg was averted.

Mine Run was the regiment's last campaign, and the men spent the next several months in winter quarters, planning their postwar lives. They came under heavy pressure to reenlist in sufficient numbers to keep the regiment intact, but many of them resisted out of dislike for Lt. Col. Charles P. Adams, who would be their new commanding officer. Others were tempted to sign up again by the prospect of generous bonuses and furloughs.

In February 1864, they began their journey home, stopping first in the capital, where most of official Washington turned out to honor the regiment whose feats at Gettysburg had made it famous. Lincoln never made it to the lavish banquet at the National Hotel, but Vice President Hannibal Hamlin and Secretary of War Edwin Stanton led an outpouring of cabinet members, senators, congressmen, and other officials in heaping praise on the new heroes from the West. Colonel Colvill, just released from a hospital in Philadelphia but still unable to walk, was carried into the room by two members of the regiment to loud cheers from the rest.

The First Minnesota retraced the route that had brought it east nearly three years before, passing through Pennsylvania, Ohio, Indiana, and Illinois before reaching LaCrosse, Wisconsin, where the railroad ended. The men completed the final leg of their journey wrapped in buffalo robes and riding in horse-drawn sleighs over the three-foot-thick ice of the Mississippi.

They were almost home now, the war behind them, or at least behind those who had no plans to reenlist. As they traveled up the frozen Mississippi, they surely thought back on the summer of 1861, when they had come down the river by steamboat. The trip then had been a frolic, almost as if they were on holiday; they were off on a great adventure that would be over quickly and successfully and at little cost.

They had been brimming with enthusiasm, patriotism, and supreme confidence in themselves and in their cause. They had also been brimming with innocence—the innocence of youth and inexperience.

That innocence was lost forever at the first battle of Bull Run, where they suffered staggering losses and bitter defeat. The frustration of the Seven Days on the Peninsula—winning battles but constantly in retreat—sapped their enthusiasm. These early setbacks shook their confidence, but then victory at Antietam partially restored it. Their patriotism—their conviction that what they were doing was necessary to preserve their country—never wavered. They expressed it in different ways, but they universally believed in their country, and they were prepared to risk hardship, pain, and even death to preserve it. This was the belief that saw them through Fredericksburg, Chancellorsville, and finally Gettysburg. It saw them through the ineptitude of a seemingly endless string of Union commanders. It saw them through cold and wet nights, twenty-two-hour marches, stale hardtack, and days without their cherished coffee. It would have seen them through Mine Run had the assault not been called off.

What caused most of them to endure all this was duty, although few actually used the word. They questioned their superiors and virtually everything else in the army at one time or another, but they never questioned the need to win the war. These were ordinary men, without pretense or guile, who happened to live at a time that was anything but ordinary. They had the same human shortcomings as any other group of men, but they also had an inner strength—perhaps stemming in part from life on the frontier—that helped them survive their incredible ordeal.

James J. Hill, who had been refused admission to the regiment for defective eyesight, thought he understood what set them apart. "Their virtues were large, simple and candid," Hill said more than forty years after the war ended. "They saw things straight and the struggle for existence in their daily life has taught them to do things quickly and well. There was no better making of a soldier."[2]

At both Bull Run and Gettysburg the First Minnesota had suffered the highest percentage of casualties of any Northern regiment. There and elsewhere, too many Minnesotans had given what Lincoln, in dedicating a cemetery just a few months earlier at Gettysburg, had called "the last full measure of devotion." Of the more than twelve hundred officers and men who had served in the First Minnesota, nearly two hundred lay in eastern graves. At least fifty-six of them, including Isaac Taylor, would find their final resting place in the Minnesota plot at Gettysburg, just a few feet from where Lincoln had spoken.* At least another thirty had died from disease or accident. Still others were missing in action or languishing in Southern prisons. Approximately half the survivors, about five hundred, had been wounded, many of them two or three times. Lieutenant Colonel Adams carried scars from Bull Run, Malvern Hill, Antietam, and Gettysburg. Many, like William Colvill, would feel the painful effects of their wounds for the rest of their lives. Others, like Charley Goddard, would see those effects shorten their lives.

The regiment's remaining 16 officers and 309 enlisted men were greeted as returning heroes in the Mississippi River towns they passed as they traveled north. They reached St. Paul on the afternoon of 15 February 1864, their odyssey finally complete. Henry Taylor recorded that "a delegation of butchers came out to meet us a mile from the city to let us know the 'fatted calf' had been slain. As we neared the city, a roar of artillery greeted us—flags were floating all over the city. The day was extremely cold but thousands of people crowded around to welcome us home, and as we marched through the streets to Atheneum Hall, I noticed now and then a falling tear. The tables in the hall were loaded with edibles and many 'fairy forms' were ready to wait on us."[3] Gov. Stephen Miller, a veteran of the regiment, gave a welcoming speech. The next day the men were released for thirty-day furloughs.

They returned to Fort Snelling on 18 March, but they had little to occupy them before their mustering-out date a month later. Finally, on 28 April, exactly three years after most of them had enlisted, the men formed on the fort's parade ground for a final review. They heard themselves praised lavishly by Miller and Adams before breaking ranks to surround the carriage holding Colvill, whose wounds prevented his participation in the ceremony. The regiment's fifth colonel had by now become a symbol of all they had accomplished and endured, at Gettysburg and elsewhere, and therefore an object of adulation.

---

* According to National Park Service records at Gettysburg, Isaac Taylor's remains lie in grave 12, row B, of the Minnesota plot. The headstone on the grave is marked "Unknown."

Over the next several days, those who had not reenlisted were formally mustered out of service by Maj. A. D. Nelson, the same regular army officer who had mustered them in three years before. Of the thousand men who had been part of the mustering ceremony at Fort Snelling then, fewer than a fifth were at the fort to participate in the regiment's last formation.

Patrick Henry Taylor, who declined an opportunity to reenlist for three years as a lieutenant, received his discharge papers on 3 May. "By sunset," he wrote, "the paymaster had furnished us with 'needful.' I received $203.85—go it, you gay soldiers! What do we CITIZENS care for now?"[4]

As most of the men of the First Minnesota fanned out across the state and beyond to their homes, those who had reenlisted stayed behind at Fort Snelling. There were 135 of them, not enough to keep the regiment intact but enough to form the nucleus of the First Battalion Minnesota Infantry Volunteers. Joined by new recruits and veterans whose enlistments had not yet expired, they spent several weeks drilling under new officers, all of whom had been enlisted men in the First Regiment. James C. Farwell of Company A was named captain of the new battalion, and Henry D. O'Brien, who had led the regiment's charge into Pickett's men on the third day at Gettysburg, was one of the lieutenants.

The battalion left Fort Snelling in mid-May on the familiar trip east. It passed through Washington and Alexandria before boarding a steamer for the Peninsula, where McClellan's Army of the Potomac had suffered ignominy less than two years earlier. Landing at White House, on the Pamunky River, the men proceeded to Cold Harbor, where one of the bloodiest battles of the war was just concluding, but they arrived too late to be thrown into the senseless slaughter. Some of the old-timers must have had thoughts of the similar luck they had enjoyed at Fredericksburg and Chancellorsville and Mine Run.

In fact they had missed not only Cold Harbor but also the Wilderness and Spotsylvania in the Union's relentless drive for Richmond. The Army of the Potomac was now led by Ulysses S. Grant, and he was a commander unlike any it had seen before. Where McClellan had been cautious and protective of his men's lives, Grant was bold, always determined to press Lee to his limits, even when it meant sending wave after wave of young men in blue coats to their almost certain death. This was a different kind of warfare—brutal, unyielding, and total.

The battalion was assigned the same position the First Regiment had vacated just a few months earlier in the First Brigade, Second Division, of the Second Army Corps, which was once again under the command of the man who had caused the regiment to find its destiny at Gettysburg, Winfield Scott Hancock. It didn't take the Minnesotans long to discover the extremely heavy casualties Hancock's men had suffered at Cold Harbor.

Once more they marched across the Peninsula, but this time they were not in retreat. They were in full pursuit of Lee's Army of Northern Virginia, which, though ill-fed, badly equipped, battered, and on the run, was still an effective fighting force. Crossing the broad James River on 14 June, the men of the battalion got their first look at Grant as he stood on the riverbank quietly smoking a cigar. They were watching him just as closely as he was watching them. The veterans had seen generals come and go, and they knew everything depended on what kind of a man he was.

Three days later they arrived at Petersburg, an important communications center south of Richmond, where the Army of the Potomac would spend most of the next year refining the art of siege warfare. It was a grim and grisly business, with both sides suffering heavy casualties but neither gaining a decisive advantage. The First Battalion was engaged in a number of secondary actions near Petersburg, including Deep Bottom, Reams's Station, and Hatcher's Run, and the Minnesotans suffered their share of casualties. Sgt. W. N. Irvine, who had been captured on Marye's Heights while on a nighttime reconnaissance mission but who was otherwise unscathed during three years in the First Regiment, was mortally wounded shortly after arriving at Petersburg. The two men who would be awarded the Medal of Honor for heroism at Gettysburg were both badly wounded at Deep Bottom: Marshall Sherman lost a leg, while Henry D. O'Brien was hit in the chest and carried off the field by a comrade who was himself awarded the medal for the feat. By December the regiment was down to only thirty men, wounds and sickness having disabled the rest, until a new recruiting drive in Minnesota produced replacements.

The Minnesotans participated in the decisive assault on Lee's Petersburg fortifications during the first two days of April 1865, and, with the rest of the Union army, pursued the fleeing Confederates west toward Appomattox. They were on picket duty when the final surrender came on 9 April 1865, and helped gather up the defeated Southerners.

Two months later the battalion was ordered to Washington, and then to Louisville, Kentucky, where it served briefly as part of the Army of the Tennessee. Within a few weeks it was ordered to Fort Snelling, where, on 15 July 1865, its members were finally mustered out.

Not all those who survived their experience with the First Minnesota survived the war. William "Billy" Acker, who at age twenty-six had been the unanimous choice of Republican and Democratic activists to lead Company C, was killed at Shiloh in 1862, after transferring to a regular army unit. Alfred Carpenter, who had written eloquently of the two harrowing days at Gettysburg, died in 1864 of yellow fever, while commanding a unit of black soldiers on Key West, Florida.

Some members of the First Regiment who had chosen not to reenlist when the First Battalion was formed later changed their minds and joined other units. After three years in the army, a number of them, including Edward Bassett and Henry Taylor, had found the routine of life on the farm or in the classroom too tame. Bassett served as a sergeant in the First Minnesota Heavy Artillery in Tennessee during the final year of the war. Henry returned to Belle Prairie for ten months before restlessness drew him back to the army. He was commissioned a lieutenant in Hancock's Veteran Corps, which took only those who had already served two years, and he spent close to a year at Fort Snelling, training new recruits.

Most of the men of the First Minnesota came back from their experience in the East to resume the lives they had left when the war began. Bassett returned from his second enlistment to his father's farm in Rice County, but soon he moved to southwestern Minnesota, where he worked a farm of his own and raised a large family. For the rest of his life he would be afflicted with catalepsy, the result of his head wound at Bristoe Station. Edward Walker, the prolific letter writer, returned to his machine shop in Clearwater before moving back East to Philadelphia. James A. Wright, who missed the charge of 2 July at Gettysburg but who experienced and chronicled the events of 3 July, worked at a livery stable in Red Wing before moving to Massachusetts, where he took up railroading. Hezekiah Bruce, who led a small group of volunteers up Marye's Heights and behind enemy lines during the second battle of Fredericksburg, resumed farming the land he had homesteaded in Goodhue County. Marshall Sherman became an insurance salesman in St. Paul and later opened a boardinghouse.

A good many of the First's veterans became prominent citizens in their communities by virtue of their service in the regiment. A number took advantage of their prominence to seek elective or appointive public office, and most who tried were successful. Henry D. O'Brien was appointed postmaster of St. Anthony before moving to St. Louis, where he was made a government pension agent. Thomas Pressnell, the audacious teenager who managed to see Lincoln at the White House, was enticed to Duluth by the prospect of publishing one of the young city's newspapers; he ended up holding a series of positions in the U.S. Land Office and the federal and state courts.

Some successfully established themselves in business. Chris Heffelfinger started a shoe company in Minneapolis, became an important civic leader, and sired a family that would be among the state's most prominent for several generations. Edward Neill, the regiment's unpopular chaplain, found prominence in other ways. He served as a private secretary to President Lincoln and President Johnson before returning to Minnesota, where for many years he was widely recognized as one of the state's most distinguished clergymen.

Charley Goddard, who enlisted at fifteen and was discharged at eighteen, returned to Winona to try to support his mother, but he was increasingly plagued by his wounds and the illnesses that had followed him through the war. He decided to seek public office nonetheless, and he won the Republican nomination for county register of deeds. He won the election too, but a few weeks later he was dead. He was twenty-three years old.

John Plummer, who as a sergeant in Company D had written a graphic letter of the fighting at Gettysburg, also died young. Promoted to captain after leaving the First Minnesota and then made provost marshal general of Tennessee, he returned to Minnesota to be elected the clerk of Hennepin County (Minneapolis) District Court. Within months, however, he was stricken with kidney and liver disease; he died at age twenty-nine.

Mathew Marvin, although destined to live a full life, had much in common with Goddard. He too was from Winona, he too was seriously wounded at Gettysburg, and he too significantly improved his spelling and grammar after three years of regular writing. Marvin spent several years in Illinois before returning to Winona to open a harness business and eventually to become superintendent of the local cemetery. He spent much of his time helping other former members of the regiment get the pensions to which they were entitled.

Edward A. Stevens, or "Raisins" as he was known in 1861–62 to the readers of the Stillwater *Messenger,* left the army in the first days of 1863. The reasons for his early discharge are unclear, but it's not difficult to imagine that his penchant for challenging authority may have played a role. Rather than return to Stillwater he settled in the young but promising city of Minneapolis, where he worked as night editor of the *Tribune.* Soon he published and edited his own paper, the *Gopher Mirror,* until he lost everything in a disastrous fire. Forsaking journalism, he served instead in a series of minor municipal offices.

William Lochren, who had risen from sergeant to regimental adjutant, resumed his law practice in St. Anthony, but he aspired to a career in politics. He won a term in the state senate but failed in his attempts to be elected attorney general, judge of the state supreme court, and United States senator. Lochren was a Democrat, and these were Republican times. President Grover Cleveland finally made him a United States district judge. In the meantime, he wrote the official account of the First Minnesota's three-year experience that remains the basic history of the regiment.

Jasper N. Searles, who had entered the army a private and left it a captain, also returned to his law practice, first in Hastings, then in Stillwater, and eventually in St. Paul. He too was elected to the state legislature, but as a Republican. Together with four other veterans of the First, he was named to serve on a commission to oversee the writing of a more elaborate official history of the regiment. Written by Return I. Holcombe, it was published in 1916, by which time only Searles and Matthew F. Taylor (no relation to Isaac and Henry) survived as commissioners. They wrote a foreword in fulsome praise of their comrades' deeds and made it clear that it was not the purpose of the work to find fault with anyone: "We have studiously aimed to avoid criticisms of commanding officers—preferring to observe the old maxim, 'Say nothing of the dead, unless it be good.' "

The three regular army officers who led the regiment from its beginning through Fredericksburg all completed their war service in the West. Willis Gorman, the regiment's controversial first colonel, who had been sent to the western theater after Antietam, served under Grant at Vicksburg and finished out the war in Missouri, Tennessee, and Arkansas. He was mustered out of service in early May 1864. He returned to his law practice in St. Paul, where, in 1868, he made an unsuccessful bid for Congress. Believing that war veterans would rally to his support, he failed even to win the Democratic nomination—losing to another veteran.

Napoleon Jackson Tecumseh Dana, who had commanded the First Minnesota only briefly, at Camp Stone, but who had won the affection of the men, never completely recovered from the wounds he suffered at Antietam. He spent the balance of his service in quiet posts in Texas, Louisiana, and Mississippi. Following the war he engaged in trading with the Russians in Alaska before serving as an executive of several railroads and as a pension official.

Alfred Sully, who had ably led the regiment in the Peninsula and at Antietam and who as a brigade commander had saved it from certain slaughter at Fredericksburg, spent the rest of the war fighting the Sioux. Although cleared of the charges against him following the short-lived rebellion of the Thirty-fourth New York, he was never again given a war command. He distinguished himself in the Indian campaigns and remained in the army after the war. Sully became a painter—like his distinguished father, Thomas—portraying the nineteenth-century West in sketches and watercolors.

George Morgan, who started the war as captain of Company E and served as the regiment's colonel at Fredericksburg, was compelled to resign his commission in the spring of 1863 because of illness. He died of consumption a year after the war ended. Charles P. Adams, frustrated in his desire to lead the First Minnesota because too few men would reenlist if he was to be their colonel, resumed his practice as a physician. He later maintained that he, not William Colvill, had led the regiment in its famous charge at Gettysburg. Unpopular with most of the men already, he alienated them further with the claim.

Stephen Miller, Governor Ramsey's political ally, who had distinguished himself at Bull Run, was given command of the Seventh Minnesota Volunteer Regiment. Assigned to Indian duty in Minnesota, Miller prevented a mob near Mankato from lynching three hundred Sioux in his custody, who had been condemned to death for the slaughter of hundreds of white settlers. He was ordered to direct the execution of thirty-eight convicted Indians—Lincoln had spared the rest—and he saw to it that they were hung simultaneously on a single huge scaffold.* He was elected governor of Minnesota in 1863 and the following year welcomed his old regiment back to the state. Embarrassed by legal difficulties two of his sons encountered on the Pacific coast, he chose not to seek a second term and never stood for elective office again. He moved to Worthington, in southwestern Minnesota, where he became a railroad executive.

William Colvill, brevetted as a brigadier general of volunteers for his heroism at Gettysburg, was formally mustered out of service in July 1865. He returned to Red Wing, the city where he had organized the Goodhue County volunteers four years earlier. He was elected state attorney general for a term as a "Union" candidate and as such was commonly understood to be a Republican. But he fell out of Republican favor when he endorsed President Andrew Johnson's Reconstruction policy, and in 1866 he accepted a Democratic nomination for Congress. Again, the fact that he was a Democrat in a strongly Republican state was a serious handicap. He lost the election and, despite his later election to a term in the state legislature, Colvill's political career never recovered. President Grover Cleveland appointed him register of the federal land office in Duluth, but mostly he led a simple and quiet life in Red Wing, tending to his garden, befriending Indians, and—like Isaac Taylor during the war—immersing himself in local geology. His war wounds forced him to use a cane for the rest of his life and left him with what some thought a

---

* Among those witnessing the hangings was fifteen-year-old Albert Woolson, who would enlist in the First Minnesota Heavy Artillery two years later and live to be the Union army's last survivor.

listless and melancholy look. But beneath this appearance was an active and inquisitive mind. He read voraciously and entertained visitors with his knowledge of a wide range of subjects. One subject he was always reluctant to discuss, however, was the famous charge he had led at Gettysburg. He only wanted to share that experience with the men who had followed him down the slope that day, and he attended as many of the regiment's reunions as he could. On 12 June 1905, nearly forty-two years later, Colvill traveled to St. Paul to attend a reunion and to participate, the next day, in the removal of the regiment's flags from the old to the new state capitol. That night he died in his sleep at the soldiers' home. He was seventy-eight.

A few days after first being mustered out, in May 1864, Henry Taylor crossed the St. Croix River to Hudson, Wisconsin, where he married Mary Ann Colgan. When he decided to reenlist ten months later, he served at Fort Snelling before he was ordered to Washington to receive his commission as a lieutenant. In October 1865, six months after the war ended, he took his bride to Prairie City, Illinois, where she stayed with the Taylor family while he was stationed not far away, in Springfield. That spring Henry received a telegram informing him of his wife's death. He was discharged from the army two months later and returned to Prairie City to teach school. He left Illinois for a farm in Cass County, Missouri, in the spring of 1867, but he returned in the fall to marry Harriet Thomas. For most of the next decade he farmed and taught school in Cass County. In 1875 he entered the insurance business in nearby Harrisonville, and by all accounts he was a success at it. Henry settled comfortably into the routine of small-town life, becoming the father of seven children and a pillar of Harrisonville. When he died of pneumonia in December 1908, the local newspaper said the county had lost "one of its most estimable citizens. He was honored and respected by everybody for his manhood and his broad intellectual capacity. No higher tribute can be paid his memory than the encomium that he was a good citizen. His life and the manner in which he lived is a eulogy in itself."[5]

Like most other survivors of Civil War combat, those who served in the First Minnesota never saw anything approaching the experience again.

The duration and intensity of the ordeal and the range of emotions it inflicted on them—exhilaration and despair, hope and frustration, joy and grief—ensured that it would remain with them forever. The fact that they had performed as well as they did, often exceeding their expectations of themselves, was naturally a matter of enormous satisfaction. "Every member justly regards his own connection with the regiment as the highest honor of his life,—the one thing respecting himself to which his own posterity will always refer with greatest pride," William Lochren wrote a quarter of a century after the war ended.[6] The ordeal also guaranteed that they would remain close to one another, because it had fused them. Like all other soldiers in every war, they believed that no one else could understand what it had been like.

After resuming their civilian lives, they started coming together again, at first irregularly but soon every year. The reunions validated all that they had been through by renewing the bonds between them and by intensifying the public aura that quickly formed around their deeds, particularly the heroic charge of 2 July 1863. James J. Hill, who had gone on to build the Great Northern Railroad after he failed to get into the First, hosted some of the reunions at his mansion on Summit Avenue in St. Paul. He attached so much importance to them that he occasionally paid the expenses of those who couldn't afford to travel great distances. For his dedication and friendship, the men made Hill an honorary member of the First Minnesota.

Several of the regiment's companies held their own reunions. When the veterans of Company B met in Stillwater on 21 July 1886 to commemorate the twenty-fifth anniversary of Bull Run, they decided to make reunions an annual event. Adolphus C. Hospes donated "a large and commodious bottle of wine," to be placed on the table at each year's gathering but not to be opened until there was only one survivor. Thus was born the Last Man's Club. The roster, with space for each man's date of death, was affixed to an expensive bottle of burgundy that made its appearance at every reunion—unopened. Gradually the club's numbers diminished—for each deceased veteran, the survivors would drape an empty chair with crepe—until the forty-second annual meeting, in 1927, when there were only three remaining, two of whom were in failing health. Fearing that this would be the last reunion, they decided to open the bottle and together toast their departed comrades. The wine having turned to vinegar, Charles Lockwood lamented that they hadn't agreed to employ "a bottle of good Irish whiskey."[7] Lockwood became the club's last man, dying only in 1935. The bottle of burgundy still resides in a specially designed octagonal case of rosewood in the care of the Washington County Historical Society.

Over the years the State of Minnesota and its citizens honored its most distinguished regiment by commissioning official histories, paintings, and statues. No public ceremony of any importance could be held without some homage to the men of the First Minnesota. Admirers compared the charge at Gettysburg to the feats of the warriors at Marathon, Thermopylae, and Yorktown and, especially, to the Charge of the Light Brigade at Balaklava, never failing to mention that the Minnesotans suffered a higher percentage of casualties. Several commemorated the great event in verse, but none, unfortunately, had the ability to give the First Minnesota the immortality that Alfred, Lord Tennyson had given the Light Brigade.

On 2 July 1897, 165 veterans of the First Minnesota and a host of Minnesota's officials arrived at Gettysburg on a special train that included sixteen sleeping cars provided by James J. Hill. At the point on Cemetery Ridge where Hancock had ordered the regiment to commence its charge, they dedicated a larger-than-life bronze statue of an infantryman running with bayonet fixed toward the swale where so many of their comrades had died thirty-four years earlier. The state legislature had appropriated $20,000 for the monument—a huge sum at the time—and commissioned a Norwegian-born sculptor, Jacob Fjelde, to craft it. A bronze plaque on the granite base succinctly describes the events that happened there that day and concludes: "In self-sacrificing desperate valor their charge has no parallel in any war."

A quarter of a mile north on Cemetery Ridge, a smaller monument in the form of an obelisk was dedicated a few years later, to commemorate the role of the Minnesotans in repelling Pickett's charge.

In 1903 the citizens of St. Paul erected a statue of Josias R. King, the man who professed to be the first Union volunteer after Fort Sumter. King never fully proved the claim, but no one ever disproved it either.

In 1909 the state unveiled a statue of Col. William Colvill, the symbol of the heroic charge, in the new state capitol building. A duplicate of the statue was placed on a hilltop overlooking Colvill's grave in Cannon Falls, not far from his home at Red Wing. President Calvin Coolidge came to Cannon Falls several years later to dedicate the statue and to offer, at long last, the nation's gratiude for the Minnesotans' sacrifice at Gettysburg.

"In all the history of warfare this charge has few, if any, equals and no superiors," Coolidge said. "It was an exhibition of the most exalted heroism against an apparently insuperable antagonist. By holding the Confederate forces in check until other reserves came up, it probably saved the Union army from defeat. . . . So far as human judgment can determine, Colonel Colvill and those eight companies of the First Minnesota are entitled to rank among the saviors of their country."[8]

Fourscore and seven years ago our fathers brought forth on this continent, a new nation, conceived in Liberty, and dedicated to the proposition that all men are created equal.

Now we are engaged in a great civil war, testing whether that nation or any nation so conceived and so dedicated can long endure. We are met on a great battlefield of that war. We have come to dedicate a portion of that field, as a final resting place for those who here gave their lives that that nation might live. It is altogether fitting and proper that we should do this.

But, in a larger sense, we cannot dedicate—we cannot consecrate—we cannot hallow—this ground. The brave men, living and dead, who struggled here, have consecrated it far above our poor power to add or detract. The world will little note nor long remember what we say here, but it can never forget what they did here. It is for us, the living, rather to be dedicated here to the unfinished work which they who fought here have thus far so nobly advanced. It is rather for us to be here dedicated to the great task remaining before us—that from these honored dead we take increased devotion to that cause for which they gave the last full measure of devotion; that we here highly resolve that these dead shall not have died in vain; that this nation, under God, shall have a new birth of freedom; and that government of the people, by the people, for the people, shall not perish from the earth.

Abraham Lincoln
November 19, 1863
Gettysburg, Pennsylvania

NOTES

1. FORT SNELLING

1. Patrick Henry Taylor, 26 Nov. 1863. Diary, 1861–64, rpt. Cass County (Missouri) *Democrat*, 22 June 1933–11 Oct. 1934 (copies). In private possession.
2. P. H. Taylor, diary, 27 Nov. 1863.
3. P. H. Taylor, diary, 30 Nov. 1863.
4. M. H. Bassett, *From Bull Run to Bristow Station* (St. Paul: North Central Publishing Co., 1962), 35.
5. William Lochren, "Narrative of the First Regiment," *Minnesota in the Civil and Indian Wars, 1861–1865*, vol. 1 (St. Paul: Pioneer Press Co., 1891), 41.
6. Lochren, 41.
7. Lochren, 41.
8. P. H. Taylor, diary, 30 Nov. 1863; Lochren, 41.
9. Lochren, 41; Bassett, 35.
10. Charles Goddard, letter to mother, 4 Dec. 1863. Orrin F. Smith and Family Papers, 1861–64. Minnesota Historical Society.
11. Lochren, 2.
12. Roy P. Basler, ed., *The Collected Works of Abraham Lincoln*, vol. 4 (New Brunswick: Rutgers University Press, 1953), 332.
13. *Minnesota in the Civil and Indian Wars*, vol. 2 (St. Paul: Pioneer Press Co., 1899), 1, 3.
14. Basler, ed., *Collected Works of Abraham Lincoln*, vol. 4, 332.
15. *Minnesota in the Civil and Indian Wars*, vol. 2, 2–3.
16. Franklin Curtiss-Wedge, ed., History of Winona County (1913), vol. 1, 383.
17. Wedge, ed., History of Goodhue County (1909), 507–08.
18. St. Paul *Press*, 2 May 1861.
19. Thomas H. Pressnell, "Incidents in the Civil War," 1. Unpublished ms., St. Louis County (Minnesota) Historical Society.
20. Stillwater *Messenger*, 7 May 1861.

21. Basler, ed., *Collected Works of Abraham Lincoln,* vol. 4, 332.
22. Jasper N. Searles, letter to father, 10 Aug. 1861. Letters, 1861–63, Minnesota Historical Society.
23. Bell Irvin Wiley, *The Life of Billy Yank: The Common Soldier of the Civil War* (Baton Rouge: Louisiana State University), 1978.
24. Hazel C. Wolf, ed., "Campaigning with the First Minnesota: A Civil War Diary [of Isaac Lyman Taylor]," *Minnesota History* 25 (1944), 14.
25. P. H. Taylor, letter to parents, 17 May 1861 (copy). Morrison County (Minnesota) Historical Society.
26. P. H. Taylor, letter to parents, 22 May 1861 (copy).
27. P. H. Taylor, diary, 22–26 May 1861.
28. Lochren, 27.
29. *Minnesota in the Civil and Indian Wars,* vol. 2, 4.
30. Joseph E. Spencer, letter to sister, 4 May 1861. Letters, 1861–65, Wisconsin Historical Society.
31. Pressnell, part 1.
32. Stillwater *Messenger,* 7 May 1861.
33. Edward L. Davis, letter to Emma, 4 May 1861. Letters, 1861, Wisconsin Historical Society.
34. Lochren, 5.
35. Pressnell, part 1.
36. Jasper N. Searles, "The First Minnesota Infantry, U.S. Volunteers," *Glimpses of the Nation's Struggle,* vol. 2 (St. Paul: St. Paul Book and Stationery Co., 1890), 82.
37. Stillwater *Messenger,* 7 May 1861.
38. Stillwater *Messenger,* 7 May 1861.
39. Stillwater *Messenger,* 7 May 1861.
40. Stillwater *Messenger,* 21 May 1861.
41. Pressnell, part 1.
42. Stillwater *Messenger,* 21 May 1861.
43. Pressnell, part 1.
44. Stillwater *Messenger,* 21 May 1861.
45. Stillwater *Messenger,* 28 May 1861.
46. Stillwater *Messenger,* 7 June 1861.
47. Stillwater *Messenger,* 7 June 1861.
48. Stillwater *Messenger,* 10 June 1861.
49. Spencer, letter to sister, 8 June 1861.
50. *Minnesota in the Civil and Indian Wars,* vol. 2, 15.
51. Lochren, 5.
52. P. H. Taylor, diary, 5 June 1861.
53. Stillwater *Messenger,* 25 June 1861.
54. Faribault *Central Republican,* 26 June 1861.
55. P. H. Taylor, diary, 21 June 1861.
56. William Watts Folwell, *A History of Minnesota* (St. Paul: Minnesota Historical Society, 1961), vol. 2, 84.
57. Pressnell, part 1.

58. Stillwater *Messenger*, 25 June 1861.
59. Winona *Republican*, 24 June 1861.
60. Mathew Marvin, diary, 23 June 1861. Mathew Marvin Papers, 1861–63, Minnesota Historical Society.
61. Faribault *Central Republican*, 10 July 1861.
62. Return I. Holcombe, *History of the First Regiment Minnesota Volunteer Infantry 1861–1864* (Stillwater: Easton & Masterson, 1916), 27–28.
63. Searles, letter to "Friends at Home," 27 June 1861.
64. Lochren, 6.
65. Lochren, 6.
66. Marvin, diary, 27 June 1861; Bassett, 5.
67. Stillwater *Messenger*, 9 July 1861.
68. Bassett, 6.
69. Searles, letter to "Friends at Home," 27 June 1861.

2. BULL RUN

1. Lochren, 7.
2. Pressnell, part 2.
3. Stillwater *Messenger*, 6 July 1861.
4. Stillwater *Messenger*, 9 July 1861; Searles, letter to "Friends at Home," 2 July 1861.
5. Faribault *Central Republican*, 10 July 1861.
6. Marvin, letter to brother, 28 June 1861.
7. Bassett, 6.
8. Stillwater *Messenger*, 7 July 1861.
9. Stillwater *Messenger*, 9 July 1861.
10. Searles, letter to "Friends at Home," 4 July 1861; Lochren, 7; Bassett, 6; Davis, letter, 3 July 1861.
11. Stillwater *Messenger*, 6 July 1861.
12. Spencer, letter to sister, 7 July 1861.
13. T. Harry Williams, *Lincoln and His Generals* (New York: Dorset Press, 1952), 21.
14. Faribault *Central Republican*, 10 July 1861.
15. P. H. Taylor, diary, 3 July 1861.
16. Bassett, 6.
17. Holcombe, 33–34.
18. Faribault *Central Republican*, 17 July 1861.
19. Faribault *Central Republican*, 17 July 1861.
20. Spencer, letter to sister, 7 July 1861.
21. Stillwater *Messenger*, 16 July 1861; Searles, letter to "Friends at Home," 4 July 1861; Faribault *Central Republican*, 17 July 1861.
22. Bassett, 6–7.
23. Faribault *Central Republican*, 17 July 1861.
24. Lochren, 7–8.
25. *Minnesota in the Civil and Indian Wars*, vol. 2, 29.
26. Bassett, 6.

27. Faribault *Central Republican,* 31 July 1861.
28. Bassett, 7; Holcombe, 39.
29. Winona *Republican,* 7 Aug. 1861.
30. P. H. Taylor, diary, 17 July 1861.
31. Holcombe, 40; Faribault *Central Republican,* 31 July 1861.
32. Winona *Republican,* 7 Aug. 1861.
33. *Minnesota in the Civil and Indian Wars,* vol. 2, 21.
34. Lochren, 9.
35. Lochren, 9.
36. Winona *Republican,* 7 Aug. 1861.
37. *Minnesota in the Civil and Indian Wars,* vol. 2, 21.
38. Lochren, 9; *Minnesota in the Civil and Indian Wars,* vol. 2, 21.
39. Lochren, 9.
40. Bassett, 103; P. H. Taylor, diary, 21 July 1861; P. H. Taylor, letter to William Lochren, 3 Feb. 1882.
41. Bassett, 104.
42. Winona *Republican,* 7 Aug. 1861.
43. Faribault *Central Republican,* 31 July 1861; Spencer, letter to sister, 30 July 1861.
44. Marvin, letter to brother, 1 Aug. 1861.
45. Stillwater *Messenger,* 6 Aug. 1861.
46. Lochren, 10.
47. *Minnesota in the Civil and Indian Wars,* vol. 2, 24.
48. Winona *Republican,* 7 Aug. 1861.
49. Josias R. King, "The Battle of Bull Run: A Confederate Victory Obtained but Not Achieved," *Glimpses of the Nation's Struggle,* vol. 6 (Minneapolis: Aug. Davis Publisher, 1909), 501.
50. King, 501, 503–04.
51. John McEwen, letter to "Robert," n.d. [1861]. Library of Congress.
52. Lochren, 10.
53. King, 506.
54. *Minnesota in the Civil and Indian Wars,* vol. 2, 22; Bassett, 7.
55. Winona *Republican,* 7 Aug. 1861.
56. Lochren, 11.
57. Lochren, 11.
58. Lochren, 12.
59. Searles, "First Minnesota Infantry," 86.
60. King, 508–09.
61. Stillwater *Messenger,* 6 Aug. 1861.
62. Winona *Republican,* 7 Aug. 1861.
63. Searles, 86.
64. Lochren, 12.
65. Davis, letter to "Emma," 27 July 1861.
66. Lochren, 12.
67. Winona *Republican,* 7 Aug. 1861.
68. *Minnesota in the Civil and Indian Wars,* vol. 2, 27.

69. Davis, letter to "Emma," 27 July 1861; Lochren, 12; Faribault *Central Republican,* 7 Aug. 1861.
70. Lochren, 10; Spencer, letter to sister, 30 July 1861.
71. Lochren, 13, 10.
72. Stillwater *Messenger,* 8 Aug. 1861.
73. *Minnesota in the Civil and Indian Wars,* vol. 2, 22.
74. Spencer, letter to sister, 30 July 1861.
75. Winona *Republican,* 14 Aug. 1861.

3. EDWARDS' FERRY

1. Lochren, 13.
2. Daniel Hand, "Reminiscences of an Army Surgeon," *Glimpses of the Nation's Struggle* vol. 1 (St. Paul: St. Paul Book and Stationery Co., 1887), 276.
3. Faribault *Central Republican,* 7 Aug. 1861.
4. *Minnesota in the Civil and Indian Wars,* vol. 2, 37, 34, 31–32.
5. *Minnesota in the Civil and Indian Wars,* vol. 2, 37.
6. Spencer, letter to "Emma," 27 July 1861.
7. John Quinn Imholte, *The First Volunteers: History of the First Minnesota Volunteer Regiment 1861–1865* (Minneapolis: Ross & Haines, Inc., 1963), 57.
8. Winona *Republican,* 13 Sept. 1861.
9. Charles Goddard, letter to mother, 2 Aug. 1861.
10. Imholte, 59.
11. Imholte, 58–60.
12. Faribault *Central Republican,* 7 Aug. 1861.
13. Imholte, 64–65.
14. Stillwater *Messenger,* 10 Sept. 1861.
15. Stillwater *Messenger,* 10 Sept. 1861.
16. For a detailed account of the controversies surrounding Gorman and the issue of enlistment, see Imholte, 56–69.
17. Marvin, diary, 2 Aug., 4 Aug. 1861.
18. Stillwater *Messenger,* 13 Aug. 1861; Lochren, 13.
19. Bassett, 8.
20. Lochren, 11; Holcombe, 61–62.
21. Faribault *Central Republican,* 2 Oct. 1861.
22. Holcombe, 62.
23. Faribault *Central Republican,* 4 Sept. 1861.
24. Bassett, 10; Searles, 88.
25. P. H. Taylor, diary, 7 Sept. 1861.
26. Holcombe, 63–64.
27. Faribault *Central Republican,* 4 Sept. 1861.
28. Winona *Republican,* 9 Oct. 1861.
29. Spencer, letter to sister, 1 Sept. 1861; Marvin, letter to brother, 26 Aug. 1861.
30. Marvin, diary, 27 Oct. 1861.
31. Bassett, 9.

32. Stillwater *Messenger,* 17 Sept. 1861.
33. P. H. Taylor, diary, 7 Sept. 1861.
34. Stillwater *Messenger,* 17 Sept. 1861.
35. Bassett, 9.
36. Goddard, letter to mother, 14 May 1861.
37. Holcombe, 68; Bassett, 9.
38. Searles, 89; Bassett, 8.
39. Holcombe, 81; Pressnell, part 4.
40. Stillwater *Messenger,* 22 Oct. 1861.
41. Bassett, 9, 13.
42. Marvin, letter to brother, 4 Oct. 1861; Pressnell, part 4; Lochren, 2.
43. Isaac Taylor, letter to Mary Taylor, 7 Sept. 1861 (copy). In private possession.
44. Pressnell, part 3.
45. P. H. Taylor, diary, Sept. 19, 1861.
46. Lochren, 14; Searles, 89; Pressnell, part 3.
47. Bassett, 13.
48. Napoleon Dana, letter to Rufus W. Peckham, 27 Oct. 1861. Library of Congress.
49. Stephen W. Sears, ed., *The Civil War Papers of George B. McClellan: Selected Correspondence, 1860–1865* (New York: Tichnor & Fields, 1989), 70.
50. Marvin, letter to brother, 19 Sept. 1861.
51. Holcombe, 74.
52. Holcombe, 74.
53. Isaac Taylor, letter to sister, 18 Oct. 1861 (copy). Morrison County (Minnesota) Historical Society.
54. John McEwen, letter to "Maggie & Jennie," 18 Oct. 1861. Library of Congress.
55. *Minnesota in the Civil and Indian Wars,* vol. 2, 49.
56. Goddard, letter to mother, 16 Nov. 1861.
57. Hand, 279–80.
58. *Minnesota in the Civil and Indian Wars,* vol. 2, 49; Bassett, 12.
59. Holcombe, 79.
60. Searles, 88.
61. Stillwater *Messenger,* 18 Nov. 1861.
62. P. H. Taylor, diary, 11 Nov. 1861;Wolf, 27.
63. Stillwater *Messenger,* 19 Nov. 1861.
64. I. Taylor, letter to "Aunt," 2 Jan. 1862; Wolf, 28;Stillwater *Messenger,* 31 Dec. 1861.
65. Searles, letter to parents, 28 Sept. 1861; *Minnesota in the Civil and Indian Wars,* vol. 2, 35.
66. Goddard, letter to mother, 14 Sept. 1861; *Minnesota in the Civil and Indian Wars,* vol. 2, 35; Stillwater *Messenger,* 22 Oct. 1861.
67. Goddard, letter to mother, 24 Jan. 1864.
68. Lochren, 14; Bassett, 13;I. Taylor, letter to "Aunt," 2 Jan. 1862.
69. Winona *Republican,* 11 Sept. 1861.
70. Wolf, 25.
71. Goddard, letter to mother, 22 Feb. 1862; Winona *Republican,* 23 Oct. 1861.

72. Bassett, 9; Spencer, letter to sister, 23 Nov. 1861; P. H. Taylor, diary, 26 Sept., 28 Nov. 1861; Hand, 280–81.
73. Pressnell, part 4.
74. Stillwater *Messenger*, 29 Oct., 19 Nov. 1861.
75. Hand, 278.
76. Lochren, 14.
77. Hand, 276–77.
78. Lochren, 15.
79. Imholte, 86.
80. Bassett, 11; Wolf, 26; Imholte, 86.
81. Stillwater *Messenger*, 21 Jan., 18 Feb. 1862.
82. Stillwater *Messenger*, 22 Oct. 1861.
83. *Minnesota in the Civil and Indian Wars*, vol. 2, 60.
84. Faribault *Central Republican*, 4 Dec. 1861.
85. Stillwater *Messenger*, 4 March 1862.
86. Wolf, 26, 24; Bassett, 9–10; *Minnesota in the Civil and Indian Wars*, vol. 2, 60.
87. Faribault *Central Republican*, 20 Nov. 1861.
88. Hand, 277.
89. Winona *Republican*, 23 Oct. 1861.
90. Faribault *Central Republican*, 11 Sept. 1861.
91. McEwen, letter to "Maggie & Jennie," 18 Oct. 1861.
92. Goddard, letter to mother, 2 Aug. 1861, 22 Feb., 7 Aug. 1862.
93. Jacob Marty, letter to "Friend," 11 July 1861. Minnesota Historical Society.
94. James Ghostley, diary. In private possession.
95. Bassett, 11, 9.
96. Amos A. Berry, diary, 25 Dec. 1861. Diary, 1861–63, Washington County (Minnesota) Historical Society.
97. Wolf, 20.
98. Wolf, 20.
99. Wolf, 22.
100. Berry, diary, 1 Jan. 1862; I. Taylor, letter to "Aunt," 2 Jan. 1862.
101. Bassett, 13–14.
102. Wolf, 25, 26; Bassett, 9.
103. Goddard, letter to mother, 22 Feb. 1862.
104. Imholte, 77.
105. Dana, letter to Rufus W. Peckham, 23 Nov. 1861.
106. Stillwater *Messenger*, 21 Nov. 1861.
107. Dana, letter to Rufus W. Peckham, 31 Oct. 1861.
108. Imholte, 78–79.
109. Stillwater *Messenger*, 22 Oct., 19 Nov. 1861.
110. Imholte, 70–76.
111. Hand, 279.
112. Stillwater *Messenger*, 19 Nov. 1861; I. Taylor, letter to "Aunt," 2 Jan. 1862.
113. Goddard, letter to mother, 29 Jan. 1862.
114. Stillwater *Messenger*, 18 Feb. 1862.

115. Marvin, diary, 3 Feb. 1862.

116. Imholte, 86–87.

117. *Minnesota in the Civil and Indian Wars,* vol. 2, 59.

118. Pressnell, part 4.

119. Willis Arnold Gorman, letter to Henry Wilson, 22 Dec. 1861. Library of Congress.

120. Marvin, letter to brother, 19 Jan. 1862.

121. Goddard, letter to mother, 10 Feb. 1862; Imholte, 87–88.

122. Bassett, 12, 14.

123. Searles, letter to parents, 20 Jan. 1962; Spencer, letter to sister, 11 Jan. 1862; McEwen, letter to "Robert," 23 Jan. 1862.

124. Spencer, letter to sister, 25 Feb. 1862.

125. Goddard, letter to mother, 2 Dec. 1861.

126. Bassett, 11.

127. McEwen, letter to "Robert," 23 Jan. 1862.

128. Bassett, 11; I. Taylor, letter to "Aunt," 2 Jan. 1862; Marvin, letter to brother, 10 Feb. 1862.

129. P. H. Taylor, diary, 18 Feb. 1862.

130. P. H. Taylor, diary, 23 Feb., 24 Feb. 1862.

131. P. H. Taylor, diary, 25 Feb. 1862.

132. Wolf, 30; P. H. Taylor diary, 25 Feb. 1862.

133. Lochren, 17.

134. Wolf, 30–31; Marvin, diary, 26 Feb. 1862.

135. Lochren, 17; Bassett, 14; Wolf, 31.

136. Wolf, 31–32; Bassett, 14.

137. Marvin, diary, 28 Feb. 1862.

138. Bassett, 15.

139. Wolf, 32, 33; Marvin, diary, 9 March 1862; P. H. Taylor, diary, 9 March 1862.

140. Lochren, 17.

141. Holcombe, 88–89n.

142. Lochren, 17.

143. Holcombe, 90.

144. Wolf, 33–34; Bassett, 15.

145. Marvin, diary, 12 March 1862.

146. Searles, 91.

147. Searles, 91.

148. Wolf, 34; Stillwater *Messenger,* 1 April 1862.

149. Wolf, 35, 37.

150. Searles, 91–92; Wolf, 37–38; P. H. Taylor, diary, 24 May 1862.

151. Wolf, 38.

152. Lochren, 18.

4. THE PENINSULA

1. Wolf, 38.

2. Edward A. Walker, letter, 24 April 1862. Walker Letters to George W. Knight, 1862–65 (copies). In private possession.

3. Marvin, diary, 13 June 1862.
4. Wolf, 39.
5. P. H. Taylor, diary, 28 March 1862; Wolf, 117.
6. Wolf, 118; Walker, letter to Knight, 24 April 1862.
7. Wolf, 118; Lochren, 18; Walker, letter to Knight, 24 April 1862.
8. Hand, 282; Lochren, 18; Walker, letter to Knight, 24 April 1862; Wolf, 118.
9. Stillwater *Messenger*, 29 April 1862; Hand, 282.
10. Lochren, 18; Pressnell, part 5; Walker, letter to Knight, 24 April 1862.
11. Lochren, 18; Wolf, 119.
12. Lochren, 18; Wolf, 119–20.
13. Stillwater *Messenger*, 29 April 1862.
14. Stillwater *Messenger*, 29 April 1862.
15. Hand, 282–83; Lochren, 18.
16. Marvin, diary, 16 April 1862.
17. Lochren, 18; Wolf, 120.
18. Wolf, 122, 124.
19. Walker, letter to Knight, 24 April 1862; Wolf, 124.
20. Pressnell, part 5; Lincoln to McClellan, 9 April 1862, Basler, ed., *Collected Works of Abraham Lincoln*, vol. 5 (New Brunswick: Rutgers University Press, 1953), 185.
21. Marvin, letter to brother, 26 April 1862.
22. Wolf, 125.
23. Marvin, diary, 4 May 1862.
24. Wolf, 125–26; Stillwater *Messenger*, 20 May 1862.
25. Marvin, letter to brother, 6 May 1862.
26. Marvin, letter to brother, 6 May 1862; Wolf, 126.
27. Stillwater *Messenger*, 29 April 1862.
28. Wolf, 126–27.
29. P. H. Taylor, diary, 12 April, 2–5 May 1862.
30. Wolf, 127–28.
31. Pressnell, part 5.
32. Wolf, 130.
33. Wolf, 129.
34. P. H. Taylor, diary, 12 May, 14 May 1862.
35. Bassett, 19–20; Marvin, diary, 15 May, 16 May 1862.
36. Wolf, 131–32.
37. Stillwater *Messenger*, 27 May 1862.
38. Stillwater *Messenger*, 29 April 1862; Pressnell, part 6.
39. Bassett, 20; Wolf, 133; P. H. Taylor, diary, 26 May 1862.
40. Wolf, 133.
41. Lochren, 19; Marvin, diary, 27 May 1862; Bassett, 20.
42. Wolf, 134.
43. Lochren, 20; Wolf, 134.
44. Holcombe, 124.
45. Edward D. Neill, "Incidents of the Battles of Fair Oaks and Malvern Hill," *Glimpses of the Nation's Struggle*, vol. 3 (St. Paul: D. D. Merrill Co., 1893), 456–57.

46. Hand, 284.
47. Lochren, 20.
48. *Minnesota in the Civil and Indian Wars*, vol. 2, 100; Wolf, 135.
49. *Minnesota in the Civil and Indian Wars*, vol. 2, 100–01; Marvin, diary, 31 May 1862.
50. Neill, 459.
51. Lochren, 20; P. H. Taylor, diary, 31 May 1862; Hand, 284–85.
52. Marvin, diary, 31 May 1862; Marvin, letter to brother, 6 June 1862.
53. Neill, 460; Hand, 285.
54. *Minnesota in the Civil and Indian Wars*, vol. 2, 101.
55. Hand, 285.
56. Lochren, 20; Wolf, 135.
57. Lochren, 20.
58. *Minnesota in the Civil and Indian Wars*, vol. 2, 101, 103, 105.
59. Hand, 461; Marvin, diary, 31 May 1862; Bassett, 20.
60. Neill, 463–64.
61. Wolf, 135.
62. Pressnell, part 6; Goddard, letter to mother, 15 June 1862.
63. Hand, 286–87, 283, 287.
64. Goddard, letter to mother, 6 June 1862; Hand, 287–88.
65. Hand, 288–89.
66. P. H. Taylor, diary, 3–7 June 1862.
67. Lochren, 21; Pressnell, part 6.
68. Pressnell, part 6.
69. Wolf, 136; Neill, 467.
70. Lochren, 21; Ghostley, diary, 24 July 1862; Hand, 289.
71. Hand, 289; Bassett, 20; Wolf, 139.
72. Wolf, 136–40.
73. P. H. Taylor, diary, 26 June 1862; Wolf, 140.
74. Wolf, 140.
75. Wolf, 140; P. H. Taylor, diary, 28 June 1862.
76. Neill, 469–70.
77. Hand, 289–90.
78. I. Taylor to "Cousin," 19 Oct. 1862 (copy). In private possession.
79. Neill, 471.
80. Hand, 290; Lochren, 22.
81. Pressnell, part 7.
82. *Minnesota in the Civil and Indian Wars*, vol. 2, 106–07.
83. I. Taylor, letter to "Cousin," 19 Oct. 1862.
84. Pressnell, part 8.
85. Holcombe, 96.
86. *Minnesota in the Civil and Indian Wars*, vol. 2, 107, 109.
87. Pressnell, part 8.
88. Hand, 290; Wolf, 141; I. Taylor, letter to "Cousin," 19 Oct. 1862.
89. Hand, 290.
90. P. H. Taylor, diary, 29 June 1862; Wolf, 141.

91. I. Taylor, letter to "Cousin," 19 Oct. 1862.
92. Hand, 290; Pressnell, part 7.
93. Lochren, 22; Bassett, 21.
94. Marvin, diary, 30 June 1862; Goddard, letter to mother, 6 July 1862.
95. Hand, 291.
96. Lochren, 23.
97. Lochren, 23; Hand, 291–92.
98. Pressnell, part 8.
99. Neill, 472–73.
100. Lochren, 23.
101. Neill, 474–75.
102. Hand, 294; Lochren, 23; Bassett, 21.
103. Pressnell, part 8.
104. Goddard, letter to brother, 6 Feb. 1863; Bassett, 21; Marvin, diary, 4 July 1862.
105. Marvin, letter to brother, 25 July 1862; Hand, 294.
106. Goddard, letter to mother, 10 July 1862; Hand, 294.
107. Goddard, letter to mother, 10 July 1862.
108. Marvin, letter to brother, 25 July 1862.
109. Bassett, 21.
110. Marvin, letter to brother, 8 Aug. 1862; Lochren, 24.
111. Marvin, diary, 9 Aug. 1862.
112. Imholte, 97–98.
113. Walker, letter to Knight, 5 Oct. 1862.
114. Wolf, 148.
115. Wolf, 141.
116. Wolf, 141n.
117. Wolf, 141–42.
118. I. Taylor, letter to "Cousin," 19 Oct. 1862.
119. Wolf, 142–43.
120. Wolf, 143.
121. Wolf, 143–44.
122. Wolf, 143–44.
123. I. Taylor, letter to "Cousin," 19 Oct. 1862.
124. Wolf, 144–45.
125. Wolf, 145–46.
126. Wolf, 146–47.
127. Wolf, 147–48.

5. ANTIETAM

1. Walker, letter to Knight, 5 Oct. 1862; Ghostley, diary, 26 Aug. 1862.
2. Lochren, 24.
3. Walker, letter to Knight, 5 Oct. 1862.
4. Lochren, 24.
5. Walker, letter to Knight, 5 Oct. 1862.

6. Holcombe, 179.

7. Lochren, 24.

8. Lochren, 24–25.

9. Walker, letter to Knight, 5 Oct. 1862.

10. Holcombe, 179; Walker, letter to Knight, 5 Oct. 1862.

11. Goddard, letter to mother, 2 Sept. 1862.

12. Walker, letter to Knight, 5 Oct. 1862.

13. Walker, letter to Knight, 5 Oct. 1862.

14. Little Falls (Minnesota) *Herald*, 26 June 1942.

15. Walker, letter to Knight, 5 Oct. 1862.

16. Lochren, 26.

17. *Minnesota in the Civil and Indian Wars*, vol. 2, 127.

18. Walker, letter to Knight, 5 Oct. 1862.

19. Walker, letter to Knight, 5 Oct. 1862.

20. Stephen W. Sears, *Landscape Turned Red: The Battle of Antietam* (New York: Warner Books, 1983), 247.

21. *Minnesota in the Civil and Indian Wars*, vol. 2, 127.

22. Walker, letter to Knight, 5 Oct. 1862.

23. Lochren, 26.

24. Walker, letter to Knight, 5 Oct. 1862.

25. Lochren, 26.

26. Sears, *Landscape*, 250.

27. *Minnesota in the Civil and Indian Wars*, vol. 2, 128.

28. *Minnesota in the Civil and Indian Wars*, vol. 2, 125; Goddard, letter to mother, 5 Oct. 1862.

29. *Minnesota in the Civil and Indian Wars*, vol. 2, 128.

30. Walker, letter to Knight, 5 Oct. 1862.

31. Pressnell, part 10.

32. Pressnell, parts 10, 11.

33. *Minnesota in the Civil and Indian Wars*, vol. 2, 125.

34. Holcombe, 221–22.

35. Little Falls *Herald*, 26 June 1942.

36. *Minnesota in the Civil and Indian Wars*, vol. 2, 125.

37. Walker, letter to Knight, 5 Oct. 1862.

38. Little Falls *Herald*, 26 June 1942.

39. Ghostley, diary, 17 Sept. 1862.

40. Walker, letter to Knight, 5 Oct. 1862.

41. *Minnesota in the Civil and Indian Wars*, vol. 2, 125.

42. Bassett, 22.

43. Walker, letter to Knight, 5 Oct. 1862; Lochren, 27.

44. Pressnell, part 10.

45. Goddard, letter to mother, 19 Sept. 1862; Bassett, 22.

46. Goddard, letter to mother, 28 Sept. 1862; Walker, letter to Knight, 5 Oct. 1862.

47. Little Falls *Herald*, 26 June 1942.

48. Wolf, 148–50.

49. I. Taylor, letter to "Cousin," 19 Oct. 1862.
50. Wolf, 148–51.
51. Wolf, 149–51.
52. P. H. Taylor, diary, 12 Sept. 1862; Wolf, 151.
53. P. H. Taylor, diary, 13 Sept. 1862.
54. Wolf, 151.
55. P. H. Taylor, diary, 14 Sept. 1862; Wolf, 152; P. H. Taylor, diary, 16 Sept. 1862.
56. Wolf, 225.
57. Wolf, 226.
58. I. Taylor, letter to "Cousin," 2 Oct. 1862. In private possession.
59. Wolf, 227.
60. P. H. Taylor, diary, 9 Oct. 1862; Wolf, 227–28.
61. P. H. Taylor, diary, 12 Oct. 1862.

6. FREDERICKSBURG

1. Walker, letter to Knight, 5 Oct. 1862.
2. Lochren, 27; Pressnell, part 11.
3. Bassett, 22–23.
4. Goddard, letter to mother, 9 Oct. 1862.
5. Wolf, 228–29.
6. Walker, letter to Knight, 23 April 1863.
7. Wolf, 229–30.
8. Wolf, 230.
9. Little Falls *Herald,* 26 June 1942.
10. Lochren, 28.
11. Wolf, 231.
12. Lochren, 28; Wolf, 232.
13. Bassett, 23; Wolf, 231.
14. Lochren, 28.
15. Marvin, diary, 7 Nov. 1862.
16. Wolf, 232; Marvin, diary, 16 Nov. 1862.
17. Lochren, 29–30.
18. Goddard, letter to mother, 23 Nov. 1862, 6 Feb. 1863.
19. Pressnell, part 12.
20. Wolf, 232.
21. Goddard, letter to mother, 14 Feb. 1863.
22. Wolf, 232–33.
23. Wolf, 233.
24. Bassett, 23–24.
25. Goddard, letter to mother, 4 Dec. 1862.
26. Wolf, 235.
27. Pressnell, part 11.
28. Pressnell, part 12.
29. Bassett, 24; Imholte, 108; Goddard, letter to mother, 16 Dec. 1862.

30. Walker, letter to Knight, 24 June 1863.
31. Lochren, 29.
32. Wolf, 236.
33. *Minnesota in the Civil and Indian Wars*, vol. 2, 159; Wolf, 236–37; P. H. Taylor, diary, 13 Dec. 1862.
34. Lochren, 29–30.
35. Bassett, 24; Lochren, 30.
36. Marvin, diary, 13 Dec. 1862; Imholte, 110.
37. *Minnesota in the Civil and Indian Wars*, vol. 2, 161; Marvin, letter to brother, 24 Dec. 1862.
38. P. H. Taylor, diary, 14 Dec. 1862; Lochren, 30.
39. Lochren, 30; Wolf, 237.
40. Pressnell, part 12.
41. *Minnesota in the Civil and Indian Wars*, vol. 2, 159; Marvin, letter to brother, 24 Dec. 1862.
42. Wolf, 237; Bassett, 24.
43. Lochren, 30.
44. Marvin, diary, 15 Dec. 1862.
45. Walker, letter to Knight, 24 Jan. 1863; Wolf, 237–38.
46. Marvin, letter to brother, 24 Dec. 1862; Wolf, 238.
47. Wolf, 238.
48. Ghostley, diary, 25 Dec. 1862; Marvin, diary, 25 Dec. 1862.
49. Wolf, 240; P. H. Taylor, diary, 1 Jan. 1863.
50. Walker, letter to Knight, 21 April 1863.
51. Bassett, 24–25; Wolf, 240.
52. Wolf, 239n.
53. Bassett, 25; Wolf, 243.
54. Goddard, letter to mother, 24 Jan. 1863; Walker, letter to Knight, 24 Jan. 1863.
55. Marvin, letter to parents, 18 Jan. 1863.
56. Goddard, letter to mother, 20 Jan. 1863.
57. Wolf, 243.
58. Walker, letter to Knight, 24 Jan. 1863.
59. Wolf, 244.
60. Wolf, 245; Walker, letter to Knight, 24 Jan. 1863.
61. Lochren, 31.
62. Marvin, letter "to all," 20 March 1863; Wolf, 247–48.
63. Wolf, 246, 247.
64. Wolf, 250; Walker, letter to Knight, 20 March 1863; Marvin, letter "to all," 20 March 1863.
65. Wolf, 255; Marvin, diary, 2 April 1863.
66. Wolf, 250, 248.
67. Wolf, 250.
68. I. Taylor, letter to Mary Jane Taylor, 17 March 1863. In private possession; Bassett, 25.
69. Walker, letter to Knight, 20 March 1863.

70. Goddard, letter to mother, 20 Feb. 1863.
71. Wolf, 254; Walker, letter to Knight, 20 March 1863.
72. Wolf, 250; Faribault *Central Republican*, 11 Feb. 1863.
73. Imholte, 111.
74. Lochren, 31.
75. Wolf, 242.
76. Wolf, 252, 254.
77. Walker, letter to Knight, 20 March 1863.
78. Wolf, 249, 247.
79. Bassett, 25; Wolf, 249, 251.
80. Bassett, 25.
81. Bassett, 26; Wolf, 251.
82. Wolf, 251, 256.
83. Wolf, 253, 254–55.
84. Wolf, 250–51; Goddard, letter to mother, 7 March 1863.
85. Walker, letter to Knight; 21 April 1863; Bassett, 25; Wolf, 256.
86. Walker, letter to Knight, 21 April 1863.
87. Wolf, 255–56.
88. Bassett, 25; Goddard, letter to mother, 14 March 1863.
89. Marvin, letter to brother, 2 April 1863.
90. Marvin, diary, 1 April 1863.
91. Wolf, 255, 256.
92. Walker, letter to Knight, 21 April 1863; Bassett, 25–26.
93. P. H. Taylor, diary, 14 April 1863.
94. Walker, letter to Knight, 21 April 1863.

7. CHANCELLORSVILLE

1. Walker, letter to Knight, 26 May 1863; Wolf, 344.
2. Walker, letter to Knight, 26 May 1863.
3. Wolf, 344–45; Walker, letter to Knight, 26 May 1863.
4. P. H. Taylor, diary, 1 May 1863.
5. Walker, letter to Knight, 26 May 1863.
6. Wolf, 345.
7. Red Wing *Republican*, 1905 (copy). Goodhue County (Minnesota) Historical Society.
8. P. H. Taylor, diary, 3 May 1863; Red Wing *Republican*, 1905; Wolf, 345.
9. Walker, letter to Knight, 26 May 1863.
10. Red Wing *Republican*, 1905; P. H. Taylor, diary, 3 May 1863.
11. Wolf, 345; Walker, letter to Knight, 26 May 1863.
12. Red Wing *Republican*, 1905.
13. Walker, letter to Knight, 26 May 1863.
14. Red Wing *Republican*, 1905.
15. *Minnesota in the Civil and Indian Wars,* vol. 2, 335.
16. Walker, letter to Knight, 26 May 1863; Wolf, 346.
17. Walker, letter to Knight, 26 May 1863.

18. Wolf, 346; Walker, letter to Knight, 26 May 1863.
19. Marvin, letter to brother, 8 May 1863.
20. P. H. Taylor, diary, 5 May 1863; Walker, letter to Knight, 26 May 1863.
21. Walker, letter to Knight, 26 May 1863.
22. P. H. Taylor, diary, 6 May 1863; Wolf, 347; Walker, letter to Knight, 26 May 1863; P. H. Taylor, diary, 7 May 1863.
23. Wolf, 347; Walker, letter to Knight, 26 May 1863.
24. Bassett, 26.
25. Wolf, 347.
26. Lochren, 32.
27. Wolf, 348.
28. Goddard, letter to mother, 24 May 1863; P. H. Taylor, diary, 11 May 1863; Wolf, 348, 350.
29. Lochren, 32.
30. Walker, letter to Knight, 26 May 1863.
31. Wolf, 343, 344, 348, 350, 351, 353.
32. P. H. Taylor, diary, 15 May 1863.
33. P. H. Taylor, diary, 15 May 1863; Wolf, 349, 352.
34. Wolf, 348, 349; Goddard, letter to mother, 24 May 1863.
35. P. H. Taylor, diary, 9 June 1863; Wolf, 353.
36. P. H. Taylor, diary, 9 June 1863; Bassett, 26.
37. Walker, letter to Knight, 26 May 1863.
38. Wolf, 350–51, 354–55.
39. P. H. Taylor, diary, 14 June 1863.
40. P. H. Taylor, diary, 15 June 1863; Wolf, 355; Goddard, letter to mother, 20 June 1863.
41. James A. Wright, "Story of Company F," 538. Unpublished ms., Minnesota Historical Society.
42. Marvin, diary, 17 June 1863.
43. Wolf, 356; Goddard, letter to mother, 20 June 1863.
44. Marvin, diary, 18 June 1863.
45. Goddard, letter to mother, 20 June 1863; Wolf, 356.
46. Wright, 545; Marvin, diary, 20 June 1863.
47. Wolf, 357, 358.
48. Lochren, 33.
49. William Lochren, "The First Minnesota at Gettysburg," *Glimpses of the Nation's Struggle,* vol. 3 (St. Paul: D. D. Merrill Co., 1893), 44–45.
50. Wright, 548.
51. P. H. Taylor, diary, 25 June 1863; Wolf, 358; P. H. Taylor, diary, 26 June 1863.
52. Marvin, diary, 26 June 1863; Wolf, 358.
53. Wolf, 358; P. H. Taylor, diary, 26 June 1863; Wolf, 358.
54. Wolf, 359; Marvin, diary, 27 June 1863.
55. William Colvill, "The Old First Minnesota at Gettysburg," Minneapolis *Daily Tribune,* 28 July 1884. Goodhue County (Minnesota) Historical Society.
56. P. H. Taylor, diary, 29 June 1863.
57. Wolf, 359.

58. Lochren, 34.
59. Marvin, diary, 29 June 1863.
60. Lochren, 34.
61. P. H. Taylor, diary, 29 June 1863; Bassett, 27.
62. Lochren, "The First Minnesota at Gettysburg," 46.
63. Wolf, 359–60; Marvin, diary, 30 June 1863.
64. John W. Plummer, letter to brother, n.d. Rpt. Minneapolis *Atlas,* 26 Aug. 1863 (copy), Gettysburg National Military Park.
65. Lochren, 34.
66. Marvin, diary, 7 July 1863; Wolf, 360.
67. Wolf, 360; Marvin, diary, 7 July 1863.
68. P. H. Taylor, letter to "Sister" [Sarah], 19–20 July 1863 (copy).

8. GETTYSBURG

1. Wolf, 360.
2. Plummer, letter to brother, n.d.
3. "Sergeant," letter to St. Paul *Pioneer,* 9 Aug. 1863 (copy). Gettysburg National Military Park.
4. Lochren, 35.
5. William Colvill, letter to John R. Bachelder, 9 June 1886 (copies). New Hampshire Historical Society.
6. Lochren, "The First Minnesota at Gettysburg," 47; Plummer, letter to brother, n.d.
7. Alfred P. Carpenter, letter, 30 July 1863, (copy). Minnesota Historical Society.
8. "Sergeant," letter to St. Paul *Pioneer,* 9 Aug. 1863.
9. P. H. Taylor, diary, 2 July 1863.
10. Marvin, diary, 2 July 1863.
11. "Sergeant," letter to St. Paul *Pioneer,* 9 Aug. 1863; Lochren, 35.
12. Plummer, letter to brother, n.d.
13. "Sergeant," letter to St. Paul *Pioneer,* 9 Aug. 1863.
14. Lochren, 35.
15. Carpenter, letter, 30 July 1863.
16. Colvill, "The Old First Minnesota at Gettysburg."
17. Carpenter, letter, 30 July 1863.
18. Colvill, letter to Bachelder, 9 June 1886.
19. Lochren, 35.
20. Charles Muller, "History Written by Charles Muller of Company A, First Minnesota Regiment of the Civil War." Unpublished ms., Minnesota Historical Society.
21. Colvill, letter to Bachelder, 9 June 1886; Colvill, "The Old First Minnesota at Gettysburg."
22. Lochren, 35; Carpenter, letter, 30 July 1863.
23. Marvin, diary, 3 July 1863.
24. "Sergeant," letter to St. Paul *Pioneer,* 9 Aug. 1863.
25. Lochren, 35–36.
26. "Sergeant," letter to St. Paul *Pioneer,* 9 Aug. 1863.

27. Plummer, letter to brother, n.d.
28. Colvill, "The First Minnesota at Gettysburg."
29. Lochren, 36.
30. Carpenter, letter, 30 July 1863.
31. Colvill, statement to William W. Folwell, 22 Dec. 1904. Folwell Papers, Minnesota Historical Society.
32. Muller, "History Written by Charles Muller."
33. Marvin, diary, 2 July 1863.
34. P. H. Taylor, diary, 2 July 1863.
35. Plummer, letter to brother, n.d.
36. Lochren, 36.
37. P. H. Taylor, diary, 2 July 1863; Colvill, "The First Minnesota at Gettysburg."
38. P. H. Taylor, diary, 2 July 1863; Bassett, 107.
39. Carpenter, letter, 30 July 1863.
40. Plummer, letter to brother, n.d.
41. "Sergeant," letter to St. Paul *Pioneer,* 9 Aug. 1863; Plummer, letter to brother, n.d.
42. P. H. Taylor, diary, 3 July 1863.
43. Wolf, 360–61.
44. P. H. Taylor, letter to "Parents," 6 July 1863 (copy).
45. P. H. Taylor, letter to "Sister" [Sarah], 19–20 July 1863 (copy).
46. "Sergeant," letter to St. Paul *Pioneer,* 9 Aug. 1863; Plummer, letter to brother, n.d.
47. Wright, 599–602.
48. Wright, 604, 607.
49. William Harmon, "Co. C at Gettysburg," Minneapolis *Journal,* 30 June 1897. Gettysburg National Military Park.
50. Plummer, letter to brother, n.d.
51. Lochren, 37; Wright, 608–09.
52. "Sergeant," letter to St. Paul *Pioneer,* 9 Aug. 1863.
53. P. H. Taylor, letter to "Sister" [Sarah], 19–20 July 1863.
54. Marvin, diary, 3 July 1863.
55. Carpenter, letter, 30 July 1863.
56. Lochren, 37.
57. Wright, 610.
58. "Sergeant," letter to St. Paul *Pioneer,* 9 Aug. 1863.
59. Wright, 610.
60. Wright, 611; Carpenter, letter, 30 July 1863.
61. Walker, letter to Knight, 29 July 1863.
62. Harmon, "Co. C at Gettysburg."
63. Lochren, 37–38.
64. Wright, 611.
65. Harmon, "Co. C at Gettysburg."
66. Plummer, letter to brother, n.d.; "Sergeant," letter to St. Paul *Pioneer,* 9 Aug. 1863.
67. Plummer, letter to brother, n.d.
68. Carpenter, letter, 30 July 1863.
69. Daniel Bond, "Bonds Recollaction," Minnesota Historical Society.

70. Wright, 612.
71. Harmon, "Co. C at Gettysburg."
72. Wright, 613, 616.
73. Plummer, letter to brother, n.d.; Carpenter, letter, 30 July 1863.
74. Bassett, 32–33.
75. Wright, 616.
76. Wright, 617–618, 616–617.
77. *Minnesota in the Civil and Indian Wars*, vol. 2, 373.
78. Robert W. Meinhard, "The First Minnesota at Gettysburg." *Gettysburg: Historical Articles of Lasting Interest*, 1 July 1991, 83.
79. *Minnesota in the Civil and Indian Wars,* vol. 2, 379.
80. Glenn Tucker, *Hancock the Superb* (Indianapolis, Bobbs-Merrill Co., 1960), 144–45.
81. Folwell, vol. 2, 311.
82. P. H. Taylor, diary, 3 July 1863.

EPILOGUE

1. "Lady," letter, St. Paul *Press*, 9 Sept. 1863. Rpt. Imholte, 126–27.
2. James J. Hill, address at the unveiling of a statue of William Colvill in the state capitol at St. Paul, 31 March 1909. Rpt. Holcombe, 450.
3. P. H. Taylor, diary, 15 Feb. 1864.
4. P. H. Taylor, diary, 3 May 1864.
5. Cass County (Missouri) *Democrat,* 26 Dec. 1908.
6. Lochren, 48.
7. Anita Buck, "To the Last Man," *Army,* March 1989.
8. Rpt. *Southern Minnesota,* Jan. 1932.

BIBLIOGRAPHY

PRIMARY SOURCES

Bassett, M. H. *From Bull Run to Bristow Station*. St. Paul: North Central Publishing Co., 1962.

Berry, Amos Askon. Diary, 1861–63. Washington County (Minnesota) Historical Society.

Board of Commissioners, ed. Vol. 2 of *Official Reports and Correspondence. Minnesota in the Civil and Indian Wars, 1861–1865*. St. Paul: Pioneer Press Co., 1899.

Bond, Daniel. "Bonds Recollection." Minnesota Historical Society.

Carpenter, Alfred P. Letter, 30 July 1863 (copy). Minnesota Historical Society.

Colvill, William. Letters to John R. Bachelder (copies). New Hampshire Historical Society.

———. "The Old First Minnesota at Gettysburg." Minneapolis *Daily Tribune*, 28 July 1884. Goodhue County (Minnesota) Historical Society.

———. Statement Concerning Participation in Battle of Gettysburg. Given to William W. Folwell, 22 Dec. 1904. Folwell Papers. Minnesota Historical Society.

"D." Letters to Faribault *Central Republican*, 1861. Rice County (Minnesota) Historical Society.

Davis, Edward L. Letters, 1861. Wisconsin Historical Society.

Ghostley, James T. Diary, 1862–63. Washington County (Minnesota) Historical Society.

Goddard, Charles. Letters, 1861–64. Orrin F. Smith and Family Papers. Minnesota Historical Society.

Hand, Daniel. "Reminiscences of an Army Surgeon," *Glimpses of the Nation's Struggle*. Vol. 1. St. Paul: St. Paul Book and Stationery Co., 1887. 276–307.

Harmon, William. "Co. C at Gettysburg." Minneapolis *Journal*, 30 June 1897 (copy). Gettysburg National Military Park.

King, Josias R. "The Battle of Bull Run: A Confederate Victory Obtained but Not Achieved." *Glimpses of the Nation's Struggle*. Vol. 6. Minneapolis: Aug. Davis Publisher, 1909. 497–510.

Lochren, William. "The First Minnesota at Gettysburg," *Glimpses of the Nation's Struggle*. Vol. 3. St. Paul: D. D. Merrill Co., 1893. 42–56.

————. "Narrative of the First Regiment." *Minnesota in the Civil and Indian Wars, 1861–1865.* Vol. 1. St. Paul: Pioneer Press Co., 1891. 1–66.

Marvin, Mathew. Papers, 1861–63. Minnesota Historical Society.

Muller, Charles. "History Written by Charles Muller of Company A, First Minnesota Regiment of the Civil War." Unpublished ms. Minnesota Historical Society.

Neill, Edward D. "Incidents of the Battles of Fair Oaks and Malvern Hill." *Glimpses of the Nation's Struggle.* Vol. 3. St. Paul: D. D. Merrill Co., 1893. 454–79.

————. Papers, 1861–63. Minnesota Historical Society.

Plummer, John W. Letter to Brother. Rpt. Minneapolis *Atlas,* 26 Aug. 1863 (copy). Gettysburg National Military Park.

Pressnell, Thomas H. "Incidents in the Civil War." Unpublished ms. St. Louis County (Minnesota) Historical Society.

Searles, Jasper N. "The First Minnesota Infantry, U.S. Volunteers." *Glimpses of the Nation's Struggle.* Vol. 2. St. Paul: St. Paul Book and Stationery Co., 1890. 80–113.

————. Letters, 1861–63. Minnesota Historical Society.

"Sergeant." Letter to St. Paul *Pioneer,* 9 Aug. 1863 (copy). Gettysburg National Military Park.

Spencer, Joseph E. Letters, 1861–65. Wisconsin Historical Society.

Stebbins, Samuel. Letters to Winona *Republican,* 1861. Winona County (Minnesota) Historical Society.

Stevens, Edward A. Letters of "Raisins" to Stillwater *Messenger,* 1861–62. Washington County (Minnesota) Historical Society.

Taylor, Isaac Lyman. Letters, 1861–63 (copies). Morrison County (Minnesota) Historical Society.

————. Letters, 1861–63 (copies). In private possession.

Taylor, Patrick Henry. Diary, 1861–64. Rpt. Cass County (Missouri) *Democrat,* 22 June 1933–11 Oct. 1934 (copies). In private possession.

————. Letters, 1861–64. Morrison County (Minnesota) Historical Society.

————. Letters, 1861–64 (copies). In private possession.

Walker, Edward A. Letters to George Knight, 1862–65. In private possession.

Wolf, Hazel C., ed. "Campaigning with the First Minnesota: A Civil War Diary [of Isaac Lyman Taylor]," *Minnesota History* 25 (1944): 11–39, 117–52, 224–57, 342–61.

Wright, James A. "Story of Company F." Unpublished ms. Minnesota Historical Society.

SECONDARY SOURCES

Basler, Roy P., ed. *The Collected Works of Abraham Lincoln.* Vols. 4, 5. New Brunswick: Rutgers University Press, 1953.

Blegen, Theodore C. *Minnesota: A History of the State.* St. Paul: University of Minnesota Press, 1963.

Boatner, Mark Mayo III. *The Civil War Dictionary.* Rev. ed. New York: David McKay Co., 1988.

Carley, Kenneth. *Minnesota in the Civil War.* Minneapolis: Ross & Haines, 1961.

Catton, Bruce. *The Civil War.* Boston: Houghton Mifflin Co., 1987.
———. *Glory Road: The Bloody Route from Fredericksburg to Gettysburg.* New York: Cardinal, 1964.
———. *Mr. Lincoln's Army.* New York: Doubleday, 1990.
———. *Reflections on the Civil War.* New York: Berkley Books, 1982.
Curtiss-Wedge, Franklyn, ed. *History of Goodhue County, Minnesota.* Chicago: H. C. Cooper, Jr., & Co., 1909.
———. *The History of Winona County, Minnesota.* Chicago: H. C. Cooper, Jr., & Co., 1913.
Folwell, William Watts. *A History of Minnesota.* Vols. 1, 2. St. Paul: Minnesota Historical Society, 1956, 1961.
Foote, Shelby. *The Civil War: A Narrative.* Vols. 1, 2. New York: Random House, 1958, 1963.
Griffith, Paddy. *Battle Tactics of the Civil War.* New Haven: Yale University Press, 1989.
Hage, Anne A. "The Battle of Gettysburg as Seen by Minnesota Soldiers." *Minnesota History* 38 (1963): 245–57.
Holcombe, Return I. *History of the First Regiment Minnesota Volunteer Infantry, 1861–1864.* Stillwater: Easton & Masterson, 1916.
Imholte, John Quinn. *The First Volunteers: History of the First Minnesota Volunteer Regiment, 1861–1865.* Minneapolis: Ross & Haines, Inc., 1963.
Kunz, Virginia Brainard. *Muskets to Missiles: A Military History of Minnesota.* St. Paul: Minnesota Statehood Centennial Commission, 1959.
Lass, William E. *Minnesota: A History.* New York: W. W. Norton & Co., 1977.
Leckie, Robert. *None Died in Vain.* New York: HarperCollins, 1990.
MacDonald, John. *Great Battles of the Civil War.* New York: Macmillan Publishing Co., 1988.
McPherson, James M. *Abraham Lincoln and the Second American Revolution.* New York: Oxford University Press, 1990.
———. *Battle Cry of Freedom: The Civil War Era.* New York: Oxford University Press, 1988.
Meinhard, Robert W. "The First Minnesota at Gettysburg." *Gettysburg: Historical Articles of Lasting Interest,* 1 July 1991.
Mitchell, Joseph B. *Decisive Battles of the Civil War.* New York: Dorset Press, 1955.
Mitchell, Reid. *Civil War Soldiers: Their Expectations and Their Experiences.* New York: Viking, 1988.
Pelowski, Gene. *Colonel William Colvill.* Unpublished ms., n.d. In private possession.
Pfanz, Harry W. *Gettysburg: The Second Day.* Chapel Hill: University of North Carolina Press, 1987.
Pierce, Lynn E. "The 1st Minnesota Regiment at the Battle of Gettysburg." Unpublished M.S. thesis, Mankato State College, 1959.
Sears, Stephen W. *George B. McClellan: The Young Napoleon.* New York: Ticknor & Fields, 1988.
———. *Landscape Turned Red: The Battle of Antietam.* New York: Warner Books, 1983.
Sears, Stephen W., ed. *The Civil War: The Best of American Heritage.* Boston: Houghton Mifflin Co., 1991.

————. *The Civil War Papers of George B. McClellan: Selected Correspondence, 1860–1865.* New York: Ticknor & Fields, 1989.

Sifakis, Stewart. *Who Was Who in the Civil War.* New York: Facts on File, 1988.

Tucker, Glenn. *Hancock the Superb.* Indianapolis: Bobbs-Merrill Co., 1960.

Ward, Geoffrey C., with Ken Burns and Ric Burns. *The Civil War.* New York: Alfred A. Knopf, Inc., 1990.

Wheeler, Richard. *Witness to Gettysburg.* New York: New American Library, 1987.

Wiley, Bell Irvin. *The Life of Billy Yank: The Common Soldier of the Union.* Baton Rouge: Louisiana State University Press, 1978.

Williams, Kenneth P. *Lincoln Finds a General: A Military Study of the Civil War.* Bloomington: Indiana University Press, 1949.

Williams, T. Harry. *Lincoln and His Generals.* New York: Dorset Press, 1952.

INDEX

Jackson, Cal, 276
Jackson, General Thomas J. "Stonewall,"
    112, 114, 116, 117, 177, 192, 197, 205,
    264
  at Antietam, 186, 188
  at Bull Run, 48, 50, 52, 55, 172
  at Chancellorsville, 239, 244
  at Fredericksburg, 211
  at Mechanicsville, 149
  at Savage Station, 166
Jefferson, Emmet, 15–16
Jefferson, Ernest R., 126, 273, 276
Jefferson, Thomas, 14
Jenny Lind (steamer), 123
Johnson, Andrew, 306, 309
Johnson, Captain Leonard, 228
Johnston, General Joseph E., 39, 46, 54, 61,
    123, 137, 148

Kearny, General Philip, 148
Kelly's Ford, battle of, 1
Kemper, General, 288
Keyes, Dency E., 244
Keyes, Mattie, 281
King, Lieutenant Josias R., 15, 54, 55, 58,
    126, 198, 312
King, Oscar, 42–43, 80
Kirby, Lieutenant, 138–41, 187, 212
Knight, George, 224, 225, 227, 289

Lander, General, 87
Last Man's Club, 311
Leach, Lieutenant William B., 30
LeBoutiller, C. W., 57
Lee, General Robert E., 1–3, 148, 149,
    164, 172, 176–79, 202, 233, 242,
    247–50, 252, 253, 257, 303–5
  at Antietam, 179, 188, 189
  at Bristoe Station, 299
  at Chancellorsville, 239
  at Fredericksburg, 206, 207, 260
  at Gettysburg, 261, 263–64, 267, 279,
    281, 286–87, 295, 298
  at Malvern Hill, 160
  at Mine Run, 300
Lee, Robert E., Jr., 187
Lester, Colonel Henry C., 10, 79, 105–6
Libby Prison, 169
Lincoln, Abraham, 7, 12, 19, 84–85, 87,
    108, 115, 120, 135, 260, 264, 300, 306
  Burnside and, 205, 221

calls for volunteers, 6, 8–9, 13, 70, 71
  conscription and, 223
  election of, 8
  Emancipation Proclamation of, 194, 207,
    217, 226
  Gettysburg Address of, 301–2, 314
  Hooker and, 221, 253
  McClellan and, 85, 124, 128–29, 164,
    176, 202, 204–6
  McDowell and, 38–39, 85
  Pressnell and, 209
  reviews troops, 36, 118, 229
Lincoln, Mary Todd, 264
Lincoln Guard, 10, 25
Little Giants, 12, 13
Lochren, William, 3–5, 16, 19, 31, 43, 72,
    81, 84, 95, 115, 119, 172, 174–75,
    202–5, 242–43, 244, 251, 253–56, 307,
    311
  at Antietam, 182, 183, 189
  at Bolivar Heights, 198
  at Bull Run, 57–60, 62
  at Edwards' Ferry, 88, 91
  at Falmouth, 222, 226
  at Fredericksburg, 211–16
  at Gettysburg, 262, 267–70, 272, 275,
    283–84, 286, 289–90
  at Harpers Ferry, 113
  in Peninsula campaign, 124–28, 137,
    139, 141, 145–47, 152, 157, 158
  in Washington, 37, 65
Lockwood, Charles, 312
Long Branch (steamer), 132
Longstreet, General James, 172, 213, 258,
    263–65, 266, 286
Louisiana Purchase, 14
Lyons, Lord, 118

McClellan, General George B., 85–86, 88,
    104, 109, 112, 172, 176, 177, 200–202,
    204–6, 216, 220, 221, 242, 253, 254,
    260, 303
  at Antietam, 178, 179, 188, 189, 194
  Peninsula campaign of, 123–31, 136,
    137, 143–44, 147–49, 156, 159–64,
    166–67, 192
McDowell, General Irvin, 38–40, 43–47,
    53–54, 57, 85, 205, 249
McEwen, John, 54, 86, 99, 110, 111, 186
McKune, Captain Lewis, 50
McLaws, General Lafayette, 183, 184